Talk to the Hand

Talk to the Hand

The Utter Bloody Rudeness of the World Today,
or Six Good Reasons to Stay Home and Bolt the Door

LYNNE TRUSS

GOTHAM BOOKS

GOTHAM BOOKS
Published by Penguin Group (USA) Inc.
375 Hudson Street, New York, New York 10014

Penguin Group (Canada), 90 Eglinton Avenue East, Suite 700, Toronto, Ontario,
Canada M4P 2Y3 (a division of Pearson Penguin Canada Inc.); Penguin Books
Ltd, 80 Strand, London WC2R 0RL, England; Penguin Ireland, 25 St Stephen's
Green, Dublin 2, Ireland (a division of Penguin Books Ltd); Penguin Group
(Australia), 250 Camberwell Road, Camberwell, Victoria 3124, Australia (a
division of Pearson Australia Group Pty Ltd); Penguin Books India Pvt Ltd, 11
Community Centre, Panchsheel Park, New Delhi - 110 017, India; Penguin Group
(NZ), cnr Airborne and Rosedale Roads, Albany, Auckland 1310, New Zealand (a
division of Pearson New Zealand Ltd); Penguin Books (South Africa) (Pty) Ltd, 24
Sturdee Avenue, Rosebank, Johannesburg 2196, South Africa

Penguin Books Ltd, Registered Offices: 80 Strand, London WC2R 0RL, England

Published by Gotham Books, a division of Penguin Group (USA) Inc.

First printing, November 2005
10 9 8 7 6 5 4 3 2 1

Gotham Books and the skyscraper logo are trademarks of
Penguin Group (USA) Inc.

Library of Congress Cataloging-in-Publication Data has been applied for.

ISBN: 1-592-40171-6
Also available in a Gotham Books Large-Print Edition: 1-592-40192-9

Printed in the United States of America

Contents

Other people are quite dreadful. The only possible society is oneself.
Oscar Wilde

An apology is a gesture through which an individual splits himself into two parts: the part that is guilty of the offence, and the part that dissociates itself from the delict and affirms a belief in the offended rule.
Erving Goffman

Fuck off, Norway.
Paul Gascoigne, on being asked if he had a message for the people of Norway

Acknowledgements

As is pretty clear in the text, *Talk to the Hand* owes a heavy debt to two excellent books: Mark Caldwell's *A Short History of Rudeness* and Kate Fox's *Watching the English*. A book about rudeness should start with as many thanks and apologies as possible, so I would like first to thank the many friends who have provided examples, sent me cuttings, or assured me I wasn't barmy not to write the expected follow-up book on grammar: Cate Olson and Nash Robbins, John Robbins, Vybarr Cregan-Reid, Margaret and Bob Cook, Mary Walker, Cathy Stewart, Bruce Holdsworth, Philip Hensher, Faynia Williams, Richard Crane, Gideon Haigh, and Anne Baker. Andrew Hadfield told me the joke about Carnegie Hall. Douglas Kennedy had the experience in the French record shop. To my badminton pals – Andrew, Vybarr, Alan,

Tom, Dan, Vicky, Martin, John, and Caroline – I say sorry (as always). I would also like to thank the nameless people who were quite rude to me during this period. Without them, this book would not have been possible.

Talk to the Hand shares only two things with *Eats, Shoots & Leaves*: (1) a title comprising four one-syllable words; and (2) its origins in radio. I would like to thank the BBC Radio 4 commissioning editors who keep allowing me to appear on the airwaves, and in particular Kate McAll, the producer who supervised the original table-thumping rants on which this book is based. "Don't bang the table" being the first law of radio broadcasting, incidentally, I have devised a rather strange method of expressing my feelings in studio, which is to sit at the microphone with arms stretched out to the sides, flapping them slowly up and down in imitation of a giant pterodactyl. Kate has always disguised her alarm at this magnificently.

Continuing the pattern of apology and thanks, I would like to apologise to the many *Telegraph* readers to whose interesting and supportive letters I have not personally replied. I would very much like to apologise – *again* – to the kind stickler from North Carolina who sent me a beautiful wooden semi-colon, hand-carved, and received no thanks until he wrote to check I had received it. And I'd like to thank my publishers and agents: Andrew Franklin, Bill Shinker, Erin Moore, Anthony Goff and George Lucas. Finally, I'd like to thank Miles Kington in the *Independent* for coming up with my logical follow-up title, *Presses, Pants & Flies* (entailing a joke about a laundryman who goes into a bar, does a few press-ups, breathes heavily and then jumps out of the window). I may still use it next time.

Author's note

The author apologises for the high incidence of the word "Eff" in this book. It is, sadly, unavoidable in a discussion of rudeness in modern life. Variants such as Effing, mother-Effing, and what the Eff? positively litter the text.

If you don't Effing like it, you know what you can Effing do. (That's a joke.)

Introduction:
When Push Comes to Shove

If you want a short-cut to an alien culture these days, there is no quicker route than to look at a French phrase book. Not because the language is different, but because the first lesson you will find there usually takes place in a shop.

"Good morning, madam."

"Good morning, sir."

"How may I help you?"

"I would like some tomatoes/eggs/postage stamps please."

"Of course. How many tomatoes/eggs/postage stamps would you like?"

"Seven/five/twelve, thank you."

"That will be six/four/two Euros. Do you have the exact money?"

"I do."

"Thank you, madam."

"Thank you, sir. Good day!"

"Good day!"

Now the amazing thing is, this formal and civil exchange actually represents what happens in French shops. French shopkeepers really say good morning and goodbye; they answer questions; they wrap things ever so nicely; and when it's all over, they wave you off like a near relation. There is none of the dumb, resentful shrugging we English shoppers have become so accustomed to. Imagine an English phrase book for French visitors, based on the same degree of verisimilitude – let's call it "*Dans le magasin*".

"Excuse me, do you work here?"

"What?"

"I said, excuse me, do you work here?"

"Not if I can help it, har, har, har."

"Do you have any tomatoes/eggs/postage stamps?"

"Well, make your mind up, that's my mobile."

This book has quite a modest double aim: first, to mourn, without much mature perspective or academic rigour, the apparent collapse of civility in all areas of our dealings with strangers; then to locate a tiny flame of hope in the rubble and fan it madly with a big hat. Does this project have any value? Well, in many ways, no. None at all. First, it is hardly original or controversial to declare oneself against rudeness. (One is reminded of that famous objection to the "Women Against Rape" campaign: "Are there any women *for* rape?") Secondly, it seems that an enormous amount of good stuff has been written on this subject already, and the plate has been licked pretty clean. Thirdly, and even more discouragingly, as long ago as 1971, the great sociologist Erving Goffman wrote that "concern about public life has heated up far beyond our capacity to throw light on it". So, to sum up: it's not worth saying; it's already been said; and it's impossible to say anything adequate in any case. This is the trouble with doing research.

However, just as my book on punctuation was fundamentally about finding oneself mysteriously at snapping point about something that seemed a tad trivial compared with war, famine, and the imminent overthrow of Western civilisation, so is *Talk to the Hand*. I just want to describe and analyse an automatic eruption of outrage and frustration that can at best cloud an otherwise lovely day, and at worst make you resolve to chuck yourself off the nearest bridge. You are lying in a dentist's chair, for example, waiting quietly for an anaesthetic to "take", and the dental nurse says, next to your left ear, "Anyway, I booked that flight and it had gone up forty quid." At which the dentist says, in your right ear, "No! What, in two hours?" And you say, rather hotly, "Look, I'm not unconscious, you know", and then they don't say anything, but you know they are rolling their eyes at each other, and agreeing that you are certifiable or menopausal, or possibly both.

Whether it's merely a question of advancing years bringing greater intolerance I don't think I shall bother to establish. I will just say that, for my own part, I need hardly defend myself against any knee-jerk "grumpy old woman" accusations, being self-evidently so young and fresh and liberal and everything. It does, however, have to be admitted that the outrage reflex ("Oh, that's so RUDE!") presents itself in most people at just about the same time as their elbow skin starts to give out. Check your own elbow skin. If it snaps back into position after bending, you probably should not be reading this book. If, on the other hand, it just sits there in a puckered fashion, a bit rough and belligerent, then you can probably also name about twenty things, right now, off the top of your head, that drive you nuts: people who chat in the cinema; young people sauntering four-abreast on the pavement; waiters who say, "There you go" as they place your bowl of soup on the table; people not even attempting to lower their voices when they use the "Eff" word. People with young, flexible elbow skin spend less time defining themselves by things they don't like. Warn a young person that "Each man becomes the thing he hates", and he is likely to reply, quite cheerfully, that that's OK, then, since the only thing he really hates is broccoli.

By contrast, I now can't abide many, many things, and am actually always on the look-out for more things to find completely unacceptable. Whenever I hear of someone being "gluten intolerant" or "lactose intolerant", for example, I feel I've been missing out. I want to be gluten intolerant too. I mean, how much longer do we have to put up with that gluten crap? Lactose has had its own way long enough. Yet I still, amazingly, deny a rightward drift in my thinking. I merely ask: isn't it odd, the way many nice, youngish liberal people are beginning secretly to admire the chewing-gum penalties of Singapore? Isn't it odd, the way nice, youngish liberal people, when faced with a teenaged boy skateboarding in Marks & Spencer's, feel a righteous urge to stick out a foot and send him somersaulting into a rack of sensible shoes? I will admit that the mere thought of taking such direct and beautiful vengeance – "There he goes!" – fills me with a profound sort of joy.

! # * !

Why is this not a handbook to good manners? Why will you not find rules about wielding knives and forks, using a mobile phone, and sending thank-you notes? I have several reasons for thinking that the era of the manners book has simply passed. First, what would be the authority of such a book, exactly? Why would anyone pay attention to it? This is an age of lazy moral relativism combined with aggressive social insolence, in which many people have been trained to distrust and reject all categorical answers, and even (I've noticed with alarm) to dispute points of actual law without having the shadow of a leg to stand on. However, this is not to say that manners are off the agenda in today's rude world. Far from it. In fact, what is so interesting about our charming Eff-Off society is that perceived rudeness probably irritates rough, insolent people even more than it peeves polite, deferential ones. As the American writer Mark Caldwell points out in *A Short History of Rudeness* (1999), if you want to observe status-obsessed people who are exquisitely sensitive to slights, don't read an Edith Wharton novel, visit San Quentin. Rudeness is a universal flashpoint. My main concern in writing this book is to work out why, all of a sudden, this is the case.

Another argument against laying down rules of etiquette is that we no longer equate posh behaviour with good behaviour, which is a splendid development, posh people being notoriously cruel to wildlife and apt to chuck bread rolls at each other when excited. Who wants to behave like a posh person? I know I don't. I recently met a very posh person, the husband of (let's say) a theatrical producer, and when I asked if he was himself in (let's say) theatrical producing, he just said, "Oh God, no", and refused to elaborate. Is this good manners? Well, the best you can say about it is that it's very English, which is not the same. As the anthropologist Kate Fox points out in her fascinating *Watching the English* (2004), it is a point of honour in English society to effect all social introductions very, very badly. "One must appear self-conscious, ill-at-ease, stiff, awkward, and above all, embarrassed," she writes. The handshake should be a confusion of half-gestures, apologies, and so on. And as for cheek-kissing, it is an established rule that someone will always have to say, "Oh, are we doing *two*?" Also essential in the introductory process, she says, is that on no account should you volunteer your own name or ask a direct question to establish the identity of the person you are speaking to.

I must admit that this last rule explained quite a lot to me. My standard behaviour at parties is to announce straight away who I am, and then work quite strenuously to ascertain the name and profession of the person I'm speaking to – mainly because I wish to avoid that familiar heart-stopping moment at the end of the evening when the host says, "So what did you make of my old friend the Archbishop of Canterbury, then? Looks good in mufti, doesn't he? You seemed to be telling him off-colour jokes for hours." However, it turns out that asking direct questions is socially naff, while the "Oh God, no" response is the one that is actually demanded by the compensatory instincts of good breeding. No wonder I have so often ended up playing Twenty Questions with chaps who seem to pride themselves on being Mister Clam the Mystery Man.

"So. Here we are at Tate Modern," I say. "I'm afraid I didn't catch your name. I expect you are front-page famous which will make this an embarrassing story to tell all my clued-up friends."

"Oh no."

"No?"

"Well, I'm known to a select few, I suppose. Mainly abroad. Nineteen."

"Pardon?"

"You've got nineteen questions left. You've just used one."

"Oh. Oh, I see. All right. Are you in the arts?"

"No, no. Nothing like that. Eighteen."

"Are you animal, vegetable, or mineral, ha ha?"

"Mm. Like everybody, I believe, I'm mainly water. Seventeen."

"I see. Well. Look. Are you the Archbishop of Canterbury?"

"No. Although there have been some notable clerics in the female line. Sixteen."

"Do your bizarre trousers hold any clue to your profession?"

"How very original of you to draw attention to my bizarre trousers. Fifteen."

"Do you own a famous stately home in the north of England?"

"Um, why do you ask?"

"Just a wild stab."

"Well, I like your style, but no. Fourteen."

"I give up. Who are you?"

"Not allowed. Thirteen."

"All right. I was trying to avoid this. If I got someone strong to pin your arms back, where would I find your wallet?"

It's always been this way, apparently, in so-called polite society. People go out and meet other people, but only so that they can come home again without anyone piercing the veil of their anonymity in the period in between. George Mikes made a related point in his wonderful *How to be an Alien* (1946): "The aim of introduction [in England] is to conceal a person's identity. It is very important that you should not pronounce anybody's name in a way that the other party may be able to catch it."

Until recently, of course, people did aspire to posh manners. Hence the immense popularity, in the nineteenth and twentieth centuries, in both Britain and America, of books that satisfied middle-class anxieties and aspirations – and incidentally fuelled snobbery. Books such as Letitia Baldrige's *Complete Guide to the New Manners for the '90s* (referring to the 1890s) or the umpteen editions since 1922 of Emily Post's *Etiquette: The Blue Book of Social Usage* existed because they were needed: as society became more fluid, people found themselves in unfamiliar situations, where there was a danger that they would embarrass themselves by punching the hotel porter for stealing their suitcase, or swigging from a finger-bowl, or using the wrong fork to scratch their noses. Cue the loud, general gasp of well-bred horror. Well, sod all that, quite frankly, and good riddance. Old-fashioned manners books have an implicit message:

"People better than you know how to behave. Just follow these rules and with a bit of good luck your true origins may pass undetected." It is no accident that the word "etiquette" derives from the same source as "ticket". It is no accident, either, that adherence to "manners" has broken down just as money and celebrity have largely replaced birth as the measure of social status.

All of which leaves the etiquette book looking a bit daft. "Wait until the credits are rolling before standing up to leave," I see in one recent guide to polite behaviour. "Don't text when you're with other people," says another. "A thank-you letter is not obligatory, although one can be sent to the Lord Steward of the Royal Household." I experience a great impatient ho-hum in the face of such advice. Once you leave behind such class concerns as how to balance the peas on the back of a fork, all the important rules surely boil down to one: *remember you are with other people; show some consideration.* A whole book telling you to do that would be a bit repetitive. However, I do recommend *Debrett's* for its incidental *Gosford Park* delights. There is, for example, a good, dark little story in the most recent edition about a well-bred country gentleman with suicidal intent who felt it wasn't right to shoot himself before entering his own name in the Game Book. You have to admire such dedication to form. For anyone wishing to follow his example, by the way, he listed himself under "Various".

Manners never were enforceable, in any case. Indeed, for many philosophers, this is regarded as their chief value: that they are voluntary. In 1912, the jurist John Fletcher Moulton claimed in a landmark speech that the greatness of a nation resided not in its obedience to laws, but in its abiding by conventions that were not obligatory. "Obedience to the unenforceable" was the phrase that was picked up by other writers – and it leads us to the most important aspect of manners: their philosophical elusiveness. Is there a clear moral dimension to manners? Can you equate civility and virtue? My own answer would be yes, despite all the famous counter-examples of blood-stained dictators who had exquisite table manners and never used their mobile phone in a crowded train compartment to order mass executions. It seems to me that, just as the loss of punctuation signalled the vast and under-acknowledged problem of illiteracy, so the collapse of manners stands for a vast and under-acknowledged problem of social immorality. Manners are based on an ideal of empathy, of imagining the impact of one's own actions on others. They involve doing something for the sake of other people that is not obligatory and attracts no reward. In the current climate of unrestrained solipsistic and aggressive self-interest, you can equate good manners not only with virtue but with positive heroism.

Philosophers are, of course, divided on all this – but then most of them didn't live in the first years of the twenty-first century. Aristotle said that, if you want to be good, it's not a bad idea to practise (I'm paraphrasing). In the seventeenth century, Thomas Hobbes said that the rights and wrongs of picking your teeth weren't worthy of consideration (I'm paraphrasing again). In the 1760s, Immanuel Kant said that manners could not be reckoned as virtues, because they called for "no large measure of moral determination"; on the other hand, he thought they were a means of developing virtue. In November 2004, however, the philosopher Julian Baggini wrote in *The Guardian*, rather compellingly, that our current alarm at the state of manners derives from our belated understanding that, in rejecting old-fashioned niceties, we have lost a great deal more than we bargained for:

> The problem is that we have failed to distinguish between pure etiquette, which is simply a matter of arbitrary social rules designed mainly to distinguish between insiders and outsiders; and what might grandly be called quotidian ethics: the morality of our small, everyday interactions with other people.

My small, personal reason for not writing a traditional etiquette book is not very laudable, but the phrase "a rod for one's own back" is a bit of a clue to the way I'm thinking. If my experience as Queen of the Apostrophe has taught me anything, it has impressed on me that, were I to adopt "zero tolerance" as my approach to manners, I would never again be able to yawn, belch, or scratch my bottom without someone using it as watertight proof that I know not whereof I speak. Is it worth it? *Zero Tolerance Manners Woman Ignores Person Who Knows Her Shock. "She walked straight past me," said wounded friend of 25 years, who was recovering yesterday at home. "She is also rubbish at punctuation, if you ask me. You should see her emails."*

Plus, in all seriousness, there are many etiquette issues on which a zero tolerance position cannot be sensible. Take the everyday thorny problem of modern forms of address. I receive many letters which begin, "Dear Ms/Miss/Lynne Truss", immediately followed by a heartfelt paragraph on the difficulty of addressing women whose marital status is unclear. Well, I sympathise with this difficulty, of course, and I am sorry to be the cause of it. I know there are many people who dislike being addressed without a title, so I appreciate that my correspondents are worthily trying to avoid being rude. However, as it happens, I loathe the whole business of titles, and prefer to do without one wherever possible, considering this a simple solution to an overelaborate problem. True, having ticked "Other" on a number of application forms, I now receive post bizarrely addressed to "Other Lynne Truss", which is a bit unsettling for someone with a rocky sense of identity, but this is still better (in my view) than going along with this outmoded Miss/Ms/Mrs thing. My point is: there is no right and wrong in this situation. Who could possibly legislate?

We all draw the wavy contour line between polite

and rude behaviour in a different place, much as we draw our own line in language usage. That's why we are always so eager to share our experiences of rudeness and feel betrayed if our best friends say, "Ooh, I'm not sure I agree with you there; perhaps you've got this out of proportion." In *Eats, Shoots & Leaves*, I alluded to Kingsley Amis's useful self-exempting system of dividing the world into "berks" and "wankers": berks being those who say, "But language has to change, surely? Why don't we just drop that silly old apostrophe?", and wankers being those who say, "I would have whole-heartedly agreed with you, Ms Truss, if you had not fatally undermined your authority by committing a howler of considerable dimensions quite early in the book, on page 19. I refer, of course, to the phrase 'bow of elfin gold'. Were you to consult *The Letters of J. R. R. Tolkien* (Boston: Houghton Mifflin, 1981), you would find in letter 236 that Professor Tolkien preferred the term 'elven' to 'elfin', but was persuaded by his editors to change it. Also, it was the dwarves who worked with gold, of course; not the elves. Finally, as any student of metallurgy would instantly confirm, gold is not a suitable element from which to fashion a bow, being at once too heavy and too malleable. With all good wishes, enjoyed your book immensely, keep up the good work, your fan."

The idea of the Berk–Wanker system is that each of us feels safe from either imputation, because we have personally arrived at a position that is the fulcrum between the two. You may remember how the BBC always answered criticism years ago: "I think we've got the balance *just about right*." Well, my point is: our attitude to manners is similarly self-defined and self-exonerating. Each of us has got it just about right. If there is something we are particularly good at, such as sending thank-you notes, we are likely to consider the thank-you note the greatest indicator of social virtue, and will be outraged by its breach. In an essay on press freedom in 1908, "Limericks and Counsels of Perfection", G. K. Chesterton saw this subjective rule-making as sufficient reason in itself for not attempting to enforce manners:

> We are justified in enforcing good morals, for they belong to all mankind ... [but] we are not justified in enforcing good manners, for good manners always means *our* manners.

Basically, everyone else has bad manners; we have

occasional bad moments. Everyone else is rude; we are sometimes a bit preoccupied.

! # ⋆ !

So, if this book is not a guide to manners, what is it? And what are those six good reasons to stay home and bolt the door? Well, my only concern in this book is to define and analyse six areas in which our dealings with strangers seem to be getting more unpleasant and inhuman, day by day. It seemed to me, as I thought about the problem of rudeness, that it might be useful to break it down. Manners have so many aspects – behavioural, psychological, political, moral – yet we react to rudeness as if it is just one thing. Understanding things sometimes helps to defuse them. Maybe I will save the world from philistinism and yobbery with my six good reasons. Failing that, however, I have the small, related hope that I may at least save myself from going nuts.

1 *Was That So Hard to Say?*

"What ever happened to thank you?" we mutter. Ask

anyone about the escalation of rudeness, and their first example is likely to be a quite animated description of how they allowed another car to pass last Wednesday, and received no thanks or acknowledgement; not even an infinitesimal nod accompanied by a briefly extended index finger, which is (curiously) usually good enough for most of us.

What has happened to the rituals of what Goffman called "supportive interchange"? They have gone disastrously awry, that's what. Last year I was a passenger in another woman's car in Denver, Colorado. Waiting at a junction, we received a wave from two young men in a car alongside. I smiled back, and then asked my companion whether the chaps might want something. She opened my window and called across, "Can I help you?" At which the driver of the other car stopped smiling and yelled, "What do you mean, can I help you? I was only being Effing friendly! Why don't you get back to your Cherry Creek Country Club, you rich bitches!" and drove off. Of course, we were both taken aback. My companion, interestingly, was upset most by the insulting accusation of wealth. It annoyed her very much to be called a rich bitch. For my own part, however,

I just kept thinking, "But surely a simple 'No, thank you' would have sufficed? What was wrong with 'No, thank you' in that situation?"

There is a theory of manners that uses the fiscal image of balancing the books, and I consider it a good one to begin with. For every good deed there is a proportionate acknowledgement which precisely repays the giver; in this world of imaginary expenditure and income, the aim is to emerge from each transaction with no one in the red. This involves quite a lot of sophisticated mental micro-calculation and fine moral balancing, so it's small wonder that many people now find that they simply can't be arsed. Nowadays, you open a door for somebody and instead of saying, "Thank you", they just think, "Oh good" and go through it. This can be very annoying if you are standing there expectantly with your pen poised and your manners ledger open at the right page. All you can enter in the credit columns is flower doodles, and these in no way salve your shock and disappointment.

Why are people adhering less to the Ps and Qs? Where does that leave those of us who wince every day at the unspoken "thank you" or the unthought-of "sorry"? Is there a strategy for cancelling the debt? Should we abandon our expectations of reciprocity? And isn't it confusing that our biggest experience of formal politeness comes from the recorded voices on automated switchboards – who patently don't mean it? "We are sorry we cannot connect you at this time," says the voice. But does it sound sorry? No, it doesn't. It is just saying the politeness words in as many different combinations as it can think of. "Please hold. Thank you for holding. We are sorry you are having to hold. We are sorry to say please. Excuse us for saying sorry. We are sorry to say thank you. Sorry, please, thank you. Thank you, sorry, please." An interesting rule applies here, I find: the more polite these messages, the more apoplectic and immoderate you become, as you lose twenty-five minutes from your life that could have been spent, more entertainingly, disinfecting the S-bend. "Thank you for choosing to wait for an adviser," says the voice. "Choose?" you yell back. "I didn't Effing choose this! Don't tell me what I Effing chose!"

2 Why am I the One Doing This?

This is quite a new source of irritation, but it goes deep. As I noted in Eats, Shoots & Leaves, good punctuation is analogous to good manners. The writer who neglects spelling and punctuation is quite arrogantly dumping a lot of avoidable work onto the reader, who deserves to be treated with more respect. I remember, some years ago, working alongside a woman who would wearily scribble phone messages on a pad, and then claim afterwards not to be able to read her own handwriting. "What does that say?" she would ask, rather unreasonably, pushing the pad at me. She was quite serious: it wasn't a joke. I would peer at the spidery scrawl, making out occasional words. "Oh, you're a big help," she would say, finally chucking the whole thing at me. "I'm going out for a smoke." This was an unacceptable transfer of effort, in my opinion. I spotted this at the time, and have continued to spot it. In my opinion, there is a lot of it about.

Just as the rise of the internet sealed the doom of grammar, so modern communications technology contributes to the end of manners. Wherever you turn for help, you find yourself on your own.

Say you phone a company to ask a question and are blocked by that Effing automatic switchboard. What happens? Well, suddenly you have quite a lot of work to do. There is an unacceptable transfer of effort. In the past, you would tell an operator, "I'm calling because you've sent my bill to the wrong address three times", and the operator, who (and this is significant) *worked for this company*, would attempt to put you through to the right person. In the age of the automated switchboard, however, we are all co-opted employees of every single company we come into contact with. "Why am I the one doing this?" we ask ourselves, twenty times a day. It is the general wail of modern life, and it can only get worse. "Why not try our self-check-in service?" they say, brightly. "Have you considered on-line banking?" "Ever fancied doing you own dental work?" "DIY funerals: the modern way."

People who object to automated switchboards are generally dismissed as grumpy old technophobes, of course. But to me it seems plain that modern customer relations are just rude, because switchboards manifestly don't attempt to meet you half-way. Manners are about imagination, ultimately. They are about imagining being the other person. These systems force us to navigate ourselves into channels that are plainly for someone else's convenience, not ours. And they then have the nerve, incidentally, to dress this up as a kind of consumer freedom. "Now you can do all this yourself!" is the message. "Take the reins. Run the show. Enjoy the shallow illusion of choice and autonomy. And by the way, don't bother trying to by-pass this system, buddy, because it's a hell of a lot smarter than you are."

This "do-it-yourself" tactic occurs so frequently, in all parts of life, that it has become unremarkable. In all our encounters with businesses and shops, we now half expect to be treated not as customers, but as system trainees who haven't quite got the hang of it yet. "We can't deal with your complaint today because Sharon only comes in on Tuesdays," they say. "Right-oh," you say. "I'll remember that for next time." In a large store, you will be trained in departmental demarcations, so that if you are buying a towel, you have to queue at a different counter – although there is no way you could discover this without queuing at the wrong counter first. Nothing is designed to put the customer's requirements above those of the shop. The other day, in a chemist's on Tottenham Court Road, the pharmacist accidentally short-changed me by £1, and then, with sincere apologies, said I would have to wait until he served his next customer (whenever that might be), because he didn't have a password for the till. While we were discussing the likelihood of another customer ever happening along, another till was opened, a few yards away. I asked if he could get me my change from the other till, and he said, with a look of panic, "Oh no, it has to come from this one." Now, this was not some callow, under-educated youth. This was a trained pharmacist; a chap with a brain. I suggested that he could repay the other till later – and it was as though I had explained the theory of relativity. He was actually excited by such a clever solution, which would never have occurred to him. Lateral thinking on behalf of the customer's convenience simply wasn't part of his job.

3 My Bubble, My Rules

This is the issue of "personal space", about which we are growing increasingly touchy. One of the great principles of manners, especially in Britain, is respecting someone else's right to be left alone, unmolested, undisturbed. The sociolinguists P. Brown and S. C. Levinson, in their book *Politeness: Some Universals in Language Usage* (1987), coined the useful term "negative politeness" for this. The British are known to take this principle to extremes, because it chimes with our natural reticence and social awkwardness, and we are therefore simply outraged when other people don't distinguish sufficiently between public and private space. The advent of the mobile phone was a disaster for fans of negative politeness. We are forced to listen, open-mouthed, to other people's intimate conversations, property transactions, business arrangements, and even criminal deals. We dream up revenges, and fantasise about pitching phones out of the window of a moving train. Meanwhile, legislation on smoking in public places has skewed our expectations of negative politeness, so that if a person now lights a cigarette in our presence *anywhere*, we cough and gag and mutter, and furiously fan the air in front of our faces.

There is an episode of *The Simpsons* in which Bart

has a contagious mosquito bite, and is encased in an isolation bubble, and when he is told off for slurping his soup, invokes the memorable constitutional right: "Hey, my bubble, my rules." Increasingly, we are all in our own virtual bubbles when we are out in public, whether we are texting, listening to iPods, reading, or just staring dangerously at other people. Concomitantly, and even more alarmingly, our real private spaces (our homes; even our brains) have become encased in a larger bubble that we can't escape: a communications network which respects no boundaries. Our computers are fair game for other computers to communicate with at all times. Meanwhile, people call us at home to sell us things, whatever the time of day. I had a call recently from a London department store at 8pm to arrange a delivery, and when I objected to the hour, the reply was, "Well, *we're* here until *nine*." There is no escape. In a Miami hotel room last year, I retrieved the message flashing on my phone, and found that it was from a cold caller. I was incensed. Someone in reception was trying to sell me a time share. In my hotel room! No wonder people are becoming so self-important, solipsistic, and rude. It used to be just CIA agents with ear-pieces who walked round with preoccupied, faraway expressions, and consequently regarded all the little people as irrelevant scum. Now, understandably, it's nearly everybody.

4 *The Universal Eff-Off Reflex*

It ought to be clear by now that manners fulfil a number of roles in social life. Arguably, their chief role is to make us feel safe in the company of strangers. In his book *The English* (1998) Jeremy Paxman says that manners seem to have been developed by the English "to protect themselves from themselves"; there is an attractive theory that, back in the mists of time, language evolved in humans simply as a less ghastly alternative to picking fleas off each other. We *placate* with good manners, especially when we apologise. Erving Goffman, in his *Relations in Public* (1971), wrote that an apology is a gesture through which an individual splits himself into two parts: the part that is guilty of the offence, and the part that dissociates itself from the crime and says, "I know why this was considered wrong. In fact, I think it's wrong myself." Goffman also explains what is going on when a person tells off a naughty child or dog in public: he is signalling to other people that while he loves the child/dog, he is also responsible for the child/dog, and since he clearly shares the general view of how the child/dog has just behaved, the matter is in hand and everyone can calm down.

Increasingly, it seems, this splitting does not occur – and to those who expect this traditional nod towards shared standards, the new behaviour can be profoundly scary. Point out bad manners to anyone younger than thirty-five, and you risk a lash-back reflex response of shocking disproportion. "Excuse me, I think your child dropped this sweet wrapper." "Why don't you Eff Off, you fat cow," comes the automatic reply. A man on a London bus recently told off a gang of boys, and was set on fire. Another was stabbed to death when he objected to someone throwing food at his girlfriend. How many of us dare to cry, "Get off that skateboard, you hooligan!" in such a moral climate? In the old days, when the split-ting occurred, a person would apply a bit of moral honesty to a situation and admit that he deserved to be told off. Not any more. Criticism is treated (and reacted to) as simple aggression. And this is very frightening. As Stephen L. Carter points out in his book *Civility* (1998), people now think that "I have a right to do X" is equal to "I am beyond censure when I do X." The comedian Jack Dee tells the true story of a health visitor friend who was appalled to find a quite large child still suckling from his mother. "I wonder whether we should be putting a stop to this?" she said. At which, the boy detached himself from the breast, told her to Eff Off, and then went back to his dinner.

One hesitates to blame television for all this because that's such an obvious thing to do. But, *come on*. Just because it's obvious doesn't mean it's not true. Popular culture is fully implicated in the all-out plummeting of social standards. Abuse is the currency of all reality shows. People being vulgar and rude to each other in contrived, stressful situations is TV's bread and butter. Meanwhile the encouragement of competitive, material self-interest is virtually its only other theme. The message and content of a vast amount of popular television can be summed up in the words, "And you can Eff right Off, too." No wonder people's aspirations are getting so limited, and their attitude to other people so cavalier. I got in a taxi recently and the driver said, "Do you know what I'd do if I had a lot of money?" I thought, well, take a holiday, buy a smallholding, give it to the Royal Society for the Protection of Birds? He said, "I'd crash the car through the wall of that pub, drive right up to the bar, wind down the window and say, 'Mine's a pint, landlord, and you can Eff Off if you don't like it coz I'm buying the place.'"

5 Booing the Judges

The timing was significant. Emerging, bruised and a bit horrified, from encounters with the uppity British public in the 2005 election campaign, the Prime Minister, Tony Blair, launched a campaign for the restoration of "respect". "A bit late," some of us muttered, when we heard. Respect was surely already a huge area for public concern. The humblest lip-reading TV viewer can spot a labio-dental fricative (or "F") being formed on the lips of a footballer, with the result that when a permanently livid chap such as Wayne Rooney, with his veins sticking out on his neck, and his jug-ears burning with indignation, hurls seventeen assorted labio-dental fricatives at the referee, there is no interpreting this as, "Actually, it *was* a bit of a dive, sir, but now I've learned my lesson and I shan't be doing it again." Sport is supposed to be character-forming, but people are turning out like Wayne Rooney, and we are in deep trouble. Blaming the parents is an attractive option here, by the way. In 2002, the American research unit Public Agenda published *Aggravating Circumstances: A Status Report on Rudeness in America*, in which only 9 per cent of those questioned thought that children behaved respectfully towards adults, and 71 per cent reported seeing parents at sports events "screaming" at coaches, referees, and players.

Disrespect for older people; disrespect for professional people; disrespect for property – every day we are newly shocked at the prevalence of this kind of rudeness. Egalitarianism was a noble aim, as was enlightened parenting, but both have ploughed up a lot of worms. Authority is largely perceived as a kind of personal insult which must be challenged. On TV competitions, judges are booed and abused for saying, "Look, I'm sorry, he *can't dance!*", because it has become a modern tenet that success should have only a loose connection with merit, and that when "the people" speak, they are incontestably right. Meanwhile, old people are addressed by their first names, teachers are brusquely informed, "That's none of your business!" by small children, judges are abused in court by mouthy teenagers, and it turns out that even if you've got the exact money, you can't buy this jumper because Jason's got the key to the till and he's a muppet, he's out the back at the moment, texting his girlfriend who's just come back from Rhodes which was all right but she wouldn't go again, she's more of a Spain person, if you know what I mean, I like Spain, I've been there twelve times, but then I'm a bit of an iconoclast.

The most extreme form of non-deference, of course, is to be treated as actually absent or invisible. People talk across you on planes, or chat between themselves when they are serving customers. Nothing – *nothing* – makes me more angry than this. I get sarcastic. I wave in people's faces. I say aloud, "I'm sure I'm standing here. Can you see me standing here? Why don't you just catch my eye for a second to acknowledge that I am standing here?" For some time now, I have been carrying a Sooty glove-puppet on shopping expeditions, so that I can at least have a decent conversation when buying stuff in Ryman's. "What's that, Sooty? That will be £3.99? What's that, Sooty? Thank you very much? What's that, Sooty? Goodbye?"

6 Someone Else Will Clean It Up

Of all forms of rudeness, the hardest for a lot of people to understand is the offence against *everybody*. The once-prevalent idea that, as individuals, we have a relationship with something bigger than ourselves, or bigger than our immediate circle, has become virtually obsolete. For this reason, many people simply cannot see why they shouldn't chuck their empty burger box out of the car window. They also don't see any reason to abide by traffic laws unless there is a speed camera advertised. "That's so selfish!" is a cry that has no judgemental content for such people, and little other meaning either. Yes, we have come a long way from Benjamin Rush, in 1786, writing, "Let our pupil be taught that he does not belong to himself, but that he is public property." These days, of course, the child is taught to believe quite the opposite: that public property, in the natural way of things, belongs to him.

The interesting thing is that, cut free from any sense of community, we are miserable and lonely as well as rude. This is an age of social autism, in which people just can't see the value of imagining their impact on others, and in which responsibility is always conveniently laid at other people's doors. People are trapped in a kind of blind, brute state of materialism. "There is no such thing as society," Mrs Thatcher said. Well, there certainly isn't now. The latest Keep Britain Tidy campaign has thrown up an interesting moral puzzler for traditionalists by targeting the obvious self-interest of teenage litterers. It trades on – well, what else? Oral sex. Ingenious, or what? "While you're down there ..." runs the slogan, over the sort of come-and-get-it-big-boy pictures you normally see on little cards in phone booths before they are removed by the police. The idea is that, while you're down there, you will also place empty beer cans in the bins provided.

I have to report that my reaction to the "While you're down there ..." posters is, to say the least, mixed. I am actually revolted by their cynicism, disgusted by the explicitness, concerned that teenage promiscuity might be a high price to pay for less litter, but on the other hand relieved and pleased that, in a poster aimed at young people, the ellipsis has been used correctly and that there is an apostrophe in the "you're". In other words, it actually could have been worse.

!#*!

This book is, obviously, a big, systematic moan about modern life. And the expression "Talk to the hand" sort of yokes it all together. "Talk to the hand" specifically alludes to a response of staggering rudeness best known from *The Jerry Springer Show* – "Talk to the hand, coz the face ain't listening", accompanied by an aggressive palm held out at arm's length. I chose it for the title because it's the way I've started to see the world. Nearly sixty years ago, George Orwell wrote in *Nineteen Eighty-Four* that the future was a boot stamping on a human face for ever. I see it as a forest of belligerent and dismissive palms held up to the human face instead. Thank you for choosing to hold for an assistant. There's no one here to help you at this time. Nobody asked you to hold the Effing door open. An error of type 506 has occurred. Please disconnect, check your preferences, then go off and die. Do NOT type PIN until requested. Please continue to hold, your call is important to us. Sharon's in charge of envelopes and she isn't in on Fridays. You need to go to the other till. Have you considered on-line banking? Eff Off, fat cow. If you would like to speak to an assistant, please have your account details ready and call back in 200 years.

People tell me, by the way, that it is possible to get terribly rude service in France, and that I've just had a lot of unusually nice experiences. Ho hum. I also hear from Americans that Britain is friendly and ever so polite, to which I reply, "Surely *America* is friendly and ever so polite (except at immigration)?" and they say, oh no, we're the rudest country on earth. In her book about the English, Kate Fox conducted field experiments, such as bumping into people to see if they would say "Sorry" – which 80 per cent of them duly did. She concluded that manners have not declined, and that when we exclaim at the standards of courtesy on the roads, we ought to remember what it's like to drive in Italy. We still queue up nicely, maintain a belief in fair play, and when we don't like something, we make an ironic joke about it (because we don't like to make a scene). And yet, if you ask people, they will mostly report with vehemence that the world has become a ruder place. They are at breaking point. They feel like blokes in films who just. Can't. Take. Any. More. So what on earth is going on?

THE FIRST GOOD REASON

THE FIRST GOOD REASON

Was That So Hard to Say?

The trouble with traditional good manners, as any fool knows, is judging where to draw the line. Politeness is, after all, a ritual of tennis-like exchange and reciprocity, of back-and-forth *pick* and *pock*, and unfortunately there is rarely an umpire on hand to stop play when the tie-break has been going on for four hours already and it's got so dark you can no longer see the net. "Thank you," says one polite person to another. "No, thank YOU," comes the response.

"No, thank YOU."

"No, really, the gratitude is all mine."

"Look, take it, you swine."

"No, please: I insist."

"After you, I said."

"No, please: after YOU."

"Look, I said after you, fatso."

"No, please, after you."

"After YOU."

"After YOU."

Did they ever discover perpetual motion in physics? In manners, it has been around for aeons. In 1966, Evelyn Waugh famously issued a warning to Lady Mosley that, if she wrote to him, she would always receive an answer. "My father spent the last twenty years of his life answering letters," he wrote. "If someone thanked him for a wedding present, he thanked them for thanking him, and there was no end to the exchange but death."

But although it can get out of hand, the principle of civil reciprocity is a solid one, for which reason it is an occasion for total, staggering dismay that it appears to be on its way out. The air hums with unspoken courtesy words, these days. You hold a door open for someone and he just walks through it. You let a car join traffic, and its driver fails to wave. People who want you to move your bag from a seat just stare at you until you move it; or sometimes they sit on it, to make the point more forcibly. As for the demise of "please", you may overhear a child demanding in a supermarket at the top of its voice,

"I want THAT ONE!" Hope briefly flares when the harassed mother bellows back, "You want that one, WHAT?" But you might have known how this would turn out. "I want that one, YOU EFFING BITCH!" shouts the kid in response.

Please, thank you, excuse me, sorry – little words, but how much they mean. Last week, a young woman sitting opposite me on a train picked up my discarded *Guardian* and just started reading it, and I realised afterwards that, had I wanted to do something similar, I would have used the maximum of politeness words ("Excuse me, sorry, may I? Thank you") instead of none at all. The near extinction of the word "sorry" is a large subject we will treat elsewhere, but it seems appropriate to repeat here the story of the *Independent*'s Janet Street-Porter, who, while filming a documentary about modern education last year, tried to prompt the children at a school assembly to grasp the importance of apology. "Children," she said, "in every family home, there's a word which people find it really hard to say to each other. It ends in 'y'. Can anyone tell me what it is?" There was a pause while everyone racked their brains, and then someone called out, "Buggery?"

As this book progresses, we will be dealing with sources of true, eye-watering horror and alienation, but the decline of courtesy words seems a good, gentle place to start because the saying of such words appears quite a simple matter. Unfortunately, however, it is not quite as simple as it looks. Besides being the *sine qua non* of good manners, what do these words really do? Well, they are a ritual necessary to life's transactions, and also magic passwords, guaranteed to earn us other people's good opinion and smooth the path to our own desires. Politeness is itself a complicated matter. When it works, does it draw people comfortably together, or does it actually keep them safely apart? And what of its moral content? Surely if we hold doors open, we are acting altruistically? Yet our furious, outraged, jumping-up-and-down reaction when we are not thanked would indicate that we hold doors open principally to procure the reward of a public pat on the back. Why is it so important to us that everyone should affirm a belief in the same codes of behaviour? Why is it so scary when someone doesn't? Should we get out more? Or is going out the problem, and we should actually *stay in*?

Any study of the history of the subject of manners begins with Norbert Elias's pioneering work *The Civilizing Process*, which began life as two volumes, *The History of Manners* and *State Formation and Civilization*, in 1939. It is not, sadly, the easiest of books to read, and I have gone quite pale and cross-eyed in the attempt, but it famously includes a section on the advance of etiquette in the early modern period which has been plundered by historians of society ever since it was first translated into English in the 1960s. Taking such etiquette issues as urinating, nose-blowing and spitting, Elias traces the norms for these activities in western Europe over several hundred years. For example, in the Middle Ages, "Do not spit into the bowl when washing your hands" becomes, by the time of Erasmus' *De civilitate morum puerilium* (*On Good Manners for Boys*) in 1530, "Turn away when spitting, lest your saliva fall on someone ... It is unmannerly to suck back saliva." By 1714, we find in a French manual the excellent advice: don't spit such a great distance that you have to hunt for the saliva to put your foot on it.

Obviously, a modern person is hoping, sooner or later, for the plain injunction, "Look, just stop *spitting!* What is it with all this *spitting*?" – but that's quite a long time coming. For hundreds of years, people were advised that saliva (not phlegm, which is odd) was better out than in, and that placing your foot over your own little pool of spittle marked you out as a toff with finer feelings. What a relief when, at last (in 1774), it becomes the mark of a gent not to spit on the walls or the furniture. Only in 1859, however, does a book called *The Habits of Good Society* flip the whole subject to a modern perspective. You might even say that it overturns expectorations (ho ho). "Spitting is at all times a disgusting habit ... Besides being coarse and atrocious, *it is very bad for the health.*"

Of course, it's no surprise that over a period of hundreds of years standards of behaviour should change and (from the perspective of a modern sensibility) improve. But some less obvious, and very intriguing, points arise from even a cross-eyed and incompetent reading of *The Civilizing Process*, because it's not just about people gradually doing fewer revolting things in public. It deals also with two related shifts: in politics, the inexorable centralising of power; and in society, the flattening and broadening of social differentiations ("diminishing contrasts, increasing varieties"). Not being a sociologist or historian, I am on very thin ice here, but I think I can see why manners might have risen in importance over a period marked by that kind of change. After all, the individual is subject to two opposing tides here, both pulling his feet from under him. When traditional class and power structures break down, people are apt to study each other feverishly for clues, and attach all kinds of judgement to forms of behaviour. Somewhere in the course of this paragraph, by the way, I let go of Norbert and struck out on my own. I couldn't even tell you where it happened.

However, what Elias does argue is that, working outwards from a courtly nucleus, standards of behaviour developed under the influence of two evolving "fears": shame and repugnance. It seems that once the rigidities of feudal society have given way to complex and diverse social networks, the Freudian super-ego inside each one of us becomes responsible for us having manners. Thus, the individual judges his own actions against a standard set by his own super-ego, and feels shame; he judges other people's actions against the same super-ego, and feels repugnance. W. B. Yeats once said that we make rhetoric out of the quarrels with others, but poetry out of the quarrels with ourselves. What Elias sees in the history of manners is a similarly creative internal wrestling match between a person's natural savagery and his own psychological organ of self-restraint:

> A major part of the tensions which were earlier discharged directly in conflicts with other people must be resolved as an inner tension in the struggle of the individual with himself ... In a sense, the danger zone now passes through the self of every individual.

I promise this is the most boring part of this book (I certainly hope it is). But I feel it's important to establish that reeling in horror at other people's everyday impoliteness may just go with the territory of being civilised. Concern over the collapse of public behaviour is not a minor niggling thing. Nor is it new. The manners books quoted by Elias unwittingly tell two stories at once: their very existence proves that concern over the state of manners has followed the same upward graph, over time, as the civilizing process itself. If one takes the view that modern-day manners are superior to the cheerful spit-and-stamp of olden times, a paradox begins to emerge: while standards have been set ever higher, people have become all the more concerned that standards are actually dropping. Basically, people have been complaining about the state of manners since at least the fifteenth century. The discomfiting behaviour of others is one of humanity's largest preoccupations, and is incidentally the basis of quite a lot of literature. Blame the damn super-ego. If we feel doomed and miserable when we consider the rudeness of our world, we are not the first to feel this way, and we certainly won't be the last.

However, we exist at a particular moment, and there can be no harm in analysing what is happening to manners right now, at the start of the twenty-first century. Theory is all very well, I hear you cry, but I'm still holding this door open and beginning to realise I could die here before anybody thanked me for doing it. So let's just take the holding-the-door example for a moment and see what can be learned from it about the function of courtesy words. Let's imagine that you hold the door open and everything goes

TALK TO THE HAND

to plan: the person says, "Thank you" and you say, "You're welcome" and the whole episode is success-fully closed. When that perfect scene unfolds, how do you feel? Well, (1) relieved that they weren't rude, of course. On the personal level, you feel (2) vindi-cated, (3) validated, and (4) virtuous. On a social or political level, you feel (5) safe. What is quite inter-esting is that you also feel (6) completely indifferent to the individual who has thanked you, because no personal relationship has been established between you. It is very, very rare for lifelong friendships to be built on a holding-the-door incident. Addresses are not often exchanged. All that happens is that a small obligation is raised, then swiftly cancelled, and normal life is immediately resumed.

So, what happens when the "thank you" does not come? The reverse reactions apply.

1   In place of feeling relieved, you are exasper-ated – but, crucially, not surprised. Oh no, you are definitely not surprised. "Typical!" you say. As Kate Fox points out, "Typical!" is one of our default modes, along with making jokes instead of complaining, claiming to prefer everything in

moderation, and prizing modesty above all other social gifts. The "Typical!" response is actually quite self-flattering, of course. It suggests that fate can never wrong-foot us because we are always prepared for the worst or most unlikely event. "So then my sister-in-law had a sex change and went off to live in Krakatoa. Typical!" we exclaim. "So then they started bombing Baghdad. Typical!" "The cat turned out to be a reincarnation of a seventh-century Chinese prophet. Typical!"

2 Instead of feeling vindicated, you are dismayed by the rejection of your kindness. Your dignity is wounded. You feel that the world is laughing at you for holding this door open.

3 Far from feeling validated, you feel obliterated. Are you invisible, then? Have you disappeared? Do doors hold themselves open these days? Do I *look* like a doorman? Would they like to *pay* me as a doorman? (You are bound to wax weakly sarcastic at this point.)

4 Instead of feeling coolly virtuous, you feel a flame of righteous indignation. A good deed has been thrown back in your face! Ha! "Did you see what that woman did? I held the door and she walked

right through! I was doing the *right* thing, and she did the *wrong* thing!" The sensation of being morally superior to everyone else in the world is, of course, secretly the best bit about the whole experience, but beware. What it brings out is not the most attractive aspect of your personality.

5   Instead of feeling safe, you are frightened. You succumb to accelerated moral reasoning. This person has no consideration for others, therefore has no imagination, therefore is a sociopath representative of a world packed with sociopaths. When someone is rude to you, the following logic kicks in: "I have no point of connection with this person ... A person who wouldn't say thank you is also a person who would cut your throat ... Oh my God, society is in meltdown and soon it won't be safe to come out."

6   Finally, you HATE the person who did not say thank you. Indifference is no longer an option. The whole incident has now become intensely personal, although you daren't say anything for fear of reprisal (see chapter four). This person has, through casual and ignorant discourtesy, made you seethe with a mixture of virtuous

affront, fury, and fear – and don't forget, you are STILL holding the door open. No wonder we shout after people, "A thank-you wouldn't kill you!" It's amazing we don't wrench doors from their hinges, run after people, and say, "Here! Open it yourself next time, OK?"

Of course, what we want is for everyone to be as polite as us. The reason I have begun with "please" and "thank you" is that nothing could be simpler than to learn these words. That's what we say to ourselves every day. They are only words! They cost nothing! Also, they are in limitless supply and are miraculously immune to the dangers of over-use. I have recently started playing badminton in the eve-nings, and last Thursday I managed to say, "Sorry" nearly 500 times in a two-hour period, but here's the marvellous thing: I can still say it any time I want. Obviously, I wish I were as skilful at foot-work and bat-work as I am at apologising – but that's another story. What is so interesting, of course, is that we all apologise to each other; even the really good players. So quite a lot of energy that might be usefully diverted to running and hitting goes into consoling and exonerating, as well. "No, not your fault! That shot was mine! I should have gone for that! You are completely in the clear! You really shouldn't apologise!" Every so often, we try to ban apology from the court, but we can't manage without it. We implode from the effort of swallowing all the "sorry"s. So the soundtrack of our matches goes sorry-sorry-sorry-sorry-SORRY-sorry-SORRY-sorry-sorry, interrupted by the occasional brisk "Yours!" (from my partner) and the responding "Oh no!" (from me), followed by another bout of sorry-sorry-sorry-sorry-sorry.

But the world is changing. Those of us who automatically deal out politeness words in suitable contexts are becoming uncomfortably aware that we earn less credit for it than we used to. It is becoming obvious that we are the exception rather than the rule, and that our beautiful manners fall on stony ground. People who serve the public are becoming impervious to rudeness, either because they are young and don't care, or because they are older and have learned to toughen up or suffer a nervous breakdown. Either way, if you attempt to sympathise with a shop-worker who has just served a rude customer, the response is rarely the one you expect. Mainly you will get a blank shrug, which carries the worrying implication: this person doesn't care whether customers are polite or not. This makes it quite hard to go through the ensuing politeness display without feeling self-conscious, or even quaint. "May I please have it wrapped separately?" you ask, with your smile fading. "Thank you, that's perfect, how kind you are." The ground starts to slip from under you, as no validating response comes your way, yet you are powerless to stop being polite and old-fashioned. "And what a fine morning, forsooth!" you exclaim. "Ha. By God's breath, thou hast a cunning way with yon mechanical abacus! Hast thou a quill-pen prithee? Or mayhap I must digitate upon yon artful keypad?"

At least we are generally spared the enforced perkiness of American service workers, for whom a positive attitude and excessive civility are non-negotiable. Trawling the internet, I discovered an article from 2000 intriguingly titled "The Civility Glut", in which Barbara Ehrenreich paints a grim picture of life under the system of "Have a nice day", "Have a great day", and "Have a really great day". She reveals that Wal-Mart workers are subjected to video-training in the art of "aggressive hospitality" and complains that call-centre workers have started to exclaim, "Perfect!" and "Great!" when she gives them her account number and home address. She has to remind herself not to get too big-headed about how great and perfect her zip code appears to be, in the admiring eyes of others. Meanwhile, she has started to feel embarrassed by her own ritual "Goodbye", because it has begun to sound a bit terse and dismissive in the context of "Have a really wonderful special day with knobs on." What struck me was the example, "I sure don't!", which is evidently the cheerful response you can get if you ask, "Do you have any seats on that flight?" Imagine where this "cruel new locution" could lead. "May I sit here?" "You sure can't!" "Excuse me, officer, is my house still standing?" "It sure isn't!" "Will I ever see you again, my darling?" "You sure won't!" "Doctor, did he leave me one final message?" "He sure didn't!"

However, any effort is better than none. So what is to be done? In terms of making the world go round, these words used to mean a lot. Courtesy words are our most elementary way of indicating that we are aware of the presence of other people, and of the impact we may be having on them. Consideration for others being the foundation of manners, children ought to be taught to use the courtesy words because they thereby learn an important social habit: to remember there are other people in the world. I think it is right to say, "Excuse me" when answering one's phone on the train. I think it is right to say, "Thank you" to the driver when alighting from a bus. We are not invisible to one another. Attention must be paid. The problem, as I hope to explore later, is that people are increasingly unwilling to admit, when they are out in public, that they are not nevertheless – through sheer force of will – actually in private. When they are on trains, or in the street, or in a queue for taxis, they can't say the courtesy words because to do so would explode their idea of the entire experience, which is that they are alone and that nobody else exists. They are, I believe, *afraid* to speak to other people. Hence the astonishing aggression that is unleashed if you challenge them. If you speak to them, you scare them.

However, the magical nature of these words needs to be admitted, too. There is a rather unpleasant aspect to courtesy words which we conveniently overlook because it does not reflect well upon us. As children, we were taught that saying the right words at the right moment had just one function: it was the key to gaining parental approval, which was in turn the key to getting what we wanted. From a moral point of view, this was pretty bad educational practice, but what the hey, people have been doing it for centuries, training children to be crafty hypocrites. In his play *Heartbreak House* (1919) George Bernard Shaw provides the great line: "If you will only take the trouble always to do the perfectly correct thing, and to say the perfectly correct thing, you can do just what you like." None of us can deny that our attitude to courtesy words contains an element of this cynicism. Make the right noises and you get the reward. Deep in our hearts, we recognise that we are merely graduates of successful behavioural training. This does not sit well with our feelings of social virtue. However, the greater happiness gets served under this system, and we can rightly feel proud to be part of that.

Where this magical thinking is now a bit dangerous is in the corollary lesson we learned as children: that if we make the right noises, we may deflate danger, or disarm aggression. Politeness words are not just concerned with making the world friendly and smooth-running: they are an acknowledgement that to negotiate human society we require overt appeasement strategies, such as are adopted by devious chimpanzees in wildlife documentaries. We may draw the line at grooming the alpha male or rolling over on our backs with our tummies in the air, but if we just say sorry at the exact right point, we believe that we may avoid being brained by a screeching savage wielding a bleached thigh-bone.

Politeness is a signal of readiness to meet someone half-way; the question of whether politeness makes society cohere, or keeps other people safely at arm's length, is actually a false opposition. Politeness does both, and that is why it's so frightening to contemplate losing it. Suddenly, the world seems both alien and threatening – and all because someone's mother never taught him to say, "Excuse me" or "Please". There is an old German fable about porcupines who need to huddle together for warmth, but are in danger of hurting each other with their spines. When they find the optimum distance to share each other's warmth without putting each other's eyes out, their state of contrived co-operation is called good manners. Well, those old German fabulists certainly knew a thing or two. When you acknowledge other people politely, the signal goes out, "I'm here. You're there. I'm staying here. You're staying there. Aren't we both glad we sorted that out?" When people don't acknowledge each other politely, the lesson from the porcupine fable is unmistakeable. "Freeze or get stabbed, mate. It's your choice."

! # ★ !

Two years ago, in Christiansburg, Virginia, a psychology professor came up with a technological solution to the problem of road rage. It was a little green light that could be installed at the back of a car and that could be flashed to say "please", "thank you", and "sorry". I believe a patent is actually in place, which makes me somehow want to burst into tears. This academic's reasoning was that, by means of his "Courteous Communicator", a driver could signal "thank you" (two flashes) or "I'm sorry" (three flashes) after cutting in front of another car.

Naturally, the invention was immediately quashed as unworkable and confusing, not to mention illegal and a bit daft. A spokesman for the American Automobile Association Foundation for Traffic Safety in Washington, DC, pragmatically pointed out that there already existed a courteous communicator in all cars: "It's called a turn signal," he said, "and some people don't even use that."

But how far this chap had missed the point! This nice Virginian man thought there might be a market for his invention – that motorists were crying out for a means of apologising to other road-users and thereby defusing bad feeling. Maybe he imagined it would ultimately lead to an even more sophisticated system of five flashes for "You're welcome" and six flashes for "Nice car, by the way!" and seven flashes for "Hey! You must come to dinner sometime!" and eight flashes for "That would be terrific!" In fact, of course, if he marketed a device for flashing, in orange neon, "Out of my way, asshole!" it would be an instant hit. No, there is one very good reason for not expecting motorists to start, suddenly, interacting with other road-users as if they are present in person. It is that the opposite is happening. When present in person, people are interacting with each other as if they are in cars.

So, one lesson can be drawn from all this courtesy-word malarkey. "Please" and "thank you" may not be so very hard to say, but they perform any number of sophisticated functions that are of no interest whatsoever to a growing number of people. Study the works of Erving Goffman, and you will find exquisite analysis of subtle transaction rituals between people in public – but the main effect will be to make you weep, because his wry observations of "remedial interchange" and "appeasement gestures" are built on the supposition that people are actually aware of each other, and are not concentrating all their attention on their iPods or mobile phones. Blame the conditions of modern life in any combination you prefer. I blame the parents, television, the internet, the mobile phone, the absence of war, the under-valuing of teachers, and I also blame the culture of blame. Richard Layard, in his recent book *Happiness: Lessons from a New Science* (2005), argues that "Our problem today is a lack of common feeling between people – the notion that life is essentially a competitive struggle." Well, that about sums it up. As I mentioned in the introduction, the only context in which you can expect to hear a "please" or "thank you" nowadays is in recorded messages – and hey, guess what, they are not extending courtesy at all, because they are not attempting to meet you half-way. "Please have your account number ready as this will help us do our job more efficiently. Thank you for waiting. I'm sorry you are having to wait." In a world increasingly starved of courtesy words, it's no wonder that when we hear these messages, we want to put back our heads and scream. As Goffman points out so beautifully, traffic cops may ask you politely to get out of the car, but that doesn't mean you have a choice.

THE SECOND GOOD REASON

THE SECOND GOOD REASON

Why am I the One Doing This?

I used to write a weekly newspaper column about the internet. This was in the mid-1990s, when newspapers were still in love with the newness of the information super-highway, and had launched special supplements, touchingly unaware that they were playing host to the mortal enemy of print culture, which would ultimately displace newspapers altogether. What an irony. Anyway, my column had no time for this over-excited supping-with-the-devil stuff: it was called "Logged Off" and was mainly a true record of my agonising difficulties just loading the software, dragging icons to the Stuffit Expander ("What the hell is a Stuffit Expander?"), and manfully trying to enjoy the impenetrable humour of computer jokes with punch-lines such as, "Excuse my friend, he's null-terminated." My column included, in its second week, the useful advice: "Things to do while awaiting connection to the internet: (1) Lick finger and clean keys of keyboard; (2) Lick finger and clean mouse; (3) Adjust earwax and stare at wall; (4) Lick finger and clean space bar; (5) Run out of fingers." From this you can deduce what species of fun I was having.

Looking back, it is now clear that my computer's memory was far too small for the stuff I was trying to do, and that the internet was pretty primitive, too. Thus I often waited twenty-five minutes for a website that was crushingly disappointing, mysteriously defunct, or had absolutely nothing on it. Entertainingly, on many occasions the search would reach its eighteenth minute and then just disconnect without explanation. Writing in the column about this disconnection problem, I received many helpful letters from readers, one of which suggested that, if my computer was located at some distance from the telephone socket (it was), I should wrap the phone cable around an item of furniture, ideally a tall bookcase. In my desperation, I tried it. Astonishingly, it worked.

Anyway, the final blow to the column came when,

one week, I had been examining a recommended website about the *Titanic* and found a rare clickable option, "About the creators". I clicked it, chewed the edge of the desk for the next twenty-five minutes, and then discovered the full, bathetic truth. The creator of this website was a schoolboy in Canberra. He was fourteen. This *Titanic* site was his science project. I had just spent four hours laboriously accessing the homework of a teenage Australian. It was time for the madness to stop.

When I wrote in the introduction to this book about the unacceptable transfer of effort in modern life, this was the sort of thing I was talking about. In common with many people today, I seem to spend my whole life wrestling resentfully with automated switchboards, waiting resentfully at home all day for deliveries that don't arrive, resentfully joining immense queues in the post office, and generally wondering, resentfully, "Isn't this transaction of mutual benefit to both sides? So why am I not being met half-way here? Why do these people never put themselves in my shoes? Why do I always have to put myself in theirs? *Why am I the one doing this?*"

And I lump the internet into this subject because

it is the supreme example of an impersonal and inflexible system which will provide information if you do all the hard work of searching for it, but crucially (a) doesn't promise anything as a reward for all the effort, (b) will never engage in dialogue, (c) is much, much bigger than you are, and (d) only exists in a virtual kind of way, so never has to apologise. It seems to me that most big businesses and customer service systems these days are either modelling themselves on the internet or have learned far too much from a deep reading of Franz Kafka. Either way, they certainly benefit from the fact that our brains have been pre-softened by our exposure to cyber-space. Our spirits are already half-broken. We have even started to believe that clicking "OK" is an act of free will, while "Quit" and "Retry" represent true philosophical alternatives.

Fuming resentment is the result. You might remember the old *Goon Show* catchphrase, "Foiled again!" Well, we are being foiled again from morning till night, in my opinion; foiled and thwarted and frustrated; and they wonder why so many people are on repeat prescriptions. Everywhere we turn for a bit of help, we are politely instructed in ways we can navigate a system to find the solution for ourselves – and I think this is driving us mad. "Do it yourself" was a refreshing and liberating concept in its day, but it has now got completely out of hand. In his book *Grumpy Old Men* (2004), which accompanied the BBC series, Stuart Prebble memorably refers to the culture of DIYFS (Do it your Effing self) and I think he is on to something that extends well beyond the trials of flat-pack self-assembly furniture. I am now so sensitive on this DIYFS issue that when I see innocent signs for "Pick Your Own Strawberries" I shout, as I drive past, "No, I won't bloody pick my own bloody strawberries! You bloody pick them for me!"

Say a replacement credit card arrives in the post. "Oh, that's nice," you say, innocently. "I'll just sign it on the back, scissor the old one, and away I go!" But close inspection reveals that you must phone up first to get it authorised. "Okey-dokey!" you cry. You dial a long number and follow instructions to reach the card-authorisation department (press one, press one, press two), then are asked to input the card number (sixteen digits) then the card expiry date (four digits) then your date of birth (six digits), then your phone number (eleven digits), then told to wait. Naturally, your initial okey-dokeyness has started to wane a bit by this time. You start to wonder whether the card will actually expire before this process is complete. "Please enter card number," comes the instruction. "What? Again?" you ask. But, listening to the menu, there is no button assigned to this reaction ("For *What? Again?* press four"), so off you go again with the sixteen digits and the four digits and then the six digits and the eleven digits, and then you hear the clipped, recorded message, "Sorry. We are unable to process your inquiry. Please call back at another time," and the line goes dead. Unable to believe your ears, you stare at the receiver in your shaking hand. It is at this point, in my experience, that a small cat always comes up behind you and emits a quiet "Miaow" and makes you actually scream and jump up and down with agitation and rage.

But such is modern life. Armies of underpaid call-centre workers have now been recruited and trained, not to help us, but to assure us, ever so politely, that the system simply does not allow us to have what we want, and no, you cannot speak to a supervisor because the system isn't organised that way. We are all slaves to the system, madam; that's just the way it is. An error of type 3265 has occurred; you're stuffed before you start, basically; click OK to exit; quit or retry, it's your funeral; anything else I can help you with?; thank you for calling, goodbye. Sometimes I think wistfully of that old TV series *The Prisoner* and how Patrick McGoohan finally blew up the computer by asking it the question "Why?" At the time, I thought it was a bit of a bizarre cop-out, what with the chimp and the space rocket and everything. Now, however, I think the notion of blowing up such an instrument of tyranny by asking it, "Why?" was quite profound. I am always wanting to ask, "Why?" – but stopping myself just in time, because I know the effect would be fatally weakening to my cause. When you ask, "Why?" these days, you instantly lose status. Asking, "Why?" usually signals the end of all meaningful exchange.

So they get away with it, the bastards. Steadily, the companies are shifting more and more effort onto their customers, and even using guilt-trip lines such as "Please have your account details ready, as this will help speed up the process, so that we can deal with more inquiries." The message here is that, yes, you may be waiting for twenty minutes while we make money from your call, but don't waste our time when you eventually get through because this would be rude and inconsiderate to others. "We are busy taking other calls," they say, sometimes. Does this placate you? No, it makes you hop up and down, especially when they suggest you call back later. "We are busy taking other calls. Perhaps you would like to call back later at a time more convenient to us? Half-past two in the morning tends to be quiet. It is a very small matter to set your alarm. Another option is to bugger off and give up; we find that a lot of our clients are choosing this option these days."

I could go on. In fact, I will. So here's a little personal story that still makes me scream. A few months ago, I was in New York (hooray). I had used my Visa card to book some theatre tickets and had then attempted to buy dinner with it. At this point I was told that a block had been put on the card, and that I would have to call customer services back in the UK. I am always okey-dokey-ish at the beginning of these processes; perhaps that is the key to my problem. So I called Barclaycard from my mobile phone, neatly navigated the automated answering service, and finally reached a very pleasant and reasonable woman, who seemed quite sympathetic when I told her what had happened.

Now, I am fully aware that credit-card fraud is an enormous problem for the companies, and that they had every right to check that I wasn't a criminal wielding someone else's cards. However, what the pleasant, reasonable woman said was that, card-fraud being what it is, the card companies now expect customers to make a courtesy call before travelling abroad. I started to hyperventilate. I was about to fly home after spending eight months travelling in America, Canada, Australia, New Zealand, Hong Kong, Singapore, France, Greece and Italy. I had been on forty-four flights. My legs were permanently ribbed from the flight socks. I had seen *DodgeBall* twenty-six times. It was as much as I could do to remember my own name. And now Barclaycard wanted me to clear my itineraries with them before leaving home? I had the brief, familiar sensation that I was going actually insane. "But I don't work for Barclaycard," I protested. "I pay Barclaycard so that it works for me." There was no point pressing the point, however. I had no power in this situation, and we both knew it. I have not ventured abroad since, and I must admit, it's partly out of pique.

My feeling about customer relations in general is that they all adopt this high-handed attitude for one simple reason: *they can*. They are insiders. They are authorised agents of the system. In face-to-face encounters, while one deals every day with nice people in shops and post offices, there is no forgetting the power relation that pertains: as agents of the system, they are in a position to condescend. As mere supplicants, we can petition for attention, but not make demands. Years ago, when I worked in shops, things were different. We deferred to customers because they had the power to spend or withhold money, and therefore controlled the ultimate destiny of our jobs. The old power ratio of shop-worker to customer was 40:60. Now it's 80:20, or maybe 100:0.

"Oh no, till's down again," they say, not looking you in the eye, and definitely not apologising, while reaching for a bell switch. "This is always happening to me," they continue, gloomily. And that's it. You are trapped. The bell sounds. Nobody comes. Time passes. Your train departs. A clock ticks. Somewhere in the Arctic Circle, a wall of ice drops into a crystal sea. The assistant plucks at your purchases with a look of mild curiosity and then resumes a prior conversation with a colleague about the final instalment of *Star Wars* and whether it's worth going because the last couple weren't up to much but there's nothing else on, apart from that thing with Orlando Bloom, oh yeah, but Jazza said that was crap, and what about *Batman Begins*, well, that's an idea. Finally, some dim race-memory prompts you to ask, "I suppose you couldn't hurry this along?" But you know the answer in your heart of hearts. "Nah," they say, rolling their eyes. "Till."

Life ebbs away. A tree grows in Brooklyn. Finally, a supervisor comes huffing to the rescue and, without catching your eye, taps a password into the till, and your liberated card is returned to you. No apology, of course. But on the plus side, there is now no need to buy any movie magazines for a while. But shouldn't *somebody* say sorry? Well, the inevitable happens. "Sorry for all that," you say. "No problem," they say, forgivingly.

! # * !

Now, there is a theory – advanced chiefly by Steven Johnson in his 2005 book *Everything Bad is Good for You* – that interactivity with machines and virtual worlds is making people smart in new and important ways. You were hoping for a bright side and here it is. Evidently, the neurotransmitter called dopamine (associated with craving) responds with high excitement when there is seeking and searching to be done. Johnson is specifically referring to – and defending – the attraction of video games, but I think the science applies also to the mental habits that attach to people who spend a lot of time on the internet or learning unfamiliar systems. "Where our brain wiring is concerned," he writes, "the craving instinct triggers a desire to explore. The [dopamine] system says, in effect, 'Can't find the reward you were promised? Perhaps if you just look a little harder you'll be in luck – it's got to be around here somewhere.'" Games playing may have negligible effects on our morality or understanding of the world, Johnson admits, but it trains the brain wonderfully in decision-making. "Novels may activate our imagination, and music may conjure up powerful emotions, but games force you to decide, to choose, to prioritize."

Now, *Everything Bad is Good for You* is certainly well-argued and important. Impatient old fuddy-duddies such as myself tend not to research the chemistry of neurotransmitters before making sweeping judgements about the harm "interactivity" is having on a generation of people who seem, more than ever, not to know how to interact. Johnson explains, rather elegantly, that old measures of IQ are becoming outmoded because intelligence nowadays is all about application: it is the ability "to take in a complex system and learn its rules on the fly". For young people, this ability is second nature. Any fool knows that, if you need a new and unfamiliar VCR programmed in a hurry, you commandeer any small passing child to do it. But the technology moves on too quickly for some of us to keep up, that's all. Looking back at my "Logged Off" columns, I find that, less than ten years ago, I was working with Eudora and AddMail, and attempting to change search engines from Infoseek to MacWAIS (but MacWAIS demanded a mysterious "key" that I did not have). New email was signalled by a cock-crow, and "No new messages" indicated by an icon of a black snake. I promise you I have no mental picture of this black snake icon. A multitude of techie advances has displaced it.

But enough of this self-pity. Johnson is clearly on to something here. But he seems to be deliberately avoiding a less comforting aspect of all this: that the kind of enhanced brain activity he celebrates not only has a known male gender bias, but is associated with Asperger's syndrome and autism. Confidently defying any such alarmist suggestions, in fact, he argues that, through the miracle of internet connectivity, people are now *more* socialised, not less! It is at this point that I start to make impatient harrumphing and snorting noises. The new social networking applications are "augmenting our people skills", Johnson jaw-droppingly avers. They are "widening our social networks, and creating new possibilities for strangers to share ideas and experiences".

It is true that we are becoming instantly familiar with strangers, and I'll be discussing in chapter five why a lot of older people consider that to be rude rather than liberating. But "widening our social networks"? Well, Johnson is not the first to fall into this little trap of virtuality, of course. Bill Clinton famously said in a State of the Union address that the internet was the new town square. Kate Fox calls it the new garden fence. It isn't, though, is it? It's people sitting on their own, staring straight ahead, tapping keyboards, often in dim light, surrounded by old coffee cups and plates with crumbs on. True, each of us has a virtual social group in our email address book, but the group has no existence beyond us; it is not a "group" at all. True, hot information whizzes around the world with the speed of supersonic gossip, but, crucially, we can choose to ignore it. Many aspects of our screen-bound lives are bad for our social skills simply because we get accustomed to controlling the information that comes in, managing our relationships electronically, deleting stuff that doesn't interest us. We edit the world; we select from menus; we pick and choose; our social "group" focuses on us and disintegrates without us. This makes it rather confusing for us when we step outdoors and discover that other people's behaviour can't be deleted with a simple one-stroke command or dragged to the trash icon. Sitting at screens and clicking buttons is a very bad training for life in the real world.

Also, this god-like privilege of the double-click

is dangerous for a philosophical reason. It blinds us to something significant: that we can pick and choose only *from what is offered*. We have choice, choice, enormous amounts of choice. But that does not amount to free will. In fact, what we do is *select*. We can actively click, and click, and click, but our role is still essentially passive because we have no influence over the list of selections. Years ago, I was asked in the street to answer market-research questions about a new yoghurt lolly. I was asked, "Is it A: creamy, B: fruity, C: refreshing?" When I said it was, if anything, a bit cheesy, the woman looked confused for a moment and then said brightly, "Look, don't worry, I'll put you down as a Don't Know!" Choice from menus is a burden dressed up as a privilege. It is bondage with bells on. And, of course, it still makes us do all the work.

But it is also beguilingly self-aggrandising, which is why we won't call a halt. This is my grand theory of social alienation in the early twenty-first century, by the way, so don't miss it, pay attention. The thing is, we are kings of click-and-buy. We can customise any service. We can publish a blog on the internet. We are always reachable by phone, text or email.

Our iPods store 4,000 of our own personal favourite tracks. Well, sod the gratification of our dopamine neurotransmitters in such an alarming context. The effect of all this limitless self-absorption is to make us isolated, solipsistic, grandiose, exhausted, inconsiderate, and anti-social. In these days of relative affluence, people are persuaded to believe that more choice equals more happiness, and that life should be approached as a kind of happiness expedition to the shops. This attitude is not only paltry and degenerate, but it breeds misery and monsters. And in case you can't hear me thumping the table, that's what I'm doing. Right. Now.

! # * !

Of course, I am not against personal freedom. As a woman from a working-class background, I never stop thanking my lucky stars for the good fortune of my birth; if I had been born even a few decades earlier, my only hope would have been that an obstinate phonetics professor would trip over me in Covent Garden, make a bet with an old colonel that he could pass me off as a duchess, and teach me to stop saying "I'm a good girl, I am." Born in the 1950s, however, I managed without a Professor Higgins – or, indeed, help from anyone at all. I benefited from a combination of post-war prosperity, liberal social change, the 1944 Education Act, equal pay, and the rise of reliable contraception. I used all the freedoms that came my way. The result of all this is that I have, unlike the huge majority of women of my class in history, done more or less what I liked with my life, my body, and my career. I believe in people taking responsibility for their own lives. I believe in being allowed to make choices.

But I really think this has gone too far, this worship of choice. I take my mum out for a cup of coffee and I say, "What would you like?" and I get quite impatient if she says, with surprise, "Um, a cup of coffee?" I want her to specify what size, what type, whipped cream or no whipped cream, choice of sprinkle, type of receptacle, type of milk, type of sugar – not because either of us cares about such stuff, but because I'm expecting all these questions at the counter, and you look daft if you dither. A friend of mine was in America for the first time, ordered a modest breakfast sausage, and was dismayed by the barked question, "Links or patties?" because it appeared to be meaningless. "Can I have a sausage?" she repeated. "Uh-huh," said the waitress, pen hovering above her order pad. "Links or patties?" "Sausage?" she kept saying, pathetically. "Er, sausage?" In Britain at that time, we were unused to there being a choice of sausage type. She had never heard the words "links" or "patties" before. Besides which, in her defence, a patty is surely not a genuine sausage within the meaning of the word.

Meanwhile the choice impulse is being exploited to the utmost degree. "More choice than ever before!" say the advertisers. "Click and find anything in the world!" says the internet. "What people want is more choice," say the politicians. "Eight thousand things to do before you die!" offer the magazines. No wonder we are in a permanent state of agitation, thinking of all the unpicked choices and whether we've missed something. Every day, you get home from the shops with a bag of catfood and bin-liners and realise that, yet again, you failed to have cosmetic surgery, book a cheap weekend in Paris, change your name to something more glamorous, buy the fifth series of *The Sopranos*, divorce your spouse, sell up and move to Devon, or adopt a child from Guatemala. Personally, I'm worn down by it. And I am sure it isn't good for us. I mean, did you know there is a website for people with internet addiction? I will repeat that. There is a WEBSITE for people with INTERNET ADDICTION. Meanwhile, a friend of mine once told me in all seriousness that having children was definitely "on the shopping list"; another recently defined her religious beliefs as "pick and mix". The idea of the world's religions forming a kind of candy display, down which you are free to wander with a paper bag and a plastic shovel, struck me as worryingly accurate about the state of confusion and decadence we've reached. Soon they'll have signs outside the churches. "Forget make-your-own pizza. Come inside for make-your-own Sermon on the Mount!" The mystery of voter apathy is explained at a stroke here, by the way. How can I vote for *all* the policies of either the government or the opposition? How can I give them a "mandate"? I like some of their policies, but I don't like others, and in any case I'd like to chuck in some mint creams and pineapple chunks. I insist on my right to mix and match.

Oh well. In his lovely 1997 book *Deeper*, about his

early-adopter adventures on the internet, John Seabrook charts a very different experience from mine
in my days of "Logged Off". For one thing, he got
the hang of the technology a lot more quickly, and
never wrapped his phone cable around a bookcase
on the principle that anything is worth a try. While
I was still bewailing the sound-to-noise ratio of the
internet, he was conducting an email correspondence with Bill Gates. While I was putting my head
through plate glass windows at instructions such as
"You can change the default FTP download directory
by holding down the options menu item, selecting
preferences and changing the directories and applications dialog box", Seabrook was actually being
flamed. But he was led to similar questions in the
end.

> When you start out on-line, it seems as though
> politics, ethics and metaphysics ... are reduced to
> their original elements, and are yours to remake
> again ... Why should individuals obey other
> individuals? What are the benefits of individual
> liberty, and what harm does that liberty do society
> as a whole? Why is honesty necessary? What is a
> neighborhood? What is a friend? Who am I?

In the past decade and a half, the world has changed immensely because of the internet, with the virtual colliding with the real. Email, in particular, has had a huge impact on our perception of relative status. For our purposes here, however, the important thing is that all the clicking and searching may appear to be an active pursuit of knowledge, but it is still hard work with no guarantee of reward in the context of cold impersonality. Two and a half millennia of Socratic educational practice have been swept aside in fifteen years. The message now is, if you want knowledge, go and find it, good luck, sit there, don't move, see you later. And make friends with your dopamine. You won't get anywhere without it.

Doesn't the same alienating, laborious impotence mark our everyday dealings with the people who ought to be serving us? We make all the effort, just to find out how far we can get, and sometimes it isn't very far. The individual is now virtually brainwashed into accepting that clicking menus, punching buttons, and self-channelling are the nearest you can get to asking a question. "Why am I the one doing this? Shouldn't they be meeting me half-way?

Isn't this *rude*?" we cry – but we will probably be the last ones to see things this way. And now I must get on with calling Barclaycard. I am thinking of taking a trip, and I need to make sure they will let me.

THE THIRD GOOD REASON

THE THIRD GOOD REASON

My Bubble, My Rules

In October 2004, a fifteen-year-old girl at a school near Swindon became the centre of a news story when she spearheaded a rebellion. Apparently, the school's head teacher had "reminded" pupils that they were not allowed to hold hands, kiss, or otherwise parade their sexuality in "the workplace". Outraged, the pupils fought back. They staged a 200-strong strike plus a rally, and then set about petitioning the governors. This was an infringement of their human rights! "At sixteen, you can get married," argued the fifteen-year-old who got herself into the papers. "So to say you're not allowed to touch each other is ridiculous."

In February 2005, the Virginia State House of Representatives voted by a 60–34 majority to outlaw the wearing of low-slung jeans. The so-called

Droopy-Drawer Bill forbade the exposure of underwear in a way that was "lewd or indecent". The bill's sponsor told the house: "To vote for this bill would be a vote for character, to uplift your community and to do something good not only for the state of Virginia, but for this entire country." "Underwear is called underwear for a reason," commented one of his colleagues.

In June 2005, the London *Evening Standard* broke the news we had all been waiting for: "Soon We'll Watch TV As We Travel on the Tube." Evidently a trial of the new service will begin in 2006, and full service should be in place by the following year. "London Underground is planning to install the necessary technology to access broadcasts via the phone and digital radio. It also plans to offer wireless internet access in stations and on trains so that commuters using laptops can check their email or surf the net." Might there be "quiet" carriages, where people could escape the TV, radio, phoning, and surfing? No. "We will focus on education instead," said a spokesman. "People need to be told to be tolerant, so we will be running ads similar to those found on overground trains."

In March 2005, the *New York Times* ran a story headlined "No Need to Stew: A Few Tips to Cope with Life's Annoyances", about people who were taking small revenges on the annoyances of modern life. One Mr Williams (of Melrose, NY) had devised a way of settling the score against junk-mailers, which entailed inserting heavy paper and small strips of sheet metal in the business-reply envelopes, thus forcing the junk-mailers to pay huge extra postage. "You wouldn't believe how heavy I got some of those envelopes to weigh," he said. A spokesman for the United States Postal Service said that Mr Williams's actions sounded legal, as long as the envelope was properly sealed.

In papers everywhere for the past year or two, there has been larky but desperate advice from columnists and stand-up comedians on how to deal with cold callers, either on the phone or in person. First prize goes to the *Independent*'s Charles Nevin, who came up with: "Thank goodness! Do you have experience in restraining people?" as a way of dealing with nuisance callers on the doorstep. Close runner-up was his colleague Deborah Ross, who described how her partner always asks flatly, "Are you selling something?" When this is hastily denied, he says, "That's a pity. I was in the mood for buying something over the phone, whatever the cost. But now I fear the moment has passed. Goodbye."

Finally, in *The Guardian* in April 2005, came the story of research conducted by a psychiatrist from King's College London, which proved that the distractions of constant emails, text and phone messages were a greater threat to concentration and IQ than smoking cannabis. "Respondents' minds were all over the place as they faced new questions and challenges every time an email dropped into their inbox," wrote Martin Wainwright. "Manners are also going by the board, with one in five of the respondents breaking off from meals or social engagements to receive and deal with messages. Although nine out of ten agreed that answering messages during face-to-face meetings or office conferences was rude, a third nonetheless felt that this had become 'acceptable and seen as a sign of diligence and efficiency'."

! # ⋆ !

Sometimes I think we were better off before the term "personal space" escaped from sociology and got mixed up with popular ideas of entitlement. It is now, however, firmly in the *Oxford Dictionary of English*, defined as "The physical space immediately surrounding someone, into which encroachment can feel uncomfortable or threatening." You will note that there is no measurement indicated in this definition, such as "Generally accepted to be about a yard behind and two yards in front", which is an oversight on the part of the ODE, I think, because a lot of people would like to know their precise rights where personal space is concerned. As it is, everyone is tiresomely free to define their personal space subjectively, and to appeal to it when it suits them. Rude people are especially fond of the personal-space defence. Children insist on their right to personal space. Even my cat knows about it. You should see the way he looks at me when I attempt to share the comfy chair with him in front of the telly. "Budge up," I say, cheerfully. "The golf's on. You don't even like golf. Name me one player you recognise." And he purses his lips in that peculiar long-suffering, affronted-cat way, and I can hear him thinking, "I don't believe it. She's invading my personal space *again*."

I have to admit, I am rather keen on keeping other people at arm's length. If a chap stands an inch behind me and loudly crunches and slurps an apple, I suffer and moan and clench all the clench-able parts of my anatomy, but what I really want to do (please don't tell anybody) is to turn round on the spot with fists raised, and with an efficient, clean one-two, knock all his teeth out. What I would really appreciate is a kind of negative polarity I could switch on in personal-space emergencies; in fact, now I think of it, is there any lovelier, more comforting four-word combination than "Activate the force field"? All my life, I seem to have seen wonderful, battery-draining force fields demonstrated in science-fiction movies, but let me tell you: if you try to buy one, you draw a blank. You can't even get an automatic apple-atomiser that will detect inappropriately propinquitous apple-consumption, blow the fruit to smithereens and deliver a mild incidental electric shock to the genitals. No, personal space is still an ideal rather than a solid reality off which bullets would bounce and swords glance. The best mental picture I can come up with for personal space as we know it is a spherical membrane eight feet in diameter with a person inside it, bowling along like a hamster in a ball.

All the news stories above – about the Swindon schoolgirl, the man sending sheet metal through the post, and so on – are concerned with the notion of "space", one way or another. The trouble is, our own personal space always seems to be up for grabs in unacceptable ways. Other people don't respect our personal space and are conducting private phone conversations in public places, regardless of the annoyance they cause. Which is very, very rude of them. Ask people about rudeness, and after "Why don't people say thank you?" and "Why am I always the one doing everything?", the subject of annoying mobile phone users comes up more quickly than you can say "I'm on the train." What is happening? Why is this such a big issue? Have some people truly lost all sense of being out in public? Has some vital inhibitor in their brains been switched off? Surely we all agree that the question "Should I do this?" ought to have an automatic subsidiary question, "Should I do this *here*?" But on the other hand, are some of us extending our personal space an unreasonable distance – basically, for as far as the eye can see or the ear can hear? Why don't we accept that being out of doors means being with other people who do things we can't control?

In reality, mostly people on public transport listen inoffensively to iPods, or quietly text on their mobile phones, which are private activities designed simply to remove them from their surroundings, in pretty much the same way that reading a newspaper both passes the time and sends out the barrier signal, "Leave me alone." Yet there is something more profound going on. Our hamster balls just keep clashing with other people's hamster balls, and it isn't comfortable. The fifteen-year-old Swindon girl feels she has a right to canoodle at school. Academic friends say their students answer calls during lectures. Lovers lolling on the public grass on a sunny day glare at you if you look at them, as if you have just walked into their living-room. People chat in the cinema during the film, and sometimes in the theatre during the play. Air travellers on long-haul flights change into pyjamas in the lavatories. It's as if we now believe, in some spooky virtual way, that wherever we are, it's home.

! # * !

I have a rather heretical view when it comes to mobile phones, so I'd better confess to it at once. I don't mind people saying, "I'm on the train." It truly doesn't annoy me. Here are the things that drive me nuts when I'm out. I can't stand people talking in the cinema. I can't stand other people's cigarette smoke, especially outdoors. I am scared and angry when I hear the approach of young men drunkenly shouting. I can't stand children skateboarding on pavements, or cyclists jumping lights and performing speed slaloms between pedestrians, and I am offended by T-shirts with ugly Eff-Off messages on them. It was, however, the rather mild "Bored of the Beckhams" that was my least favourite T-shirt slogan of recent years, for the usual shameful pedantic reasons. "Bored *with* the Beckhams!" I would inwardly moan, reaching for the smelling salts in my lavender portmanteau. "Or even bored *by* the Beckhams, if you must! But bored *of* the Beckhams? Never, my dear, *never!*"

What else? Well, I am incensed by graffiti, and would like to see offenders sprayed all over with car-paint and then strung up for public humiliation. (As you can tell, I've given a lot of thought to that one.) I also can't abide to see people drop litter; it truly shocks me. People of all ages evidently think nothing of reaching into a bag, discovering something surplus to requirements, holding it out at arm's length and then insouciantly *letting go*. Walking along the Brighton seafront one balmy evening, I saw a woman perform a nappy-change on a public bench and then just leave the old nappy and the paper towels behind, when there was a litter-bin about fifteen feet away. Occasionally I will confront a litter-bug, running after them and saying, "Excuse me, I think you dropped this." But, well, I say "occasionally"; I've done it twice. Sensibly I weigh the odds. If the person is bigger than me, or is (very important consideration, this) *accompanied by* anyone bigger than me, I walk away. As a litter-bug vigilante, I know my limits. If they are over five foot two, or older than four, I let it go.

But as I say, the thing that doesn't drive me nuts is other people's mobile phones – mainly, I suspect, because I have one myself, but also because hearing a stranger on the phone humanises them in (to me) a generally welcome way, whereas watching them blow smoke in the air or drop soiled tissue or deface a building does quite the opposite. It seems to me obvious that "I'm on the train" is the main thing you will hear other people say, because – being reasonable about it – the train is the main place you are likely to hear people talking on mobile phones. If they said instead, "I'm in the bath" you'd think, hang on, no you're not, you're on the train. Actually, the only depressing aspect of this is how boringly honest people are. They seem to have no imagination at all. When they say, "Just pulling into Haywards Heath, dear," I look up optimistically every time, but dammit, we always are just pulling into Haywards Heath. I yearn to hear someone say, "Yes, dear; next stop Albuquerque", when the train is arriving in Ramsgate. "Yes, the dog's with me, he sends a woof, don't you, boy, eh, yes you do, yes you do (ruff, ruff!)" when there's actually no dog anywhere in sight.

To me, the delight of people answering or making calls is that they suddenly – and oblivious to the enforced eavesdropping – reveal enormous amounts about themselves, as if they had, under the influence

of hypnosis, stood up on a table and started stripping, and then, just as suddenly, got down again,
adjusted their clothing, and resumed the anonymity of the everyday humdrum passenger. Of course,
I have overheard – and resented – banal, annoying,
and even obscene mobile calls. A friend of mine
travelling from Victoria to Brighton was obliged
to overhear all the arrangements for the felonious
handover of counterfeit money ("That last lot was
like bog paper!" the bloke yelled, striking terror in
all his fellow passengers). I once stood in misery in
a taxi queue while a huge drunk man behind me bel-
lowed a rather vile account of the evening's sexual
exploits ("I said to her, 'No nails, love! No nails! The
wife'll Effing kill me!'"). But on the whole, I rather
welcome the chance it gives us to overhear other
people's business. And of course one day I'll hear
someone standing outside Waterloo station saying,
"Yes, Istanbul is so magical in the springtime!" and
it will make me very happy.

But just because I find it quite interesting doesn't
mean that it isn't yet another symptom of our almost
insane levels of self-absorption. The trouble is, the
telephone has always had the ability to distract us

from our duty to our surroundings; it is, quite simply, an anti-social instrument. When you are talking to someone face-to-face and the phone interrupts you, you can be as polite as you like about it ("Excuse me, do you mind, I'm sorry"), but it's still a snub to the person present. I used to visit a friend in her office, and would often go through a very painful pantomime when she answered the phone, because she would launch into an animated conversation immediately, but when I mimed a discreet "I'll go, then", she would wave and frown at me, insisting I stay, and roll her eyes exaggeratedly at how annoying it was to be on the phone to this total bore, all the while laughing and chatting, and giving no verbal indication that she had someone present in her office and therefore ought to cut it short. "And *then what?*" she would ask, beckoning me back as I tried to escape. "No! Really? I've always thought that about him!" I would writhe in agony at how rude she was being to me, how rude she was being to the other person (who didn't know), and how miserable I was, having to listen to all this. Imagine calling her up, after witnessing scenes like this. "Is this a bad moment?" I would ask. "Is there anyone there? Who's there? I bet there's someone there!" "No, of course there isn't!" she would assure me, but I still imagined her scribbling my name on a piece of paper, pushing it across the desk, and miming being sick down a lavatory.

When people look for a piece of technology to blame for modern manners, it is often television that cops the lot, but we forget what an impact the telephone had when it was first introduced. With the advent of the phone, people could choose to conduct real-time private conversations with people *who weren't there*. Having grown up with universal telephone technology, we find this idea pretty unremarkable, but Carolyn Marvin's fascinating book *When Old Technologies were New* (1988) points out that there were considerable fears in the last quarter of the nineteenth century about the impact the telephone would have – quite common-sense fears, actually, that mainly came true, and that neatly parallel our current concerns about the internet. The telephone was an instrument for speaking to someone who couldn't see you, and who could be many miles away. It cut through normal social etiquette. Because of these factors, it would make people more confiding and open, but also less civil, less deferential, and less honest. It would facilitate crime. Children would become furtive, anti-social, and uncontrollable. Young people could make assignations with it. None of this seems ridiculous or alarmist to me, incidentally, except perhaps for the warning from the editor of a Philadelphia newspaper in 1894 who cautioned his readers "not to converse by phone with ill persons for fear of contracting contagious diseases".

The impact of the phone on the "proprieties of presence" was immediately worrying. People spoke more freely on the telephone. Women gossiped on it. Formerly, there was a code for speaking when at home, and a code for speaking when outside the home. Both codes were posited on observing the presence of others and the etiquette of the surroundings. But the phone was one-to-one, and neither indoors nor outdoors, and the four walls of domestic privacy were breached for ever. "The home wears a vanishing aspect," lamented *Harper's* in 1893. Carolyn Marvin quotes from *The Times* in 1897 the astonishingly modern prediction, "We shall soon be nothing but transparent heaps of jelly to each other." She also quotes, from the same year, a presentation by W. E. Ayrton to the British Imperial Institute which exactly predicted the weirdness of the mobile phone, anticipating it by about a century:

> When a person wants to telegraph a friend, he knows not where, he will call in an electromagnetic voice, which will be heard loud by him who has the electromagnetic ear, but will be silent to everyone else, he will call, "Where are you?" and the reply will come loud to the man with the electromagnetic ear, "I am at the bottom of a coal mine, or crossing the Andes, or in the middle of the Pacific."

My point is, we have to place our annoyance at the mobile phone in this context. For over a hundred years, we have been pretty useless at juggling the relative claims of the *there* and the *not-there*. Perhaps that's why we are so miserable about the way people now use mobiles in public: it reminds us that we didn't deal with this problem adequately when it first arose. We let things slide. We pretended it didn't matter. We loved the phone too much to care. But phones have always obtruded; they have always trapped us in their tracker beams and transported us instantaneously to another planet. A phone conversation, being both blind and one-to-one, is a more intense and concentrated form of communication than talking face-to-face. Inevitably, then, when a phone call competes for attention with a real-world conversation, it wins. Everyone knows the distinctive high-and-dry feeling of being abandoned for a phone call, and of having to compensate – with quite elaborate behaviours – for the sudden half-disappearance of the person we were just speaking to. "Go ahead!" we say. "Don't mind us! Oh look, here's a magazine I can read!" When the call is over, other rituals come into play, to minimise the disruption caused, and to restore good feeling. "Oh, it was your *mother*, was it? Well, I wondered, naturally, but I wasn't really listening."

And now people are yelling, "So I said to her, no nails!" or "That last lot was like bog paper!" down their mobile phones in public places, and we don't know what to do about it besides boil and seethe. If only you could ignore it. In fact, why *can't* you ignore it? Do you see how the person sitting next to the caller – their boyfriend, their mum – is usually quite happily gazing out of the window or doing a word-search puzzle? Why are they so unaffected? Isn't that a bit perverse of them? What's going on?

Well, let's say you are with someone you know, at his house or in his office, and he has to take a phone call. A void opens up, doesn't it? It's a kind of limbo. A positive becomes, as it were, a temporary negative. You were plus a person; now you are minus a person. While the phone call unfolds, you sympathetically adopt a minus position yourself. When it's over, and you get the person back, you both become positive again (i.e. both are present and aware of each other).

But when the person who goes on the phone is a stranger, it's entirely different. In a train compartment where all are strenuously activating their feeble force fields, the void, the limbo, is implicitly agreed to be the desired state of all. Then the phone rings, a young woman answers it, and a bizarre thing happens: she duly absents herself from her surroundings, but the result is not a double negative, as you might suppose. She becomes a positive! "Ange! I was gonna phone ya! Wha' appened? Djoo gow off wiv im?" Yes, two negatives make an intensely annoying positive! Not only that, but her sudden vivid presence demands that everyone else become positive too, hanging on every word. It's awful. The old healing rituals don't apply in this situation, since there is no conciliatory "Do you mind?" beforehand, or explanatory "That was my mother" afterwards. And a different, unsatisfactory kind of positive is achieved, in any case. You are now intensely aware of this intensely present woman. "Yer, well, she's a slag in't she?" But of course she is not remotely aware of you.

! # * !

Why don't we object more often? Why is advice on this issue always facetious, unrealistic, and only weakly amusing?

"Switch on a tape recorder and place it in front of the person speaking. They will soon shut up."

"Note down their number and call it immediately, pretending to be someone from the office."

"When they have loudly broadcast their address and credit card details, text this information to them with the accompanying message, For God's sake, we can all hear you, shut up."

"Wait for the call to finish, then go over and start talking to the user, but *just mouth the words.*"

"Pick up their phone and throw it out of the window."

There are many reasons why we don't do these things. Ingrained politeness and fear of reprisal are prominent among them. Also, any fair-minded person is bound to ask, "Why am I taking this personally? I know perfectly well that it's not personal." So we grumble and sigh and fidget, and occasionally catch the eye of another passenger similarly fed up, because we feel that a public space should be neutral and shared. We don't want to dominate it ourselves; we just don't want anyone else to dominate it, either – and the idea of people being able to tune in to telly stations on the underground drives me close to despair. In that *New York Times* story of the business-reply envelope guerrilla, there is a tantalising reference to illegal hand-held "jammers" that can block all phone signals in a forty-five-foot radius; also a gadget called "TV-B-Gone", which can switch off televisions, rather as the name implies. I am urgently in the market for both these wonderful inventions – especially if they operate secretly, as I am getting quite bold (not to say stroppy) in this regard already, and am generally asking for a punch in the face. I now automatically ask taxi drivers to switch off their annoying talk radio; at the self-storage warehouse, where a pop channel is left blaring amid the units for the supposed entertainment of the patrons, I just march in and unplug the hi-fi; at Broadcasting House, if I am waiting alone in reception, I switch off Radio 2. When I am thwarted in my mission to restore neutral quiet to public areas, by the way, I get quite confused. "Anyone listening to this?" I said the other day in the dentist's waiting-room, finger already poised above the "Off" button (which wasn't easy, as the hi-fi was fixed quite high up on the wall). "Yes, I am," said a woman. I was completely taken aback. If she hadn't looked pained and swollen, I think I would have called her a liar.

Back with the mobile phone, however, I have started to think that the rudeness is not in answering them, because answering a ringing phone is a kind of conditioned reflex that few of us can resist. I am beginning to think it is much more rude to call one. I find that people I've never spoken to before are increasingly choosing to call me on my mobile before even checking whether I am at my desk. They then leave a message involving a lot of numbers that I'm in no position to write down. Since my mobile doesn't work properly indoors (insufficient signal), it will merely indicate that I have a message. Sighing and muttering, I have no choice but to put some shoes on, leave the house, climb a hill, and pace up and down with my eyes closed and my fist to my head. Then I come back downhill, come indoors, grab a pen and paper, go up the hill again and listen again, taking notes. When I finally get back indoors again, huffing and fuming, I reach for the phone and discover that, while I've been outside doing this Grand Old Duke of York impression for the neighbours, the bastards have called me at my desk as an afterthought.

The most touching aspect of that 1897 prediction about the electromagnetic voice communicating with the electromagnetic ear is that the voice cries out, "Where are you?" and the reply comes, so splendidly, "In the Andes!" This, of course, is the key to the universal jumping-up-and-down reaction to "I'm on the train." Surely a technology so miraculous deserves to convey communication that's a bit less banal? Other people's overheard conversations fall into four categories, it seems to me, and each carries its own objection:

1   business conversations that, in an office setting, would be conducted behind closed doors;
2   intimate conversations that ought to be conducted behind closed doors;
3   humdrum domestic arrangements which would keep perfectly well for later; and
4   dross.

All these types are uncomfortable to listen to. But it's hard to see what can be done. On the one hand, it is a natural thing in humans to communicate. Putting the mobile phone in context, with the birth of each new form of communication technology (the penny post, the postcard), there has been a similar explosion of superfluous usage, just for the hell of it. On the other hand, however, the inconsiderateness is a proper cause for concern, and in particular it highlights a new development of relations in public: that group pressure no longer operates in the way that it once did. Formerly, a person might weigh it up: I want to do this anti-social thing, but there are twenty other people here, so I won't. The calculation now is different. I want to do this anti-social thing, and if anyone objects, I'll tell him to Eff Off. I can

TALK TO THE HAND

bank on him not getting support from other people, incidentally, because that's the way things are.

The Eff-Off reflex is where we will pick up the story of modern rudeness in the next chapter. But in the meantime, there was one particular point from those news stories I want to pick up. Of course, I'm hoping that other people share my reaction to those stories, which is, broadly:

1 *The schoolgirl story*
Reaction: outrage; bit of teeth-grinding; "Not in my day", etcetera

2 *Virginia banning low-slung jeans*
Reaction: knee-jerk despair at reactionary legislation, followed by honest anxiety about my politics because, actually, I'm a bit sick of seeing young people's underwear as well

3 *Television on the tube*
Reaction: gloom; Cassandra-ish tearing of hair; searching on internet for "TV-B-Gone" and other gadgets

4 *The small revenges story*
Reaction: supportive cheering; resolve to buy strips of sheet metal and clear all other work from routine

5 *Dealing with doorstep callers by ingenious means*
Reaction: slightly louder supportive cheering; resolve to practise "Quick! I tied him to a kitchen chair but he's wriggling free!"

6 *People are losing the ability to concentrate*
Reaction: self-righteous nodding and arm-folding; muttering of, "I told you so", followed by, "Hang on, what are we talking about, I've forgotten."

"Whatever happened to consideration?" we cry. Well, the prerequisite of consideration is the ability to imagine being someone other than oneself, and that's a bit of a lost cause. For me, the detail that springs out and alarms me most from the news stories at the start of this chapter is the word "tolerant" in the London Underground report. *"We will focus on education instead,"* said a spokesman. *"People need to be told to be tolerant, so we will be running ads similar to those found on overground trains."* The spokesman is, I think, suggesting that those who make calls or watch TV in a crowded Northern Line carriage should be *considerate* of other passengers; oddly, however, he uses the word "tolerant" instead.

Why? Well, it is possible that he just has a small vocabulary, but it's still a significant slip. From his point of view, you see, the nuisance-makers will soon be the ones operating within their rights. Therefore, if trouble is to be avoided, the nuisance-makers are the ones who must be tolerant; they must exercise saintly forbearance when they find people around them shouting, "Turn that Effing thing off! Turn that Effing thing off! It's driving me Effing mad!" Being tolerated by selfish people who don't understand that they're in public may be the final straw for some of us. We may have no alternative – and I didn't want to get quite so gloomy when I'm only half-way through the book – but we may have no alternative but to stay home and bolt the door.

THE FOURTH GOOD REASON

THE FOURTH GOOD REASON

The Universal Eff-Off Reflex

The world has changed a lot since the Hungarian-born George Mikes published his classic work *How to be an Alien* in 1946. What he observed about the British in those early post-war days was our habit of reserve, irony, and understatement; our determination to avert unpleasantness mainly by ignoring it. J. B. Priestley famously lamented that the difficulty of writing plays about the non-confrontational English is their refusal to "make a scene". Mikes, in his chapter "How to be Rude", nailed this trait beautifully.

> If someone tells you an obviously untrue story, on the Continent you would remark, "You are a liar, Sir, and a dirty one at that." In England you just say "Oh, is that so?" Or "That's rather an unusual story, isn't it?"

Turned down for a job as a translator, for which he was completely unqualified, Mikes was told, "I am afraid your English is somewhat unorthodox." He found this hilarious. In any other European country, he says, the equivalent brush-off would have taken the form of calling to the commissionaire, "Jean, kick this gentleman down the steps!" The proper British way is, in the words of Arnold Bennett, "always to behave as if nothing has happened, no matter what has happened". We esteem it our highest national virtue that we can look back on a day of total disaster and say, "Well, I think that went pretty well, don't you?"

The question is: why do we have such a horror of directness? Why do we place value on not saying what we mean? Why do we think it's *funny*? Why do we think the word "irony" gives us magical permission to confuse less devious foreigners about whether we're serious or not? Given that it is now commonplace to be told to Eff Off by eight-year-olds, are we just finally paying the price for confusing directness with rudeness for so long? Kate Fox, by the end of *Watching the English*, is clearly exasperated by our stubborn refusal to assert ourselves, and is convinced that the recent rise of verbal aggression is not some strange, illogical departure from traditional reserve; it is just the flipside of the same behaviour.

> We are always oblique, always playing some complex, convoluted game. When we are not doing things backwards (saying the opposite of what we mean ...), we are doing them sideways (addressing our indignant mutterings about queue-jumpers to other queuers ... rather than actually tackling the offenders). Every social situation is fraught with ambiguity, knee-deep in complication, hidden meanings, veiled power struggles, passive-aggression and paranoid confusion.

She goes on:

> When we feel uncomfortable in social situations (that is, most of the time) we either become over-polite, buttoned up and awkwardly restrained, or loud, loutish, crude, violent and generally obnoxious. Both our famous "English reserve" and our infamous "English hooliganism" are symptoms of this social dis-ease, as is our obsession with privacy.

This really is an affliction. Call it the absence of frankness. Call it passive aggression. If there is a chance that we can call a spade an everyday long-handled horticultural implement for the purpose of digging, we would genuinely prefer it. As for our cowardly attitude to quite straightforward confrontation, well, here is a story illustrative of the British–US divide. I was complaining recently to a New Yorker about a British man who annoys me by joshingly referring to me as "World-Famous Author" when we are out with mutual friends. He has a generally mocking and sardonic tone, this chap; when I'm around, his technique is to invent headlines. I might say, "Mm, I don't know what to have," and he says, "Oh. World-Famous Author *can't decide what to eat.*" This gives me the utter pip. It is clearly hostile, but I feel I'm not allowed to say so. And so it goes on. "Oh, World-Famous Author gets a haircut but *isn't sure she likes it.*" "World-Famous Author thinks it may be time to re-read *Great Expectations.*"

Now, I think I make it plain enough that this annoys me, but of course I employ the time-honoured British method of conveying my rancour: I smile along with everyone else, and say afterwards,

"Well, how lovely to see you again. We ought to make this a regular occasion! What a card you are!" My New Yorker friend listened rather impatiently to the problem, then set me straight. And I'll admit, when he did, he scared me.

"Listen," he snapped. "What's the name of this jerk?"

"Er, Mick," I said.

"OK, this is what you do. Next time you see him, you take him to one side and you say, 'Mick. Cut it out.' "

I laughed. "I can't do that," I said.

My friend did not laugh. He was serious. "Yes you can. You say, 'Mick, cut it out, you're being an Effing jerk, and it's not funny.' Trust me, he'll stop."

I looked at him in amazement. Could it really be as simple as that? Should I just tell him to stop? I could honestly have lived to the end of my life and not come up with such a brilliant and original strategy on my own.

My suspicion is that we have to accept what very, very strange and perversely indirect people we are before we can understand where the Universal Eff-Off Reflex has come from. It is so brutally defensive, so swingeingly final, that it clearly comes, itself, out of a sense of affront and outrage. People don't expect to be spoken to directly; it is interpreted as sheer hostility. I keep thinking of an incident twenty years ago when I was travelling by train to the seaside with my sister and her children. We were in the buffet compartment, consuming crisps and drinks, when a woman came in with a dog. "Oh, that's charming!" announced my sister, folding her arms and pulling a face. "What a thing to do in a place where food is served. Stop eating, children. I suppose I'll have to throw all this food away now, won't I? And just because certain people can't read signs!" Now, this scene would play out very differently today, because what happened next was that I went over and spoke to the woman. It was, for me, an unusually assertive thing to do, but I felt it was necessary to act, if only to prevent more of this pointed harrumphing. "Excuse me," I said, "there's a notice above the door that says you can't bring dogs in here." The woman – who would nowadays, of course, tell me to Eff Off – said she was sorry and took the dog away. What has always intrigued me about this incident, however, was that my sister was horrified by what I had done. "That was so rude," she said. "Going over and speaking to that woman was so rude."

! # ⋆ !

The Universal Eff-Off Reflex is generally agreed to be something new in the world of manners. I wrote a piece in the *Daily Telegraph* while preparing this book, and I received a number of letters and emails afterwards about rudeness, a high proportion of which dealt with the holy shock of being told to Eff Off by someone they'd never met. Some people say Eff Off all the time, of course – and this is shocking and worrying enough in itself, but what I'm really interested in here is the way we are getting less and less prepared to accept criticism or admonishment, or ever to say sorry. An overtaking car endangers your life. You flash your lights. The driver makes the wanker signal at you. A pedestrian steps out in front of a bus. The bus brakes abruptly, spilling its passengers on the floor, and toots its horn. The pedestrian turns his back, holds up a finger, and saunters away. No one is ever in the wrong, it seems. If you point out to someone that he is in the wrong, you must be prepared for the consequences, which may include violence, but will automatically include Eff Off.

This is not just at street level, either. We are all Teflon people, on whom criticism cannot stick. Abuse is becoming accepted as the quickest and smartest way of dealing with criticism in all areas of life. I had an interesting experience in 2004 when my book *Eats, Shoots & Leaves* received a mauling in the *New Yorker*, and my London publisher riposted on my behalf that the author of the critical article was "a tosser". Now, I loved my publisher for doing this, of course. He was defending my honour. He is a famously maverick character. And although I have never read the article, I have heard enough about it to suspect that the chosen epithet actually had some merit in this case. But good grief, how embarrass-ing. Meanwhile, ripostes of this sort made by public figures are reported in the news, and quoted as if they were witty or thoughtful. In April 2005, when the football manager Harry Redknapp was heckled and booed at Portsmouth, he was reported as saying, "If people have got nothing better to do than shout abuse at me, they must have sad lives, and I feel sorry for them." And I repeat, *this was on the news*.

So there are several things contributing to the Universal Eff-Off Reflex. The state of manners is driving some of us to be direct, which makes us uncomfortable enough in the first place. And this directness is whacked straight back at us by people who are never in the wrong, who interpret directness as sheer hostility, and who say Eff Off so much in their normal conversations anyway that it springs automatically to their cherry-red lips. The prison psychiatrist Theodore Dalrymple (whom we shall meet again in chapter six) notes, in his book *Life at the Bottom* (2001), that Eff Off is a favourite tattoo among the people he meets.

> Why anyone should want these words indelibly imprinted on his skin is a mystery whose meaning I have not yet penetrated ... but I recall a patient who had the two words tattooed in mirror writing upon his forehead, no doubt that he might read them in the bathroom mirror every morning and be reminded of the vanity of earthly concerns.

But why don't people take the criticism on board? Why doesn't telling-off *work*? I'm sure it used to. In the past, if someone was so offended by your actions that they broke the directness taboo, you would take it to heart. You felt *ashamed*.

Now, you may remember that Norbert Elias identified shame as one of the twin engines of the civilising process. Shame is now such a quaint, bygone concept that one feels almost embarrassed to bring it up. "Have you no *shame?*" is a question merrily kicked aside; indeed, shamelessness is not only a highly regarded modern attribute, but the *sine qua non* of most successful TV and entertainment formats, which compete to push shamelessness to ever further limits. Things used to be different. My own childhood, and the childhood of many others of my generation, was marked by episodes of this red-hot, moiling state of self-blame, and I am not going to say it never did me any harm. I am obliged to admit, on the contrary, that it left me so psychologically flailed, scorched, eviscerated, and hobbled that it's a miracle I can drag myself about.

I can appreciate, therefore, why modern parents would want to shield their own children from such a terrible awareness of personal worthlessness. But surely they go too far? Modern parents from all classes seem genuinely to believe they are doing the right thing by protecting their children from blame or accountability of any sort. Every time the little chaps get themselves on a hook, the parents gently lift them down and tell them to run along and forget about it. While working-class parents pride themselves on how quickly they can march to the school and pin a teacher against a blackboard, middle-class people spend a lot of time worrying, "Is it right to tell off other people's children?" and wringing their hands amid the shards of their favourite Chinese jardinière. This is one of the big etiquette dilemmas of our times. Families arrive at your house and you wait for the parents to say, "Remember, children, this is Uncle Robert's house, and it has lovely things in it that don't belong to you. So please be very good and don't touch anything." But they don't do this. They say, "Say hi to Bob, kids. Yes, darling, this is the man we call Fatty Bob, how clever you are to remember. Now, why don't you all run off and see how many things beginning with the letter H you can collect for mummy? All right, Freddie, you can use a screwdriver. Take your sticky drinks with you, darlings, that's right." Later, if you confront a child with its bad behaviour, the parents will step in at once. "Fatty Bob didn't mean to be nasty to you, darling. He's just a bit materialistic, which means he prefers things to people. *We* prefer people to things, don't we? Besides, Fatty Bob shouldn't leave such irreplaceable heirlooms just lying about, should he? Silly Fatty Bob."

So what is shame? Why is it socially useful? Elias defines shame as an "anxiety" and explains it as a sophisticated act of self-division, when a person is forced to judge his own behaviour against an internal moral censor ("the sector of his consciousness by which he controls himself"). The idea is that we import a sense of social opinion, internalise it, and measure ourselves against it. But he isn't talking about judging oneself on a scale of good–bad. Interestingly, what Elias sees in shame is that we place ourselves on a scale of superior–inferior, which is probably much, much harder to take. "It is a conflict within his own personality; he himself recognizes himself as inferior ... This is what makes him so defenceless against gestures of superiority by others which somehow trigger off this automatism within him."

Saying sorry involves the same sort of process.

Taking Erving Goffman's "splitting" description of apology, it seems that this division now takes place a lot less than it used to. People have been brought up not to split under any circumstances – least of all when an apology is demanded. Quite the reverse. Under attack, the individual personality wastes no time bolstering its defences. It circles the wagons and starts firing. Not a second is allowed for self-examination. Where this comes out in a most peculiar way is in our dealings with people who, we feel, are obliged to apologise on behalf of the company they represent, but who don't see how they are personally involved. My favourite story from the many sent in by *Daily Telegraph* readers concerned a man buying a book. He had entered a reputable bookshop and been treated in an off-hand manner when he asked for help. Then, having located the book, he paid for it with his credit card. The assistant put the bill in the bag, and he said, "I'd like to put the bill separately, please," at which he was told, "Well, you know where it is; you can do that yourself." He felt aggrieved, and said so. "I've been in this shop for five minutes and spent thirty pounds, and no one has been polite to me." At which the assistant retaliated,

"Just because you spent thirty pounds doesn't mean you've *bought my soul.*"

! # * !

Deference is a topic for another chapter. What I think marks out the Universal Eff-Off Reflex is contained in the name: it's a reflex. It's as if you touch someone lightly on the shoulder and *snick, snack,* the next thing you know, your hand has been severed at the wrist. It is startling partly because it's so primitive, so *animal.* Through shielding children from feelings of low self-worth, we have created people who simply will not stand to be corrected in any way. "Excuse me, I think you dropped this," you say. "Eff Off," they say, with heat. "There ought to be an apostrophe on that sign." "Eff Off." A contestant on a quiz who is told, "The answer to 'Who wrote *Pride and Prejudice?*' was Jane Austen" will not bite a lip and look embarrassed. He will say, "I didn't know that because it's not a thing worth knowing!" – and get a little cheer from the audience for sticking up for himself.

But the last aspect of the Universal Eff-Off Reflex I want to consider is just why so many of us are speaking up anyway. "Don't cycle on the pavement, you hooligan!" we shout, even though experience now tells us that it's dangerous, and our built-in inhibition begs us not to. Moreover, we are beginning to realise that if we appeal for other people to agree with us, they will either make themselves scarce or concentrate very hard on a bit of urgent texting. Whatever happened to our famous controlling characteristic of "negative politeness" – of minding one's own business?

Back with George Mikes, he wrote several follow-up books to How to be an Alien, including How to be Inimitable (1960). All the books are collected in How to be a Brit. This is how he describes British non-confrontational habits forty-five years ago, in his chapter, "On Minding One's Own Business":

> If a man happens to be standing on your foot in the bus, you must not ask him to get off, since it is clearly his business where he chooses to stand; if your neighbour's television or radio is blaring military marches till midnight, you may not remonstrate with him because it is his business what he pleases to listen to and at what time; if you are walking peacefully in the street and

someone pours two gallons of boiling water over your best bowler through his bathroom overflow ... you should proceed without uttering a word – however short – because it is obviously the other fellow's business when he has his bath and how hot he likes it.

I have an awful feeling that I used to agree with this. Now, however, it is unrecognisable as British behaviour. Personally, I have turned into a bug-eyed mad person who must either speak up or explode – which is as much of a departure from previous norms as the Eff-Off Reflex is. For example, I was recently in a check-out queue, being served by a young woman. From his place at the next till, an odious boy of about seventeen was loudly and unselfconsciously telling her the story of a friend who had discovered the decomposing body of an old woman in her house. "She hadn't been seen for *seven days*," he said, at the beginning, with all the relish of the fat boy in Dickens who wants to make your flesh creep. As he absently scanned somebody else's shopping – Whiskas, Double Gloucester, etcetera – it became obvious that no detail was going to be omitted from his grisly tale.

I didn't know what to do. This situation offended me on so many levels. For a start, the two of them were ignoring their customers. Yet the woman who was being served by the boy (and who had far more right than me to be offended) seemed unconcerned. If anything, she was amused. The girl at my till just rolled her eyes at me, as if to say, "What can you do?" Again, I don't think she was remotely bothered by the content of the story, or struck by its inappropriateness; she merely thought the boy was a bit of a tosser. So he had just described the bluebottles buzzing in the curtained window, and the door being broken down, and the smell coming out, when I finally broke. "Stop telling that story, for pity's sake!" I said. The boy stopped. His customer pulled a face and shrugged. Looking back, I suppose I'm lucky that nobody actually laughed. As far as I was concerned, I could not possibly mind my own business in this situation. *I had to say something.* But having done so, I have never felt so alone and alienated in my life.

Drugs are probably the only solution, unfortunately. Strong, mood-altering drugs will ultimately stop me from Speaking Up. It was the same with being a stickler for punctuation, of course. It's the same urge to correct the world, and drag it into line; and it is bound to be met with the same consternation. Look into the eyes of someone who is telling you to Eff Off and what you will often find there, along with aggression, is pure surprise. "What's up with *her*?" the look says. "Where did *that* spring from?" For the boy at the check-out, when I yelled at him, it was as if a tin of beans had suddenly jumped up from the conveyor belt and biffed him in the eye; unaware of anyone else within ear-shot, he believed he was having a private conversation. Why couldn't I mind my own business? Why had I broken the basic rules of "negative politeness"? Why had I been so *rude*?

There is one positive aspect to all this. It's quite a feeble one, but worth mentioning. Even though there were hundreds of complaints from BBC viewers about the swearing at the Live8 concert, the word Eff every day loses some of its shock power. I would still be horrified to hear my mum say it, and I always apologise to her if I let it slip out when I'm talking to her, but it's clearly the case that through sheer constant over-use, "Effing" is becoming a meaningless intensifier and will soon hardly be worth saying. There is a hilarious section about gossip in *Watching the English*, in which the three ways an English man can react to news are anatomised:

1   with surprise
2   with anger
3   with elation and triumph

In each case, Kate Fox explains, "expletives" must be used. In other words, he can say:

1   "Effing hell!"
2   "Oh, Eff that!"
3   "Eff, yes! Effing fantastic!"

And they say the language of Shakespeare and Milton is dead. Television, as always, delights in accelerating the process of social change by normalising the entertainingly shocking. In the first five minutes of a recent *Gordon Ramsay's Kitchen Nightmares*, the famously robust chef said:

> You are Effing useless, this is Effing disgusting, this is Effing frozen in the centre, it's as authentic

as an Effing Chinese takeaway, that was Effing dire,
you're giving the customer Effing food poisoning,
I am so Effing glad the customers can't see what's
going on, I don't know where to Effing start.

Well, strike that man's head a glancing blow
with a frying pan, but I suppose he is ultimately
serving the greater good, even if he doesn't know
it. Blue Peter viewers wait for the day a children's TV
presenter says with a big smile, "And now it's time
to make an Effing model car park out of an Effing
corn-flake packet!" At that point, all-clear sirens will
sound throughout the land and the reign of Eff will
be officially over. By great good fortune, the word
that is far more shocking than Eff – you probably
know the one I mean – can't really step up to take its
place, being an incontrovertible noun with far less
scope for use as a verb, adverb, adjective and intensifier. Tee hee. Those Effing Eff people may know Eff
All about grammar, but grammar will ultimately Eff
them in the end.

Wasn't it amusing, incidentally, that when Jerry
Springer briefly visited the UK to make a British
version of his show, he was reportedly astonished
by the amount of foul language he heard? Perhaps,

in common with many other Americans, he thought that in Britain we talked like something out of *Mary Poppins*. He thought we said things like, "Stripe me pink, I am proper peeved and no mistake. Do you know, I'd like to give that scallywag a piece of my mind. Heavens, yes indeedy." In fact, of course, it's easier to shield yourself from bad language in America than it is here. There is an old joke about an English tourist asking a New York taxi-driver, "Excuse me, can you tell me the way to Carnegie Hall, or shall I just go and Eff myself?" Nowadays the joke works better with an American asking the way to Piccadilly Circus.

In the meantime, however, the Universal Eff-Off Reflex looks set to stay and I am clearly destined to keep running foul of it. Each of us is inside a bubble, after all. Most of us grow more grumpy and misanthropic every day. Pascal said, "I have discovered that all human misery comes from a single thing, which is not knowing enough to stay quietly in your room." Sometimes I have a little dream that it is eight o'clock on a fine wintry morning, and as I leave my house to walk to the station, I notice I'm feeling rather lighthearted. No one about. No cars. No noise except the faraway hum of a milk float. Mm. Nice. The street is clean as if washed by recent rain. I walk briskly, humming to myself, cross a quiet road and arrive at the station in good time for the 8.49. As I buy my paper (putting coins in a slot), I notice that the concourse is empty, utterly empty, and I begin to think well, this is a bit too good to be true, but never mind, they cleared Times Square for Tom Cruise that time, didn't they? And *Vanilla Sky* was rubbish. I buy a ticket (no queue), board the train (no other passengers), and feel blissfully happy.

Now, this may be a dream, I think, as the train begins to move. This may even be – and that distant milk float was rather a giveaway – a long-forgotten episode of *The Avengers* that has somehow lodged in my brain and is now repeating itself as a kind of benign near-death experience as I lie unconscious at the bottom of some stairs. Either way, I don't care. Somehow, overnight, other people have been eradicated, expunged, annihilated, or just ordered to stay indoors and keep out of my bloody way. And you know how it feels? It feels *right*.

THE FIFTH GOOD REASON

THE FIFTH GOOD REASON

Booing the Judges

A young woman of my acquaintance once wrote to Tommy Steele. You may remember him from such films as *Half a Sixpence* and such chart-topping songs as "Little White Bull". For many years, he lived in a rather grand eighteenth-century house behind a high wall on the main road between Richmond and Kingston in Surrey, near to where I grew up, and we council-estate locals were jolly pleased to have him in the neighbourhood, even though we never actually saw him. Whenever the song "'Old it flash bang wallop what a picture!" was played on *Two-Way Family Favourites*, we turned up the volume with a glow of pride. Anyway, one day, about fifteen years ago, this young woman wrote to him, but it was not a fan letter. It was an accusation, expressed in quite belligerent terms. "I have been past your house on the top deck of a bus for years and years," she wrote, "yet I have never seen you. As a famous person, don't you have a duty to appear for people? You'd be nobody without us, you know." Unbelievably, she received a reply. Tommy Steele wrote to say that, if she cared to catch a bus on Sunday afternoon between two and three, he would be in the garden and would give her a wave. "Well, was he there?" I asked, when she told me about it, some months later. She snorted with laughter. "How should I know?" she said. "I didn't go."

When people applaud the "end of deference" in our society, they tend to evoke the old British class system, with its sepia-coloured peasants clutching cloth caps to their waistcoats and refusing to make a fuss about dying of industrial chest ailments. Words such as "servile" and "repressive" crop up, as the bad old days are given a glad good riddance. People will even resort (as I did, earlier) to the slightly dubious argument that posh people are quite unworthy of special respect, in any case, being genetically stupid from the in-breeding, laughably out of touch with popular entertainment, apt to pelt each other with bakery products in London's club land, and absolute bastards where foxes are concerned. The end of deference is presented as politically progressive and therefore a good thing. Nobody "looks up" to anyone any more: Hooray! The media don't allow anyone to get too big for their boots: Hooray! In the bad old days ordinary people often had to cope with feelings of inferiority, which sometimes drove them to exert themselves: Boo! But now we have relativism and entitlement: Hooray! Oh yes, everything is grandy and dandy. Hooray, hooray, hooray!

What a brave new world we have, then, that glorifies rudeness in the name of egalitarianism. The British have always enjoyed the sport of abusing public figures; we regard it as hilarious as well as cathartic. I was once at Madison Square Garden in New York, to report on a heavyweight title bout between Lennox Lewis and Evander Holyfield, and yes, I know how odd that sounds, but this isn't the place to explain. The point is that, before the fight, the ring announcer made a fatal error: addressing a crowd with a large, rowdy British element, he listed the celebrities in the audience. He evidently thought we would be impressed. "Ladies and gentlemen, we have Paul Simon in the Garden tonight!" he said.

And what happened? "Booo!" yelled the Brits. "We have John Kennedy Junior!" "BOOOO!" "We have Michael Douglas!" "BOOOO!" Only two people were given a cheer by the British contingent: Jack Nicholson and Keith Richards. I felt embarrassed by my chippy countrymen. Abuse is the weapon of the weak. But at the same time, I did feel very proud. I mean, I like Paul Simon. I have nothing against him. But nobody deserves uncritical acclaim just for filling a ringside seat at a punch-up.

This traditional weapon of the weak is, however, becoming heavier and more blunt. There seems to be an avid and self-righteous movement to make public figures pay the price for too much deference in the past. It is getting a bit bloody. The royal family is brutally cut down to size whenever the opportunity arises, and you certainly don't have to be Jeremy Paxman any more to be rude to a politician. In fact, if you see John Prescott in a motorway service station, the accepted MO seems to be that first you insult him, then you go and get a bunch of friends in hoods with a video camera so that you can perform a "happy slap" (i.e., a filmed assault). As for famous people – well, who the hell would want to be famous any more? You'd have to be insane. People demand you appear for them in your garden, and then they don't even show up to give you a wave. On a recent *Have I Got News for You*, Les Dennis told the story of a celebrity (whose name meant nothing to me) being struck in the street by a woman with an umbrella, who then said, "You see? I told you it was him!" There is a well-worn dictum that, in Britain, "they build you up and then they tear you down", but it's getting to the point where the tearing-down is far too much fun to hang about for. There was once a story in *Private Eye* about a bloodsports enthusiast so excited by the delivery of some pheasant chicks that he shot them in the box. This is, I think, a pretty good image for the way public life now works in this country.

All this would be all right if it actually served the cause of egalitarianism, but it plainly doesn't. Look around. We don't even have social mobility any more. Just because newspapers refer to HRH The Prince of Wales as "Chazza" (and everyone feels free to say vile things about his uncomplaining wife) does not make him the same as you and me. There seems to be an idea that the more disrespect you show towards the rich or famous (for example, squirting

TALK TO THE HAND

water in the face of Tom Cruise), the nearer you move towards achieving equality, but the effect is quite the opposite: rudeness highlights difference. In a truly egalitarian society, everyone would show respect to everyone else. It is very bad news for our society that overt disrespect is such a big game these days, because it just stirs people up without enlightening them. Mass entertainment that demeans public figures satisfies popular base instincts but leaves nobody better off. Besides, at the same time as it's become fashionable never to look up to anyone, it has become nastily acceptable to look down.

The "end of deference" is about a lot more than the flattening of class distinctions, in any case. This is where the baby has been so thoughtlessly poured down the drain with the bath water. Respect and consideration are traditionally due to other people for all sorts of reasons, some big, some small. Here are twenty (mostly lapsed) reasons to show special politeness to other people that have nothing to do with class.

1 they are older
2 they know more than you do

3 they know less than you do

4 they got here first

5 they have educational qualifications in the subject under discussion

6 you are in their house

7 they once helped you financially

8 they have been good to you all your life

9 they are less fortunate than you

10 they have achieved status in the wider world

11 you are serving them in a shop

12 they are in the right

13 they are your boss

14 they work for you

15 they are a policeman/teacher/doctor/judge

16 they are in need

17 they are doing you a favour

18 they paid for the tickets

19 you phoned them, not the other way round

20 they have a menial job

The utter bloody rudeness of the world today is about a lot of things, as we have already seen, but I think what most dismays many honourable people is the way "deference" has become a dirty little demeaning word, while its close relative "respect" has become a cool street-crime buzz-word mainly associated with paying feudal obeisance to those in possession of firearms. Both words have lost their true meaning. Deference is not about lying down and letting someone put their foot on your head. It is not about kow-tow. It is about assessing what is due to other people on all sorts of grounds. The dictionary definition of "in deference to" is: "out of respect for; in consideration of". To show deference does not mean "I hereby declare I am inferior to you." But that's what people seem to think it means, so they refuse to defer to anybody, on any grounds at all. The same misunderstanding prevents people from apologising. They think that if they say "Sorry", it means "I am 100 per cent to blame. And now that I've admitted it, you can sue the pants off me."

! # * !

Contempt is the word. Although I don't know why I bother continuing with this; most of you are too stupid to follow it, let's be honest. All right, I suppose I'll have to spell it out. Contempt, also known as "attitude", is the new behavioural default mode. And what breeds contempt? Oh, come on, you muppets! I'm working with idiots here. What breeds contempt? Familiarity! Blimey, I thought you were cleverer than that, mate. Although judging by the way you've been moving your lips while you read this, I don't know where I got that idea.

It goes against the grain just to sit here applauding the sagacity of a proverb, but I find that I have no choice. So here goes. What breeds contempt? Familiarity breeds contempt. I used to be confused by this saying, incidentally, because I thought it meant "familiarity" in the sense of being familiar with the lay-out of Exeter, or familiar with the problem plays of Shakespeare, and I thought, "Hang on, the more I know about *Measure for Measure*, the more I admire it! When Claudio pleads so eloquently for his life at the expense of his sister's chastity, I am absolutely fit to be tied. And that Cathedral Close in Exeter is lovely. Familiarity really boosts things in one's estimation. What on earth are these proverb-coiners talking about?"

But it isn't that kind of familiarity. It's the sort that has you call your maths teacher "Jeff". It's going up to the Prime Minister and saying, "Nice jacket; how much?" It is using someone's loo without asking, and leaving the seat up as evidence. It is calling someone you've never met, on their mobile, to settle a dispute about punctuation. Few issues divide generations more than the issue of familiarity. It is one of the main rudenesses cited by older people, and it is easy to see why. People who have spent their whole lives as "Mr Webster" or "Mrs Owen" do not want to find, at the ends of their lives, that younger people who don't know them are calling them "Alf" and "Joyce". To them, it is sheer impertinence (and usually takes place when they are in a weakened state, which makes it all the more insensitive). Sometimes you really do have to admire the French. They would never stand for this kind of thing. An American writer-friend who is quite proficient in French once attempted to use a slang term with a record-shop owner, and the chap did not let it pass. "Have we *met*?" he asked, horrified at the breach of decorum.

Several of my *Daily Telegraph* correspondents objected to being called "mate" or "love" by strangers, and one particularly loathed being served in restaurants with the words "There you go." Which for some reason, always makes me laugh, because I can picture the scene: man waiting for roast dinner to be served, pouring wine for wife, practising deep breathing. "He might not say it, dear," whispers the wife, patting his hand. "I know. Don't go on about it," says the man, biting his lip. Along come two plates of dinner. "There you go!" says the waiter. "Aaaagh!" yells the man. I would include "No problem" alongside "There you go" under the heading "Unacceptable Insouciance", incidentally. I always want to administer a clip round the ear to people who accept my thanks with "No problem". The "There you go" man and I ought to go out together, I realise. We could spend most of our time jumping up and down, ranting. "*Where* do I go? Just tell me, *where do I go*? Did I *ask* whether it was a problem? Was a problem *ever* mentioned?"

It is tempting to blame the parents and the teachers for this end-of-deference state of affairs, and do you know what? I am not going to resist that temptation. As a non-parent, I naturally feel I am writing with one hand tied behind my back: after all, many of my best friends are parents, and I know they have done their best. But if I had both hands tied behind my back, I would be obliged to type this with my nose: those damned breeders know they should carry the can, so why pretend otherwise? They have let their kids manipulate, insult and bully them. They have taught them to demand respect, but not to show it. And by doing this, they have failed the kids as much as they have failed the rest of us. There is a great exchange in Arthur Miller's *Death of a Salesman* when Willy says proudly of his sons, "Two fearless characters!" and Charley dryly remarks, "The jails are full of fearless characters." Many parents nowadays seem to share Willy's view – that if a child has reached maturity and is not intimidated by anyone or anything, a fine job of parenting has been done. Who cares if the result is a generation of unhappy sociopaths? Just so long as the unhappy sociopaths regard their parents as their pals.

However, there is a big plus side to the breakdown of formality. Every day I have an encounter of some kind that is friendlier than it would have been ten years ago. The painter who decorated my living room chatted to me about his cats, which was nice. At the station, the person selling tickets says, "That's a nice bag." Not standing on ceremony softens the edges of a sharp world, perhaps? As someone who sits at home all day, banging a keyboard, I am quite grateful for a bit of friendly contact on the phone, even if the chumminess is ultimately empty of meaning, and even if I leap on it with disproportionate gratitude. For example, I give my address to a ticket agency man and he says, "Hey, I know that street. I used to live just round the corner in Buckingham Place!" and I say, "Were you at University down here?" and he says, "No, actually, I worked at the dog track" and I say, "That's really interesting" and he says, "That'll be £88 including the booking fee" and I say, "What's it like at the dog track? I've never been," and he says, "These tickets are non-refundable, and your booking reference is 127565," and I say, "Great. Well, nice to talk to you. And if you ever find yourself in Buckingham Place on a visit to old friends, or just to see the sea, ha ha, there'll be a cup of tea waiting for you at my house, absolutely, just quote booking reference 127565, hello, hello, oh he's gone, oh well." And I'm not making it up; that's the sort of fleeting human contact that can really make my day.

However, it does sometimes go wrong. I recently had a rather instructive friendly cold call from my gas supplier – instructive because it turned out to be extremely complicated, from the familiarity point of view. First of all, you see, the chap was very polite. He apologised for calling me at home, and addressed me as "Miss Truss" throughout. This kept me in a state of placation, obviously. He explained that he was calling about domestic appliance insurance, and asked if this was a good time to talk. Here are the bare bones of what happened next. I said no, sorry, writing book, can't talk. If you must ring back, give it month.

HIM: OK, fair enough.
ME: Bye.
HIM: Writing book, you say?
ME: Yes.
HIM: Mm. Well, Miss Truss, that's v. interesting. I'm bit of writer myself.
ME: Really? (Thinks) Oh no.
HIM: Written rather good story, wondering how to proceed. Any ideas?
ME (incredulous, thinks): Didn't I just say v. busy?

ME: Er, quite busy.

HIM: Appreciate anything. V. tough starting out.

ME (*deep breath; save document; turn attention*): OK, buster, here's deal. Get latest *Writer's Handbook*. Blah blah. Maybe join writing group. Send to agent. Blah blah. Copyright first? Ha ha, are you kidding, you must be kidding. Right. Not kidding. OK, send part of it, précis rest. Blah blah. Send to magazine. How long story? Well, too long BBC. Two thousand two hundred tops. Shorten it poss? Course not. Not poss. That's it. Sorry. Blah blah. Good luck. Blah blah. Hope it helps. Bye.

HIM: That's very helpful, Miss Truss. Thank you. What's your book then?

ME (*big sigh; growing impatient*): About rudeness. Big rant. Short. No discernible value. Oh, look at time. Must rush. Still on chap five.

HIM: That sounds very interesting, Miss Truss. Now, would it be rude if I point out that for as little as 38 pence a week, *which is less than the price of a Yorkie bar*, you could insure all your domestic appliances with us this afternoon?

! # * !

A bulldozer has knocked down a myriad fine distinctions that used to pertain. I deliberately omitted gender from my list of twenty ("they are a member of the weaker sex"), but it's clear that many men are particularly upset that when they show traditional politeness to women nowadays, it's a form of Gallantry Russian Roulette. One time in six, their courtesy makes someone's day. Four times out of six, they get a lecture in gender politics. And one in six, they get their heads blown off. "Are you holding that door open because I'm a woman?" they are asked, aggressively. And the clever ones respond, "No, I'm doing it because I am a gentleman." The problem is, many of the old forms of politeness (such as addressing slaves by their first names) are better abandoned, because they were designed to serve inequality. I was outraged recently when a bill was divided after a rather jolly group dinner, and I was told, "Only the men need pay." While I'm sure there were good intentions behind this, I was furious and made quite a noise, which was awkward for everybody – especially, I have to say, for the more easy-going women who had already said, "Great! Thanks!" and put their bags back on the floor.

In some ways it's quite proper that we should all walk permanently on egg-shells. But it is still tiresomely hard to do the right thing. Give up your seat to a pregnant woman and she will thank you. Give up your seat to a woman who just *looks* pregnant, and she may punch you on the nose. I have started agonising on the train because I happen to know that people sitting in first-class compartments without first-class tickets run the risk of being fined on the spot. There are ugly scenes when this happens. The fine is large, and there ought to be a warning notice, but there isn't. I am thinking of writing to a problem page. How can I inform my fellow passengers of this without giving offence? My inference would be too obvious. "Excuse me, you look like a hard-up person/scoundrel/fare dodger/idiot. Allow me to give you a tip."

Thus our good intentions are often thwarted by fear in today's politically sensitive world. Offence is so easily given. And where the "minority" issue is involved, the rules seem to shift about: most of the time, a person who is female/black/disabled/

gay wants this *not* to be their defining characteristic; you are supposed to be blind to it. But then, on other occasions, you are supposed to observe special sensitivity, or show special respect. I was recently given a lift by a friend who thoughtfully reversed at a road junction to allow a motorised wheelchair to cross. But having done this highly decent thing, for which he was smilingly thanked, he worried about it. "I shouldn't have done that," he said. "Why, was there someone behind you?" I asked, confused. "No," he said, "but I wouldn't have done that for someone who *wasn't* disabled, would I?"

I mention all this because "political correctness" is sometimes confused with respect, but it operates quite differently. It is not about paying due regard to other people for their individual qualities, needs, or virtues; it's mainly about covering oneself and avoiding prosecution in a world of hair-trigger sensitivity. Hence the escalation of euphemism, and the moral panic that breaks out when a public figure uses the word "niggardly" in a perfectly correct way. In a hundred years' time, anyone wanting to know the moral contortions necessary to well-intentioned and intelligent people in the first years of the twenty-first century should just buy a DVD set of Larry David's *Curb Your Enthusiasm* – and I hope they will laugh, but there's no guarantee that things won't be a whole lot worse by then. Robert Hughes, in his 1993 book *Culture of Complaint: The Fraying of America*, writes, "It's as though all human encounter were one big sore spot, inflamed with opportunities to unwittingly give, and truculently receive, offence ... We want to create a sort of linguistic Lourdes, where evil and misfortune are dispelled by a dip in the waters of euphemism." And I would say, "Amen" to that, if it didn't potentially offend people of other faiths who employ a different form of holy affirmation.

What is left of pure deference? In Britain, I think the last thing we do well (and beautifully) is pay respects to the war dead. "When this goes, it all goes," I have started to think. The controlled emotion of Armistice Day tugs at conscience, swells the commonality of sorrow, and swivels the historical telescope to a proper angle, so that we see, however briefly, that we are not self-made: we owe an absolute debt to other people; a debt that our most solemn respect may acknowledge but can never repay. We stop and we silently remember.

Personally, I sob. I am sobbing now. It is a miracle that some sort of political relativism has not contaminated this ceremony of public grief, a full sixty years after the end of the Second World War. The first cannon fires at 11am, and one is overwhelmed by a sense of sheer humility, sheer *perspective*. We are particles of suffering humanity. For two minutes a year, it's not a bad thing to remember that. If we looked inside ourselves and remembered how insignificant we are, just for a couple of minutes a day, respect for other people would be an automatic result.

! # * !

Of the many reasons for retaining a little bit of deference and respect, the most compelling, I think, must be this common-sense appeal to self-interest. It is a well-observed fact that people are happier when they have some idea of where they stand and what the rules are. It's a basic-instinct, primal-chimp thing that is the basis of many vivid behavioural experiments. Tell an orang-utan that he answers to no one and in a couple of weeks he's lost all idea of himself. His eyes roll back, he bangs his head against trees, he eats his own deposits and wears his hair just any old how. Similarly, when people have no "boundaries" or discipline, they can't relax and it drives them nuts. Every so often, a television experiment will place ungovernable modern schoolchildren in a mocked up old-fashioned school with bells and a merit system, and they not only visibly flourish and calm down, they even learn the capital of Iceland and a bit of Latin grammar. Virtually every day on television, unruly toddlers undergo miraculous transformations when their parents are taught to stop ingratiating themselves and start imposing discipline. Not having respect for other people is clearly incredibly tiring and alienating, if only because the ego never gets a rest.

Of course, with "knowing one's place", we are flirting with class issues again. One of the traditional functions of manners was, obviously, to identify an individual with his own social group. The way you crooked your little finger when raising a tea-cup betokened either your solidarity with other people who crooked their little finger in precisely the same way, or your superiority over those who tipped the tea in the saucer and slurped happily from that. According to the famous "U" and "Non-U" system (coined by Professor Alan Ross to identify upper-class usage and popularised by Nancy Mitford), people who said "lavatory" were better than those who said "toilet". People who had fish-knives were beneath contempt. It was ever so common to say "ever so". This has largely passed, of course. In a very short time, snobbery based on vocabulary and the milk-first/milk-second issue has virtually disappeared. Honestly, you can say "serviette" at me all day until you are blue in the face, and I promise I won't even flinch.

But something useful got lost with all this. Surely one of the reasons that rudeness is such a huge issue for people today is that we worry about it more; it is a source of anxiety. We recount situations to each other, just to check our own reactions. "Was that rude? I thought that was rude. Do you think that's rude? Oh thank goodness you agree with me, because I thought it was rude but then I thought maybe I was being over-sensitive." I mentioned Larry David's *Curb Your Enthusiasm* earlier, because every episode entails anxiety over what's acceptable in a world where people are free to disagree, but still hold fiercely to their own rules. There is a whole episode, for example, about "cut-off time". Someone tells Larry you can't call people at home after 10pm. Is that true? It can't be true. How can that be a *rule*? He tries it and gets into trouble. The next night he calls someone before 10pm and gets into trouble because *their* cut-off time is 9.30. Rules exist, it seems, but there are no rules about the rules. This, in a nutshell, is the insanity of the modern condition.

But how can we go back? As Mark Caldwell points out, in his *Short History of Rudeness*, many rules of etiquette are mere conventions with no moral content or usefulness – which is the sort of thing we don't put up with these days. The reason table manners always played such a large part in etiquette guides was that so many of the intricate rules of eating had no other function than to trip the ignorant. Piling peas on the back of the fork is the usual example given of an etiquette rule that was contrived from the start as pure class-indicator, being otherwise daft, strange, counter-intuitive, and instrumental in letting your dinner get cold. Knives and forks were for a long time the main concern of manners guides, not to mention of posh people. There is an excellent clerihew on this subject about the Duke of Fife:

It looked bad when the Duke of Fife
Left off using a knife;
But people began to talk
When he left off using a fork.

Caldwell cites a rather extreme example of sheer class-solidarity etiquette from a sixteenth-century German chronicle: an old aristocratic Christmas tradition in which dinner companions "festively pelted each other with dog turds". No doubt this tradition arose out of one of those tragic mistranslations from scripture one is always hearing about (scholars will one day discover that the Aramaic for "dog turd" is very close to the word for "season's greetings"), but the point remains: if everyone's doing it, do it. You will be accepted by your peers. You can relax.

The tragedy is that we have swept away class snobbery largely without grasping the opportunity to respect different things. So now, in place of a hierarchy of class, or a system of respect for other people, we mainly have stuff. The glory of stuff has swept most other considerations aside. I would say that respect is now allowable in very few fields: we respect sportsmen (but only when they are playing sport), and we respect charisma, but mainly we respect anyone who's got the latest iPod. Manners guides have actually reflected this shift. Look at modern ones and you will find that instead of teaching you to consider the feelings of others, they tell you what gift to take to a dinner party, how much to spend on flowers for a wedding, and what range of social stationery to buy. In other words, how you act is less important, in terms of status, than what you have. But is this ultimately satisfying? There is a *New Yorker* cartoon that says it all. Dog says to dog: "I've got the bowl, the bone, the big yard. I know I *should* be happy."

It's not just children or members of shaven-headed bling-bling street gangs who are infected with this stuff-anxiety, either. I have sophisticated, left-leaning friends who visibly cheer up when the subject turns to designer clothes, and I have long been aware that my refusal to care about clothes as status symbols gives them actual pain. How proud I was when, a few years ago, an unpolitically correct boyfriend of mine had the following conversation with a leftie journalist friend.

LEFTIE FRIEND: Is that a Paul Smith shirt?

BOYFRIEND: Yes.

LEFTIE FRIEND: That's the same Paul Smith shirt you wore last time I met you, isn't it?

BOYFRIEND: Yes, it must be.

LEFTIE FRIEND: This skirt is by Issey Miyake.

BOYFRIEND: Really? (*Pause*) Correct me if I'm wrong, but isn't it usually aspiring gangsta rappers who set such store by designer labels?

Leftie friend's jaw drops; end of conversation

It has been amusing to note, of course, while writing this book, that the government has drawn up a "Respect Agenda". It will be interesting to see how they sell this optimistic document to the British people. Have you ever noticed how many role models there are in popular culture for rudeness, crassness, laddishness, and nastiness? "Ooh, Anne Robinson! She so *rude*!" "Oh, Jonathan Ross! He's so *rude*!" "Oh, Graham Norton! He's so *rude*!" "Oh, Ali G! He's so *rude*!" "Oh, Jeremy Paxman! He's so *rude*!" Count the role models for respectfulness, on the other hand, and after a couple of hours you will have to admit there is only one: Babe. That's it.

Just one small sturdy imaginary sheep-pig stands between us and total moral decay. "Excuse me," he says, gently tilting his little snout upwards. "I wonder if you'd care to follow me this way towards the hillside of enlightenment?" At which point a passer-by tragically fells him with a blow to the head with an umbrella and shouts, "You see? I told you it was him!"

THE SIXTH GOOD REASON

THE SIXTH GOOD REASON

Someone Else Will Clean It Up

Theodore Dalrymple has been called "the best doctor-writer since William Carlos Williams". He recently stopped working as a psychiatrist in a hospital and prison in the Midlands. As a writer and columnist, he is noted for his savage anti-claptrappery, his unpopular but irrefutable ground-level reports of the poor and the criminal, his sublime prose, and the tremendous quality of his anecdotes. In his collection of essays *Life at the Bottom*, he quotes time and again from anti-social offenders. And time and again, he establishes – through his patients' unconscious "locutions of passivity" – that they have no concept whatever of accountability. "The beer went mad," they say. "Heroin's everywhere." "The knife went in." "Something must have made me do it."

"I have come to see the uncovering of this

dishonesty and self-deception as an essential part of my work," he writes. "When a man tells me, in explanation of his anti-social behaviour, that he is easily led, I ask him whether he was ever easily led to study mathematics or the subjunctives of French verbs." One man said that he had beaten up his pregnant girlfriend because of his low self-esteem, and was quite confused when Dalrymple suggested to him that surely the feeling of low self-esteem ought to be the result of the assault, rather than the cause of it. "My trouble came on again," said another (this man's "trouble" turned out to be breaking into churches, stealing their portable silver, then burning them down to destroy the evidence). However, nothing can surpass the conversation he had with a non-criminal patient, when he asked, "How would you describe your own character?" After thinking about it for a moment, the chap replied, "I take people as they come. I'm very non-judgemental."

Crime is not the subject of this book, thank goodness. I am depressed enough already. But the prevailing psychology of non-accountability is certainly one of the six reasons that the world seems a more rude and dangerous place. George Orwell once wrote that society has always seemed to demand a little more from human beings than it will get in practice. He may have been right. The trouble is, locating the concept of "society" isn't as easy as it once was. As for knowing what society "demands" – well, that's not easy, either. Most of us wish we didn't find graffiti and litter all over the place. We wish the pavements weren't regarded as chewing-gum repositories. We wish men wouldn't urinate in doorways and telephone boxes, sometimes in the hours of daylight. We wish skateboarders didn't come trundling like juggernauts along the pavement and expect us to jump for safety from their path. We wish cyclists didn't ignore traffic lights at pedestrian crossings. When we wish these things, we do it on behalf of "society". Yes, there is a whole lot of impotent communal *wishing* going on.

Now, obviously, we must take a zero tolerance attitude to this shocking state of affairs. It is quite proper that anti-social behaviour is being criminalised, since most of it is technically crime. But, annoyingly, I find I have a problem perching on this particular spot of moral high ground. It seems to be a bit prickly. My hat keeps getting blown off. It has started raining. Something tells me that I don't belong here. It is all very well to write "IMP" and "YES INDEED" and "ABSOLUTELY" in pencil next to sympathetic passages in erudite books and articles about our "network of dependencies" and "tissues of mobile relationships", and "bands of association and mutual commitment", but I find myself nevertheless secretly thinking, "What bands of association? Do I belong to any bands? What networks of dependencies? Am I involved in any networks? What tissues of relationships? Surely I would notice if I were caught up in some tissues?" Norbert Elias, in his book *The Society of Individuals* (1939), writes:

> The idea that in "reality" there is no such thing as a society, only a lot of individuals, says about as much as the statement that there is in "reality" no such thing as a house, only a lot of individual bricks, a heap of stones.

(Next to this passage, incidentally, I have written the word "USE".)

My problem is, you see, that I honestly don't feel like a brick in the house of society. I don't even feel like a chimney pot, a roof tile, or a glazed porch. I am self-reliance personified, a bricky brick without a trace of mortar, and my proudest contribution to society is that I don't take anything away from it. I quite fervently believe in leaving things how you found them, placing litter in the bins provided (or carrying it until you find one), and never causing another motorist to brake or swerve. In other words, I aspire to be a zero impact member of society. But does this qualify me as the opposite of an anti-social person? Quite honestly, I don't think it does, because that would be pro-social, which would involve acting on society's behalf, and I don't do that. "Nothing to do with me," I think, when I observe a sea of litter. And then I bugger off home. "That's a big job for somebody." "Someone really ought to do something about this."

Who dares to be public-spirited these days? The very term "public-spirited" is so outmoded that it actually took me a couple of days to remember it. There was a character called Martha Woodford in *The Archers* years ago who, rather eccentrically, used to dust and polish inside the telephone box on the village green and leave a little vase of flowers in it, but she is long dead; in her place, the heart of Ambridge significantly now has a webcam. I can think of only one example of a real-life person who is altruistically *pro*-social: a friend who collects the litter blowing about her street in Brighton and puts it in the bins. Evidently she has as little faith as me in the "While you're down there ..." anti-litter campaign I mentioned in the introduction. Anyway, it pains me to admit that I generally try to dissuade her from performing this selfless litter-bagging, on the grounds that:

1   It is not her responsibility, so why should she?
2   It is someone else's job, so why aren't *they* doing it?
3   It looks a bit obsessive/eccentric/Martha Woodford-ish.
4   She actually hates and resents doing it, so it makes her grumpy.
5   It makes me feel guilty and worthless.
6   As a general rule you should never volunteer for anything.
7   Ugh! That's other people's litter!

Actually, there is one other example. For his 2004 Channel 4 documentary *Where's Your ****ing*

Manners? the disc jockey Nihal Arthanayake discovered a small group of well-spoken young people in London who spent their lunchtimes in the City committing "Random Acts of Kindness", often by feeding other people's parking meters. Of course, ours is too cynical an age not to shudder and mutter at such uncalled-for goody-goodiness. Some of us did not enjoy the film *Amélie*, after all, and have never been able to look a *crème brûlée* in the face again, let alone listen to warm-hearted accordion music. We are suspicious of people who do good things for no reason. Anyone who departs from the principle of overt self-interest is simply weird. I recently told a story to a couple in a check-in queue, and I think the conversation was quite instructive. The thing is, we were queuing for the chance of extra leg-room on a charter flight, so I explained how, at the start of a previous holiday, I had managed to secure just one seat with leg-room and had valiantly insisted that my companion take it. And what do you know? During the flight, my friend had a rotten time. Someone fell on her. Someone else poured orange juice on her nice suede shoes. The point of my story, of course, was of the just-my-luck variety: you see how good intentions can backfire? No good deed goes unpunished, and so on. But the other people found quite a different moral to my tale. "Bet you were glad you chose the other seat!" they laughed. "Ha ha. Clever you! Well done! Good story!"

! # * !

So is it true that people who need people are the luckiest people in the world? Mm. I suppose there are several profound-sounding axioms thrown up by popular culture that I consider completely inane, and this is one of them. Here is a short list of the worst offenders:

1   People who need people are the luckiest people in the world.
2   Love means never having to say you're sorry.
3   Life is like a box of chocolates. You never know what you're going to get.

Taking these in reverse order, life can certainly be full of possibilities and surprises, but the analogy between life and a box of chocolates breaks down almost immediately because you *do* know what you're going to get with a box of chocolates, actually, if you can be bothered to consult the diagrams that are either supplied on a handy loose sheet or printed inside the lid. By rights, *Forrest Gump*'s catch line should have been, "Life is like a box of chocolates, and if you're sensible you will avoid the cracknels or anything with a bit of candied peel on top." Meanwhile, "Love means never having to say you're sorry" is the counsel of a scoundrel, to say the least. And as for people who need people – can you imagine a condition less fortunate? "I need people!" they must cry aloud at street corners. "Tough cheese!" comes the general reply. Perhaps the lyric actually means that the desperately lonely have a good winning record at the blackjack table or the race track. Perhaps croupiers are taught to spot the tell-tale signs of people-who-need-people during their basic training (sighing, weeping, yearning, etc.), and to deal to them automatically from the bottom of the deck. In poker games on Mississippi river boats, everyone scatters at the warning, "People-who-need-people boarded at Baton Rouge!" "Dang, they are the luckiest people in the whole danged world," says a chap in a fancy waistcoat, quickly scooping his chips into his hat and then putting it on his head. "Deal me out, Miss Cora! If'n you hear a splash, it's me a-swimmin' to safety."

Forgive the flight of fancy. The issue is whether we can claim to have a society any more, against which "anti-social" behaviour offends. Much as I hate to subscribe to any relativist argument, I am aware that there is a kind of paradox: that the less we engage with each other as a society, the more we are self-righteously outraged on "society's" behalf. I keep thinking about attitudes to smoking, and how they have changed during my own lifetime. Smoking in the presence of non-smokers (or in the house of a non-smoker) is now considered excessively rude, and this is only partly because of the medical evidence that shows it is also both dangerous and stupid. There is a marvellous radio monologue by Michael Frayn called "A Pleasure Shared" that sums up how a lot of people feel about second-hand smoke. The "Khhghm" noise is throat-clearing. The "thpp!" is a spit:

Do you spit? No? You don't mind if I do, though?

Khhghm ... Hold on, can you see a spittoon on the
table anywhere? Never mind. Sit down, sit down!
I can use my empty soup bowl. Khhghm – thpp!
My God, that's better. I've been sitting here all the
way through the first course just dying for one.

Personally, I hate smoking, and am largely safe
from it, but I have to be honest: I do remember a time
when it just didn't bother me. I grew up in a house
full of smoke; I worked in offices full of smoke;
I chose the upper deck on buses because I wanted
the view and didn't mind the smoke. I once actually
shared a desk *and a chair* with a chain smoker during
a very busy time at the office, and did not complain
except about the strain to my bottom. It's not that
I wasn't affected by smoke all this time, either. It
nearly did me in. At the age of twelve, I had to spend
the whole summer holiday in bed with respiratory
problems, and I continued to cough phlegm into
hankies until I left home aged eighteen. I had chest
X-rays and pointless antibiotics. I couldn't run the
length of a netball court without seeing stars. My
family talked darkly about Beth in *Little Women* and
sometimes actually cried at the thought of my inevitable early tubercular demise. Meanwhile they each

(four adults) lit small poisonous fires in an unventilated house between twenty and forty times a day, and had to redecorate the living room on a continuous, Forth Rail Bridge basis because of the build-up of orange nicotine tar on the ceiling.

My point is not that I was harmed by all this, and that we were all blind to the obvious. My point is that I used to accept something I truly don't accept any more: that being with other people involved a bit of compromise. When you were not alone, you suspended a portion of yourself. You became a member of a crowd. You didn't judge people by your own standards. I believe we have simply become a lot more sensitive to other people's behaviour in a climate of basic fearful alienation. Instead of a little vase of flowers inside the telephone box, there is a webcam keeping an eye on it. There was recently a news story that ostensibly proved that the world is now one big caring community, in which a webcam led to an exciting rescue: a woman in a stables in Charlotte, Iowa, was kicked by a foaling horse and was unable to move; people who had been watching her on their computers in England and Australia alerted the local rescue services and saved her life.

Now, is this heart-warming to you, or just unbelievably worrying?

The breakdown of "community" has, of course, been well noted already by political scientists, both here and in America: Robert D. Putnam's powerful (and wonderfully titled) book *Bowling Alone* (2000) was a bestseller, despite the rather depressing cover illustration of an Edward Hopper-ish loner at a yellow bowling alley, with head bowed and no visible mates. Putnam sees a broad pattern that resonates in Britain as much as in America: for the first two thirds of the twentieth century, a tide bore Americans deeper into the life of their communities, but a few decades ago, the tide changed and "a treacherous rip current" started to pull everything back. "Without at first noticing, we have been pulled apart from one another and from our communities over the last third of the century."

Some will counter-argue that they have a lot more friends these days, too many to keep up with; and may even belong to more clubs and reading groups. But Putnam distinguishes usefully between two basic types of "social capital" – *bridging* and *bonding* – to rather sobering effect. Bridging is inclusive;

bonding is exclusive. The ultimate bridging group would be the Civil Rights Movement; the ultimate bonding group would be the Ku Klux Klan. Bridging is a lubricant; bonding is an adhesive. Bridging obliges you to adapt and compromise (it generates "broader identities and reciprocity"); bonding confirms you are perfectly all right defining yourself by your existing desires and connections (it "bolsters our narrower selves"). And guess which type is doing quite well at the moment? Here's a clue: think pointy hats and flaming crosses. Think Loctite superglue. Think like-minded nutcases gratefully locating each other on the internet and secretly watching women getting kicked by horses in faraway Charlotte, Iowa.

! # * !

In the introduction to this book, I quoted Benjamin Rush from 1786, to the effect that a schoolboy should learn that "he does not belong to himself, but that he is public property". Is there any chance of a general return to the idea that the individual just owes *something* to the world around him? I have just remembered, incidentally, that in the absence of adequate street-lighting near my house, I do keep an outside light constantly burning in a spirit of general helpfulness, so maybe I am a modern saint after all. Phew. When they make lists of heroines in the future, this outside-light thing will doubtless ensure me a place alongside women who rowed lifeboats in tempests and tended the gangrenous in the Crimea. They can put it on my gravestone: "She lit the way for others." And underneath, "On the other hand, she was a shockingly bad recycler."

I tend to think in terms of bits of the brain. I once got interested in phrenology and dabbled in primitive neuro-science, and now I can't sort things out any other way. So here's how I see the present situation vis-à-vis our instinct for civic responsibility. I think we all have, hard-wired, a bit of the brain that makes a moral calculation on behalf of the common good and decides to act on it. This bit of the brain has, however, been through some tough, attenuating times recently. It has not been much called upon, and has therefore shrunk and dwindled and dried out. In fact, if I can get technical for a moment, our prevailing mode of selfishness has *sucked all the juice* out of that bit of the brain, and it is now just a tragic handful of dust, like that old sibyl in ancient times who asked Apollo for everlasting life and forgot to ask for everlasting youth – condemned to exist eternally, without hope, thirsty, in pain and loneliness and everlasting dark.

But it does still live! You see a vestige of it (oddly enough) in the way we drive: we sometimes calculate that, if we drop back a bit in the middle lane, it will allow someone in the slow lane to move out, which will allow someone else on the slip-road to join later – and no one will have to slow down and everyone will be safer and happier. In cars hurtling at 70 miles per hour, such calculations have quite a large element of self-preservation in them, admittedly; but I do uphold that they employ the bit of the brain marked "FOR THE COMMON GOOD", nevertheless. For the split second of that decision, we acknowledge that we are part of a bigger picture, and that we have a duty to improve the bigger picture if we can. We have absolutely no personal feelings about the people in the other cars. Their right to share the road with us is incontestable. They have our respect. We are all equal in the sight of the Highway Code.

According to some analysts, we can't extend this

sense of civic duty to individuals, because we feel we have to be friends with people – or at least know them – in order to be decent towards them. "Civility is not the same as affection," writes Stephen L. Carter in his book *Civility*. Richard Sennett likewise argues that the desire for some sort of intimacy in all our relationships is the enemy of civility. Our eagerness to make friends with the plumber and chat about dog tracks with the man at the booking agency is based on the idea that, once you know someone, you can respect them. But it reinforces the corollary idea: that if you *don't* know someone, you needn't have any time for them at all. Sennett, in *The Fall of Public Man* (1977), warns that we can't relate to each other as a polity until we rediscover the value of "bands of association and mutual commitment ... between people who are not joined by ties of family or intimate association".

Kindness is still in the world, of course. Morality is still in the world, too. But the old connection between manners and morality has been demolished. Many people now believe that it is harmful, unhelpful and simply wrong to judge a person by the way he behaves. To demand consideration from others is to offend against a kind of modern propriety which understands that each of us has a personal morality, but is under no obligation to prove it. We regard our morality less as a guide to action or conscience, more a hidden jewel – enshrined within, inviolable, and nobody else's business. There is a line in the new *Batman* film which I can't quote exactly but is, in other words: "It's not who you are deep inside that matters, Bruce Wayne; it's what you do that defines you." Morally speaking, however, *Batman Begins* is a bit confused and should not be taken as a model for good living. For one thing, the morally squalid city of Gotham does not appear to be worth saving from obliteration; in fact, the obliteration of Gotham looks like a dandy idea. And for another, the myth of the lone superhero who swoops down and saves everybody with his bat-cunning and bat-ability may provide vicarious moral bat-pleasure (especially when he spreads his wings with a wonderful *Wump!*), but let's face it, it also lets us off the bat-hook. It is, after all, the ultimate confirmation of the view, "Someone else will clean it up."

! # ★ !

What can be done? Well, ha ha, search me. All I know is that I am sick of hearing mothers tell their children, "That was a bad thing to do, Timmy, but you are not bad for doing it." I am also horrified by scenes in gritty TV dramas (presumably based on some sort of middle-class family reality beyond my own experience) where solemn, self-possessed children sit down at kitchen tables with their parents and tick them off for the rotten job they are doing. "It's time you treated us with respect, Alan," they say to their Dad. Or, "Shape up, John. Floy and I have decided you're disgusting." And the Dad hangs his head and mumbles an apology. Something seems to have gone seriously awry here. Topsy-turvy is the word. A few years ago, a friend of mine, with a difficult two-year-old, explained to me, "She didn't ask to be born, did she? Therefore I have to spend my whole life making it up to her." It took me quite a while to pin down what was odd about this statement, but I finally nailed it. It was the contrast to the old days, when the parental attitude was, "We didn't ask to have this child, did we? Therefore she had better spend her whole life making it up to us."

We all knew from the very start that this book

would end up as a moral homily. I have used every angle I could think of before reaching this point; I have even experimented with a bit of relativism, which probably didn't fool anybody. However, it is time to be plain at last. Rudeness is bad. Manners are good. It feels very daring to come out and say it, but I've done it and I feel better. I have used the words "bad" and "good", and thereby committed the ultimate political fuddy-duddiness, and doubtless undermined all my good work. Modern people are impatient with the bad–good distinction; they consider it intellectually primitive. But rudeness is a moral issue and it always has been. The way people behave towards each other, even in minor things, is a measure of their value as human beings. Henry James wrote: "Three things in human life are important. The first is to be kind. The second is to be kind. And the third is to be kind."

Ignore the small niceties and what happens? There is a splendid passage in Dickens's *Martin Chuzzlewit*, when Martin is appalled (as Dickens himself had been) by the brutish manners in 1840s America, and is told that America has better things to do than "acquire forms". He is enraged – and warns what tolerance of bad manners can lead to:

> "The mass of your countrymen begin by stubbornly neglecting little social observances, which have nothing to do with gentility, custom, usage, government, or country, but are acts of common, decent, natural, human politeness. You abet them in this, by resenting all attacks upon their social offences as if they were a beautiful national feature. From disregarding small obligations they come in course to disregard great ones; and so refuse to pay their debts. What they may do, or what they may refuse to do next, I don't know; but any man may see if he will, that it will be something following in natural succession, and a part of one great growth, which is rotten at the root."

Substitute modern relativist values for pioneering American ones, and the point is quite well made. Bad manners lead to other kinds of badness. If we each let the "FOR THE COMMON GOOD" bit of our brains shrivel on the vine, the ultimate result is crime, alienation and moral hell. Manners are easy to dismiss from discussions of morality because they seem to be trivial; the words "moral panic" were invented to belittle those of us who burst into tears at the news that 300,000 bits of chewing-gum sit, newly spat, on the pavements of Oxford Street at any one time. But if we can't talk about the morality of manners, we can't talk about the morality of anything. As Mark Caldwell puts it, in his *Short History of Rudeness*, "Manners are what is left when serious issues of human relations are removed from consideration, yet without manners serious human relations are impossible."

The problem is that it has become politically awkward to draw attention to absolutes of bad and good. In place of manners, we now have doctrines of political correctness, against which one offends at one's peril: by means of a considerable circular logic, such offences mark you as reactionary and *therefore a bad person*. Therefore if you say people are bad, *you* are bad. And to state that a well-mannered person is superior to an ill-mannered one – well, it is to invite total ignominy. Yet I can't not say this. I believe it. Manners are about showing consideration, and using empathy. But they are also about being connected to the common good; they are about being *better*. Every time a person asks himself, "What would the world be like if everyone did this?"

or "I'm not going to calculate the cost to me on this occasion. I'm just going to do the right thing", or "Someone seems to need this seat more than I do", the world becomes a better place. It is ennobled. The crying shame about modern rudeness is that it's such a terrible missed opportunity for a different kind of manners – manners based, for the first time, not on class and snobbery, but on a kind of voluntary charity that dignifies both the giver and the receiver by being a system of mutual, civil respect.

Instead of which, sadly, we have people who say, "The beer went mad" when what they mean is, "I drank too much and then I got violent." Far from taking moral responsibility for other people, we have started refusing to take moral responsibility even for ourselves. I once heard someone say, in all seriousness, "If I contract salmonella from eating this runny egg, they'll be sorry." Someone else is always the repository for blame. Someone else will clear it up. Someone else will pay for this. Even when we are offended, we don't feel comfortable saying, "This offends me." Instead, we say, "This could offend people more sensitive to this kind of thing." There was recently a hoo-ha about a TV advertisement for

Kentucky Fried Chicken in which call-centre staff sang, with their mouths full, about how great the new KFC chicken salad was – with subtitles, because their words were so unclear. Now, the Advertising Standards Authority received over a thousand complaints in two weeks, and the complaints were that:

1 It set a bad example to children.
2 It encouraged dangerous behaviour because of the risk of choking.
3 It presented emergency call-centre staff in a bad light.
4 It mocked people with speech impediments.

Evidently the true reaction, the true objection – that watching people talk with their mouths full is something you perhaps shouldn't be subjected to in your own home – simply could not be voiced, because such a point would be judgemental and therefore inadmissible.

I mentioned, in the introduction to this book, a tiny flame of hope, and here it is. Let's try *pretending* to be polite, and see what happens. Old Aristotle might have been right all those centuries ago: that if

you practise being good in small things (I'm paraphrasing again), it can lead to the improvement of
general morality. I promise I will stop shouting at
boys on skateboards, if that will help. Being friendly
and familiar with strangers is not the same as being
polite (as we have seen), but if it helps us overcome
our normal reticence, all right, be friendly. Yes, we
live in an aggressive "Talk to the hand" world. Yes,
we are systematically alienated and have no sense of
community. Yes, we swear a lot more than we used
to, and we prefer to be inside our own individual
Bart Simpson bubbles. But just because these are the
conditions that promote rudeness does not mean
that we can't choose to improve our happiness by
deciding to be polite to one another. Just as enough
people going around correcting apostrophes may
ultimately lead to some restoration of respect for the
English language, so enough people demonstrating
kindness and good manners may ultimately have
an impact on social morality. Evelyn Waugh wrote
that, historically, ceremony and etiquette were the
signs of an advancing civilisation; but he went on,
rather wonderfully: "They can also be the protection
of [civilisations] in decline; strong defences behind

which the delicate and the valuable are preserved."
Or, if we can't go quite that far, let's just remember
to put the empty beer can in the bin *while we're down
there* ...

Bibliography

Allan Bloom, *The Closing of the American Mind*, Simon
    and Schuster, 1987

P. Brown and S.C. Levinson, *Politeness: Some
    Universals in Language Usage*, Cambridge
    University Press, 1987

Mark Caldwell, *A Short History of Rudeness: Manners,
    Morals and Misbehavior in Modern America*, Picador
    USA, 1999

Stephen L. Carter, *Civility: Manners, Morals, and the
    Etiquette of Democracy*, 1998

Theodore Dalrymple, *Life at the Bottom: The Worldview
    That Makes the Underclass*, Ivan R. Dee, 2001

Barbara Ehrenreich, "The Civility Glut", *The
    Progressive*, vol. 64, issue 12, December 2000

Norbert Elias, *The Civilizing Process: Sociogenetic and Psychogenetic Investigations* (1939), Blackwell, 1994; rev. edn 2000

Norbert Elias, *The Society of Individuals* (1983), Blackwell, 1991

Kate Fox, *Watching the English: The Hidden Rules of English Behaviour*, Hodder and Stoughton Ltd, 2004

Michael Frayn, "A Pleasure Shared", from *Listen to This: Sketches and Monologues*, Methuen, 1990

Erving Goffman, *Behavior in Public Places: Notes on the Social Organization of Gatherings*, Free Press, 1963

Erving Goffman, *Interaction Ritual: Essays on Face-to-Face Behavior*, Pantheon, 1967 (Aldine Transaction, 2005)

Erving Goffman, *The Presentation of Self in Everyday Life*, Anchor Books, 1959 (Penguin, 2005)

Erving Goffman, *Relations in Public: Microstudies of the Public Order*, Allen Lane, 1971

Robert Hughes, *Culture of Complaint: The Fraying of America*, Oxford University Press USA, 1993 (Harvill Press, 1994)

Steven Johnson, *Everything Bad is Good for You*, Allen Lane, 2005

Bibliography

Richard Layard, *Happiness: Lessons from a New Science*, Allen Lane, 2005

Carolyn Marvin, *When Old Technologies were New: Thinking about Electric Communication in the Late Nineteenth Century*, Oxford University Press USA, 1988

George Mikes, *How to be a Brit*, André Deutsch, 1984 (Penguin, 1986)

John Morgan, *Debrett's New Guide to Etiquette and Modern Manners*, Headline, 1999

Jeremy Paxman, *The English: A Portrait of a People*, Michael Joseph, 1998 (Penguin 1999)

Stuart Prebble, *Grumpy Old Men*, BBC, 2004

Public Agenda, *Aggravating Circumstances: A Status Report on Rudeness in America*, 2002

Robert D. Putnam, *Bowling Alone: The Collapse and Revival of American Community*, Simon and Schuster, 2000

John Seabrook, *Deeper: A Two-Year Odyssey in Cyberspace*, Faber and Faber, 1997

Richard Sennett, *The Fall of Public Man*, Knopf, 1977 (Penguin, 2003)

Richard Sennett, *Respect in a World of Inequality*, W. W. Norton, 2003 (Penguin, 2004)

Evelyn Waugh, "Manners and Morals", from *The Essays, Articles and Reviews of Evelyn Waugh*, ed. Donat Gallagher, Methuen, 1984

Contents

MECHANICS

8
Manuscript Form   82

9
Capitals   92

10
Italics

11
Abbreviations and Numbers

PUNCTUATION

12
The Comma

Contents

13
Superfluous Commas   128

14
The Semicolon   132

15
The Apostrophe 140

16
Quotation Marks 145

17
The Period and Other Marks 154

Contents

SPELLING AND DICTION

18
Spelling and Hyphenation

19
Good use — Glossary

20
Exactness

21
Wordiness

22
Omission of Necessary Words

EFFECTIVE SENTENCES

23
Unity and Logical Thinking

24
Subordination

25
Coherence: Misplaced Parts, Dangling Modifiers

Contents

26
Parallelism   282

27
Point of View   290

Contents

28
Reference of Pronouns 296

29
Emphasis 302

30
Variety 314

xxiv

LARGER ELEMENTS

31
The Paragraph

32
Planning and Writing the Whole Composition

33
Library Paper

34
Letters   458

GRAMMAR

Sentence Sense

1

Master the essentials of the sentence as an aid to clear thinking and effective writing.

Acquiring sentence sense means developing the ability to recognize what *makes* a sentence. An understanding of the grammar of English sentences is a key to good writing.

Study the structure of the sentence below; focus attention upon how meaning is expressed by the arrangement and the forms of words.

> The hijacked airliner has landed safely.

Note the importance of word order. Other arrangements of the same words are possible:

> The hijacked airliner has safely landed. [No appreciable difference in meaning]
> Has the hijacked airliner landed safely? [A change in meaning]

But not every arrangement of words is possible in an English sentence:

> NONSENSICAL   Hijacked safely airliner has landed the.

Note also that changing the forms of words affects sentence meaning:

> The hijacked airliners have landed safely. [A change in meaning]

Observing the forms and the positions of words can help you to understand the relationship between parts of sentences.

The following sentences have two main parts:

Enthusiastic freshmen | were registering.

An explosion of knowledge | creates problems.

The first part of each sentence above functions as the subject; the second part functions as the predicate. Most simple sentences follow this pattern:

> PATTERN **SUBJECT—PREDICATE.**

Speakers and writers combine sentences and in the process rearrange, add, delete, and substitute words.

The air is dirty.   We can purify it.

VARIOUS COMBINATIONS

The air is dirty, but we can purify it.
We can purify the air that is dirty.
We can purify the dirty air.
Although dirty, the air can be purified.

A study of Sections 1 through 7 of this handbook should help you understand how words are related to one another, why their forms change, and what order they take in sentence patterns. For explanations of any unfamiliar grammatical terms, see the Glossary of Grammatical Terms beginning on page 467.

1a

Learn to recognize verbs.

A verb may function as the predicate of a sentence or as a part of the predicate:

SUBJECT + PREDICATE

William	*drives.*
William	*drives* carefully in heavy traffic.
William	always *drives* his car to work.

You can learn to recognize a verb by observing its meaning and its form.

Meaning   Often defined as a word expressing action or a state of being, a verb is used to make a statement, to ask a question, or to give a command or a direction.

Charles *slept* well.   *Leave* the computer alone!

Was it necessary?   *Turn* left at Akard Street.

Form   When converted from the present to the past tense, nearly all verbs change form (*eat—ate*). In the present tense, all verbs change form to indicate a singular subject in the third person (I *eat*—he *eats*). Used with a form of *be*, all verbs in the progressive tense end in *-ing* (*was eating*). Some verbs have a special ending when used with a form of *have* in the perfect tense (*has eaten*).

PRESENT	I *play.* It *plays.*	We *eat* early. He *eats* early.
PAST	Tom *played* well.	All of them *ate* here today.
PROGRESSIVE	He *is playing.*	They *were eating* breakfast.
PERFECT	He *has played.*	They *have eaten* all the pie.

In addition, certain suffixes like *-ize* and *-ify* often indicate that a word is a verb (*legalize, beautify*).

Verb phrases   A verb consisting of more than one word is often referred to as a *verb phrase*. A verb phrase comprises the main verb together with the auxiliary words, or verb helpers.

The fight *had started.*   He *may be sleeping.*
I *am going to try.*   [Compare "I *will try.*"]
She *has to rest.*   [Compare "She *must rest.*"]

Words commonly used in verb phrases are *has, have, had,*

be, am, is, are, was, were, been, do, does, did, used to, may, might, must, has to, have to, had to, shall, will, am (is, are, and so on) going to, am (is, are, and so on) about to, would, should, ought to, can, and *could.* These words are often called *verb markers* because they precede and act as signals for verbs. Notice, however, that other words may intervene between the verb marker and the verb:

> Television *will* never completely *replace* the radio. [The auxiliary *will* signals the approach of the verb *replace.*]

Note: The contraction for *not* may be added to such verb markers as *does, have, can: doesn't, haven't, can't.* The full word *not* following a verb marker is written separately: *does not, have not.* An exception is *cannot.*

Verbs with particles Many verbs are used with particles like *in, up, up with, off, on, down, over,* and *out.* Notice that the verb-particle combinations below are single units in meaning.

> He *gets up* early and *turns in* late. [Compare "He *rises* early and *retires* late."]
> We *put up with* the noise for hours. [Compare "We *tolerated* the noise for hours."]
> She will *look over* the books and *pick* one *out.* [Notice that a word intervenes between the verb *pick* and the particle *out.*]

■ **Exercise 1** Write sentences (1) using *left* and *flies* as single-word predicates and (2) using *up, bargaining,* and *experiment* as parts of predicates.

■ **Exercise 2** In the following paragraph, underline the twenty verbs, including any auxiliaries.

¹ Jim angrily called himself a fool, as he had been doing all the way through the woods. ² Why had he listened to Fred's mad idea? ³ What were ghosts and family legends to him, in this year of grace and nuclear fission? ⁴ He had mysteries enough of his own, of a highly complex electronic sort, which

5

would occupy him through the rest of a lifetime. ⁵ But now he was plodding along here, like the Mississippi schoolboy that he had been a dozen years before; this ghost chase in the middle of the night was preposterous. ⁶ It was lunacy. ⁷ It was—he swallowed the truth like a bitter pill—frightful! ⁸ The legend and the ghost had been a horror to him as a child; and they were a horror still. ⁹ As he stood at the edge of the weed-choked, briar-tangled slope, on the top of which the old mansion waited evilly, he felt almost sick. ¹⁰ The safe, sure things of every day had become distant, childish fantasies. ¹¹ This grotesque night and whatever ghoulish and monstrous inhabited it were clammily and horribly real.

1b

Learn to recognize subjects and objects of verbs.

Nouns and noun substitutes are used as subjects and objects of verbs. In the following sentence, the three nouns are italicized: the first functions as a *subject* (or *simple subject*), the second as an *indirect object,* and the third as a *direct object.*

> A persuasive *clerk* quickly sold these *freshmen* the expensive *encyclopedias.*

The basic sentence pattern is as follows:

```
PATTERN
SUBJECT—VERB—INDIRECT OBJECT—DIRECT OBJECT.
```

clerk   sold   freshmen   encyclopedias

You can learn to recognize subjects and objects of verbs by observing their meaning, their form, and their position in sentences.

Meaning   To identify a subject, first find the verb; then use the verb in a question beginning with *who* or *what* as shown in the following examples:

The dogs in the pen ate.	The pen was built by Ed.
Verb: *ate*	Verb: *was built*
WHO or WHAT ate? *The dogs* (not the pen) *ate.*	WHAT was built? *The pen* (not Ed) *was built.*
Subject: *dogs*	Subject: *pen*

To identify a direct object, find the subject and the verb; then use them in a question ending with *whom* or *what* as shown below:

> Margaret happily greeted the reporters at the airport.
> Subject and verb: *Margaret greeted*
> Margaret greeted WHOM or WHAT? *the reporters*
> Direct object: *reporters*

A verb that has a direct object to complete its meaning is called a *transitive* verb. Notice that a direct object in a sentence like the following is directly affected by the action of the verb:

> High winds leveled a *city* in West Texas.

Some verbs (such as *give, offer, bring, take, lend, send, buy,* and *sell*) may have both a direct object and an indirect object. An indirect object states *to whom* or *for whom* (or *to what* or *for what*) something is done.

> Richard sent *Mildred* an invitation. [Richard sent an invitation *to whom? Mildred* is the indirect object.]

Form   Although other words or word groups may function as subjects or objects, nouns and pronouns are most frequently used in this way.

Most nouns (words used to name persons, places, things, ideas, animals, qualities, or actions) change their form to indicate number (*movement, movements; city, cities; woman, women*) and to indicate the possessive case (*John's* car, the *boys'* dogs, the *men's* job). Such suffixes as *-ance, -ation, -ence, -ment, -ness,* and *-ship* frequently indicate that a word is a noun (*appearance, determination, reference, atonement, boldness, hardship*). The articles *a, an,* and *the* are sometimes called *noun markers* because they regularly signal that a noun is to follow (a *chair*, an *activity*, the last *race*).

Form makes it a simple matter to recognize some pronouns. Pronouns such as *I, we, she, he, they,* and *who* function as subjects; when used as objects, these words change to the forms *me, us, her, him, them,* and *whom.* Other pronouns—such as *you, it, mine, ours, yours, hers, his, theirs, that, which*—resemble nouns in that they function as either subjects or objects without a change in form.

Position   Becoming thoroughly aware of the meaningfulness of English word order—normally SUBJECT—VERB—OBJECT—will help you to recognize subjects and objects. Study carefully the following commonly used sentence patterns, observing the importance of word order (especially in Pattern 2) in determining meaning. (For patterns with subject and object complements, see **4b** and **5f.**)

> PATTERN 1 **SUBJECT—VERB.**

Coyotes often *howl.*
The *lights* on the boat *were flashing* brightly.

> PATTERN 2 **SUBJECT—VERB—OBJECT.**

Elephants frighten mice.
Mice frighten elephants.
A tiny *battery* in the handle *provided* much *power.*

> PATTERN 3
> **SUBJECT—VERB—INDIRECT OBJECT—DIRECT OBJECT.**

Mary baked Fred a *cake.*
Candidates often rashly *promise voters* lower *taxes.*

Remember, however, that subjects and objects of verbs do not always take the position indicated by these basic patterns.

There *were* no *objections*. [Verb precedes subject. *There* used as an introductory word or filler is an expletive, which is never the subject.]

Over the door *were sprigs* of mistletoe. [Verb precedes subject. Compare "Sprigs of mistletoe were over the door."]

His last *question I did* not *answer*. [Here the pattern is OBJECT—SUBJECT—VERB.]

Look carefully at the structure of the following sentences, which show a basic pattern and several common variations.

STATEMENT His *secretary typed* the *letters*.
[Pattern 2: SUBJECT—VERB—OBJECT.]

COMMAND OR REQUEST *Type* the *letters*. [VERB—OBJECT.]

EXCLAMATION What *letters* his *secretary typed!*
[OBJECT—SUBJECT—VERB!]

QUESTIONS *Has* his *secretary typed* the *letters?*
[AUXILIARY—SUBJECT—VERB—OBJECT?]

What *letters should* his *secretary type?*
[OBJECT—AUXILIARY—SUBJECT—VERB?]

A test for an object Knowing how to change an active verb to the passive voice can also help you to identify an object, since the object of an active verb can usually be made the subject of a passive verb.

ACTIVE The Eagles finally *defeated* the *Lions*. [*Lions* is the direct object of *defeated.*]

PASSIVE The *Lions were* finally *defeated* by the Eagles. [*Lions* is the subject of *were defeated.*]

Notice above that a form of *be* is added when an active verb is changed to the passive.

Note: Subjects, verbs, and objects may be compound.

Cobras and *pythons* both lay eggs. [Compound subject]

A capable student *can face* and *solve* his *problems* or *difficulties*. [Compound verb and compound object]

9

■ **Exercise 3**   Label all subjects of verbs, direct objects, and indirect objects in the quotations below. Prepare for a class discussion of the basic sentence patterns and the variations used.

1. Even senators quail before a group of angry women.
   —RODERICK A. CAMERON
2. Scarcely anything awakens attention like a tale of cruelty.
   —SAMUEL JOHNSON
3. We have found the world in our own souls.
   —TEILHARD DE CHARDIN
4. Only a moral idiot with a suicidal mania would press the button for a nuclear war.   —WALTER LIPPMANN
5. Signs of the future float in our smoggy skies and on our greasy surf.   —GEORGE B. LEONARD
6. Consider the intellectual climate in most of our colleges today.   —RALPH E. ELLSWORTH
7. There is a built-in trouble with age segregation.
   —TOM WOLFE
8. Philosophy and science give us knowledge of men in the aggregate, or in essence.   —MARK VAN DOREN
9. Should our personal philosophy toward government include an element of fear?   —MARIO PEI
10. Neither intelligence nor integrity can be imposed by law.
    —CARL BECKER

1c

Learn to recognize all the parts of speech.

Two methods of classifying words in a sentence are shown below:

Waitresses usually offer us free coffee at Joe's café.

1. SUBJECT—MODIFIER—VERB—INDIRECT OBJECT—
   MODIFIER—DIRECT OBJECT—PREPOSITION—
   MODIFIER—OBJECT OF PREPOSITION.

2. NOUN—ADVERB—VERB—PRONOUN—ADJECTIVE—
   NOUN—PREPOSITION—NOUN—NOUN.

The first method classifies words according to their function in a sentence; the second, according to their part of speech.

Notice here that one part of speech—the noun (a naming word with a typical form)—is used as a subject, a direct object, a modifier, and an object of a preposition.

Words are traditionally grouped into eight classes or parts of speech: *verbs, nouns, pronouns, adjectives, adverbs, prepositions, conjunctions,* and *interjections.* Verbs, nouns, adjectives, and adverbs are sometimes called *vocabulary words* because they make up more than 99 percent of all words listed in the dictionary. But pronouns, prepositions, and conjunctions—though small in number—are important because they are used over and over in our speaking and writing. Prepositions and conjunctions—as well as small subgroups of the other main classes, such as auxiliaries (a subgroup of verbs) and articles (a subgroup of adjectives)—are often called *function words.* They serve to relate the vocabulary words to one another.

Of the eight word classes, only three—prepositions, conjunctions, and interjections—do not change their form. For a summary of the form changes of verbs, nouns, pronouns, adjectives, and adverbs, see **inflection**, page 479.

Carefully study the forms, meanings, and functions of each of the eight parts of speech listed on the following pages.

VERBS   *notify, notifies, are notifying, notified*
        write, writes, is writing, wrote, has written

A verb can function as the predicate of a sentence or as a part of the predicate: see **1a.**

> Herman *writes.*
> He *is* no longer *writing* those long, dull historical novels.

Note: Verb forms classified as participles, gerunds, or infinitives cannot function as the predicate of a sentence: see **1d.**

PARTICIPLE	She gave him *written* instructions. [Modifier]
GERUND	His *writing* all night long disturbed his whole family. [Subject]
INFINITIVES	Herman wants *to write.* [Direct object]
	The urge *to write* left him. [Modifier]

NOUNS	*man, men; kindness, kindnesses*
	nation, nations; nation's, nations'
	Carthage, United States, William, DNA
	prudence, the *money,* an *understanding*

In sentences, nouns function as subjects, direct or indirect objects, objects of prepositions, subject complements (predicate nouns), object complements, appositives, modifiers, and subjects and objects of participles, gerunds, and infinitives; they are also used in direct address and in absolute constructions. Nouns may name persons, places, things, ideas, animals, qualities, or actions.

> *Edward* paid the *men* for the *work.*

Note: Words such as *father-in-law, forest ranger, swimming pool, dropout,* and *breakthrough* are generally classified as *compound nouns.*

PRONOUNS	*I, me, my, mine, myself; they, you, him, it*
	this, these; who, whose, whom; which, that
	one, ones, one's; both, everybody, anyone

Pronouns serve the function of nouns in sentences.

> *He* paid *them* for *it.*   *Everyone* knows *this.*

ADJECTIVES	*young, younger, youngest; a, an, the*
	three men, *sturdy* chairs, *this* day, *the* one

Adjectives modify or qualify nouns and pronouns; sometimes they modify gerunds. Generally adjectives are placed near the words they modify.

> *Lonely* and *sleepy,* he was *glad* to see *familiar* landmarks.

In the sentence above, *glad* is a predicate adjective (subject complement), a word that helps to complete the meaning of a linking verb (*be, am, is, are, was, were, been, seem, become, feel, look, smell, sound, taste,* and so on) and that modifies the subject: see **4b.**

ADVERBS   *rarely* saw, call *daily*, *soon* left, left *sooner*
                 very short, *too* angry, *never* shy, *not* fearful
                 practically never loses, *nearly always* cold

In the first series of examples above, the adverbs modify
verbs; in the second, the adverbs modify adjectives. In the
third, *practically* modifies the adverb *never; nearly,* the adverb *always.* In addition to modifying verbs, adjectives, and
other adverbs, an adverb may modify an infinitive, a gerund,
a participle, or a phrase or clause. It may even modify the
rest of the sentence in which it appears:

   Honestly, she lies about her age.

PREPOSITIONS   *at* times, *between* us, *because of* rain
                     to the door, *by* them, *before* class

Words commonly used as prepositions are *across, after, as,
at, because of, before, between, by, for, from, in, in front
of, in regard to, like, near, of, on, over, through, to, together
with, under, until, up, with.* A preposition, a function word,
always has an object, which is usually a noun or a pronoun;
the preposition with its object (and any modifiers) is called
a *prepositional phrase.*

   Byron expressed *with great force* his love *of liberty.*

The preposition may follow rather than precede its object,
and it may be placed at the end of the sentence.

   What are you selling it *for?*   Faith is what we live *by.*

Note: Words like *in, up, off, on, down, over,* and *out* may
be classified as prepositions, as adverbs, or as particles (used
with verbs: see page 5).

PREPOSITIONS	He ran *up* the hill. I was a mile *off* shore.
ADVERBS	Look *up.* He marched *off.*
PARTICLES	Look *up* George. OR Look George *up.*
	[Compare ''Find George.'']
	I put *off* work. OR I put work *off.*
	[Compare ''I postpone work.'']

CONJUNCTIONS   Ida *and* Bill, in *or* out, long *but* witty
She acts *as if* she cares.
I left *because* I had finished the job.

Conjunctions function as connectors. They fall into two
classes: the coordinating conjunctions (*and, but, or, nor, for,*
and sometimes *so* and *yet*), used to connect words or phrases
or to connect clauses that are of equal rank; and the subordinating conjunctions (such as *after, as if, because, if, since,
till, when, where, while*), used to connect subordinate clauses
with main clauses.

> According to one biographer, Bacon did not look at friends
> *when* he talked with them, *for* he was concerned chiefly
> with ideas, not people.

INTERJECTIONS   *Ouch! Oh,* pardon me.

Interjections are exclamations, which may be followed by
an exclamation point or by a comma: see **17c**.

The dictionary shows the word class (often the several
word classes) in which a given word may be used, but the
actual classification of any word is dependent upon its use
in the sentence. Notice how the classification of *round* varies
in accordance with its use in the following sentences:

> The second *round* was tiring.   [Noun]
> Any *round* table will do.   [Adjective]
> Some drivers *round* corners too rapidly.   [Verb]
> The sound goes *round* and *round*.   [Adverb]
> He lives *round* the corner.   [Preposition]

Suffixes can often serve as clues to word classification:

> recre*ation*, recreation*al*   [Noun, adjective]
> beaut*iful*, beaut*ify*   [Adjective, verb]

■ **Exercise 4**   Study the use of the words in the following
quotations, paying special attention to the form and the position

of each word. Prepare for a class discussion of the parts of speech.

1. Biology has always recognized inborn individuality.
   —ROGER J. WILLIAMS
2. Of all persons, adolescents are the most intensely personal; their intensity is often uncomfortable to adults.
   —EDGAR Z. FRIEDENBERG
3. He felt as though he had stepped with both feet into a Sherwood Anderson story.   —BERNARD MALAMUD
4. Romantic love also obscures the realities of female status and the burden of economic dependency.   —KATE MILLETT

1d

Learn to recognize phrases and subordinate clauses.

PHRASES

A phrase is often defined as a group of related words without a subject and a predicate. Phrases are generally classified as follows:

VERB PHRASES   The rose *has wilted.   Did* you *see* it?
Mr. Kelly *may run up* the bill.   The roof *used to leak.*

NOUN PHRASES   *The severe drought* struck *many midwestern states.*

PREPOSITIONAL PHRASES   A special program *on the growth of flowers* fascinated audiences everywhere.   *In fact,* the timed photography was spectacular.

PARTICIPIAL PHRASES   A person *seeing an accident* should stay on the scene.   *Seeing the accident,* a woman stopped. *Seen by three men,* the accident was reported at once.

GERUND PHRASES   *Riding a horse* takes skill.   I prefer *riding a bicycle.*

INFINITIVE PHRASES   Does James like *to swim in the ocean?* That is the problem *to be solved now.*

Notice in the examples above that the gerund *riding,* like

the present participle *seeing,* ends in *-ing,* and that the two
are distinguished only by their use in the sentence: the
participle functions as an adjective and the gerund functions
as a noun.

Participles, gerunds, and infinitives are derived from verbs.
(See also the Glossary of Grammatical Terms.) They are
much like verbs in that they have different tenses, can take
subjects and objects, and can be modified by adverbs. But
they cannot serve as the only verb form in the predicate
of a sentence. Participial, gerund, and infinitive phrases
function as adjectives, nouns, or adverbs and are therefore
only parts of sentences, as the following examples illustrate.

SENTENCES

He explained the process.   *He drew simple illustrations.*

PHRASES IN SENTENCES

Explaining the process, he drew simple illustrations.   OR
Drawing simple illustrations, he explained the process.
   [Participial phrases]
He explained the process by *drawing simple illustrations.*
   [Gerund phrase]
He drew simple illustrations *to explain the process.*
   [Infinitive phrase]

(1) Phrases used as nouns

Gerund phrases are always used as nouns. Infinitive phrases
are often used as nouns (though they may also function as
modifiers). Occasionally a prepositional phrase functions as
a noun.

NOUNS

The *decision* is important.

She likes the *job.*

PHRASES USED AS NOUNS

Choosing a major is important.
   [Gerund phrase—subject]

She likes *to do the work.*
   [Infinitive phrase—direct
   object]

His *action* prompted the *change.*	*His leaving the farm* prompted *her to seek a job in town.* [Gerund phrase—subject; infinitive phrase—direct object]
The lesson in *speech* began.	The lesson in *speaking correctly* began. [Gerund phrase—object of a preposition]
That *hour* is too late.	*After supper* is too late. [Prepositional phrase—subject]

■ **Exercise 5**   Make a list of the gerund phrases and the infinitive phrases used as nouns in the following sentences (selected from *Time*).

1. Merely to argue for the preservation of park land is not enough.
2. Successfully merchandising a product is creative.
3. "We just want to take some of the blindness out of blind dates," explains the founder of Operation Match.
4. He insisted on calling every play from the bench; he tried installing a radio receiver in his quarterback's helmet, and when other teams started tuning in on his broadcast, he switched to shuttling "messenger guards" back and forth with his orders.

(2) Phrases used as modifiers

Prepositional phrases nearly always function as adjectives or adverbs. Infinitive phrases are also used as adjectives or adverbs. Participial phrases are used as adjectives.

ADJECTIVES	PHRASES USED AS ADJECTIVES
It is a *significant* discovery.	It is a discovery *of significance.* [Prepositional phrase]
Appropriate language is very important.	Language *to suit the occasion* is very important. [Infinitive phrase]

17

Destructive storms lashed the Midwest.	Storms, *destroying many crops of corn and oats,* lashed the Midwest. [Participial phrase containing a prepositional phrase]
The *icy* bridge was dangerous.	*Covered with ice,* the bridge was dangerous. [Participial phrase containing a prepositional phrase]

ADVERBS	PHRASES USED AS ADVERBS
Drive *carefully*.	Drive *with care on slick streets.* [Prepositional phrases]
Certainly Mary Ann radiates self-confidence and poise.	*To be sure,* Mary Ann radiates self-confidence and poise. [Infinitive phrase]

The preceding examples demonstrate how phrases function in the same way as single-word modifiers. Remember, however, that phrases are not merely substitutes for single words. Many times phrases express more than can be packed into a single word.

> The gas gauge fluttered *from empty to full.*
> He telephoned his wife *to tell her of his arrival.*
> *Walking down Third Avenue,* I noticed many new buildings.

■ **Exercise 6** Each italicized phrase below is used as a modifier. First classify each phrase as *prepositional, infinitive,* or *participial;* then state whether the phrase functions as an adjective or as an adverb. (These sentences were selected from *Life.*)

1. The great highways [1] *lancing into the suburbs* are changing the tone and the pace [2] *of the city.*
2. [3] *Imprisoned in the narrowness* [4] *of our human scale,* we are blind [5] *to the vast reaches* [6] *of reality.*
3. She is too shy [7] *to employ the hustle and muscle necessary* [8] *to win the honor.*
4. Watch the jaywalker [9] *in action:* one of nature's noblemen, [10] *dodging and feinting* [11] *among the sullen monsters* [12] *of chrome.*

18

SUBORDINATE CLAUSES

A clause is often defined as a group of related words that contains both a subject and a predicate. Like a phrase, a subordinate or dependent clause is not a sentence. The subordinate clause functions as a single part of speech—as a noun, an adjective, or an adverb. Notice the relationship of the sentences below to the clauses that follow.

SENTENCES

That fact I must admit.
Ralph was my first and only blind date.
I married him.

SUBORDINATE CLAUSES IN SENTENCES

I must admit *that Ralph was my first and only blind date.*
   [Noun clause—direct object]
The first blind date *that I ever had* was Ralph.
   [Adjective clause]
Ralph was my first and only blind date *because I married him.* [Adverb clause]

In the examples above, *that* and *because* are used as *subordinators:* they subordinate the clauses they introduce, making these clauses dependent. The following words are commonly used to mark subordinate clauses:

RELATIVE PRONOUNS that, what, which, who, whoever, whom, whomever, whose
SUBORDINATING CONJUNCTIONS after, although, as, as if, as though, because, before, if, in order that, since, so that, that, though, unless, until, when, whenever, where, wherever, while

The subordinator *that* commonly functions either as a conjunction or as a pronoun:

He admits *that* the theory disturbs him. [Conjunction]
The theory *that* disturbs him is not new. [Pronoun—subject of *disturbs*]

(3) Subordinate clauses used as nouns

NOUNS	NOUN CLAUSES
The newspaper *accounts* may be false.	*What the newspapers say* may be false. [Subject]
I do not know his *address*.	I do not know *where he lives.* [Direct object]
Give the tools to *Paul.*	Give the tools to *whoever can use them best.* [Object of a preposition]
That fact—his *protest*—amazed me.	The fact *that he protested* amazed me. [Appositive]

(4) Subordinate clauses used as modifiers

Two types of subordinate clauses, the adjective clause and the adverb clause, are used as modifiers.

ADJECTIVE	ADJECTIVE CLAUSE
The *golden* window reflects the sun.	The window, *which shines like gold,* reflects the sun.

ADVERB	ADVERB CLAUSE
The work stops *then.*	The work stops *when it rains.*

Adjective clauses   Any clause that modifies a noun or a pronoun is an adjective clause. Adjective clauses, which nearly always follow the words modified, are most frequently introduced by a relative pronoun, which is often a subject or an object in the subordinate clause.

> A man *who knows the truth* is fortunate. [The relative pronoun *who* is the subject of *knows* in the adjective clause.]
> He is a man *whom I have always admired.* [The relative pronoun *whom* is the direct object of *have admired.*]

Other words, such as adverbs, may introduce adjective clauses:

It was a time *when all things went well for him.*
That is the reason *why I changed my mind.*

Note: If not used as a subject, the word introducing an adjective or a noun clause may sometimes be omitted. See also **22a**.

He is a man [*whom* or *that*] I admire. [Relative pronoun]
I know [*that*] she is right. [Subordinating conjunction]

Adverb clauses   An adverb clause may modify a verb, an adjective, an adverb, an infinitive, a gerund, a participle, or even the rest of the sentence in which it appears.
Like a number of adverbs, many adverb clauses can take various positions in a sentence.

Immediately other guests expressed regret. [Adverb]
When Bill decided to leave, other guests expressed regret.
 [Adverb clause. See also **12b**.]

Other guests *immediately* expressed regret.
Other guests, *when Bill decided to leave,* expressed regret.
 [See also **12d**.]

Other guests expressed regret *immediately.*
Other guests expressed regret *when Bill decided to leave.*
 [See also **12b**.]

■ **Exercise 7** In the paragraph that follows, find each subordinate clause and label it as a *noun clause,* an *adjective clause,* or an *adverb clause.*

[1] Whenever today's militant feminists get together, the words "sexist" and "sexism" play a large part in the conversation. [2] Although both are too new to be found in the dictionaries, the parallel with "racist" and "racism" makes their meanings clear enough. [3] Sexism is the belief that men are superior to women and that the difference between the sexes justifies a sharp distinction in roles. [4] A sexist is a man who holds such a belief and practices male domination of women. [5] Of course, the meaning *could* be reversed with sexism used to mean female superiority, but this usage is rare even though many women

secretly believe that men are just irresponsible little boys who must be protected and cajoled without letting them know that a woman is really making the decisions. —PAUL WOODRING[1]

1e

Learn to recognize main clauses and the various types of sentences.

Unlike a subordinate clause (see 1d), a main clause can stand alone as a sentence, a grammatically independent unit of expression, although it may require other sentences to complete its meaning. (Used alone, a subordinate clause is a sentence fragment.)

SENTENCE   When Kay discusses pollution, she mentions noise first.   [SUBORDINATE CLAUSE, MAIN CLAUSE.]
FRAGMENT   When Kay discusses pollution
SENTENCE   She mentions noise first.

One way to classify sentences is to label those with only one subject and one predicate (either or both of which may be compound) as *simple* and to call all others *complex*. Another way is to divide sentences into four categories:

1. *simple sentences*—those with only one subject and one predicate (either or both of which may be compound);
2. *compound sentences*—those that consist of at least two main clauses;
3. *complex sentences*—those made up of one main clause and at least one subordinate clause; and
4. *compound-complex sentences*—those made up of at least two main clauses and at least one subordinate clause.

Compare the structure of the following sentences. As you study their patterns, give special attention to punctuation.

---

[1]From "A View from the Campus: Sexism on the Campus" by Paul Woodring, *Saturday Review*, May 16, 1970. Copyright 1970 Saturday Review, Inc. Reprinted by permission.

SIMPLE SENTENCE   One part of the TV screen carried the football game. [SUBJECT—VERB—OBJECT. See also the various patterns of the simple sentence on pages 8–9.]

COMPOUND SENTENCE   One part of the TV screen carried the football game, and the other part showed the launch countdown. [MAIN CLAUSE, *and* MAIN CLAUSE. See 12a.]

COMPLEX SENTENCE   Because two pictures were on the TV screen, we could watch both the football game and the launch countdown. [ADVERB CLAUSE, MAIN CLAUSE. See 12b.]

COMPOUND-COMPLEX SENTENCE   While one part of the TV screen carried the football game, another part showed the launch countdown; at times printed scores of other games appeared across the bottom of both pictures. [ADVERB CLAUSE, MAIN CLAUSE; MAIN CLAUSE. See 12b and 14a.]

Sentences may also be classified as *statements, commands* or *requests, questions,* or *exclamations.* Notice differences in the punctuation of the following examples.

STATEMENT   He refused the offer.

COMMAND OR REQUEST   Refuse the offer.

QUESTIONS   Did he refuse the offer?   He refused, didn't he? He refused it?

EXCLAMATIONS   What an offer!   He refused it!   Refuse it!

■ **Exercise 8**   Classify each of the following sentences as *simple, compound, complex,* or *compound-complex.*

1. The discrepancy between the reality and the dream burns into their consciousness.   —KENNETH B. CLARK

2. The atomic power which can cure cancers can also broil us up in cauliflower clouds of radioactive chaff.
   —RAY BRADBURY

3. We sometimes think that we hate flattery, but we hate the manner in which it is done.   —LA ROCHEFOUCAULD

4. When two lovers look into each other's eyes, they see a unity.   —IRA WOLFERT

23

5. A round trip to Mars using the now conventional liquid hydrogen and oxygen would require millions of tons of fuel.
—JOHN P. WILEY, JR.

compound
6. In the Middle Ages the lives of children were separated from those of their parents; this practice endured for a long time, especially among the aristocracy and among the poor.
—JOHN LUKACS

complex
7. Student revolt, black revolt, women's liberation, rock music, new dress and hairstyles—none of these things is conceivable as it exists without some assistance from the media.
—PETER SCHRAG

simple
8. In his war experience he has acquired new confidence and new skills, among them the skills of guerrilla warfare, of killing, of subversion, and the gamut of tricks of military combat. —WHITNEY M. YOUNG, JR.

complex
9. A word changes meaning according to the music you play it in with your voice. —BENJAMIN DE MOTT

10. If a man does not keep pace with his companions, perhaps it is because he hears a different drummer.
—HENRY DAVID THOREAU

■ **Exercise 9** Observing differences in emphasis, convert each pair of sentences below to (a) a simple sentence, (b) a compound sentence consisting of two main clauses, and (c) a complex sentence with one main clause and one subordinate clause.

EXAMPLE
Male sperm whales occasionally attack ships. These whales jealously guard their territory.
a. *Jealously guarding their territory, male sperm whales occasionally attack ships.*
b. *Male sperm whales occasionally attack ships; these whales jealously guard their territory.*
c. *Since male sperm whales jealously guard their territory, they occasionally attack ships.*

1. The men smuggled marijuana into Spain. They were sentenced to six years in prison.
2. The council first condemned the property. Then it ordered the owner's eviction.

3. Uncle Oliver applied for a patent on his invention. He learned of three hundred such devices already on the market.
4. A national organization initiated the program. It recommended making all courses elective.

■ **Exercise 10** Analyze the following sentences of the Gettysburg Address as directed by your instructor.

1. Fourscore and seven years ago our fathers brought forth on this continent a new nation, conceived in liberty, and dedicated to the proposition that all men are created equal.
2. Now we are engaged in a great civil war, testing whether that nation, or any nation so conceived and so dedicated, can long endure.
3. We are met on a great battlefield of that war.
4. We have come to dedicate a portion of that field as a final resting place for those who here gave their lives that that nation might live.
5. It is altogether fitting and proper that we should do this.
6. But in a larger sense we cannot dedicate, we cannot consecrate, we cannot hallow this ground.
7. The brave men, living and dead, who struggled here, have consecrated it far above our power to add or detract.
8. The world will little note, nor long remember, what we say here, but it can never forget what they did here.
9. It is for us, the living, rather to be dedicated here to the unfinished work which they who fought here have thus far so nobly advanced.
10. It is rather for us to be here dedicated to the great task remaining before us, that from these honored dead we take increased devotion to that cause for which they gave the last full measure of devotion; that we here highly resolve that these dead shall not have died in vain; that this nation, under God, shall have a new birth of freedom, and that government of the people, by the people, for the people shall not perish from the earth.

Sentence Fragment

2

Do not write an ineffective sentence fragment.

A fragment is a part of a sentence—such as a phrase or a subordinate clause—written with the capitalization and punctuation appropriate to a sentence.

> INEFFECTIVE FRAGMENTS   When the children arrived at camp. Many dancing for joy and others weeping. Because they wanted to be back with their parents.
>
> SENTENCES   Then the children arrived at camp. Many danced for joy. Others wept because they wanted to be back with their parents.

Not all fragments are ineffective. Indeed, some types of fragments are not only standard but desirable. Exclamations often consist of single words or phrases. Questions, as well as their answers, are frequently phrases or subordinate clauses written as sentences. Written dialogue often contains parts of sentences that mirror speech habits. And assertions containing elliptical elements can be effective fragments. Compare the structures at the left and the right below:

EFFECTIVE FRAGMENTS	SENTENCES
How undemocratic!	How undemocratic it is!
By raising prices? No.	Can it be done by raising prices? No, it cannot.
"Low on oil."	"The oil is low," he said.
Examples: *mini, maxi.*	Examples are *mini, maxi.*

Despite their suitability for some purposes, however, sentence fragments are comparatively rare in formal expository writing.

A fragment may be an isolated, mispunctuated part of an adjacent sentence. As a rule, such a fragment should be repunctuated and made a part of the complete sentence.

FRAGMENT   Henry smiled self-consciously. *Like a politician before a camera.*

SENTENCES   Henry smiled self-consciously, like a politician before a camera.

OR

Henry smiled self-consciously— like a politician before a camera. [The use of the dash instead of the comma tends to emphasize the material that follows.]

Test for Sentence Completeness

Before handing in a composition, proofread each word group written as a sentence. Test each one for completeness by being sure (1) that it has at least one subject and one predicate and (2) that the subject and the predicate are not introduced by a subordinating conjunction or by a relative pronoun (see page 19).

FRAGMENTS WITHOUT SUBJECTS AND PREDICATES

Especially in the early spring. [Prepositional phrase]
To jog and to swim. [Infinitives]
Water sparkling in the moonlight. [Noun modified by a participial phrase]

FRAGMENTS WITH SUBJECTS AND PREDICATES

When I jog, especially in the early spring. [Subject and verb: *I jog.* Subordinating conjunction: *When.*]
Although I like to jog and to swim. [Subject and verb: *I like.* Subordinating conjunction: *Although.*]
Which sparkles in the moonlight. [Subject and verb: *Which sparkles.* Relative pronoun: *Which.*]

27

Revision of the Sentence Fragment

If you have difficulty eliminating ineffective fragments from your compositions, first review **1d** and **1e** as well as the sentence patterns on pages 8–9. Then find the rule (**2a**, **2b**, or **2c**) that applies to each fragment you have written, and study the appropriate examples and exercise materials. Finally, revise each fragment by including it in the preceding or following sentence or by rewriting the fragment to make it a sentence.

FRAGMENT   He registered for the summer session. *Hoping thus to graduate ahead of his class.* [Participial phrase]

REVISED   He registered for the summer session, hoping thus to graduate ahead of his class. [Fragment included in the preceding sentence]
OR
He registered for the summer session. By this means he hoped to graduate ahead of his class. [Fragment made into a sentence]

2a

Do not carelessly capitalize and punctuate a phrase as you would a sentence.

FRAGMENT   Astronauts venturing deep into space may not come back to earth for fifty years. *Returning only to discover an uninhabitable planet.* [Participial phrase]

REVISED   Astronauts venturing deep into space may not come back to earth for fifty years. They may return only to discover an uninhabitable planet. [Fragment made into a sentence]

FRAGMENT   Soon I began to work for the company. *First in the rock pit and later on the highway.* [Prepositional phrases]

REVISED   Soon I began to work for the company, first in the rock pit and later on the highway. [Fragment included in the preceding sentence]

FRAGMENT   He will have an opportunity to visit his home town. *And to talk with many of his old friends.* [Infinitive phrase]

REVISED   He will have an opportunity to visit his home town and to talk with many of his old friends. [Fragment included in the preceding sentence]

■ **Exercise 1** Eliminate each fragment below by including it in the preceding or following sentence or by making it into a sentence.

1. I enjoy reading a few types of novels. Like science fiction.
2. I spray the shrubbery twice a year. Once in the late spring and again in the early fall.
3. The pampered Dennis finally left home. Earnestly seeking to become an individual in his own right.
4. He was a beautiful child. With black hair and blue eyes.
5. Heads snap around and eyes widen as I trudge across campus. Carrying a wet towel and dripping with every step.
6. In high school I was a "discipline problem." In more ways than one.
7. My grandmother is a delightful conversationalist. Often speaking of the "days of her youth," during what she calls the "Renaissance period."
8. I think that it is wise to ignore his sarcasm. Or to make a quick exit.
9. Only three days to go. Those three days in Vietnam seemed like three lifetimes.
10. Squinting her eyes, the gossip leaned forward. To whisper this question in my ear: "Have you seen that mangy little hippie she dates?"

2b

Do not carelessly capitalize and punctuate a subordinate clause as you would a sentence.

FRAGMENT   Thousands of bumper stickers pleaded for a united America. *After the race riots, draft-card burnings, and campus killings had changed apathy to concern.* [Subordinate clause]

29

REVISED   After the race riots, draft-card burnings, and campus killings had changed apathy to concern, thousands of bumper stickers pleaded for a united America. [Fragment included in the preceding sentence]

FRAGMENT   I was trying to read the directions. *Which were confusing and absurd.* [Subordinate clause]

REVISED   I was trying to read the directions, which were confusing and absurd. [Fragment included in the preceding sentence]

OR

I was trying to read the directions. They were confusing and absurd. [Fragment made into a sentence]

■ **Exercise 2** Some of the following numbered word groups contain fragments; others do not. Label each word group as a *fragment* or a *sentence.*

1. Many students were obviously victims of spring fever. Which affected class attendance.
2. I decided to give skiing a try. After I had grown tired of watching other people fall.
3. She told us of her visit to Russia. Later she described the poverty in India.
4. Paul faints whenever he sees blood. And whenever he climbs into a dentist's chair.
5. I stopped trying to read my assignment. As soon as he started imitating my favorite comedian by doing the tango with a lamp shade on his head.
6. The poor thief was almost sick from fright. And the sheriff believed that he could handle his prisoner alone.
7. My hobby is oil painting. In fact, that is my pride, my joy, and my only dependable source of income.
8. Mr. Adams did not insist on my buying insurance. Which is more than I can say for the last agent who came here.
9. Then she would fail. This was the nightmare that haunted her, the dread of the inevitable surrender to defeat.
10. The *Titanic* crashed into an iceberg. Which took place on April 15, 1912.

2c

Do not carelessly capitalize and punctuate any other fragment (such as an appositive or a part of a compound predicate) as you would a sentence.

FRAGMENT My father was born in Cartersville. *A little country town where everyone knows everyone else.* [Appositive modified by a subordinate clause]

REVISED My father was born in Cartersville, a little country town where everyone knows everyone else. [Fragment included in the preceding sentence]

OR

My father was born in Cartersville—a little country town where everyone knows everyone else. [The use of the dash instead of the comma tends to emphasize the material that follows.]

FRAGMENT William was elected president of his class. *And was made a member of the National Honor Society.* [Detached part of a compound predicate]

REVISED William was elected president of his class and was made a member of the National Honor Society.

■ **Exercise 3** Eliminate each fragment below by including it in the preceding sentence or by making it into a sentence.

1. My roommate keeps all her cosmetics, books, papers, and clothes in one closet. The worst disaster area on campus.
2. According to Chesterton, realism is a kind of romanticism. The kind that has lost its mind.
3. The group met during the summer and made plans. And decided upon the dates for action in the fall.
4. The hydraulic lift raises the plows out of the ground. And lowers them again.
5. I had a feeling that some sinister spirit of evil brooded over the place. A feeling that I could not analyze.

■ **Exercise 4** Find the seven fragments in the following paragraphs. Revise each fragment by attaching it logically to a preceding or following sentence or by rewriting the fragment so that it stands by itself as a sentence.

[1] As a weather watcher, I am often amused by official forecasts. [2] Or, rather, by occasional prophecies made by weathermen who seldom bother to look out the window. [3] For example, one day late last spring when heavy rain and large hail lashed the city. [4] I promptly telephoned the weather bureau. [5] To ask about the possibility of a tornado. [6] A confident voice replied glibly, "Oh, don't worry about a tornado; we're not even in an alert area."

[7] Relieved, I turned on the radio, found a chair near a window, and watched the angry clouds. [8] To my amazement, I soon saw a swirling funnel emerge from a black cloud and strike toward the ground. [9] Just north of the city, about five miles away. [10] Of course, I immediately notified the weather bureau.

[11] A short time later. [12] An important message interrupted the rock music on the radio: "The weather bureau has issued a warning that a tornado may strike north of here." [13] I smiled as I repeated the words "may strike." [14] Knowing that the official prophets were busily rushing about their work. [15] As they tried to repair their radar and kept an eye on falling barometers and erratic wind gauges instead of paying attention to the turbulent weather itself.

Comma Splice
and Fused Sentence

3

Do not carelessly link two sentences with only a comma (comma splice) or run two sentences together without any punctuation (fused sentence).

SENTENCES   The current was swift. He could not swim to shore.

COMMA SPLICE   The current was swift, he could not swim to shore.   [Sentences linked with only a comma]

FUSED SENTENCE   The current was swift he could not swim to shore.   [Sentences run together with no punctuation]

If you cannot recognize an independent or main clause and distinguish it from a dependent or subordinate clause, review **1d** and **1e**.

3a
Correct either comma splices or fused sentences by one of the following methods.

(1) Subordinate one of the main clauses—usually the best method. See also **12b** and Section **24**.

COMMA SPLICE   The current was swift, he could not swim to shore.

REVISED Because the current was swift, he could not swim to shore. [First main clause changed to a subordinate clause]

(2) Make each main clause into a sentence.

FUSED SENTENCE The current was swift he could not swim to shore.

REVISED The current was swift. He could not swim to shore.

(3) Join the main clauses with a semicolon.

> PATTERN **MAIN CLAUSE; MAIN CLAUSE.**

REVISED The current was swift; he could not swim to shore.

(4) Join the main clauses with a comma plus a coordinating conjunction (*and, but, or, nor, for,* and sometimes *so* and *yet*).

> PATTERN **MAIN CLAUSE, *and* MAIN CLAUSE.**

REVISED The current was swift, and he could not swim to shore.

Exceptions: The comma may link (1) short coordinate clauses parallel in form and unified in thought or (2) main clauses in a series.

Dreams kill, dreams cure. —WILFRID SHEED

School bores them, preaching bores them, even television bores them. —ARTHUR MILLER

The semicolon may also link short main clauses parallel in form.

One is the reality; the other is the symbol. —NANCY HALE

The children shout; their bare feet fly over the spawning fish; the nets soar; sea boots grind down; the fish spill out; gulls run in the shallows under the children's feet; the flounder gorge. —FRANKLIN RUSSELL

Note 1: The comma is optional between such balanced *the . . . the* structures as those below. (A semicolon would not be appropriate.)

The more it rained, the worse they suffered. —JOSEPH HELLER

The greater the fool the better the dancer.
—THEODORE EDWARD HOOK

Note 2: The comma is used to separate a statement from an echo question.

You can come, can't you? [Statement echoed by question]

■ **Exercise 1** Link each pair of sentences below three different ways, as shown in the example.

EXAMPLE
Attacks of homesickness diminish in intensity. Immunity gradually develops.
  a. *As attacks of homesickness diminish in intensity, immunity gradually develops.*
  b. *Attacks of homesickness diminish in intensity; immunity gradually develops.*
  c. *Attacks of homesickness diminish in intensity, **and** immunity gradually develops.*

1. Dedicated ecologists do not kill wildlife. They carry Leicas instead of Winchesters.
2. The stakes were high in the political game. He played to win.
3. Amateur scientists abound in England. The United States has only a few.
4. My Canadian cousin resents the influx of Americans. He may move to Australia.

35

3b

Do not let a conjunctive adverb, a transitional phrase, or a divided quotation trick you into making a comma splice. See also 14a.

CONJUNCTIVE ADVERBS AND TRANSITIONAL PHRASES

Conjunctive adverbs (such as *accordingly, also, anyhow, besides, consequently, furthermore, hence, henceforth, however, indeed, instead, likewise, meanwhile, moreover, nevertheless, otherwise, still, then, therefore, thus*) and transitional phrases (such as *as a result, at the same time, for example, in addition, in fact, in other words, on the contrary, on the other hand, that is*) connecting main clauses are preceded by a semicolon.

> But meaning does not imply certainty; indeed, the quest for certainty blocks the search for meaning.   —ERICH FROMM
>
> I have no complaint against the existence of an intelligentsia; on the contrary, I favor it.   —ROBERTSON DAVIES

Unlike a coordinating conjunction, which has a fixed position between the main clauses it links, a conjunctive adverb or a transitional phrase can take various positions within the second main clause.

> I don't like punch, *but* I sometimes drink it at parties. [Coordinating conjunction with a fixed position]
>
> I don't like punch; *however,* I sometimes drink it at parties. [Conjunctive adverb begins the second main clause. See also 14a.]
>
> I don't like punch; I sometimes drink it, *however,* at parties. [Conjunctive adverb interrupts the second main clause. See 12d(3).]

DIVIDED QUOTATIONS

COMMA SPLICE   "Your watch is wrong," he said, "reset it."
REVISED   "Your watch is wrong," he said. "Reset it."

COMMA SPLICE	"What are you looking for?" she asked, "may I help you?"
REVISED	"What are you looking for?" she asked. "May I help you?"

■ **Exercise 2** Link each pair of sentences below, following the pattern of the examples.

EXAMPLES

At first the slogan shocked. After a year or two, however, it became a household platitude.

At first the slogan shocked; however, after a year or two it became a household platitude.

Frank worked part time until he graduated from high school. He then decided to apply for a permanent position.

Frank worked part time until he graduated from high school; then he decided to apply for a permanent position.

1. The art company sent a sample collection of famous American paintings. The work of Norman Rockwell, however, was carelessly omitted.
2. Some women look upon themselves as slaves of the System. They have, in fact, compared their plight with that of blacks.
3. A parade was organized to fight the demise of the mini-skirt. The designers still continued to push the maxi.
4. On the one hand, pessimists warn us about the inundation of the West Coast. Optimists, on the other hand, envision our enjoyment of the millennium.

■ **Exercise 3** Divide the following quotations without creating a comma splice, as shown in the example below.

EXAMPLE

Eric Sevareid has said, "Let those who wish compare America with Rome. Rome lasted a thousand years."

"Let those who wish compare America with Rome," Eric Sevareid has said. "Rome lasted a thousand years."

1. "No writer, no artist, is a lady. She can't afford to be," Catherine D. Bowen observed.
2. "What good is a salt marsh? Who needs a swamp?" Gene Marine asks ironically in *America the Raped.*

3. Lee Strout White reminisced, "The driver of the old Model T was a man enthroned. The car, with top up, stood seven feet high."

4. Goodman Ace has observed, "In today's entertainment, movies especially, nobody 'covets' a neighbor's wife. He just takes."

■ **Exercise 4** Determine which of the following sentences contain comma splices. (As an aid to your analysis, you may wish to bracket each subordinate clause and to underline the subject and verb of each main clause.) Put a checkmark after each sentence that needs no revision. Correct each comma splice in the most appropriate way.

1. Mary Queen of Scots' death warrant was written on a playing card, the nine of diamonds, as a result, this card is sometimes called "the curse of Scotland."

2. If Jay's batting average had been better, for example, he would have been the best baseball player in the league.

3. "Begin the screening," he said, "interview the applicants, and study their recommendations."

4. Washington Irving exploited local legends, he helped to start American folklore by writing "Rip Van Winkle."

5. Typhus used to kill more soldiers than actual warfare did, however, the disease is rarely heard of today.

6. Fred was lucky in his assigned room, although it was small, it was close to his classes.

7. Liechtenstein postage stamps are especially beautiful, stamp collectors eagerly buy special issues.

8. To be a baby sitter, one should know something of child care, one should know, for example, how to warm a bottle and to burp a baby.

9. The Western world is indebted to the Saracens for paper. It was the Saracens, moreover, who built Europe's first paper mill.

10. Frogs swallow only moving objects, as a matter of fact, they will die of hunger rather than strike a motionless insect.

Adjectives and Adverbs

4

Use adjectives and adverbs appropriately.

Adjectives and adverbs are modifiers that have much in common: (1) they restrict, qualify, or limit the meaning of other words or word groups; (2) they often follow linking verbs and complete the meaning of sentences; and (3) they usually have comparative forms. Modifiers sometimes follow markers or signals such as *very* and *too*. In the following examples, modifiers are italicized.

ADJECTIVES

quick punishment, *realistic* fiction, those less *familiar*
Punishment was *quick*. Those should be more *familiar*.
quicker, *quickest*, most *realistic*, least *familiar*
very *quick*, too *realistic*, somewhat *familiar*

ADVERBS

soon moved, judged *rashly*, to act *quickly*, *wholly* true
I was *there*. That will be *soon*. It must be *somewhere*.
sooner, *soonest*, more *frequently*, less *rashly*
very *soon*, too *frequently*, somewhat *rashly*

Any word modifying a noun or a pronoun functions as an adjective; an adjective may also modify a gerund. Any word modifying a verb, an adjective, or an adverb functions as an adverb; an adverb may also modify an infinitive, a gerund, a participle, a phrase, a clause, or the rest of the sentence in which it appears. Just as the modification of adjectives and adverbs differs, so do their positions in sentences: see Section **25**. Generally speaking, adverbs are more mobile than adjectives.

As a rule, suffixes such as *-al, -ic, -ish, -like, -ly,* and *-ous* convert nouns into adjectives:

NOUNS	a *nation,* a *boy,* my *friend,* the *danger*
ADJECTIVES	*national* industry, *boyish* prank, *friendly* cat, *dangerous* work

The *-ly* ending nearly always converts adjectives to adverbs:

ADJECTIVES	*formal* dress, a *sudden* turn, a *real* gem, a *sure* thing
ADVERBS	*formally* dressed, *suddenly* turning, *really* valuable, *surely* is

Note: A few words ending in *-ly* (such as *only, early, cowardly*) may be either adjectives or adverbs, and the same is true for a considerable number of common words not ending in *-ly* (such as *far, fast, late, little, near, right, straight, well*).

A good dictionary shows the appropriate form for adjective or adverb, but only the use to which the word is put in the sentence determines whether the adjective or the adverb form is required.

4a

Use adverbs to modify verbs, adjectives, and other adverbs.

(1) Modifiers of verbs

NONSTANDARD	His clothes fit him perfect. [The adjective *perfect* misused to modify the verb *fit*]
STANDARD	His clothes fit him *perfectly.*
NONSTANDARD	He ran good for the first mile. [The adjective *good* misused to modify the verb *ran*]

STANDARD	He ran *well* for the first mile.

(2) Modifiers of adjectives

NONSTANDARD	The farmer has a reasonable secure future. [The adjective *reasonable* misused to modify the adjective *secure*]
STANDARD	The farmer has a *reasonably* secure future.

(3) Modifiers of adverbs

INFORMAL	Only by working *real* hard can the men meet the builder's deadline. [The adjective *real* modifies the adverb *hard.*]
GENERAL	Only by working *really* hard can the men meet the builder's deadline. [Appropriate in both formal and informal usage]

■ **Exercise 1** In the items below, convert adjectives into adverbs, following the pattern of the examples.

EXAMPLE
abrupt reply   *replied abruptly*   OR   *abruptly replied*

1. vague answer
2. safe travel
3. fierce battle
4. quick refusal
5. hearty welcome
6. blind conformity

EXAMPLE
fine subtlety   *finely subtle*

7. remote possibility
8. unusual intelligence
9. utter chaos
10. strange harmony

4b

Use the appropriate modifiers after such verbs as *feel, look, smell, sound,* and *taste.*

As subject complements (predicate adjectives), adjectives always modify the subject. Subject complements are used with such verbs as *feel, look, smell, sound,* and *taste,* which are called *linking verbs* when they connect a subject with its predicate adjective.

PATTERN
SUBJECT—LINKING VERB—SUBJECT COMPLEMENT.

> The blind beggar felt *nervous.* [The adjective *nervous* modifies *beggar.*]
> The actress looked *angry.* [The adjective *angry* modifies *actress.*]

Variations in word order are possible, as the examples below show:

> How *nervous* he must have felt!
> How *angry* did she look?

The modifier should be an adverb when it refers to the action of the verb. In that case the verb is not used as a linking verb.

PATTERN   SUBJECT—VERB—adverb . . .

> The blind beggar felt *nervously* along the wall. [The adverb *nervously* qualifies *felt.*]
> The actress looked *angrily* at him. [The adverb *angrily* qualifies *looked.*]

Note: A modifier following a verb and its direct object is an adjective when it refers to the object rather than to the action of the verb.

PATTERN
SUBJECT—VERB—OBJECT—OBJECT COMPLEMENT.

> The boy dug the hole *deep.* [*Deep* hole]

■ **Exercise 2** Using adjectives as subject complements, write five sentences that illustrate the pattern SUBJECT—LINKING VERB—SUBJECT COMPLEMENT.

4c

Use the appropriate forms for the comparative and the superlative.

In general, the shorter adjectives (and a few adverbs) form the comparative degree by adding *-er* and the superlative by adding *-est.* The longer adjectives and most adverbs form the comparative by the use of *more* (*less*) and the superlative by the use of *most* (*least*). A few modifiers have an irregular comparison.

Positive	Comparative	Superlative
warm	warmer	warmest
warmly	more warmly	most warmly
helpful	less helpful	least helpful
good, well	better	best
bad, badly	worse	worst

Many writers prefer to use the comparative degree for two persons or things and the superlative for three or more.

COMPARATIVE   Was Monday or Tuesday *warmer?*
                    James was the *taller* of the two.

SUPERLATIVE   Today is the *warmest* day of the year.
                    William was the *tallest* of the three.

Note: In a comparison such as the following, the word *other* may indicate a difference in meaning.

Fuller runs faster than any player on the team. [Fuller is apparently not on the team. (In context, however, this may be an informal sentence meaning that Fuller is the fastest of the players on the team.)]
Fuller runs faster than any *other* player on the team. [*Other* clearly indicates that Fuller is on the team.]

4d

Avoid awkward or ambiguous use of a noun form as an adjective.

Many noun forms are used effectively to modify other nouns (as in *boat* race, *show* business, *opera* tickets, and so on), especially when appropriate adjectives are not available. But such forms should be avoided when they are either awkward or confusing.

> AWKWARD I sometimes forget basic mathematics principles.
> BETTER   I sometimes forget basic mathematical prin-
>   ciples. OR I sometimes forget principles of
>   basic mathematics.
>
> CONFUSING The Congressman Benjamin M. Landor recess
>   maneuvers led to victory.
> BETTER   Congressman Benjamin M. Landor's maneuvers
>   during the recess led to victory.

■ **Exercise 3** Revise the following sentences to correct mistakes in the formal usage of adjectives and adverbs. Put a checkmark after each sentence that needs no revision.

1. The almanac has been published continuous since 1893; that is sure a long time.
2. The A. H. Chapman *Put-Offs & Come-Ons* book clearly exposes the selfishness of the human race.
3. Fresh vegetables are some cheaper in the summer than in the winter.
4. Many do not consider the dangers of drug use very careful.
5. Although Mr. Walters owns the restaurant, he is not real interested in its success.
6. So vivid did the actress portray Hedda Gabler that she received a standing ovation.
7. Donald's explanation, the clearer of the two, indicates that he will do good at teaching.
8. Social life is as important as any other facet of campus living.
9. When the oil truck stopped so sudden, the bus almost crashed into it.

10. The Hattaway Exterminating and Fumigating Company business ventures thrive.

■ **Exercise 4**   Compose sentences containing the following constructions:

1. *good* as a subject complement
2. *well* modifying a verb
3. *sure* as a subject complement
4. *surely* modifying a verb
5. an adjective used as a subject complement after *looked*
6. an adverb modifying *looked*
7. an adjective following and modifying a direct object
8. the superlative form of *bad*
9. the comparative form of *good*
10. a noun used clearly and effectively to modify another noun

Case

5

Use the proper case form to show the function of pronouns or nouns in sentences.

The pronouns *I, me, my,* and *mine* all refer to the person who is speaking or writing. The change in form to indicate function is called *case. I* is in the subjective, or nominative, case; *me,* in the objective case; and *my* and *mine,* in the possessive, or genitive, case. Nouns and some indefinite pronouns (*anyone, someone, everyone,* and so on) have a distinctive case form only for the possessive (the *boy's* book, the *boys'* mother: see **15a**). But six common pronouns have distinctive forms in all three cases and must be used with care.

Case forms

SUBJECTIVE	I	we	he, she	they	who
POSSESSIVE	my	our	his, her	their	whose
	(mine)	(ours)	(hers)	(theirs)	
OBJECTIVE	me	us	him, her	them	whom

Note: The personal pronouns *it* and *you* change form only to indicate the possessive: *its, your* (*yours*).

Functions

SUBJECTIVE	*He* and *I* traveled together in France. [Subjects]

It was *she who* paid the bill. [*She* is used as a subject complement, and *who* as the subject of *paid.*]

POSSESSIVE
That is *your* gift, not *mine*. [Possessors]
His having to mow the acreage deadened the joy of ownership. [Before a gerund]

OBJECTIVE
Frances has already met *him*. [Direct object]
Give *them* our best regards. [Indirect object]
The cake was for *us*. [Object of a preposition]
Our guest did not expect *us* to entertain *him*. [*Us* is the subject of the infinitive; *him,* the object. See also **5e**.]

5a

Take special care with pronouns in apposition and in compound constructions.

(1) Appositives

An appositive takes the same case as the noun or pronoun with which it is in apposition.

We—John and *I*—are responsible for the damage. [*I* is in the subjective case because it is in apposition with the subject *we*.]

Let's you and *me* go together. Let us—you and *me*—go together. [*Me* and *us* are in the same case.]

Two students—John and *I*—represented our class. [*I* is in the subjective case because it is in apposition with the subject *students*.]

Our class was represented by two students, John and *me*. [*Me* is in the objective case because it is in apposition with *students,* the object of the preposition *by*.]

Note: Do not let an appositive following a pronoun trick you into using the wrong case.

We boys often study together.   [*We* is the subject of *study:* *We study.*]

He would not let *us* girls do any of the hard work.   [Since *us* is the subject of the infinitive (*to*) *do,* it is in the objective case: see **5e**.]

(2)   Compound constructions

My brother and *I* share expenses.   [*I* is a subject of the verb *share.*]

Everyone signed the petition except Hazel and *her.*   [*Her* is an object of the preposition *except.*]

Last summer my father hired Tom and *me.*   [*Me* is an object of the verb *hired.*]

Note: In formal writing, *myself* is usually avoided as a substitute for *I* or *me:* see **19i**. The *-self* pronouns (such as *myself, himself, ourselves, themselves*) are ordinarily used as either reflexive or intensive pronouns.

REFLEXIVE   James hurt *himself.*
INTENSIVE   James *himself* was hurt.

■ **Exercise 1**   Choose the correct case form within parentheses in each sentence below.

1. Both George and (she, her) have read Updike's *Bech: A Book.*
2. Both men—Mr. Adams and (he, him)—still insist upon controlling education with computers.
3. Study in Europe did not appeal to Tim or (I, me).
4. Several of (we, us) freshmen actively support the governor.
5. (We, us) Americans do not have a monopoly on freedom.
6. The newly elected officers—Ted, Pat, and (she, her)—have little experience but a great deal of enthusiasm.
7. Research on DNA continues under Dr. Bell and (they, them).
8. Let's you and (I, me) register for a course in world literature.
9. The new import shop offered jobs to (we, us) students taking merchandising.
10. In the Follies try-outs, Kit mimicked Joy and (I, me).

5b

Determine the case of each pronoun by its use in its own clause.

(1) Pronoun as the subject of a clause

The subject of a clause takes the subjective case, even when the whole clause is the object of a verb or a preposition.

> He will employ *whoever* is willing to work. [*Whoever* is the subject of *is willing.* The whole clause *whoever is willing to work* is the direct object of *will employ.*]
>
> He has respect for *whoever* is in power. [*Whoever* is the subject of *is.* The complete clause *whoever is in power* is the object of the preposition *for.*]

(2) Pronoun before *I think, he says,* and so on

Such expressions as *I think, he says, she believes,* or *we know* may follow *whom* or *who.* When one of these expressions comes between the pronoun and its verb (as in the second example below), take special care not to use the wrong case.

> Gene is a man *whom* we know well. [*Whom* is the direct object of *know.*]
>
> Gene is a man *who* we know is honest. [*Who* is the subject of the second *is.* Compare "We know that Gene is a man *who* is honest."]

(3) Pronoun after *than, as,* or *but*

A pronoun following *than* or *as* takes the subjective or the objective case according to whether the pronoun is the subject or the object of the following verb, which may be either stated or implied.

> Mr. Ames is somewhat older than *I* [am].
> Aristotle is as wise as *they* [are].
> The editor admires Hesse more than *I* [do].
> She admires him more than [she admires] *me.*

49

Note: In informal usage, *than* may be considered as a preposition and may therefore be followed by the objective case.

INFORMAL Mr. Ames is somewhat older than *me*.

But may function as a conjunction or as a preposition.

Everyone but *I* saw it. [*But* is considered a conjunction. Compare "Everyone else saw it, but *I* did not see it."]
Everyone saw it but *me*. [*But* is considered a preposition. Compare "Everyone saw it except *me*."]

■ **Exercise 2** In sentences 1, 2, and 3 below, insert *I think* after each *who;* then read each sentence aloud. Notice that *who,* not *whom,* is still the correct case form. In sentences 4 and 5, complete each comparison by using first *they* and then *them.* Prepare to explain the differences in meaning.

1. George Eliot, who was a woman, wrote *Adam Bede.*
2. It was Mr. Holland who served as the eighth president of the bank.
3. Maugham, who was an Englishman, died in 1965.
4. The professor likes you as much as _____.
5. The director praised her more than _____.

5c

In formal writing use *whom* for all objects.

The artist *whom* she loved has gone away. [*Whom* is the direct object of *loved.*]
The song was dedicated to *whom?* [*Whom* is the object of the preposition *to.*]

Speakers tend to use *who* rather than *whom,* regardless of the function in a sentence:

INFORMAL *Who* did you vote for? [*Who* may be used in an informal situation to begin any question.]
INFORMAL He is a senior *who* I talk with a lot.

Both speakers and writers may avoid *whom* by omitting it in sentences such as the following:

The artist she loved has gone away.

■ **Exercise 3** Using the case form in parentheses, convert each pair of sentences below into a single sentence.

EXAMPLES
Members of the AA helped the drunkard. He fell off the bus. (*who*)
Members of the AA helped the drunkard who fell off the bus.

Evelyn consulted an astrologer. She had met him in San Francisco. (*whom*)
Evelyn consulted an astrologer whom she had met in San Francisco.

1. The teenagers set the building on fire. We sometimes called them the "street people." (*whom*)
2. Some parents make an introvert out of an only child. They think they are protecting their offspring. (*who*)
3. Does anyone remember the name of the Frenchman? He built a helicopter in 1784. (*who*)
4. One of the officials called for a severe penalty. The players had quarreled with the officials earlier. (*whom*)

5d

As a rule, use the possessive case immediately before a gerund.

His leaving the farm was a surprise.
Mother approved of *my* (*our, his, her, your, their*) going to the game.

The *-ing* form of a verb can be used as a noun (gerund) or as an adjective (participle). The possessive case is not used before participles.

A *man's* directing traffic solved the problem.   [*Directing* is a gerund—the subject of the verb *solved.*]

A *man* directing traffic solved the problem.   [*Directing* is a participle modifying *man; man* is the subject of the verb *solved.*]

When the emphasis is on the noun or pronoun preceding the *-ing* verb form, the *-ing* word may be interpreted as a participle.

John's running away was unexpected.   [*Running* is a gerund.]
We caught *John* running away.   [*Running* is a participle.]

His acting the part was a surprise.   [*Acting* is a gerund.]
We could not imagine *him* acting the part.   [*Acting* is a participle.]

Note: Do not use an awkward possessive before a gerund.

AWKWARD   The board approved of something's being sent to the poor overseas.

BETTER   The board approved of sending something to the poor overseas.

5e

Use the objective case for the subject, the object, or the complement of an infinitive.

He asked *me* to help *him*.   [*Me* is the subject and *him* is the object of the infinitive *to help. Me to help him* is the direct object of the verb *asked.*]

We expected *him* to be *her*.   [*Him* is the subject and *her* is the complement of the infinitive *to be.*]

Note: In formal writing the complement of the infinitive *to be* is in the subjective case when the infinitive *to be* has no subject.

I would like to be *he*.

5f

Use the subjective case for the complement of the verb *be*.

> PATTERN
> SUBJECT—LINKING VERB *BE*—SUBJECT COMPLEMENT.

That may be *she*.
It was *they*.

Those writers who consider the use of personal pronouns as subject complements stilted generally avoid the structure.

Note: Informal usage accepts *It is me* (*It's me*).

■ **Exercise 4** Find and revise in the sentences below all case forms that would be inappropriate in formal writing. Put a checkmark after each sentence that needs no revision.

1. I soon became acquainted with Ruth and her, whom I thought were agitators.
2. It was Doris and she who he blamed for the accident.
3. Jack's racing the motor did not hurry Tom or me.
4. Between you and I, I prefer wood-block prints.
5. Who do you suppose will ever change Earth to Eden?
6. Since Joan eats less than I, I weigh more than she.
7. Let's you and I plan the curriculum of an ideal university.
8. The attorney who I interviewed yesterday is going to make public the records of three men who he believes are guilty of tax evasion.
9. We players always cooperate with our assistant coach, who we respect and who respects us.
10. The librarian wanted us—Kirt Jacobs and I—to choose Schlesinger's *The Bitter Heritage*.

Agreement

6

Make a verb agree in number with its subject; make a pronoun agree in number with its antecedent.

Singular subjects require singular verbs; plural subjects require plural verbs. Pronouns agree with their antecedents (the words to which they refer) in the same way. The *-s* ending of a subject is the sign of the plural; the *-s* ending of a verb is the sign of the third person singular.

> The *risk* of the workers *seems* great.
>   [Singular subject—singular verb]
> The *risks* of the workers *seem* great.
>   [Plural subject—plural verb]
>
> The *woman* washes *her* own clothes.
>   [Singular antecedent—singular pronoun]
> The *women* wash *their* own clothes.
>   [Plural antecedent—plural pronoun]

To avoid mistakes in agreement, single out each subject and its verb and connect them mentally (*risk seems, risks seem*). Do the same with each antecedent and its pronoun (*woman ← her, women ← their*). If you find it difficult to distinguish verbs and relate them to their subjects, review **1a** and **1b**.

6a

Make a verb agree in number with its subject.

(1) Do not be misled by nouns or pronouns intervening between the subject and the verb or by subjects and verbs with endings difficult to pronounce.

The *recurrence* of like sounds *helps* to stir emotions.
Every *one* of you *is invited* to the panel discussion.

Scientists sift the facts.
The *scientist asks* several pertinent questions.

The number of the subject is not changed by the addition of expressions beginning with such words as *besides, like, with, together with, accompanied by, along with, as well as, in addition to, including,* and *no less than.*

Inflation as well as taxes *influences* voters.
Taxes along with inflation *influence* voters.

John, together with James and William, *was* late.
James and *William,* like John, *were* late.

(2) Subjects joined by *and* are usually plural.

A hammer and a saw *are* useful tools.
Mary, Jane, and I *were* innocent.

Exceptions: A compound subject referring to a single person, or to two or more things considered as a unit, is followed by a singular verb.

My best friend and adviser *has gone.* [A single individual was both friend and adviser.]
The tumult and the shouting *dies.* —KIPLING [The two nouns are considered a single unit.]

Each or *every* preceding singular subjects joined by *and* calls for a singular verb.

Each boy and each girl *is* to work independently.
Every boy and girl *has been urged* to attend the play.

As a rule, *each* after a plural subject does not affect the verb form; however, *each* after a compound subject is sometimes followed by a singular verb.

> They each *have spoken.* [NOT They each *has spoken.*]
> The conservative and the liberal each *have voiced* their opinions. OR The conservative and the liberal each *has voiced* his opinion.

(3) Singular subjects joined by *or, nor, either . . . or,* or *neither . . . nor* usually take a singular verb.

> Either the man or his wife *knows* the truth of the matter.
> Neither money nor power *was winning* any friends.

When the meaning is felt to be plural, the plural verb is occasionally used in informal English:

> INFORMAL   Neither she nor I *were dancing,* for we felt tired.

If one subject is singular and one is plural, the verb usually agrees with the nearer subject.

> Neither the television nor the radios *work.*
> Neither the radios nor the television *works.*

Many writers prefer to recast such sentences and thus avoid the problem:

> The television and the radios *do* not *work.*

(4) When the subject follows the verb (especially in sentences beginning with *there is* or *there are*), special care is needed to determine the subject and to make sure that it agrees with the verb.

> On the wall *were* several *posters.*
> There *are* many possible *candidates.*
> There *is* only one good *candidate.*

Before a compound subject of which the first member is singular, a singular verb is sometimes used:

There *is Cash McCall* and *The Man in the Gray Flannel
Suit* and *Marjorie Morningstar* and *The Enemy Camp* and
Advise and Consent, and so on.   —PHILIP ROTH

Note: The expletive *it* is always followed by a singular verb:

It *is* the woman who suffers.
It *is* the women who suffer.

**(5) A relative pronoun used as a subject takes a singu-
lar or plural verb to accord with its antecedent.**

A *vegetable* that *contains* DDT can be harmful.
Vegetables that *contain* DDT can be harmful.

Mary is among the *students* who *have done* honor to the
college.   [*Students* is the antecedent of *who.*]
Mary is the only *one* of our students who *has achieved* national recognition.   [*One,* not *students,* is the antecedent
of *who.* Compare ''Of all our students Mary is the only
one who *has achieved* national recognition.'']

**(6) When used as subjects, such words as *each, either,
neither, another, anyone, anybody, anything,
someone, somebody, something, one, everyone,
everybody, everything, no one, nobody,* and *nothing*
regularly take singular verbs. Such words as *none,
any, all, more, most,* and *some* may take singular
or plural verbs, depending upon the context.**

Each *takes* his turn at rowing.
Neither *likes* the friends of the other.
Everyone in the fraternity *has* his own set of prejudices.

None *is* so blind as he who will not see.
None *are* so blind as those who will not see.

Some of the salt *was* damp.   [Compare ''Some salt *was*
damp.'']
Some of the clothes *were* damp.   [Compare ''Some clothes
were damp.'']

Note: In informal English, plural verbs are sometimes used in sentences like the following:

> INFORMAL   Each of the wives *do* their own hair.
> INFORMAL   *Do* either of the lifeguards ever *use* the pool?

(7) When regarded as a unit, collective nouns, as well as noun phrases denoting quantity, take singular verbs.

> The whole family *is* active.   [*Family* is a collective noun regarded as a unit.]
> The family *have met* their various obligations.   [The individuals of the family are regarded separately.]
>
> A thousand bushels *is* a good yield.   [A quantity or unit]
> A thousand bushels *were crated.*   [Individual bushels]

The number is singular; *a number* is plural.

> The number of students *was* small.   [*The number* is taken as a unit.]
> A number of students *were taking* tests.   [*A number* refers to individuals.]

(8) A linking verb agrees with its subject, not with its complement (predicate noun).

> His main *problem is* frequent heart attacks.
> Frequent *heart attacks are* his main problem.

Many writers prefer to recast such sentences in order to avoid the disagreement in number between subject and complement:

> He has one main problem: frequent heart attacks.

(9) Nouns plural in form but singular in meaning usually take singular verbs. In all doubtful cases, consult a good dictionary.

> News *is traveling* faster than ever before.
> Physics *has fascinated* my roommate for months.

Words regularly treated as singular include *aesthetics, astronautics, economics, genetics, linguistics, mathematics, measles, mumps, news, physics,* and *semantics.* Words regularly treated as plural include *blue jeans, slacks, trousers,* and *suburbs.*

Some nouns ending in *-ics* (such as *athletics, acoustics,* and *statistics*) are considered singular when referring to an organized body of knowledge and plural when referring to activities, qualities, or individual facts.

> Athletics *is required* of every student. [Compare ''Activity in games *is required* of every student.'']
> Athletics *provide* good recreation. [Compare ''Various games *provide* good recreation.'']
>
> Acoustics *is* an interesting study.
> The acoustics of the hall *are* good.
>
> Statistics *is* a science.
> The statistics *were* easily *assembled.*

(10) The title of a single work or a word spoken of as a word, even when plural in form, takes a singular verb.

> Bowser's "The Eggomaniacs" *describes* an egg fad.
> The New York *Times* still *has* a wide circulation.
> *They is* a pronoun.

■ **Exercise 1** The following sentences are all correct. Read them aloud, stressing the italicized words. If any sentence sounds wrong to you, read it aloud two or three more times so that you will gain practice in saying and hearing the correct forms.

1. *Everybody* in the audience *was* eager to participate.
2. One of the *men who were* fishing on the pier caught a man-eating shark.
3. The *rattles* and *knocks* under the hood *are* a warning.
4. Under the old house *were* valuable Mason *jars.*
5. *Each* of the lawyers *has* won many suits.
6. He was the *only one* of the actors *who was* bored.

59

7. *Human rights is* a term that *has* been interpreted many different ways.
8. There *are* a few *cookies* and potato *chips* left.
9. His *hobby* during his vacations *was* beautiful women.
10. Every *one* of the *boys who belong* to the organization *is* planning to help build and decorate the float.

■ **Exercise 2** Choose the correct form of the verb within parentheses in each of the following sentences.

1. Taste in magazines (differ, differs) greatly.
2. There (is, are) numerous positions available in the firm.
3. Each of the awards (carries, carry) several guarantees.
4. They each (has, have) good judgment.
5. The cat or her kittens (are, is) to blame for turning over the Christmas tree.
6. Those buttermilk clouds (presage, presages) a storm.
7. Everyone in the stands (were, was) unusually quiet.
8. Almost every illustration in these folios (has, have) been done by an amateur.
9. The booby prize (was, were) green apples.
10. A rustic lodge with tall pines and fishing waters close by (was, were) what we wanted.

■ **Exercise 3** In the following sentences, find each verb and relate it to its subject. If subject and verb do not agree according to the rules of formal English, change the verb to the correct form. Put a checkmark after each sentence that needs no revision.

1. Neither teachers nor postmen are averse to strikes.
2. Every one of the figures were checked at least twice.
3. Her flashing green eyes and her smile are hard to resist.
4. Neither of them understand the mechanism.
5. His aging parents and the provision he might make for them were his principal concern.
6. There come to my mind now the two or three people who were most influential in my life.
7. The study of words is facilitated by breaking them down into prefixes, suffixes, and roots.
8. A study of the many contrasts in the poetry of Browning and Tennyson seem a good research topic.

9. Hidden cameras, which invade the privacy of the unwary few, provides entertainment for thousands.
10. College newspapers that present only one side of the picture does an injustice to readers.

6b

Make a pronoun agree in number with its antecedent.

A singular antecedent (one that would take a singular verb) is referred to by a singular pronoun; a plural antecedent (one that would take a plural verb) is referred to by a plural pronoun.

> *Many* of the hard-core unemployed *were working* for the first time in *their* lives.   [The antecedent of *their* is *many.*]
> *One* of the hard-core unemployed *was working* for the first time in *his* life.   [The antecedent of *his* is *one.*]

(1) In formal English, use a singular pronoun to refer to such antecedents as *man, woman, person, kind, sort, each, either, neither, another, anyone, anybody, someone, somebody, one, everyone, everybody, no one,* **and** *nobody.* **See also 6a(6).**

> If a *person* reads the first few pages, *he* will finish the novel.
> *Someone* had left *his* canceled checks on the Xerox machine.

In informal English, plural pronouns are occasionally used to refer to such words:

> INFORMAL   *Someone* had left *their* canceled checks on the Xerox machine.

Caution: Avoid illogical sentences that may result from strict adherence to this rule.

> ILLOGICAL   Since every one of the patients seemed discouraged, I told a joke to cheer him up.
> BETTER   Since *all* the patients seemed discouraged, I told a joke to cheer *them* up.

(2) Two or more antecedents joined by *and* are referred to by a plural pronoun; two or more singular antecedents joined by *or* or *nor* are referred to by a singular pronoun. See also **6a(2)** and **6a(3)**.

Henry and James have completed *their* work.
Neither *Henry nor James* has completed *his* work.

If one of two antecedents joined by *or* or *nor* is singular and one is plural, the pronoun usually agrees with the nearer antecedent:

Either the *professor or* the *students* can begin to bridge the communication gap by expressing *their* opinions first.
[*Their* is closer to the plural antecedent *students.*]
Either the *students or* the *professor* can begin to bridge the communication gap by expressing *his* opinions first.   [*His* is closer to the singular antecedent *professor.*]

Caution: Avoid clumsy sentences that may result from strict adherence to this rule.

CLUMSY	When a *man or woman* enters college, *he or she* finds it different from high school.
BETTER	When *men and women* enter college, *they* find it different from high school.

(3) Collective nouns are referred to by singular or plural pronouns, depending on whether the collective noun is used in a singular or plural sense. See also **6a(7)**.

Special care should be taken to avoid treating a collective noun as *both* singular and plural within the same sentence.

INCONSISTENT	The group is writing their own music. [*Group* is followed by the singular verb *is* but is referred to by the plural pronoun *their.*]
BETTER	The *group is* writing *its* own music. [Consistently singular] OR The *group are* writing *their* own music. [Consistently plural]

■ **Exercise 4** Put a checkmark after each correct sentence below. If a sentence contains a pronoun that does not agree with its antecedent in number, substitute the correct pronoun form. Change verb forms when necessary to secure full agreement.

1. According to George Bernard Shaw, a woman delights in wounding a man's ego, though a man takes great pleasure in gratifying hers.
2. An author like Shaw, however, seldom captures the whole truth with their generalizations.
3. A generalization is frequently only partially true, though a person may quote it and think they wholly believe it.
4. For example, nearly everyone, to express their appreciation, has said with great conviction, "A friend in need is a friend indeed."
5. At the same time, probably no one will deny that far too often a successful man avoids the very shoulders that they have climbed upon.
6. Each of these quotations contains its grain of truth, but not the whole truth: "What a piece of work is a man! how noble in reason!" and "As a rule man is a fool."
7. That these quotations are contradictory anyone in their right mind can see.
8. Though contradictory, each of the quotations may be true if they are applied to specific persons in particular circumstances.
9. A great satirist like Jonathan Swift or Mark Twain in their works may often depict man as a fool.
10. Yet every reader who thinks for himself knows that the satirist—by pointing out man's foibles and follies—strives to reform man by showing him the value of making good use of his reason for lofty purposes.

■ **Exercise 5** All the following sentences are correct. Change them as directed in parentheses, revising other parts of the sentence to secure agreement of subject and verb, pronoun and antecedent.

1. Everyone in our Latin class thoroughly enjoys the full hour. (Change *Everyone* to *All students*.)

2. Every activity in that class seems not only instructive but amusing. (Change *Every activity* to *All activities.*)

3. Since the students eat their lunch just before the class, the Latin professor keeps coffee on hand to revive any sluggish thinkers. (Change *the students* to *nearly every student.*)

4. Yesterday one of the auditors was called on to translate some Latin sentences. (Change *one* to *two.*)

5. We were busily following the oral translation in our textbooks. (Change *We* to *Everyone else.*)

6. One or perhaps two in the class were not paying attention when the auditor, Jim Melton, said, "Who do you see?" (Use *Two or perhaps only one* instead of *One or perhaps two.*)

7. The Latin professor ordered, "Look at those inflections that indicate case! *Whom! Whom* do you see! Not *who!*" (Change *those inflections* to *the inflection.*)

8. Nobody in the room was inattentive as Jim translated the sentence again: "*Whom* do *youm* see?" (Change *Nobody* to *Few.*)

9. All students in the class were laughing as the professor exclaimed, "*Youm!* Whoever heard of *youm!*" (Change *All students* to *Everyone.*)

10. A student who often poses questions that provoke thought rather than the professor, Jim replied, "Whoever heard of *whom?*" (Change *questions* to *a question.*)

Tense and Mood

7

Use the appropriate form of the verb.

Verbs have *inflection*. The verb *eat*, for example, has five forms, as shown in the sentences below.

> I always *eat* pizza.　　They *ate* it yesterday.
> He *eats* it too.　　I had not yet *eaten* my pizza.
> They are *eating* pizza.

Regular verbs have only four distinct forms.

> believe, believes, believing, believed
> repeat, repeats, repeating, repeated

Some irregular verbs have four forms; others have five; and a few have three.

> become, becomes, becoming, became
> choose, chooses, choosing, chose, chosen
> put, puts, putting

Be, the most irregular verb in the English language, has eight forms.

> be, am, is, are, being, was, were, been

The principal parts of verbs are generally considered to be the *present* form, which is also the stem of the infinitive (*eat—to eat*); the *past* form (*ate*); and the *past participle* (*eaten*). (See the list of principal parts of verbs on pages 72–73.)

Verbs have *tense*. If we consider only the form changes of single-word verbs, there are just two tenses—present and past.

PRESENT	allow (allows), see (sees)
PAST	allowed, saw

Note: The *-s* form of the verb (*allows, sees*) is used only with third-person singular subjects: see **7a(2)**.

When we consider certain verb phrases along with the form changes of single-word verbs, there are six tenses.

PRESENT	allow (allows), see (sees)
PAST	allowed, saw
FUTURE	will allow, shall allow; will see, shall see
PRESENT PERFECT	have (has) allowed, have (has) seen
PAST PERFECT	had allowed, had seen
FUTURE PERFECT	will have allowed, shall have allowed; will have seen, shall have seen

This grammatical classification of tenses does not, of course, include all words commonly used in verb phrases: see the list on pages 4–5.

There are three main divisions of time—present, future, and past. Various verb forms and verb phrases refer to divisions of actual time.

PRESENT

At last I *see* what you meant by that remark.
Right now he *is seeing* double.   He *does see* double now.

FUTURE

I *will* (OR *shall*) *see* him.
Tomorrow I *see* my lawyer.
Pauline *is to see* Switzerland next summer.
He *is going to* (OR *will*) *see* justice done.
They *are about to see* their dreams in action.
   [Immediate future]
Mr. Yates *will have seen* the report by then.
   [Before a given time]

PAST

We *saw* the accident this morning. [At a definite time]
They *have* already *seen* much of the West.
  [At some time before now]
Nancy *had seen* the play before she received our invitation.
  [Before a given time in the past]
We *were to see* the dean on Monday.
We *were going to see* great changes.
I *was about to see* Paris for the first time.
I *used to see* him daily. I *did see* him daily.
In the sixteenth century the Spaniards *see* their Armada
  defeated. [Historical present]
Shakespeare writes about what he *sees* in the human heart.
  [Literary present]

Note: A present-tense verb form may be used to express a
universal truth or a habitual action.

Men *see* that death *is* inevitable. [Universal truth]
My father *sees* his doctor every Tuesday. [Habitual action]

The verb markers *do, does,* and *did* (with present and past
forms only) are used for negations, questions, and emphatic
statements or restatements.

He *pays* his bills on time. [Positive statement]
He *does* not *pay* his bills on time. [Negation]
Does he *pay* his bills on time? [Question]
He *does pay* his bills on time. [Emphatic restatement]

In the indicative mood, both active and passive verbs have
all six tense forms shown on page 66. (For definitions of
such terms as *mood* and *voice,* see the Glossary of Grammatical Terms.) In the imperative mood, verbs have only present
tense (*see, be seen*). In the subjunctive mood, verbs have only
present, past, present perfect, and past perfect tenses: see
page 474. The English language also has progressive tense
forms (used with a form of *be* and ending in *-ing*—for example, *is seeing, was seeing, will be seeing*) to show action
in progress or a state of being.

Below is a summary of the forms of the verb *see*—the simple tense forms and the progressive forms, both active and passive voices.

SIMPLE FORMS

	Active	*Passive*
PRESENT	(he) sees	is seen
PAST	(he) saw	was seen
FUTURE	(he) will see	will be seen
PRESENT PERFECT	(he) has seen	has been seen
PAST PERFECT	(he) had seen	had been seen
FUTURE PERFECT	(he) will have seen	will have been seen

PROGRESSIVE FORMS

	Active	*Passive*
PRESENT	(he) is seeing	is being seen
PAST	(he) was seeing	was being seen
FUTURE	(he) will be seeing	will be being seen
PRESENT PERFECT	(he) has been seeing	has been being seen
PAST PERFECT	(he) had been seeing	had been being seen
FUTURE PERFECT	(he) will have been seeing	will have been being seen

Infinitives, participles, and gerunds also have tense, but not all six tenses:

Infinitives

PRESENT	to see, to be seen, to be seeing
PRESENT PERFECT	to have seen, to have been seen, to have been seeing

Participles

PRESENT	seeing, being seen
PAST	seen
PRESENT PERFECT	having seen, having been seen

Gerunds

PRESENT	seeing, being seen
PRESENT PERFECT	having seen, having been seen

Such verb markers as *can, may, shall,* and *will* have past-tense forms (*could, might, should,* and *would*).

7a

Avoid confusing similar verbs or misusing the principal parts of verbs.

(1) Do not confuse the intransitive verbs *lie* and *sit* with the transitive verbs *lay* and *set*.

Become familiar with the principal parts and the meanings of *lie, lay, sit,* and *set:*

Present stem (infinitive)	Past tense	Past participle	Present participle
lie (*to recline*)	lay	lain	lying
lay (*to cause to lie*)	laid	laid	laying
sit (*to be seated*)	sat	sat	sitting
set (*to place or put*)	set	set	setting

The forms of the intransitive verbs *lie* and *sit* do not have objects and are not passive; the forms of the transitive verbs *lay* and *set* either have objects or are in the passive.

PATTERN	SUBJECT—INTRANSITIVE VERB.

You should *lie* down.   Yesterday he *lay* down awhile.
It *has lain* there for days.   Logs *are lying* on the porch.

I *did* not *sit* down.   Helen *sat* up straight.
I *had sat* there an hour.   A flowerpot *was sitting* here.

PATTERN	SUBJECT—TRANSITIVE VERB—OBJECT.

You *should lay* the package down immediately.
Yesterday he *laid* bricks.   They *are laying* plans.

I *did* not *set* it down.   We *were setting* traps.

> PATTERN   SUBJECT—PASSIVE VERB.

The foundation for the house *was laid* last week.
A date *has been set* for the reception.

■ **Exercise 1**   All the sentences below are correct. Read them aloud, stressing the italicized verb forms. Then convert each transitive active verb to passive. Put a checkmark after each sentence in which the italicized verb is intransitive.

EXAMPLE
Ellen *set* a bowl of fruit in front of us.
*A bowl of fruit **was set** in front of us.*

1. Perhaps the lost coins *lie* buried under the gravel.
2. Mrs. Rawlins *laid* the sleeping child in the back seat.
3. Political leaflets *were lying* on tables in the library.
4. Last night he *lay* awake worrying.
5. We have to *lay* aside our prejudices.
6. Louise *sits* up late on Friday nights.
7. The fence company *set* the posts in concrete.
8. Twenty freshmen *sat* waiting for orientation to begin.
9. Are the boys *setting* out the young trees?
10. Are the boys *sitting* in those young trees?

(2) Avoid misusing the principal parts of verbs.

Learn when to use the various forms of a verb. The *-s* form functions as a single-word verb with a singular subject in the third person. See also **6a**.

he *asks*, a person *asks*, she *begins*, everyone *begins*

The *-ing* form is used with a form of *be*.

I *was asking*, he *has been asking*, it *is beginning*

The principal parts of a verb include the *present* form (which is also the stem of the infinitive), the *past* form, and the *past participle*:

Present stem (infinitive)	Past tense	Past participle
ask	asked	asked
begin	began	begun

The *present* form may function as a single-word verb or may be preceded by verb markers such as *will, do, may, could, have to, ought to,* or *used to.* See also pages 4–5.

    I *ask,* he *does ask,* we *begin,* it *used to begin*

The *past* form functions as a single-word verb.

    He *asked* questions.   The show *began* at eight.

The *past participle,* when used as a part of a verb phrase, always has at least one verb marker or auxiliary.

    they *have asked,* she *was asked,* he *has been asked*
    it *has begun,* the work *will be begun,* we *have begun*

Be sure to use only standard verb forms in your writing.

NONSTANDARD	The militants were ask to speak.
STANDARD	The militants were *asked* to speak.
NONSTANDARD	The TV program had just began.
STANDARD	The TV program had just *begun.*

When in doubt about the principal parts of a verb, consult a good dictionary. For irregular verbs (such as *begin*), dictionaries give all the principal parts. For regular verbs (such as *ask*), the past tense and the past participle, when not given, are understood to be formed by adding *-d* or *-ed.*

The following list gives the principal parts of a number of commonly misused verbs. As you study it, you may find that some verb forms are more troublesome to you than others. For instance, you may tend to use *done* for *did* and *bursted* for *burst,* but you may have no trouble with *gone* or *set.* You can master the difficult verbs by associating them with similar verbs that you never misuse:

Present stem (infinitive)	Past tense	Past participle
go	went	gone
do	*did*	*done*
set	set	set
burst	*burst*	*burst*

Principal Parts of Verbs

Present stem (infinitive)	Past tense	Past participle
[I]		
become	became	become
come	came	come
run	ran	run
[II]		
begin	began	begun
drink	drank	drunk
ring	rang	rung
sing	sang OR sung	sung
sink	sank OR sunk	sunk
spring	sprang OR sprung	sprung
swim	swam	swum
[III]		
blow	blew	blown
draw	drew	drawn
fly	flew	flown
grow	grew	grown
know	knew	known
swear	swore	sworn
tear	tore	torn
wear	wore	worn
[IV]		
bring	brought	brought
catch	caught	caught
dig	dug	dug
dive	dived OR dove	dived
drag	dragged	dragged

Present stem (infinitive)	Past tense	Past participle
lead	led	led
lose	lost	lost
raise	raised	raised
[V]		
arise	arose	arisen
break	broke	broken
choose	chose	chosen
drive	drove	driven
eat	ate	eaten
fall	fell	fallen
forget	forgot	forgotten OR forgot
forgive	forgave	forgiven
freeze	froze	frozen
get	got	got OR gotten
give	gave	given
ride	rode	ridden
rise	rose	risen
shake	shook	shaken
shrink	shrank OR shrunk	shrunk OR shrunken
speak	spoke	spoken
steal	stole	stolen
take	took	taken
write	wrote	written

Note: Mistakes with verb forms sometimes involve misspelling, such as writing *payed* for *paid,* adding a *d* before the *-ed* in *drowned* or a *t* before the *-ed* in *attacked,* or omitting a *-d* or *-ed* in phrases like *am used to, was supposed to,* or *had happened to.*

■ **Exercise 2** Make your own list of principal parts of verbs, made up of verbs that you need to study and review. (Include on your list any troublesome verbs listed in the five groups on these two pages, as well as verbs you have misused in your writing.) When your list is complete, compose sentences to illustrate the correct use of each principal part.

7b

Use logical tense forms in sequence.

(1) Verbs in clauses

Notice in the examples below the relationship of each verb form to actual time.

> When the speaker *entered*, the audience *rose*. [Both actions took place at the same definite time in the past.]
>
> I *have ceased* worrying because I *have heard* no more rumors. [Both verb forms indicate action at some time before now.]
>
> When I *had been* at camp four weeks, I *received* word that my application *had been accepted.* [The *had* before *been* indicates a time prior to that of *received.*]

(2) Infinitives

Use the present infinitive to express action contemporaneous with, or later than, that of the main verb; use the present perfect infinitive for action prior to that of the main verb.

> I hoped *to go* (NOT *to have gone*). I hope *to go.* [Present infinitives—for time later than that of the main verb. At the time indicated by the main verbs, the speaker was still hoping *to go,* not *to have gone.*]
>
> I would like *to have lived* in Shakespeare's time. [Present perfect infinitive—expressing time prior to that of the main verb. Compare "I wish I *had lived* in Shakespeare's time."]
>
> I would have liked *to live* (NOT *to have lived*) in Shakespeare's time. [Present infinitive—for time contemporaneous with that of the main verb.]

(3) Participles and gerunds

Use the present form of participles and gerunds to express action contemporaneous with that of the main verb; use the present perfect form for action prior to that of the main verb.

PARTICIPLES

Walking along the streets, he met many old friends.   [The walking and the meeting were contemporaneous.]
Having walked all the way home, he found himself tired. [The walking was prior to his finding himself tired.]

GERUNDS

Writing letters to the editor is her hobby.   [Both *writing* and *is* refer to the present.]
Having won the world's championship does not make the team invincible.   [The winning took place before the present.]

■ **Exercise 3**   Choose the verb form inside parentheses that is the logical tense form in sequence.

1. When the fire sale (ended, had ended), the store closed.
2. Fans cheered as the goal (had been made, was made).
3. The team plans (to celebrate, to have celebrated) tomorrow.
4. We should have planned (to have gone, to go) by bus.
5. (Having finished, Finishing) his test, James left the room.
6. (Having bought, Buying) the tickets, Mr. Selby took the children to the circus.
7. The chairman had left the meeting before it (had adjourned, adjourned).
8. It is customary for ranchers (to brand, to have branded) their cattle.
9. Marilyn had not expected (to see, to have seen) her cousin in the beauty shop.
10. The pond has begun freezing because the temperature (dropped, has dropped).

7c

Use the subjunctive mood in the few types of expressions in which it is still appropriate.

Distinctive forms for the subjunctive occur only in the present and past tenses of *be* and in the present tense of other verbs used with third-person singular subjects.

INDICATIVE	I *am,* you *are,* he *is,* others *are* [Present]
	I *was,* you *were,* he *was,* others *were* [Past]
SUBJUNCTIVE	(with all subjects) *be* [Present], *were* [Past]
INDICATIVE	he *sees,* others *see* [Present]
SUBJUNCTIVE	(that) he *see,* (that) others *see* [Present]

Although the subjunctive mood has been largely displaced by the indicative, the subjunctive is still used in a few structures, such as the following:

> As Steinberg once remarked, it was as if he *were* guided by an ouija board. —OLIVER LA FARGE
>
> Such a school demands from the teacher that he *be* a kind of artist in his province. —ALBERT EINSTEIN
>
> *Had* the price of looking *been* blindness, I would have looked.
> —RALPH ELLISON

The subjunctive is required (1) in *that* clauses of motion, resolution, recommendation, command, or demand and (2) in a few idiomatic expressions.

> I move that the report *be* approved.
> Resolved, that dues for the coming year *be* doubled.
> I recommend (order, demand) that the prisoner *see* his lawyer.
> I demand (request, insist) that the messenger *go* alone.
> If need *be* . . . *Suffice* it to say . . . *Come* what may . . .
> *Lest* we forget . . . [Fixed subjunctive in idiomatic expressions]

Many writers prefer the subjunctive to express contrary-to-fact condition, especially in formal writing.

INFORMAL	If the apple *was* ripe, it would be good.
PREFERRED	If the apple *were* ripe, it would be good.
INFORMAL	I wish that he *was* here now.
PREFERRED	I wish that he *were* here now.

■ **Exercise 4** Prepare for a class discussion of the use of the subjunctive mood (both required and preferred verb forms) and of the indicative verb forms used informally in the following sentences.

1. If Lena was here, she'd explain everything.
2. We insist that he be punished.
3. I wish that peace were possible.
4. Americans now speak of Spain as though it were just across the river.
5. Present-day problems demand that we be ready for any emergency.
6. If there was time, I could finish my report.
7. Come what may, we will never choose anarchy.
8. I demand that he make amends.
9. If I were you, I would apply tomorrow.
10. The man acts as though he were the owner.

■ **Exercise 5** Compose five sentences in which the subjunctive is required. Compose five other sentences in which either the subjunctive or the indicative may be used, giving the indicative (informal) form in parentheses.

7d

Avoid needless shifts in tense or mood. See also **27a** and **27b**.

INCONSISTENT He came to the river and pays a man to ferry him across. [A shift in tense within one sentence]

BETTER He *came* to the river and *paid* a man to ferry him across.

INCONSISTENT It is necessary to restrain an occasional foolhardy park visitor lest a mother bear *mistake* his friendly intentions and *supposes* him a menace to her cubs. [Mood shifts improperly from subjunctive to indicative within the compound predicate.] But females with cubs *were* only one of the dangers. [A correct sentence if standing alone, but here inconsistent with present tense of preceding sentence and therefore misleading] One *has* to remember that all bears *were* wild animals and not domesticated pets. [Inconsistent and misleading shift of tense from present in main clause to past in subordinate clause] Though a bear *may seem* altogether peaceable and harmless, he *might* not *remain* peaceable, and he is never harmless. [Tense shifts improperly from present in introductory clause to past in main clause.] It *is* therefore an important part of the park ranger's duty *to watch* the tourists, and above all *don't* let anyone try to feed the bears. [Inconsistent and needless shift in mood from indicative to imperative]

BETTER   It is necessary to restrain an occasional foolhardy park visitor lest a mother bear *mistake* his friendly intentions and *suppose* him a menace to her cubs. But females with cubs *are* only one of the dangers. One *has* to remember that all bears *are* wild animals and not domesticated pets. Though a bear *may seem* altogether peaceable and harmless, he *may* not *remain* peaceable, and he is never harmless. It *is* therefore an important part of the park ranger's duty *to watch* the tourists and above all not *to let* anyone try to feed the bears.

■ **Exercise 6**   In the following passage correct all errors and inconsistencies in tense and mood as well as any other errors in verb usage. Put a checkmark after any sentence that is satisfactory as it stands.

¹ Across the Thames from Shakespeare's London lay the area known as the Bankside, probably as rough and unsavory a neighborhood as ever laid across the river from any city.   ² And yet it was to such a place that Shakespeare and his company had to have gone to build their new theater.   ³ For the Puritan government of the City had set up all sorts of prohibitions against theatrical entertainment within the city walls.   ⁴ When it became necessary, therefore, for the company to have moved their playhouse from its old location north of the city, they obtain a lease to a tract on the Bankside.   ⁵ Other theatrical companies had went there before them, and it seemed reasonable to have supposed that Shakespeare and his partners would prosper in the new location.   ⁶ Apparently the Puritans of the City had no law against anyone's moving cartloads of lumber through the public streets.   ⁷ There is no record that the company met with difficulty while the timbers of the dismantled playhouse are being hauled to the new site.   ⁸ The partners had foresaw and forestalled one difficulty: the efforts of their old landlord to have stopped them from removing the building.   ⁹ Lest his presence complicate their

task and would perhaps defeat its working altogether, they waited until he had gone out of town. [10] And when he came back, his lot was bare. [11] The building's timbers were all in stacks on the far side of the river, and the theater is waiting only to be put together. [12] It is a matter of general knowledge that on the Bankside Shakespeare continued his successful career as a showman and went on to enjoy even greater prosperity after he had made the move than before.

7e

Observe such distinctions as exist among *should, would, shall,* and *will*.

(1) Use *should* in all persons to express a mild obligation or a condition.

> I (You, He, We, They) *should* help the needy.
> If I (you, he, we, they) *should* resign, the program would not be continued.

(2) Use *would* in all persons to express a customary action.

> I (You, He, We, They) *would* spend hours by the seashore during the summer months.

Caution: Do not use *would have* as a substitute for *had*.

> If you *had* (NOT *would have*) arrived earlier, you would have seen the president.

(3) Use *shall* or *will* in accordance with general English usage.

In general English usage, *shall* and *will* are used for all subjects, whether first, second, or third person. *Will* is more frequently used than *shall*. *Shall* is used primarily in questions but may be used in emphatic statements:

> *Shall* we eat now or later?   We *shall* conquer disease.

Note: A few writers still distinguish between *shall* and *will* in the following fashion:

   (a) by using *shall* in the first person and *will* in the second and third to express the simple future or expectation:

   I *shall* plan to stay.   He *will* probably stay.

   (b) by using *will* in the first person and *shall* in the second and third to express determination, threat, command, prophecy, promise, or willingness:

   I *will* stay.   You and he *shall* stay.

■ **Exercise 7**   Revise any incorrect verb forms in the sentences below. Put a checkmark after any sentence that needs no revision. Prepare to explain the reason for each change you make.

 1. If he would have registered later, he would have had night classes.
 2. If Mary enrolled in the class at the beginning, she could have made good grades.
 3. A stone lying in one position for a long time may gather moss.
 4. The members recommended that all delinquents be fined.
 5. It was reported that there use to be very few delinquents.
 6. After Mr. Norwood entered the room, he sat down at the desk and begins to write rapidly.
 7. Until I received his letter, I was hoping to have had a visit from him.
 8. Follow the main road for a mile; then you need to take the next road on the left.
 9. The beggar could not deny that he had stole the purse.
 10. I would have liked to have been with the team on the trip to New Orleans.

MECHANICS

Manuscript Form

8

Put your manuscript in acceptable form. Divide words at the ends of lines according to standard practices. Proofread and revise with care.

8a
Use the proper materials.

Unless you are given other instructions, follow these general rules:

(1) **Handwritten papers**   Use standard theme paper, size $8\frac{1}{2}$ by 11 inches, with widely spaced lines. (Narrow spaces between lines do not allow sufficient room for corrections.) Use black, blue, or blue-black ink, and write on only one side of the paper.

(2) **Typewritten papers**   Use regular weight typing paper (not onion skin), size $8\frac{1}{2}$ by 11 inches. Double-space between lines to make room for corrections. Use a black ribbon, and make sure that the type is clean. Type on only one side of the paper.

8b

Arrange your writing in clear and orderly fashion on the page. Divide a word at the end of a line only between syllables.

ARRANGEMENT

(1) **Margins** Leave sufficient margins—about an inch and a half at the left and top, an inch at the right and bottom—to prevent a crowded appearance. The ruled lines on theme paper indicate the proper margins at the left and top.

(2) **Indention** Indent the first lines of paragraphs uniformly, about an inch in handwritten copy and five spaces in typewritten copy.

(3) **Paging** Use Arabic numerals—without parentheses or periods—in the upper right-hand corner to mark all pages after the first.

(4) **Title** *Do not put quotation marks around the title or underline it* (unless it is a quotation or the title of a book), and use no period after the title. Center the title on the page about an inch and a half from the top or on the first ruled line. Leave the next line blank and begin the first paragraph on the third line. In this way the title will stand off from the text. Capitalize the first and last words of the title and all other words except articles, short conjunctions, and short prepositions.

(5) **Poetry** Quoted lines of poetry should be arranged and indented as in the original: see **16a(2)**.

(6) **Punctuation** Never begin a line with a comma, a colon, a semicolon, or a terminal mark of punctuation; never end a line with the first of a set of brackets, parentheses, or quotation marks.

(7) **Identification** Papers are identified in the way prescribed by the instructor to facilitate handling. Usually

8b   **ms**

papers carry the name of the student and the course, the date, and the number of the assignment. Often the name of the instructor is also given.

WORD DIVISION

(8) **Word division**   You will seldom need to divide words, especially short ones, if you leave a reasonably wide right-hand margin. The reader will object less to an uneven margin than he will to a large number of broken words.

When you need to divide a word at the end of a line, use a hyphen to mark the separation of syllables. In college dictionaries, dots usually divide the syllables of words: **at·om, i·so·late, ec·u·men·i·cal.** But not every dot marks an appropriate place for dividing a word at the end of a line. The following principles are useful guidelines:

(a) Do not put a single letter of a word at the end or at the beginning of a line: **e·vade, a·lone, perk·y.**

(b) Do not put *-ed* or any other two-letter ending at the beginning of a line: **tax·is, lay·er, sure·ly, thick·en.**

(c) Do not carry forward *-ble*; if necessary, carry forward *-able* or *-ible*: **a·vail·a·ble, vis·i·ble.**

(d) Divide hyphenated words only at the hyphen: **mass=pro·duced, self=con·grat·u·la·to·ry, mer·ry-go=round.**

(e) Divide words ending in *-ing* between those consonants that you double when adding the *-ing*: **set=ting, jam=ming, plan=ning, gel=ling.**   [Compare **sell=ing, press=ing.**]

(f) Divide words between two consonants that come between vowels—except when the division does not reflect pronunciation: **pic=nic, un=tie, prac=ticed, thun=der.**   [But NOT **thin-ker** or **rec-line**]

Avoid having divisions at the ends of three consecutive lines. When possible, avoid dividing proper names like *Mexico, Agnes,* or *Mr. T. E. Jackson.*

Caution: Do not divide one-syllable words such as *through, twelfth,* or *beamed.*

■ **Exercise 1** First list the words below that should not be divided at the end of a line; then, with the aid of your dictionary, write out the other words by syllables and insert hyphens to mark appropriate end-of-line divisions.

(1) cross-examination, (2) portable, (3) fifteenth, (4) impossible, (5) combed, (6) scrubbing, (7) guessing, (8) against, (9) confetti, (10) fantastic.

8c

Write or type the manuscript so that it can be read easily and accurately.

(1) **Legible handwriting** Form each letter clearly; distinguish between each *o* and *a, i* and *e, t* and *l, b* and *f.* Be sure that capital letters differ from lower-case letters. Use firm dots, not circles, for periods. Make each word a distinct unit. Avoid flourishes.
(2) **Legible typing** Do not strike over letters; make neat corrections. Be sure to double-space between lines. Leave one space after a comma or a semicolon, one or two after a colon, and two or three after a period, a question mark, or an exclamation point. To indicate a dash, use two hyphens without spacing before, between, or after. Use ink to insert marks that are not on your typewriter, such as accent marks, mathematical symbols, or brackets.

8d

Proofread and revise the manuscript with care.[1]

(1) Proofread the paper and correct mistakes before submitting it to the instructor.

When doing in-class papers, use the last few minutes of the period for proofreading and making corrections. Changes should be made as follows:

(a) Draw one line horizontally through any word to be deleted. Do not put it within parentheses or make an unsightly erasure.

(b) In case of an addition of one line or less, place a caret (∧) at the point in the line where the addition is to come, and write just above the caret the word or words to be added.

Since you have more time for out-of-class assignments, write a first draft, put the paper aside for several hours or for a day, and then use the following check list as you proofread and make changes.

Proofreader's Check List

1. *Title.* Is there any unnecessary punctuation in the title? Is it centered on the first line? Are key words capitalized? See **8b(4)**.
2. *Logic.* Is the central idea of the paper stated clearly and developed logically? Does the paper contain any questionable generalizations? Does it contain any irrelevant material? See Section **23**.

---

[1] For marks used in correcting proofs for the printer, see the *Standard College Dictionary*, pp. 1604–06; *Webster's New World Dictionary*, 2nd College ed., p. 1687; *The American College Dictionary*, p. 1432; or *The American Heritage Dictionary*, p. 1048.

3. *Point of view.* Is the point of view in the paper consistent? Are there any needless shifts in tense, mood, voice, person, number, type of discourse, tone, or perspective? See Section 27.

4. *Paragraphs.* Is the first line of each paragraph clearly indented? Are ideas carefully organized and adequately developed? See 8b(2), 31a, and 31c-d.

5. *Transitions.* Do ideas follow one another smoothly? Do all conjunctions and transitional expressions relate ideas precisely? See 31b.

6. *Sentences.* Are there any sentence fragments, comma splices, or fused sentences? Are ideas properly subordinated? Are modifiers correctly placed? Is there any faulty parallelism? Are the references of pronouns clear? Are sentences as effective as possible? See Sections 2-3, 24-26, and 28-30.

7. *Grammar.* Are appropriate forms of modifiers, pronouns, and verbs used? Do subjects and verbs agree? See Sections 4-7.

8. *Spelling and diction.* Is the spelling correct? Are words carefully chosen, appropriate, exact? Should any words be deleted? Should any be inserted? Should any be changed because of ambiguity? See Section 18; 19i; and Sections 20-22.

9. *Punctuation.* Are apostrophes correctly placed? Are end marks appropriate? Is any one mark of punctuation overused? See Sections 12-17.

10. *Mechanics.* Do word divisions at the ends of lines follow conventional practices? Are capitals and underlining (italics) used correctly? Should any abbreviations or numbers be spelled out? See 8b(8) and Sections 9-11.

To detect errors in spelling, try reading lines backward so that you will see each word separately. To proofread individual sentences, look at each one as a unit, apart from its context.

■ **Exercise 2**   Proofread the following composition; circle mistakes. Prepare to discuss in class the changes that you as a proofreader would make.

Programmed People.

Everybody over twenty is a machine-an insensitive,

unhearing, unseeing, unthinking, unfeeling mechanism.

They act like programmed people, all their movements

or responses triggered by clocks. Take, for example

my brother. At 7:30 A.M. he automatically shuts off

the alarm, then for the next hour he grumbles and

sputter around like the cold, sluggish motor that he is.

On the way to work he did not see the glorious

sky or notice ambulance at his neighbor's house. At

8:20 he unlocks his store and starts selling auto

parts; however, all mourning long he never once

really sees a customers' face. While eating lunch

at Joe's cafe, the same music he spent a quarter for

yesterday is playing again. he does not hear it.

At one o'clock my bother is back working with invoices

and punching an old comptometer: The clock and him

ticks on and on.

When the hour hand hits five, it pushes the "move"

button of my brother: lock store, take bus, pet dog at

front door, kiss wife and baby, eat supper, read paper,

```
watch TV, and during the 10-o'clock news he starts his

nodding. His wife interrupts his heavy breathing to

say that thier neighbor had a mild heart attach while

mowing the lawn.  My brother jerks and snorts.  Then

he mumbles, "Tomorrow, honey, tomorrow.  I have got

a year and a half to go before I am twenty
```

(2) Revise the paper after the instructor has marked it.

One of the best ways to learn how to write is to revise returned papers carefully. Give special attention to any comment on content or style, and become familiar with the numbers or abbreviations used by your instructor to indicate specific errors or suggested changes.

Unless directed otherwise, follow this procedure as you revise a marked paper:

(a) Find in this handbook the exact principle that deals with each error or recommended change.

(b) After the instructor's mark in the margin, write the letter designating the appropriate principle, such as a or c.

(c) Rather than rewrite the composition, make the corrections on the marked paper. To make the corrections stand out distinctly from the original, use ink of a different color or a no. 2 pencil.

The purpose of this method of revision is to help you not only to understand why a change is desirable but also to avoid repetition of the same mistakes.

On the following page are examples of a paragraph marked by an instructor and the same paragraph corrected by a student.

A Paragraph Marked by an Instructor

3   Those who damn advertising stress its
disadvantages, however, it saves consumers time,
labor, and money. Billboards can save a traveler

12   time for many tell him where to find a meal or a

18   bed. TV commercials announce new labor-saveing

2   products. Such as a spray or a cleaner. In
addition, some advertisers give away free samples

19   of shampoo, toothpaste, soap flakes, and etc. These

24   samples often last for weeks. They save the
consumer money. Consumers should appreciate
advertising, not condemn it.

The Same Paragraph Corrected by a Student

Those who damn advertising stress its

3a   disadvantages /; however, it saves consumers time,
labor, and money. Billboards can save a traveler

12a   time, for many tell him where to find a meal or a

18c   bed. TV commercials announce new labor-~~saveing~~ *saving*

2c   products /, ~~Such~~ *such* as a spray or a cleaner. In
addition, some advertisers give away free samples

19i   of shampoo, toothpaste, soap flakes, ~~and~~ etc. These

24a   samples, *which* often last for weeks /, ~~They~~ save the
consumer money. Consumers should appreciate
advertising, not condemn it.

The method of revision shown opposite works equally well if your instructor uses abbreviations or other symbols instead of numbers. In that case, instead of putting a after 3, for example, you would put a after cs.

Individual Record of Errors

You may find that keeping a record of your errors will help you to check the improvement in your writing. A clear record of the symbols on your revised papers will show your progress at a glance. As you write each paper, keep your record in mind; avoid mistakes that have already been pointed out and corrected.

One way to record your errors is to write them down as they occur in each paper, grouping them in columns according to the seven major divisions of the handbook as illustrated below. In the spaces for paper no. 1 are the numbers and letters from the margin of the revised paragraph on the opposite page. In the spelling column is the correctly spelled word rather than 18c. You may wish to add on your record sheet other columns for date, grade, and instructor's comments.

RECORD OF ERRORS

Paper No.	Grammar 1–7	Mechanics 8–11	Punctuation 12–17	Words Misspelled 18	Diction 19–22	Effective-ness 23–30	Larger Elements 31–34
	3a 2c		12a	saving	19i	24a	

Capitals

9

Capitalize words in accordance with standard conventions. Avoid unnecessary capitals.[1]

Most capitalized words fall into three main categories: proper names, key words in titles, and the first words of sentences.

> Brigham Young led the Mormons to Utah.   [Proper names]
> I read *The Greening of America*.   [Key words in title]
> She said, "At first the bullfights made me sick." Then she
>   added, "Later I thought they were exciting."   [Words
>   beginning sentences]

A study of the principles in this section should help you use capitals appropriately. When problems arise with individual words, check the capitalization in a good college dictionary. In dictionary entries, words regularly capitalized begin with capitals.

---

[1] For a more detailed discussion of the capitalization of words and abbreviations, see the United States Government Printing Office *Style Manual* (Washington, D.C.: Government Printing Office, 1967), pp. 23–59, or *A Manual of Style*, 12th ed. (Chicago: Univ. of Chicago Press, 1969), pp. 149–94.

9a

Capitalize proper names, words used as an essential part of proper names, and, usually, derivatives and abbreviations of proper names.

Proper names begin with capitals, but names of classes of persons, places, or things do not.

> James Brady, England, Broadway, Indiana University
> the man, his country, the street, any university

(1) Proper names

Capitalize names of specific persons, places, and things; organizations and institutions; historical periods and events; members of national, political, racial, religious, social, and athletic groups; calendar designations; and words pertaining to the Deity and Holy Scripture.

> Milton, Mr. Adams, Japan, Iowa, the Alamo, the Alleghenies
> Central Intelligence Agency, the Middle Ages, War of 1812
> Republicans, Negro, Methodist, Jaycees, Cleveland Browns
> Monday, January, Memorial Day, Thanksgiving, Hanukkah
> God, the Lord, our Father, the Old Testament, the Bible

Note 1: Capitalize pronouns referring to the Deity only when necessary for clarity.

> God promised Abraham that He would bless his people.

Note 2: Capitalize names of objects, animals, or ideas when they are personified. See also **20a(4)**.

> the reign of Reason

(2) Words used as an essential part of proper names

Words like *college, lake, river, building, street, county,* and *association* are capitalized only when they are part of names.

> Central State College, Bowie Street, Empire State Building

Note: In instances such as the following, capitalization depends on word placement:

> on the Erie and Huron lakes   on Lakes Erie and Huron

(3) Derivatives

Words derived from proper names are usually capitalized.

> Miltonic, Mexican-American, New Yorker, Christian

(4) Abbreviations

As a rule, capitalize abbreviations of capitalized words.

> Y.M.C.A., FBI, NASA   [Compare *m.p.h.*]

Note 1: Both *no.* and *No.* are correct abbreviations for *number.*

Note 2: When proper names and their derivatives become names of a general class, they are no longer capitalized.

> malapropism   [Derived from *Mrs. Malaprop*]
> chauvinistic   [Derived from *Nicholas Chauvin*]

Caution: Some words may be used correctly as either proper or common nouns:

> the Democratic candidate   a democratic principle
> the Boston Tea Party   the Republican party

9b

Capitalize titles that precede a proper name, but not those that follow it.

> Governor Paul Smith, King Philip, Sister Mary[2]
> Paul Smith, the governor; Philip, the king; Mary, my sister

----

[2] This rule also applies to names of members of religious orders.

Note: Usage is divided regarding the capitalization of titles indicating high rank or distinction when not followed by a proper name, or of words denoting family relationship when used as substitutes for proper names:

> Who was the President (OR president) of the United States?
> "Oh, Dad (OR dad)!" I said. "Tell Mother (OR mother)."

9c

In titles of books, plays, student papers, and so on, capitalize the first and last words and all other words except articles (*a, an, the*), short conjunctions, and short prepositions.

> *Crime and Punishment, Midnight on the Desert*
> *The Man Without a Country*   [In titles a conjunction or a
>   preposition of five or more letters is usually capitalized.]
> "A Code to Live By," "Journalists Who Influence Elections"

Note: In a title capitalize the first word of a hyphenated compound. As a rule, capitalize the word following the hyphen if it is a noun or a proper adjective or if it is equal in importance to the first word.

> *A Substitute for the H-Bomb*   [Noun]
> *French-Canadian Propaganda*   [Proper adjective]
> "Hit-and-Run Accidents"   [Parallel words]

Usage varies with respect to the capitalization of words following such prefixes as *anti-, ex-, re-,* and *self-*:

> *The Anti-Poverty Program,* "Re-covering Old Sofas"

9d

Capitalize the pronoun *I* and the interjection *O* (but not *oh,* except when it begins a sentence).

> David sings, "Out of the depths I cry to thee, O Lord."

cap

9e

Capitalize the first word of every sentence (including quoted sentences).

> My brother said, "Tests are not fun and games."
> He did not consider tests "fun and games." [A sentence fragment within quotation marks does not begin with a capital.]

Note: Direct questions within sentences begin with a capital except after a colon, when the capital is optional.

> The question is, Can tests ever be fun and games?
> We both had one worry: Did (OR did) we pass the test?

9f

Avoid unnecessary capitals.

If you have a tendency to overuse capitals, review **9a** through **9e** and study the following style sheet.

Style Sheet for Capitalization

Capitals	*No capitals*
Chicago, Cook County	a city in that county
New Mexico	a beautiful state
Boston College	a college
Cisco High School	in high school
the Amazon River, Lake Erie	a large river, the lake
Fifth Avenue, Highway 40	a busy street, the new highway
the First Presbyterian Church	the first church built
the French Revolution	a revolution in France
Continental Casualty Company	an insurance company
the Physics Club	the society
a Baptist	baptism
the Medal of Honor	a medal for bravery
Communists in China, Marxism	communistic ideas, socialism
the Lord I worship	a lord among peons
the Stamp Act	the act

the Iron Age	an age of change
Labor Day	the holiday weekend
a Volvo or Toyota	a foreign car
Lieutenant William Jones	William Jones, the lieutenant
President C. B. Jones	C. B. Jones, president of the club
his Uncle Charles	Charles, his uncle
Chemistry B, Geology 100	courses in chemistry, geology
to take Spanish, German	to study a language
in the East, an Eastern rite	to the east, an eastern college
the West, a Westerner	to fly west, a western wind
May, July, Friday, Sunday	summer, fall, winter, spring

■ **Exercise 1**   Write brief sentences correctly using each of the following words.

(1) professor, (2) Professor, (3) college, (4) College, (5) south, (6) South, (7) avenue, (8) Avenue, (9) algebra, (10) Algebra, (11) theater, (12) Theater.

■ **Exercise 2**   Supply capitals wherever needed below.

1. The pacific ocean was discovered in 1513 by a spaniard named balboa.
2. Many americans in the northwest are of polish descent.
3. The battle of new orleans, which made general jackson famous, took place *after* the signing of the peace treaty at ghent.
4. The minister stressed the importance of obeying god's laws as set forth in the bible.
5. The west offers grand sights for tourists: the carlsbad caverns, the grand canyon, yellowstone national park.
6. Both beauty and strength desert everyman, the chief character in the morality play.
7. Many new englanders go south for part of the winter, but usually they turn back north before april.
8. During the easter vacation, after window shopping on fifth avenue and seeing the sights on broadway, I went to bedloe's island, climbed up into the crown of the statue of liberty, and took pictures.
9. My uncle rob said, ''we democrats must elect judge green.''
10. *the confessions of aleister crowley* is an autohagiography.

Italics

10

To indicate italics, underline titles of publications; foreign words; names of ships, trains, aircraft, and spacecraft; titles of works of art; and words spoken of as words. Use italics sparingly for emphasis.

In handwritten or typewritten papers, italics are indicated by underlining. Printers set underlined words in italic type.

TYPEWRITTEN
In David Copperfield Dickens writes of his own boyhood.

PRINTED
In *David Copperfield* Dickens writes of his own boyhood.

10a

Titles of separate publications (books, periodicals, newspapers, bulletins, musical works) and titles of plays and long poems are underlined (italicized) when mentioned in writing.

> Eudora Welty's *Losing Battles* is a novel about life in the Mississippi hill country.   [Note that the author's name is not italicized.]
>
> Sections of *The Tempest* echo the *Essays* of Montaigne.   [An initial *a, an,* or *the* is italicized and capitalized when part of a title.]

He pored over *Time,* the *Atlantic Monthly,* and the *New York Times* (OR the New York *Times*). [An initial *a, an,* or *the* in titles of periodicals is usually not italicized; the name of the city in titles of newspapers is sometimes not italicized.]
Mozart's *Don Giovanni* stays popular through the years.
A Man for All Seasons is one of my favorite plays.

Occasionally quotation marks are used instead of italics for titles of separate publications. The usual practice, however, is to reserve quotation marks for short stories, essays, short poems, songs, articles from periodicals, and subdivisions of books: see **16b**.

David Copperfield opens with a chapter entitled "I Am Born."

Exception: Neither italics nor quotation marks are used in references to the Bible and its parts or to legal documents.

The Bible begins with Genesis.
We must protect our Bill of Rights.

■ **Exercise 1** Underline all words below that should be italicized.

1. While waiting in the dentist's office, I thumbed through an old issue of U.S. News & World Report and scanned an article entitled "Changes Coming in American Colleges."
2. My father reads the editorials in the San Francisco Chronicle and the comic strips in the Chicago Tribune.
3. A performance of Verdi's opera La Traviata was reviewed in the Fort Worth Star Telegram.
4. Huxley's Brave New World differs greatly from Plato's Republic and More's Utopia.

10b

Foreign words and phrases not yet Anglicized are usually underlined (italicized).

What was his *raison d'être?* [French for "reason for being"]
It is the *Zeitgeist.* [German for "spirit of the times"]

Anglicized words are *not* italicized.

cliché (French)	ante-bellum (Latin)
patio (Spanish)	tomahawk (Algonquian)
psyche (Greek)	zombie (West African)

If in doubt about whether or not a word has been Anglicized, consult a dictionary. A double dagger (‡) marks foreign words in *Webster's New World Dictionary*. In the *Standard College Dictionary, The American College Dictionary,* and *The American Heritage Dictionary,* the name of the appropriate foreign language appears in italics immediately after each foreign entry.

■ **Exercise 2** With the aid of your dictionary, list and underline five foreign words or phrases generally printed in italics.

10c

Names of ships, trains, aircraft, and spacecraft and titles of motion pictures and works of art are underlined (italicized).

The *Manhattan,* a huge oil tanker, slashed through the thick ice.

The Lion in Winter is a historical motion picture that suggests modern dilemmas.

Rodin's *The Thinker* is in a garden in Paris.

10d

Words, letters, or figures spoken of as such or used as illustrations are usually underlined (italicized).

There is an obvious affinity between the words *status* and *static.* —RUSSELL LYNES [Sometimes words used as words are put in quotation marks rather than italicized: see **16c**.]

The letters *qu* replaced *cw* in such words as *queen, quoth,* and *quick.* —CHARLES C. FRIES

The first *3* and the final *0* of the serial number are barely legible.

10e

Do not overuse underlining (italics) for emphasis. Do not underline the title of your own paper.

Writers occasionally use italics to stress ideas:

> Probably the single largest group called "drug abusers" are in reality *tasters.* —KENNETH KENISTON

> A poem does not *talk about* ideas; it *enacts* them.
> —JOHN CIARDI

But overuse of italics for emphasis (like overuse of the exclamation point) defeats its own purpose. If you tend to overuse italics to stress ideas, study Section 29. Also try substituting more specific or more forceful words for those you are tempted to underline.

> Of course, Salinger is a *good* writer. [Italics used for emphasis]

> Of course, Salinger is a most skillful and original writer. —GEORGE STEINER [No italics needed]

A title is not italicized when it stands at the head of a book or an article. Accordingly, a student should not underline (italicize) the title at the head of his own paper (unless the title happens to be also the title of a book). See also 8b(4).

■ **Exercise 3** Underline all words in the following sentences that should be italicized.

1. "Our vocabulary may also identify whether we are male or female," writes Roger W. Shuy in his book entitled Discovering American Dialects. "Most high school boys, for example, are not likely to use lovely, peachy, darling, and many words ending in -ie."

2. The Saturday Evening Post, founded by Benjamin Franklin, and the New York Herald Tribune both expired in the 1960's.
3. My handwriting is difficult to read because each o looks like an a and each 9 resembles a 7.
4. In the early 1920's, Rudolph Valentino starred as "the great lover" in The Sheik.
5. To Let was completed in September, 1920, before Galsworthy sailed from Liverpool on the Empress of France to spend the winter in America.
6. In the Spirit of St. Louis, Charles A. Lindbergh made the first solo nonstop transatlantic flight from New York to Paris.
7. Nearly everyone in the office considered the promotion of Mr. Anderson a fait accompli.
8. There are two acceptable ways to spell such words as judgment and cigarette.
9. Stevenson is said to have revised the first chapter of Treasure Island no fewer than thirty-seven times.
10. Michelangelo's Battle of the Centaurs and his Madonna of the Steps are among the world's finest sculptures.

■ **Exercise 4** Copy the following passage, underlining all words that should be italicized.

[1] I was returning home on the America when I read Euripides' Medea. [2] The play was of course in translation, by Murray, I believe; it was reprinted in Riley's Great Plays of Greece and Rome. [3] I admire Medea the play and Medea the woman. [4] Both have a quality of atrocitas that our contemporary primitivism misses. [5] Characters in modern plays are neurotic; Medea was sublimely and savagely mad.

Abbreviations and Numbers

11

In ordinary writing use abbreviations only when appropriate, and spell out numbers that can be expressed simply.

Abbreviations and figures are desirable in tables, footnotes, and bibliographies (see the list on page 424) and in some kinds of special or technical writing. In ordinary writing, however, only certain abbreviations are appropriate, and numbers that can be expressed in one word or two (like *forty-two* or *five hundred*) are usually spelled out.

Abbreviations

11a

In ordinary writing use the abbreviations *Mr., Messrs., Mrs., Mmes., Dr.,* and *St.* (for *Saint*). Spell out *doctor* and *saint* when not followed by proper names.

> Dr. Bell, Mrs. Kay Gibbs, Mr. W. W. Kirtley, St. Francis
> the young doctor, the early life of the saint

Note 1: Such abbreviations as *Prof., Sen., Rep., Gen.,* and *Capt.* may be used before full names or before initials and last names, but not before last names alone.

> Sen. John Sherman Cooper   Senator Cooper
> Capt. P. T. Gaines   Captain Gaines

Note 2: In formal writing the abbreviations *Hon.* and *Rev.* may be used before full names or before initials and last names, but not before last names alone.

FORMAL   Hon. George Smith, Rev. J. C. Lee [NOT Hon. Smith, Rev. Lee]

MORE FORMAL   the Honorable (OR Hon.) George Smith, the Reverend (OR Rev.) J. C. Lee

11b

In ordinary writing spell out names of states, countries, months, days of the week, and units of measurement.

On Sunday, October 10, we spent the night in Tulsa, Oklahoma; the next day we flew to South America.

Only four feet tall, Susan weighs ninety-one pounds.

11c

In ordinary writing spell out *Street, Avenue, Road, Park, Mount, River, Company,* and similar words used as an essential part of proper names.

Fifth Avenue is east of Central Park.

The Ford Motor Company does not expect a strike soon.

Note: Avoid the use of & (for *and*) and such abbreviations as *Bros.* or *Inc.*, except in copying official titles.

A & P; Gold Bros.; Best & Co., Inc.; G. Bell & Sons, Ltd.

11d

In ordinary writing spell out the words *volume, chapter,* and *page* and the names of courses of study.

The chart is on page 46 of chapter 9.

I plan to take chemistry and physics next semester.

11e

In ordinary writing spell out first names.

> George White or James Preston will be elected. [NOT Geo. White, Jas. Preston]

Permissible Abbreviations

In addition to the abbreviations listed in **11a**, the following abbreviations and symbols are permissible and usually desirable.

1. *For titles and degrees after proper names*: Jr., Sr., Esq., D.D., Ph.D., M.A., M.D., C.P.A.

   Mr. Sam Jones, Sr.; Sam Jones, Jr.; Thomas Jones, M.D.

2. *For words used with dates or figures:* A.D., B.C., A.M. OR a.m., P.M. OR p.m., no. OR No., $

   The city of Jerusalem fell in 586 B.C. and again in A.D. 70. At 8 A.M. (OR 8:00 A.M.) he paid the manager $14.25. [Compare "At eight o'clock the next morning he paid the manager over fourteen dollars."]

3. *For the District of Columbia and for names of organizations and government agencies usually referred to by their initials:*

   Washington, D.C.
   DAR, GOP, FBI, AMA, NASA, HEW, FHA [See also 17a(2).]

4. *For certain common Latin expressions, although the English term is usually spelled out in formal writing, as indicated in parentheses*: i.e. (that is), e.g. (for example), viz. (namely), cf. (compare), etc. (and so forth, and so on), vs. (versus), et al. (and others)

If you have any doubt about the spelling or capitalization of an abbreviation, consult a good dictionary.

■ **Exercise 1**   Strike out any form below that is not appropriate in formal writing. (In a few items both forms are appropriate.)

1. in the U.S.; in the United States
2. at 4 P.M.; at four in the afternoon
3. the Rev. Miller; the Reverend James Frank Miller
4. on Magnolia St.; on Magnolia Street
5. Washington, D.C.; Charleston, S.C.
6. FBI; Federal Bureau of Investigation
7. on Aug. 15; on August 15
8. for Jr.; for John Evans, Jr.
9. e.g.; for example
10. before 6 A.M.; before six in the A.M.

Numbers

11f

Although usage varies, writers tend to spell out numbers that can be expressed in one word or two; they regularly use figures for other numbers.

after twenty-two years	after 124 years
only thirty dollars	only $29.99
one fourth OR one-fourth	$56\frac{1}{4}$
five thousand voters	5,261 voters
ten million bushels	10,402,317 bushels

Special Usage Regarding Numbers

1. *Specific time of day*

   2 A.M. OR 2:00 A.M. OR two o'clock in the morning
   4:30 P.M. OR half-past four in the afternoon

2. *Dates*

   March 5, 1973 OR 5 March 1973 [NOT March 5th, 1973]
   May sixth OR the sixth of May OR May 6 OR May 6th
   the thirties OR the 1930's OR the 1930s
   the twentieth century

in 1900[1]   in 1970–1971 OR in 1970–71
from 1940 to 1945 OR 1940–1945 OR 1940–45
[NOT from 1940–1945, from 1940–45]

3. *Addresses*

8 Wildwood Drive, Prescott, Arizona 86301
P.O. Box 14   Route 4   Apartment 3   Room 19
16 Tenth Street   2 East 114 Street OR 2 East 114th Street

4. *Identification numbers*

Channel 13   Highway 35   Henry VIII   *Apollo 14*

5. *Pages and divisions of books*

page 30   chapter 6   part 4   exercise 14

6. *Decimals and percentages*

a 2.5 average   .63 of an inch $12\frac{1}{2}$ percent

7. *Numbers in series and statistics*

two cows, five pigs, and forty-two chickens
125 feet long, 50 feet wide, and 12 feet deep
scores of 17 to 13 and 42 to 3 OR scores of 17-13 and 42-3
The members voted 99 to 23 against it.

8. *Large round numbers*

four billion dollars OR $4 billion OR $4,000,000,000
[Figures are used for emphasis only.]
12,500,000 OR 12.5 million

9. *Numbers beginning sentences*

Six percent of the students voted. OR Only 6 percent of
the students voted. [NOT 6 percent of the students voted.]

10. *Repeated numbers (in legal or commercial writing)*

I enclose ten (10) dollars. OR I enclose ten dollars ($10).

---

[1] The year is never written out except in very formal social announcements
or invitations.

■ **Exercise 2** Correct all errors in the use of abbreviations and numbers in the following sentences. Put a checkmark after any sentence that needs no change.

1. The Thanksgiving holiday begins at one P.M.
2. On June 27th, 1959, Hawaiians voted 18 to 1 for state-hood.
3. Pres. Geo. Washington was born in seventeen hundred and thirty-two.
4. When he was 20 years old, he inherited Mt. Vernon.
5. I lived in Ann Arbor, Mich., from 1968–71.
6. 125 men were sent to the stockade on Aug. 9.
7. At the age of 14 Gordon spent 12 days hunting and fishing with a group of Boy Scouts in the Ozarks.
8. The reception, to be held at 27 Jackson Street, will begin about 8 o'clock.
9. 18,500 fans watched the Eagles win their 7th victory of the season last Friday night.
10. The Tigers gained only 251 yards on the ground and 35 in the air. The final score was 17-6.

■ **Exercise 3** All items below are appropriate in formal writing. Using desirable abbreviations and figures, change each item to an acceptable shortened form.

EXAMPLES
Jude, the saint   *St. Jude*
at two o'clock that afternoon   *at 2* P.M.

1. on the fifteenth of February
2. Ernest Threadgill, a doctor
3. thirty million dollars
4. Mr. Keith, a certified public accountant
5. the United Nations
6. one o'clock in the afternoon
7. by the first of December, 1975
8. at the bottom of the fifteenth page
9. W. A. Peterson, our senator
10. four hundred years before Christ

PUNCTUATION

The Comma

12

Use the comma (which ordinarily indicates a pause and a variation in voice pitch) where it is required by the structure of the sentence.

Just as pauses and variations in voice pitch help to convey the meaning of spoken sentences, commas help to clarify the meaning of written sentences.

> When the lightning struck, James Harvey fainted.
> When the lightning struck James, Harvey fainted.

The sound of a sentence can serve as a guide in using commas.

But many times sound is not a dependable guide. The use of the comma is primarily determined by the structure of the sentence. If you understand this structure (see Section 1), you can learn to apply the basic principles governing comma usage. The following rules cover the usual practices of the best modern writers:

Commas—
a precede coordinating conjunctions (*and, but, or, nor, for*) that join main clauses;
b follow certain introductory elements;

c   separate items in a series (including coordinate adjectives);

d   set off nonrestrictive and other parenthetical elements.

Main Clauses

12a

Commas precede coordinating conjunctions (*and, but, or, nor, for*) that join main clauses.

PATTERN   MAIN CLAUSE, $\begin{cases} and \\ but \\ or \\ nor \\ for \end{cases}$ MAIN CLAUSE.

An oral culture is necessarily a highly ritualized one, and oral poetry has strong affinities with magic.   —NORTHROP FRYE

Paradise was an exclusive country club, but the gates of hell were open to all.   —ARTHUR KOESTLER

Justice stands upon Power, or there is no justice.
—WILLIAM S. WHITE

The peoples of the Sahara have never been united, nor have they even considered uniting in any common cause.
—JAMES R. NEWMAN

No one watches the performance, for everybody is taking part.   —JAN KOTT

This rule also applies to such elliptical constructions as the following:

Pessimism is no truer than optimism, nor positivism than mysticism.   —ALDOUS HUXLEY [Compare "Pessimism is no truer than optimism, nor is positivism truer than mysticism."]

111

Note 1: A comma precedes a coordinating conjunction that links the main clauses of a compound-complex sentence (that is, a sentence with at least two main clauses and one subordinate clause):

> Men who are engaged in a daily struggle for survival do not think of old age, for they do not expect to see it.
> —JOHN KENNETH GALBRAITH

Note 2: Some writers use a comma before *yet* and *so* (meaning "therefore") linking main clauses. Others use semicolons: see 14a.

> No air moves in or out of the room, yet I am curiously affected by emanations from the immediate surroundings.
> —E. B. WHITE

> They are hopeless and humble, so he loves them.
> —E. M. FORSTER

Caution: Do not confuse the compound sentence with a simple sentence containing a compound predicate.

> Colonel Cathcart had courage, and he never hesitated to volunteer his men for any target available. [Compound sentence—comma before *and*]

> Colonel Cathcart had courage and never hesitated to volunteer his men for any target available. —JOSEPH HELLER [Compound predicate—no comma before *and*]

Only occasionally, for special emphasis, do writers depart from this pattern of punctuation:

> Artists always seek a new technique, and will continue to do so as long as their work excites them. —E. M. FORSTER

Exceptions to 12a

1. *Omission of the comma*

When the main clauses are short, the comma is frequently omitted before *and* or *or*. Before the conjunctions *but* and *for,* the comma is usually needed to prevent confusion with the prepositions *but* and *for.* Sometimes, especially in narrative writing, the comma is omitted even when the clauses are long.

> The next night the wind shifted and the thaw began.
> —RACHEL CARSON

> She had never been kissed before and she was pleased to discover that it was an unexceptional experience and all a matter of the mind's control.   —FLANNERY O'CONNOR

2. Use of the semicolon instead of the comma

Sometimes the coordinating conjunction is preceded by a semicolon instead of the usual comma, especially when the main clauses have internal punctuation or reveal a striking contrast. See also **14a.**

> Whether or not America is sick or violent **,** it surely is preachy and predictable **;** and one shares in this quality oneself **,** as if it were a public utility.   —WILFRID SHEED

> Space can be mapped and crossed and occupied without definable limit **;** but it can never be conquered.
> —ARTHUR C. CLARKE

■ **Exercise 1**   Join the sentences in the following items with a coordinating conjunction, using the comma (or the semicolon) appropriately.

EXAMPLE
We cannot win the battle. We cannot afford to lose it.
*We cannot win the battle **,** nor can we afford to lose it.*

1. A crisis strikes. Another presidential fact-finding committee is born.
2. The new leash law did not put all dogs behind bars. It did not make the streets safe for cats.
3. Motorists may admit their guilt and pay a fine immediately. They may choose to appear in court within thirty days and plead not guilty.

4. They decided not to take a vacation. They needed the money to remodel their kitchen.
5. The leader of the band can sing, dance, and whistle. He cannot read music.

Introductory Elements

12b

Commas follow introductory elements such as adverb clauses, long phrases, transitional expressions, and interjections.

(1) Introductory adverb clauses

> PATTERN   **ADVERB CLAUSE, MAIN CLAUSE.**

> Whenever I tried to put chains on a tire, the car would maliciously wrap them around a rear axle. —JAMES THURBER
>
> If he is a key man on his team, an injury is often insufficient to keep him on the sidelines. —PAUL GALLICO

A writer may omit the comma after an introductory adverb clause, especially when the clause is short, if the omission does not make for difficult reading.

> As soon as I saw the elephant I knew with perfect certainty that I ought not to shoot him. —GEORGE ORWELL

Note: When the adverb clause *follows* the main clause, there is usually no pause and no need for a comma.

> PATTERN   **MAIN CLAUSE ADVERB CLAUSE.**

> The sun shone as if there were no death. —SAUL BELLOW
>
> He stands amazed while she serenely twists her legs into the lotus position. —JOHN UPDIKE

Such adverb clauses, however, are preceded by a comma

if they are parenthetical to sentence meaning or if a distinct pause is required in the reading.

> A free society cannot get along without heroes, because they are the most vivid means of exhibiting the power of free men.
> —ARTHUR M. SCHLESINGER, JR.

> Perhaps the initiative and referendum have their uses, although the governments of most eastern states have declined to give the voters so much authority. —RICHARD L. NEUBERGER

> Events recorded in the Book of Exodus are thought by many to be exaggeration or fantasy, whereas Velikovsky has shown that they are historically accurate. —MARY BUCKALEW [Here *whereas* means "when in truth."]

(2) Long introductory phrases

> In the folklore of white America, Harlem has long been considered exotic as well as dangerous territory.
> —LEONARD KRIEGEL

> Before the discovery of insulin in 1921, all young diabetics died before they could grow up and reproduce.
> —LUCY EISENBERG

Sometimes commas are omitted after long introductory phrases when no misreading would result:

> After months of listening for some meager clue he suddenly began to talk in torrents. —ARTHUR L. KOPIT

Introductory phrases containing a gerund, a participle, or an infinitive, even though short, must often be followed by a comma to prevent misreading.

> Before leaving, the soldiers demolished the fort.
> Because of his effort to escape, his punishment was increased.

Short introductory prepositional phrases, except when they are distinctly parenthetical expressions (such as *in fact* or *for example*), are seldom followed by commas.

> At ninety she was still active.
> During the night he heard many noises.

(3) Introductory transitional expressions and inter-jections

Interjections as well as transitional expressions (such as *for example, in fact, on the other hand, in the second place*) are generally considered parenthetical: see **12d(3)**. When used as introductory elements, they are ordinarily followed by commas.

> Intelligent she was not. In fact, she veered in the opposite direction.   —MAX SHULMAN

> "Well, move the ball or move the body."   —ALLEN JACKSON

■ **Exercise 2**   In each sentence below, find the main clause and identify the preceding element as an adverb clause or as a phrase. Then determine whether or not to use a comma after the introductory element.

¹In order to pay his way through college George worked at night in an iron foundry.   ²During this time he became acquainted with all the company's operations.   ³At the end of four years' observation of George's work the foundry owner offered George a position as manager.   ⁴Although George had planned to attend medical school and enter his father's profession he found now that the kind of work he had been doing had a far greater appeal for him.   ⁵In fact he accepted the offer without hesitation.

Items in a Series

12c

Commas separate items in a series (including coordinate adjectives).

The punctuation of a series depends upon its form:

> The air was *raw, dank, gray.*   [*a, b, c*]
> The air was *raw, dank,* and *gray.*   [*a, b,* and *c*]
> The air was *raw* and *dank* and *gray.*   [*a* and *b* and *c*]

(1) Words, phrases, or clauses in a series

There are no woods now, no white water, no clear pools.
—BERNARD DE VOTO

These trends discourage all compassionate people, darken our prospect, and chill our once warm faith in meliorism.
—ALLAN NEVINS

Go to your favorite drugstore tomorrow, buy yourself a bottle of the American Dream in the new economy size, shake well before using, and live luxuriously ever afterward.
—DAVID L. COHN

The comma before the conjunction is often omitted when the series takes the form *a*, *b*, and *c*. But students are usually advised to use the final comma, if only because it is sometimes needed to prevent confusion.

CONFUSING   The natives ate beans, onions, rice and honey.
               [Was the rice and honey a mixture?]
CLEAR   The natives ate beans, onions, rice, and honey.
          OR   The natives ate beans, onions, and rice and honey.

(2) Coordinate adjectives

Use a comma between coordinate adjectives not linked by a coordinating conjunction.

It was a dank and gray day.   It was a dank, gray day.

Coordinate adjectives may modify one word or a word group:

Trexler stifled a small, internal smile. —E. B. WHITE
[Compare "a *smile* that was small and internal."]

The air was full of acid and a purplish, spleeny winter mist.
—HERBERT GOLD   [Compare "a *winter mist* that was purplish and spleeny."]

■ **Exercise 3**   By omitting words and shifting word order, change each sentence in the following paragraph so that it will contain items in a series or coordinate adjectives.

EXAMPLES

Drowsiness and drunkenness are difficult to hide; so is hostility.
Drowsiness, drunkenness, and hostility are difficult to hide.

It was a football game that was close and exciting.
It was a close, exciting football game.

[1]Pete More used to carry a lunch pail that was old and battered. [2]Every morning he would go past our house and wait on the corner for his ride; he would hand his lunch pail up to one of the men on the truck and climb up himself, and then he would go rolling away. [3]Every year Pete and his lunch pail got a little older and a little more battered—a little more used up. [4]Then one awful day we heard the blast at the plant and saw the sky black with smoke, and we watched the streets fill with people who were tense and fearful. [5]That day was the end of old Pete and of his battered lunch pail, and it was the end of the jokes we made about them both.

■ **Exercise 4**   Using commas as necessary, supply coordinate adjectives to modify each of the following.

EXAMPLE
a blue ribbon   *a long, brilliant blue ribbon*

1. stock market
2. old master
3. public library
4. best seller
5. chocolate milk

Parenthetical Elements

12d

Commas set off nonrestrictive clauses or phrases and other parenthetical elements ("interrupters"). Commas do not set off restrictive clauses or phrases.

Use a comma after a parenthetical element at the beginning of a sentence, before a parenthetical element at the end of a sentence, and both before and after a parenthetical element within a sentence.

> Generally speaking, an experienced driver does not fear the open road.
> An experienced driver does not fear the open road, generally speaking.
> An experienced driver, generally speaking, does not fear the open road.

Caution: When two commas are needed to set off a parenthetical element, do not forget one of the commas.

> CONFUSING   An experienced driver generally speaking, does not fear the open road.

Your voice can help you punctuate parenthetical elements. Notice differences in the way you read the following sentences aloud.

> My mother, sitting near me, smiled knowingly.
> A mother sitting near me smiled knowingly.

Remember that adjective clauses beginning with *that* are restrictive. Adjective clauses beginning with *who* (*whom, whose*) and *which* may be restrictive or nonrestrictive.

(1) Nonrestrictive clauses and phrases are set off by commas. Restrictive clauses and phrases are not set off.

NONRESTRICTIVE CLAUSES AND PHRASES

Adjective clauses and phrases are nonrestrictive when they are not essential to the meaning of the main clause and may be omitted. Such modifiers are parenthetical and are set off by commas.

> This intrigued Newton, *who sought knowledge in many strange places.* —JOSEPH F. GOODAVAGE [The *who* clause is nonessential to the meaning of "This intrigued Newton."]

Major famines, *which were not infrequent earlier in the 1900s,* have ceased. —J. H. PLUMB [The *which* clause provides nonessential information.]

He tossed the letter aside and pulled his apple pie, *topped with a melting scoop of vanilla ice cream,* toward him. —TRUMAN CAPOTE [The nonrestrictive phrase can be changed to a nonrestrictive clause: "*which was* topped with a melting scoop of vanilla ice cream." This parenthetical element has a fixed position: after *pie,* the word modified.]

She spoke with great distinctness, *moving her lips meticulously,* as if in parlance with the deaf. —DOROTHY PARKER [The nonrestrictive phrase can be shifted to the beginning of the sentence: "*Moving her lips meticulously,* she spoke with great distinctness."]

RESTRICTIVE CLAUSES AND PHRASES

Restrictive clauses and phrases follow and limit the words they modify. They are essential to the meaning of the main clause and are not set off by commas.

Students *who use drugs* are usually treated by the mass media as an alien wart upon the student body of America. —KENNETH KENISTON [The *who* clause is essential to the meaning of the sentence: not all students are treated in this way, but only those who use drugs.]

I began writing one-act plays *that tried to capture not verisimilitude but reality.* —THORNTON WILDER [An adjective clause beginning with *that* is restrictive.]

The two things *most universally desired* are power and admiration. —BERTRAND RUSSELL [The restrictive phrase can be expanded to a clause: "*that are* most universally desired."]

Sometimes a clause or phrase may be either nonrestrictive or restrictive. The writer signifies his meaning by using or by omitting commas.

NONRESTRICTIVE He spent hours caring for the Indian guides, *who were sick with malaria.* [He cared for all the Indian guides. They were all sick with malaria.]

RESTRICTIVE He spent hours caring for the Indian guides *who were sick with malaria.* [Some of the Indian guides were sick with malaria. He cared only for the sick ones.]

■ **Exercise 5** Use commas to set off nonrestrictive clauses and phrases in the following sentences. Put a checkmark after any sentence that needs no further punctuation.

1. The James Lee who owns the bank is a grandson of the one who founded it.
2. James Lee who owns this bank and five others is one of the wealthiest men in the state.
3. The coach called out to Higgins who got up from the bench and trotted over to him.
4. The coach who chewed on cigars but never lighted them threw one away and reached for another.
5. Anyone who saw him could tell that something was troubling him.
6. All banks which fail to report by the following Saturday will be closed.
7. All banks failing to report will be closed.
8. Henry betrayed the man who had helped him build his fortune.
9. William White who had helped Henry build his fortune died yesterday.
10. My father hoping that I would remain at home offered me a share in his business.

(2) Nonrestrictive appositives, contrasted elements, geographical names, and most items in dates and addresses are set off by commas.

Notice the similarity between the appositive and the contrasted element that follow and the corresponding nonrestrictive clauses:

Those insects are termites, *distant cousins of roaches.* [Nonrestrictive appositive]

Those insects are termites, *which are distant cousins of roaches.* [Nonrestrictive clause]

He gave me a mini-car, *not a white elephant.* [Contrasted element]

He gave me a mini-car, *which was not a white elephant.* [Nonrestrictive clause]

NONRESTRICTIVE APPOSITIVES

But inertia, *the great minimizer,* provided them with the usual excuses. —MARY McCARTHY

The most visible victims of pollution, fish are only a link in a chain from microscopic life to man. —GEORGE GOODMAN [The appositive precedes rather than follows *fish.*]

The peaks float in the sky, *fantastic pyramids of flame.* —ARTHUR C. CLARKE [Notice that the appositive could be shifted to the beginning of the sentence.]

Was the letter from Frank Evans, *Ph.D.,* or from F. H. Evans, *M.D.*? [Abbreviations after names are treated like nonrestrictive appositives.]

Note: Commas do not set off restrictive appositives:

His son *James* is sick. [*James,* not his son William]
The word *malapropism* is derived from Sheridan's *The Rivals.*
Do you refer to Samuel Butler *the poet* or to Samuel Butler *the novelist*?

CONTRASTED ELEMENTS

President Roosevelt, *not Congress,* made the decision.

She prefers to camp out, *not to pay for a motel room.*

Their metaphors were of sound and smell, *but not sight.* —DANIEL BELL

The goal was achievement, *not adjustment;* the young were taught to work, *not to socialize.* —ALLEN WHEELIS [Only one comma sets off a parenthetical element before a semicolon or a period.]

Note 1: Usage is divided regarding the placement of a comma before *but* in such parenthetical elements as the following:

Other citizens who disagree with me base their disagreement, not on facts different from the ones I know, but on a different set of values. —RENÉ DUBOS

But I think I should prefer to go out laughing, not at death itself but at something irrelevantly funny enough to make me forget it. —JOSEPH WOOD KRUTCH

Note 2: When an antithetical element is considered essential to sentence meaning, it is not set off by commas:

One works for justice not in the hope that the evil of the past can be undone but in the hope that there shall be a liveable future. —LEONARD KRIEGEL

■ **Exercise 6** Use commas to set off nonrestrictive appositives and contrasted elements in the following paragraph.

¹Years ago I read *The Marks of an Educated Man* an interesting book by Albert Wiggam. ²According to Wiggam, one outstanding characteristic of the educated man is that he "links himself with a great cause" one that requires selfless service. ³Certainly many famous men whether scientists or artists or philosophers have dedicated their lives to the cause of serving others. ⁴For example, Louis Pasteur the famous French chemist devoted his life to the study of medicine to benefit mankind. ⁵And the artist Michelangelo served humanity by creating numerous works of lasting beauty. ⁶Francis of Assisi a saint of the twelfth century was also devoted to a great cause. ⁷His life was the mirror of his creed a reflection of his ardent love for others. ⁸Among twentieth-century philosophers was Albert Schweitzer a well-known missionary and physician. ⁹Schweitzer a person who worked for both peace and brotherhood was like Pasteur, Michelangelo, and St. Francis in that he linked himself with a great cause not with transitory, selfish aims. ¹⁰I think that the author Wiggam should use the adjective *committed* or *dedicated* not *educated* to describe the man who devotes himself to a noble cause.

■ **Exercise 7** Using appropriate commas, compose three sentences with nonrestrictive appositives and two sentences with contrasted elements.

**GEOGRAPHICAL NAMES, ITEMS IN DATES
AND ADDRESSES**

Pasadena **,** California **,** is the site of the Rose Bowl.
The letter was addressed to Mr. J. L. Karnes **,** Clayton **,**
Delaware 19938. [The zip code is not separated by a
comma from the name of the state.]
Tom left for Vietnam in January **,** 1968 **,** and arrived home
on Wednesday **,** May 27 **,** 1970. OR Tom left for Vietnam
in January 1968 and arrived home on Wednesday **,** 27 May
1970. [Note that commas may be omitted when the day
of the month is not given or when the day of the month
precedes rather than follows the month.]

■ **Exercise 8** Insert commas where needed below.

1. My son was born on Friday June 11 1971 in Denver.
2. He was inducted into the army at Fort Oglethorpe Georgia
on 30 September 1942.
3. William Congreve was born in Bardsey England on January
24 1670.
4. The publisher's address is 757 Third Avenue New York New
York 10017.
5. Pearl Harbor Hawaii was bombed on December 7 1941.

**(3) Parenthetical expressions and other parenthetical
elements are set off by commas.**

PARENTHETICAL EXPRESSIONS

The term *parenthetical* is correctly applied to all nonrestrictive elements discussed under **12d**. But it may also
be applied to such transitional expressions as *on the other
hand, first, in the first place, in fact, to tell the truth, however,
that is, then, therefore,* and *for example* and to such expressions as *I hope, I believe,* and *he says* (sometimes called
"interrupters"). Expressions that come at the beginning of
a sentence are treated by both **12b** and **12d**.

You will **,** *then* **,** accept our offer?
To tell the truth **,** we anticipated bad luck.

The work is, *in fact,* very satisfactory.
We think, *however,* that he should refuse. [When *however* means "no matter how," it is a subordinator, not a parenthetical word: "The trip will be hard, *however* you go."]
Organic foods will, *I believe,* gain in popularity.

Expressions such as *also, too, of course, indeed, perhaps, at least,* and *likewise,* when they cause little or no pause in reading, are frequently not set off by commas.

Your efforts will of course be appreciated. OR Your efforts will, of course, be appreciated.

OTHER PARENTHETICAL ELEMENTS

Oh, peace is a dream. [Mild interjection]
Animal lovers, write letters of protest now. [Direct address]
Win or lose, it is fun to play the game. [Parenthetical phrase]
The legends portraying the wolf as an enemy of man, *although they are widely believed,* are not based on facts. [Parenthetical clause]
Trouble seemed inevitable, *tensions among the workers mounting daily.* [Absolute construction]

Note: With direct quotations, such expressions as *he said, she asked, I replied,* and *we shouted* are also set off by commas. See also **16a(4)**.

He said, "Our rose-hips tea is really different."
"Our rose-hips tea," he said, "is really different."
"Our rose-hips tea is really different," he said.

12e

Occasionally a comma, though not called for by any of the major principles already discussed, may be needed to prevent misreading.

Use **12e** sparingly to justify your commas. In a general sense, nearly all commas are used to prevent misreading or to make reading easier. Your mastery of the comma will come through application of the more specific major principles (a, b, c, d) to the structure of your sentences.

CONFUSING   Inside the old house was gaily decorated. [*Inside the old house* may be read as a unit.]
BETTER   Inside, the old house was gaily decorated.

CONFUSING   A few weeks before I had seen him in an off-Broadway play.
BETTER   A few weeks before, I had seen him in an off-Broadway play.

■ **Exercise 9**   All commas in the following passage are correctly used. Explain the reason for each comma by referring to **12a** (main clauses joined by a coordinating conjunction), **12b** (introductory elements), **12c** (items in a series, including coordinate adjectives), or **12d** (nonrestrictive and other parenthetical elements).

[1]It is easy to dismiss the free university movement as politically impotent. [2]Like nonviolence in the civil rights movement, setting a good example on the campus (''blackmailing the institution with quality'') has not worked. [3]Habit, self-interest, and power dominate the university as they do the wider society, in spite of rebellions, confrontations, or riots. [4]The faculty and administration are in charge, and they intend to keep things that way. [5]But the university is a different place from what it was in 1962 or 1965, and we would make two claims for the free university movement: first, that it take major responsibility, through the rapid spread of counterculture, for the idea of a student-centered curriculum; second, that it take partial responsibility for raising hard questions about the elitism of universities, which we expect will be central to campus struggles in the seventies.

—FLORENCE HOWE and PAUL LAUTER[1]

---

[1]From "What's Happened to the 'Free University'" by Florence Howe and Paul Lauter, printed in the *Saturday Review*, June 20, 1970; the article is an excerpt from *The Conspiracy of the Young* by Florence Howe and Paul Lauter (1970). Copyright 1970 Saturday Review, Inc. Reprinted by permission.

■ **Exercise 10** Insert commas where needed in the following sentences (selected and adapted from the *New Yorker*). Be prepared to explain the reason for each comma used.

1. Dogs monkeys and fruit flies have already distinguished themselves in outer space but as yet neither Russia nor the United States has produced an astrohorse.
2. She wore a pince-nez which she took off to convey an armory of responses.
3. He was in truth slightly bowlegged but he concealed the flaw by standing with one knee bent.
4. A black cloud crossed the city flashed two or three fierce bolts rumbled halfheartedly and passed on.
5. The envelope beside my plate the other morning addressed in a florid feminine backhand was tinted the particular robin's-egg blue reserved for babies' bassinets.
6. For a week suspended in air we had given thought to becoming engaged—I more than she perhaps for she was engaged already.
7. When Miss Meltzer reminded Feder that there existed neither sufficiently powerful lamps nor properly designed fixtures for the project he said "Of course they don't exist Meltzer. We're going to create them."
8. Two girls one of them with pert buckteeth and eyes as black as vest buttons the other with white skin and flesh-colored hair like an underdeveloped photograph of a redhead came and sat on my right.
9. He dies of pneumonia shortly afterward but returns as a robust ghost to steal the overcoats off the backs of half the citizens in the city triumphantly righting one wrong with a dozen wrongs.
10. Technology originally associated with the civilizing arts of building and weaving has replaced Nature as the No. 1 opponent of human society.

Superfluous Commas

13

Do not use superfluous commas.

Unnecessary or misplaced commas are false or awkward signals that may confuse the reader. If you tend to use too many commas, remember that, although the comma ordinarily signals a pause (see Section 12), not every pause calls for a comma. As you read the following sentence aloud, for example, you may pause naturally at least once, but no commas are necessary.

> Incidents like the eastern Illinois spraying raise a question that is not only scientific but moral.   —RACHEL CARSON

13a

Do not use a comma to separate the subject from its verb or the verb from its object.

The encircled commas below should be omitted.

> Even women with unlisted telephone numbers⊙ receive crank calls.   [Needless separation of subject and verb]
> He assigned⊙ "ESP as a Weapon."   [A title, not direct discourse—needless separation of verb and object]
> Cicero says⊙ that luxury is the mother of avarice.   [Indirect discourse—needless separation of verb and object]

Note: When the subject is heavily modified, a comma before the verb sometimes helps to clarify.

Rain coming at frequent intervals and in sufficient amounts
to fill the ponds, the cisterns, and the many small containers
near the house⊙ is productive of mosquitoes.

13b

**Do not use an inappropriate comma with a coordi-
nating conjunction.**

The encircled commas below should be omitted.

The flight of *Apollo 13* was a brief⊙ and disappointing
venture.
What he said⊙ and what he did seemed contradictory.
In that class I did not learn⊙ or unlearn anything.
The Air Force continued to debunk UFO sightings, but⊙
the committee proceeded with its scientific investigation.

13c

**Do not use commas to set off words or short phrases
(especially introductory ones) that are not parenthetical or that are very slightly so.**

The encircled commas below should be omitted.

Today⊙ air travel is a commonplace.
It is easy to relay messages⊙ by wire⊙ to any continent.

13d

**Do not use commas to set off restrictive (necessary)
clauses, restrictive phrases, or restrictive appositives.**

The encircled commas below should be omitted.

Everyone⊙ who smokes cigarettes⊙ risks losing about ten
years of life. [Restrictive clause: see **12d(1)**.]
For years she has not eaten anything⊙ seasoned with onions
or garlic. [Restrictive phrase: see **12d(1)**.]

Only in ancient Spanish was *k* used, and the letter⊙ *w*⊙ has never had a place in the Spanish alphabet. [Restrictive appositive: see **12d(2)**.]

13e

Do not use a comma before the first item or after the last item of a series (including a series of coordinate adjectives).

The encircled commas below should be omitted.

I enjoy the study of⊙ ecology, parapsychology, and Eastern philosophy. [Needless comma before first item of series. A colon here would also be needless, since there is no formal introduction: see **17d**.]

In the garage sale were a few novels, such as⊙ *Ben Hur, Gone with the Wind,* and *Catch-22.* [Needless comma before first item of series]

Henry became a firm, stubborn, incompetent⊙ banker. [Needless comma after last item of series of coordinate adjectives]

Frogs, newts, and salamanders⊙ are all classified as amphibians. [Needless comma after last item of series; also needless separation of subject and verb]

■ **Exercise 1** Study the structure of the sentence below; then answer the question that follows by giving a specific rule number (such as **13a**, **13d**) for each item. Be prepared to explain your answers in class.

Now when you say ''newly rich'' you picture a middle-aged and corpulent man who has a tendency to remove his collar at formal dinners and is in perpetual hot water with his ambitious wife and her titled friends. —F. SCOTT FITZGERALD

Why is there no comma after (1) *Now,* (2) *say,* (3) *middle-aged,* (4) *man,* (5) *collar,* (6) *dinners,* or (7) *wife?*

■ **Exercise 2** Encircle each superfluous comma in the following sentences (selected and adapted from Henry David Thoreau).

Be prepared to explain the reason for each comma that you do not encircle.

1. I would rather sit on a pumpkin, and have it all to myself, than be crowded on a velvet cushion.
2. I, also, heard of such names as, Zoheth, Beriah, Amaziah, Bethuel, and Shearjashub.
3. We admire Chaucer, for his sturdy, English, wit.
4. The fishermen say, that the ''thundering of the pond,'' scares the fishes, and, prevents their biting.
5. Under a government, which imprisons any, unjustly, the true place for a just man is also in prison.

■ **Exercise 3**   Change the structure and the punctuation of the following sentences according to the pattern of the examples.

EXAMPLE

A motorcyclist saw our flashing lights, and he stopped to offer aid.   [An appropriate comma: see **12a.**]

A motorcyclist saw our flashing lights and stopped to offer aid.   [Comma no longer needed]

1. The hail stripped leaves from trees, and it pounded early gardens.
2. Some science fiction presents newly discovered facts, and it predicts the future accurately.
3. Carter likes the work, and he may make a career of it.

EXAMPLE

If any student destroyed public property, he was expelled.   [An appropriate comma: see **12b.**]

Any student who destroyed public property was expelled.   [Comma no longer needed]

4. If a teacher leads rather than demands, he usually gets good results.
5. If the man is willing to work, he can earn his living there.

The Semicolon

14

Use the semicolon between two main clauses not joined by a coordinating conjunction (*and, but, or, nor, for*) and between coordinate elements containing commas. Use the semicolon only between parts of equal rank.

Read aloud the following strings of words; notice the length of pauses and any voice variations.

> just as radio stretches our ears   radar extends our eyes
> radio stretches our ears   radar extends our eyes

The comma, the period, and the semicolon indicate differences in the way sentences are spoken.

> Just as radio stretches our ears, radar extends our eyes.
> Radio stretches our ears. Radar extends our eyes.
> Radio stretches our ears; radar extends our eyes.

Sometimes called a weak period, the semicolon can be used to join closely related sentences.

Although sound helps you to punctuate, you should rely chiefly on your knowledge of the structure of the sentence. If you can distinguish between phrases and clauses, between main and subordinate clauses (see 1d and 1e), you should have little trouble using the semicolon.

14a

Use the semicolon between two main clauses not joined by a coordinating conjunction (*and, but, or, nor, for*).

> PATTERN   MAIN CLAUSE; MAIN CLAUSE.

Every statement was verified; every fact was authenticated.
—VIRGINIA WOOLF

Nations no longer declare war or wage war; they declare or wage mutual suicide.   —NORMAN COUSINS

At this time we do nothing but question ourselves; rosy little Hamlets, we are forever busy with self-communion.
—J. B. PRIESTLEY

Note: The semicolon also separates main clauses not joined by a coordinating conjunction in compound-complex sentences.

A bird does not fly because it has wings; it has wings because it flies.   —ROBERT ARDREY

Remember that conjunctive adverbs and transitional phrases used as conjunctive adverbs, such as those listed below, are not grammatically equivalent to coordinating conjunctions.

accordingly	henceforth	nevertheless
also	however	on the contrary
anyhow	in addition	on the other hand
as a result	indeed	otherwise
at the same time	in fact	still
besides	in other words	that is
consequently	instead	then
for example	likewise	therefore
furthermore	meanwhile	thus
hence	moreover	

Use a semicolon before one of these words or phrases when

133

it connects main clauses: see **3b**. Use a comma after it only if you consider it distinctly parenthetical.

> John broke his ankle skiing; then he bought a snowmobile.
> The new regulation permits numerous absences; however, it does not encourage them.
> Any medicine can be dangerous; for example, even aspirin can cause illness.

Note: *Yet* and *so* (meaning "therefore") linking main clauses may be preceded either by a semicolon or by a comma: see **12a**.

> The tendency is manifestly perverse and unfair; yet it has some justification. —ERIC HOFFER
>
> The town is one of those that people pass through on the way to somewhere else; so its inhabitants have become expert in giving directions. —JOHN UPDIKE

Caution: Do not overwork the semicolon. Often compound sentences are better revised according to the principles of subordination: see Section **24** and also **14c**.

Exception to 14a: Coordinating conjunctions between main clauses are often preceded by a semicolon (instead of the usual comma) if the clauses have internal punctuation or reveal a striking contrast. See also **12a**.

> Politicians and statesmen are prime targets; and, above everyone else, our Presidents are sitting ducks.
> —JOHN STEINBECK
>
> Profound experiences stimulate thought; but such thoughts do not look very adequate on paper. —WALTER KAUFMANN

■ **Exercise 1** Change each of the following items to conform to Pattern **14a**, as shown in the examples below.

> EXAMPLES
> The new translation is not poetic. Nor is its language really modern.
>
> *The new translation is not poetic; its language is not really modern.*

Some vegetables are high in protein. Soy beans, for example, contain more protein than beef.
Some vegetables are high in protein; for example, soy beans contain more protein than beef. [Position of transitional expression is variable: see 3b.]

1. A recession is not a depression. Nor is a cigarette cough necessarily emphysema.
2. Henry VIII had Anne Boleyn executed. It was her daughter, however, who later ruled England.
3. The stickers give the point of origin. And the majority of them say "Made in Japan."
4. The one-sided contest was not over yet. The panting, tormented bull lowered his head in readiness for another charge.

14b

Use the semicolon to separate a series of items which themselves contain commas.

This use of the semicolon helps to clarify, showing the reader at a glance the main divisions, which would be more difficult to distinguish if only commas were used throughout the sentence.

> I came to this conclusion after talking in Moscow last spring with three kinds of people concerned: foreign diplomats, students, and correspondents; the new rector of Friendship University; and the harried Afro-Asian students themselves.
> —PRISCILLA JOHNSON

> The challenge of facing a large audience, expectant but unaroused; the laughter that greets a sally at the outset, then the stillness as the power of imagery and ideas takes hold; the response that flows, audibly or inaudibly, from the audience to the speaker; the fresh extemporizing without which a lecture is dead; the tension and timing as the talk nears the hour; and the unexpected conclusion—this is what every professional speaker comes to know. —EDWARD WEEKS

14c

Use the semicolon only between parts of equal rank, not between a clause and a phrase or between a main clause and a subordinate clause.

PARTS OF EQUAL RANK

A bitter wind swept the dead leaves along the street; it cast them high in the air and against the buildings. [Two main clauses]

I hope to spend my vacation in Canada; I enjoy the fishing there. [Two main clauses]

PARTS OF UNEQUAL RANK

A bitter wind swept the dead leaves along the street, casting them high in the air and against the buildings. [Main clause and phrase, separated by a comma]

I hope to spend my vacation in Canada, where I enjoy the fishing. [Main clause and subordinate clause, separated by a comma]

Note: At times a semicolon is apparently used between parts of unequal rank. However, closer examination usually reveals that the semicolon is in reality a mark of coordination: following the semicolon is an elliptical construction.

Burns compares his mistress to a "red, red rose"; Wordsworth his to "a violet by a mossy stone half hidden from the eye." —C. S. LEWIS [*Compares* is clearly understood after *Wordsworth*.]

The theory applied equally well to Mrs. Kerr's case; perhaps even better since it also confirmed the deep-rooted public conviction that no woman really knows what a car is for. —HARPER'S MAGAZINE [*The theory applied* is clearly understood after *perhaps*.]

Sometimes, as an aid to clarity, commas are used to mark omissions.

The logic and the mathematics are impeccable; the premises, wholly invalid. —ARTHUR C. CLARKE

■ **Exercise 2** In the following sentences (selected from *Look*), all semicolons are correctly used. Be prepared to give the reason for the use of each semicolon.

1. Intensity is what counts; we should all die spent and out of breath.
2. Youth is impatient; its "leaders," intractable.
3. I found an old friend, now living in California, who is almost my astrological twin; that is, we were born the same month and year, within two days of each other (her birthplace was Mexico City and mine was Nebraska).
4. We can create honest, caring politics; more pleasurable, less threatening sexuality; more humane business ethics; deeper religious concerns.

■ **Exercise 3** Compose four sentences to illustrate various uses of the semicolon.

■ **Exercise 4** Insert semicolons where they are needed in the following sentences. Substitute commas for any semicolons standing between parts of unequal rank. Put a checkmark after each sentence that needs no revision.

1. Although the educational channel at times presents uninteresting panel discussions; at least tedious advertisements do not interrupt.
2. Ever present problems are crime, poverty, strikes, and taxation cannot solve them all.
3. Don went jogging one afternoon and never returned, therefore, he was numbered among the tens of thousands who disappear every year.
4. Mac goes around in par now; he has trimmed several strokes off his game since we played together last.
5. Hank had dismantled his motor; intending to give it a complete overhaul for the following week's races.
6. He lamented that he had no suggestions to offer, however, he spent the next forty minutes offering them.
7. In our unit at that time there were Lieutenant Holmes, a criminologist by profession and a university lecturer on penology, Captain Sturm, in peacetime a United States Steel executive, and two old majors, previously retired and now writing their memoirs.

8. In a few years TV sets will replace the wrist watch; cars will speed about on airways rather than on highways.
9. In September a box of candles costs $1.49; in December, $1.98; in July, $1.05.
10. After seeing a movie that showed peasants digging in rice fields, the artist Willem de Kooning painted *Excavation,* an abstract work that now hangs in the Chicago Institute of Modern Art.

General Exercise on the Comma and the Semicolon

■ **Exercise 5** Carefully review the sentences below showing correct usage of the comma and the semicolon. Then punctuate sentences 1–10 appropriately.

12a Pat poured gasoline into the hot tank, for he had not read the warning in his tractor manual.
12b Since Pat had not read the warning in his tractor manual, he poured gasoline into the hot tank.
In very large print in the tractor manual, the warning is conspicuous.
12c Pat did not read the tractor manual, observe the warning, or wait for the tank to cool.
Pat was a rash, impatient young mechanic.
12d Pat did not read his tractor manual, which warned against pouring gasoline into a hot tank.
Pat, a careless young man, poured gasoline into the hot tank of his tractor.
12e First, warnings should be read.
14a Pat ignored the warning in the tractor manual; he poured gasoline into the hot tank.
Pat poured gasoline into the hot tank; thus he caused the explosion.
14b At the hospital Pat said that he had not read the warning; that he had, of course, been careless; and that he would never again, under any circumstances, pour gasoline into a hot tank.

1. I did not choose the "pass-fail" system of grading for I do not know yet what my major will be.

2. The professor a Mr. Redmon merely mentioned the possibility of "pop teach-ins" from that moment forward students attended all his lectures and read all his long assignments.

3. The stalls of the open market along the wharf were filled with tray after tray of glassy-eyed fish flat-topped pyramids of brussel sprouts slender stalks of pink rhubarb mounds of home-grown tomatoes and jars of bronze honey.

4. Two or three scrawny mangy-looking hounds lay sprawled in the shade of the cabin.

5. While Frank was unpacking the cooking gear and Gene was chopping firewood I began to put up our shelter.

6. Completely disregarding the machine-gun bullets that were ripping through the grass tops all around us Jerry wriggled on his belly all the way out to where I was put a tourniquet on my leg and then began dragging me back to the shelter of the ditch.

7. Still in high school we had to memorize dates and facts such as 1066 the Battle of Hastings 1914–1918 World War I 1939–1945 World War II and 1969 man's first landing on the moon.

8. The dream home that they often talk about is a split-level chalet to tell the truth however they seem perfectly happy in their mobile home which they bought in 1965.

9. Profanity had lost its power to offend obscenity its power to shock.

10. After two days of massive antiwar demonstrations the crowd dwindled however many individuals remained in the area to distribute leaflets and to canvass from door to door.

The Apostrophe

15

Use the apostrophe to indicate the possessive case (except for personal pronouns), to mark omissions in contracted words or numerals, and to form certain plurals.

15a

Use the apostrophe to indicate the possessive (or genitive) case of nouns and indefinite pronouns.

The apostrophe indicates possession or some other type of relationship. (Because possession is not the only relationship shown, the term *genitive* is often substituted for *possessive*.) This relationship may be otherwise expressed by the substitution of a modifier.

Ted's horse	the horse owned by Ted
everybody's friend	the friend of everybody
tomorrow's assignment	the assignment for tomorrow
Mrs. Harris's party	the party that Mrs. Harris gave
for clarity's sake	for the sake of clarity

Compare the following phrases, noting the use of the apostrophe.

this morning's paper	the morning paper

the students' idea	the student center
the government's duty	a government building

For inanimate objects the *'s* is usually either dropped or converted to an *of* phrase or a similar modifier.

tree trunk	trunk of the tree
the kitchen sink	the sink in the kitchen

(1) If a noun or an indefinite pronoun (either singular or plural) does not end in an *s* or *z* sound, add the apostrophe and *s.*

a man's job, a dime's worth, today's special   [Singular]
men's jobs, women's rights, children's books   [Plural]
anyone's guess, one's own   [Singular indefinite pronouns]

(2) If the plural ends in an *s* or *z* sound, add only the apostrophe.

ladies' gloves, the Joneses' gardens, three dollars' worth
Farmers' (OR Farmers) Cooperative Society   [The names of organizations frequently omit the apostrophe, as in *Ball State Teachers College*.]

(3) If the singular ends in an *s* or *z* sound, add the apostrophe and *s* for words of one syllable. Add only the apostrophe for words of more than one syllable unless you expect the pronunciation of the second *s* or *z* sound.

the boss's desk, Moses' brother, Eloise's letters

(4) Hyphenated compounds and nouns in joint possession show the possessive in the last word only. But if there is individual (or separate) possession, each noun takes the possessive form.

my brother-in-law's shop, anyone else's luggage
Helen and Mary's piano   [Joint ownership]
Helen's and Mary's clothes   [Individual ownership]

■ **Exercise 1**   Change each item below according to the pattern of the examples.

> EXAMPLES
> the boats that the Harrises bought
> *the Harrises' boats*
>
> a policy followed by the editor-in-chief
> *the editor-in-chief's policy*

1. the laughter of the girl
2. the screaming of the girls
3. suggestions that someone else made
4. suggestions that the ladies made
5. the army led by Cortez
6. the land that Robert and Bess owned jointly
7. the voices of Bill and Mary
8. the property owned by churches
9. apartment houses that Mr. Davis owns
10. the strategy that my mother-in-law uses

15b

Do not use the apostrophe with the pronouns *his, hers, its, ours, yours, theirs,* or *whose* or with plural nouns not in the possessive case.

> *His* parents sent money; *ours* sent food.
> A friend of *theirs* knows a cousin of *yours.*
> The *sisters* design *clothes* for *babies.*
>   [BUT The sisters design *babies'* clothes.]

Caution: Do not confuse *its* with *it's* or *whose* with *who's:*

> *Its* motor is small.   [The motor *of it*]
> *It's* a small motor.   [*It is* a small motor.]
>
> He is a mechanic *whose* work is reliable.   [The work *of whom*]
> He is a mechanic *who's* reliable.   [A mechanic *who is* reliable]

15c

Use an apostrophe to mark omissions in contracted words or numerals.

he will	he'll	rock and roll	rock 'n' roll
she would	she'd	of the clock	o'clock
they are	they're	class of 1972	class of '72

Caution: Place the apostrophe exactly where the omission occurs: *didn't* (NOT *did'nt*).

15d

Use the apostrophe and *s* to form the plural of lower-case letters and of abbreviations followed by periods. When needed to prevent confusion, use the apostrophe and *s* to form the plural of capital letters, of abbreviations not followed by periods, and of words referred to as words.

a's, *th*'s, p.s.'s, Ph.D.'s, P.O.W.'s
His *I*'s are illegible, and his *loss*'s look like *lass*'s.
   [NOT *I*s, *loss*s, or *lass*s]

Either *'s* or *s* may be used to form such plurals as the following:

the 1970's OR the 1970s	his 7's OR his 7s
two *B*'s OR two *B*s	the &'s OR the &s
her *and*'s OR her *and*s	the VFW's OR the VFWs

■ **Exercise 2** Write brief sentences correctly using (*a*) the possessive singular, (*b*) the plural, and (*c*) the possessive plural of each of the following words, as shown in the example below.

EXAMPLE   student
   a. *The student's attitude changed completely.*
   b. *Four students dropped the course.*
   c. *The students' parents are no longer notified.*

1. marksman
2. other
3. Thomas
4. genius

■ **Exercise 3** Insert apostrophes where needed in the following sentences. Put a checkmark after any sentence that needs no change in punctuation.

1. He puts circles instead of dots over his *i*s and *j*s.
2. The bookstores sell Marian Mannixs homemade penuche.
3. Theyre not interested in kick boxing; its roughness repels them.
4. Their friends are all cyclists; ours are mostly hikers.
5. Mr. Hesss office closes at ten.
6. She and Sandra styled each others hair.
7. ''Its just one C.P.A.s opinion, isnt it?'' Otis replied.
8. The subtitle is clever, but its only vaguely related to the main point of the article.
9. Though affluent, their parents refused to buy a TV.
10. For the class of 69, *the establishment, the pill,* and *stoned* had new meanings.

Quotation Marks

16

Use quotation marks to set off all direct quotations, some titles, and words used in a special sense. Place other marks of punctuation in proper relation to quotation marks.

Quotations usually consist of passages borrowed from the written work of others or the direct speech of individuals, especially in dialogue (conversation).

QUOTED WRITING   Margaret Mead has written: "Mankind joined the astronauts in their willowy, eerie, unweighted walks on the moon and saw the earth in all its isolated diversity. Earth became an island in space." [The words and punctuation within quotation marks are exactly as they appear in "The Island Earth," *Natural History,* 79, No. 1 (January 1970), 22.]

QUOTED SPEECH   "Sure enough, I'd like to own a slave," Donna explained. "A compact, push-button robot!" [Within quotation marks are the exactly recorded words of the speaker; the punctuation is supplied by the writer.]

Notice that quotation marks are used in pairs: the first one marks the beginning of the quotation, and the second marks the end. Be careful not to omit or misplace the second one. Also remember that the speaker and the verb of saying (such as *Donna* and *explained*) should never be within the quotation marks.

16a

Use double quotation marks to enclose direct (but not indirect) quotations; use single marks to enclose a quotation within a quotation.

> Making fun of Cooper, Mark Twain said, "He saw nearly all things as through a glass eye, darkly." [A directly quoted sentence]
> According to Mark Twain, Cooper "saw nearly all things as through a glass eye, darkly." [Part of a sentence quoted directly]
> Mark Twain said that Cooper saw nearly everything darkly, as if he were looking through a glass eye. [Indirect quotation—no quotation marks]

Notice in the following example that the quotation within a quotation is enclosed by single quotation marks; the quotation within that, by double marks.

> "It took courage," the speaker said, "for a man to affirm in those days: 'I endorse every word of Patrick Henry's sentiment, "Give me liberty or give me death!"' "
> —WILLIAM LEWIN

(1) Long prose quotations (not dialogue) In printed matter, quoted material of ten or more lines is usually set off from the rest of the text by the use of smaller type. Quotation marks are used only if they appear in the original. In typewritten papers, lengthy quoted passages are single-spaced and indented from both sides five spaces.[1] The first line is indented ten spaces when it marks the beginning of a paragraph.

---

[1] When quotation marks—instead of the usual smaller type or indention—are used to set off a passage of two or more paragraphs, the quotation marks come before each paragraph and at the end of the last; they do not come at the ends of intermediate paragraphs.

John A. Keel, whose specialty is reporting on
abominable snowmen and other monsters, tells the
following story:

> Tim Bullock and Barbara Smith were
> in a car parked near Chittyville, Illinois
> (north of Herrin), on August 11, 1968. At
> 8:30 P.M. a giant figure suddenly appeared
> from the bushes, badly frightening the
> couple. They said it was ten feet tall,
> "with a head as large as a steering wheel
> and a round, hairy face." It threw dirt
> at them through the window. Bullock
> returned to the spot the next day and
> found a large depression in the grass.
> People claimed that dogs in the area had
> been "carrying on" for the previous two
> weeks.
> The editor of the Herrin, Illinois,
> Spokesman did not publish the story.
> He felt it was the work of some local
> practical jokers.[2]

(2) Poetry In both printed matter and typewritten papers,
except for very special emphasis, a single line of poetry
or less is handled like other short quotations—run in with
the text and enclosed in quotation marks. A two-line
quotation may be handled in either of two ways. It may
be run in with the text, with a slash marking the end
of the first line:

> The poet asks, "How is it under our control / To love
>
> or not to love?"

Or it may be set off from the text like longer quotations
and quoted line by line exactly as it appears in the

---

[2] From *Strange Creatures from Time and Space* by John A. Keel. Published
by Fawcett Publishers, Inc., 1970. Reprinted by permission.

original. In printed matter, longer passages are usually set off by smaller type. In typewritten papers, they are single-spaced and indented from the left five spaces:

```
The last part of "The Leaden Echo," by Gerard

Manley Hopkins, offers no hope to those who would like

to stay young and beautiful:

        Be beginning; since, no, nothing can be done
        To keep at bay
        Age and age's evils--hoar hair,
        Ruck and wrinkle, drooping, dying, death's
            worst, winding sheets, tombs and worms,
            and tumbling to decay;
        So be beginning, be beginning to despair.
        Oh, there's none--no, no, no, there's none:
          Be beginning to despair, to despair,
          Despair, despair, despair, despair.3

    In the companion poem, "The Golden Echo," however,

Hopkins presents a cure for despair.
```

(3) Dialogue (conversation) Written dialogue represents the directly quoted speech of two or more persons talking together. Standard practice is to write each person's speech, no matter how short, as a separate paragraph. Verbs of saying, as well as closely related bits of narrative, are included in the paragraph along with the speech.

The only political discussion that I can remember from those days was with Tennessee Williams. It occurred shortly before the Italian elections in which the Communists were expected to win. "The Russians," Tennessee announced most uncharacteristically, "are not a predatory people. I

---

[3]From *The Poems of Gerard Manley Hopkins* by Gerard Manley Hopkins. Published by Oxford University Press, 1918. Reprinted by permission.

don't know why there is all this fuss about 'international communism.' "

I disagreed. "They've always been imperialists, just like us."

"That's not true. Just name me one country Russia has tried to take over. I mean recently."

"Latvia, Lithuania and Estonia," I began. . . .

"And what," asked Tennessee, "are they?"

It is his charm, and genius, to be his own world.

—GORE VIDAL[4]

(4) Punctuation of dialogue Commas are used to set off expressions such as *he said* and *she asked* in quoted dialogue: see **12d(3)**

He said, "Pro football is like nuclear warfare."
"Pro football," he said, "is like nuclear warfare."
"Pro football is like nuclear warfare," he said.

When the quoted speech is a question or an exclamation, the question mark or exclamation point replaces the usual comma.

"Pro football?" she asked. "Like nuclear warfare!" she added.

When an expression such as *he said* introduces a quotation of two or more sentences, it is often followed by a colon: see **17d(1)**

It is as Frank Gifford said: "Pro football is like nuclear warfare. There are no winners, only survivors."

■ **Exercise 1** In the following sentences, change each indirect quotation to a direct quotation and each direct quotation to an indirect one.

1. Doris said that she had a theory about me.

---

[4] From "A Memoir in the Form of a Novel" by Gore Vidal, *Esquire*, May 1970. Reprinted by permission.

2. Allen announced that he had read "The Sunless Sea."
3. An ardent Weight Watcher, Laura explained that she could eat as much as she wanted—of foods like spinach, rhubarb, and celery!
4. Clyde asked, "Will you go with me to the opera?"
5. "Read the poem once over lightly before class," he said with a wink.

16b

Use quotation marks for minor titles (short stories, essays, short poems, songs, articles from periodicals) and for subdivisions of books.

> Max Shulman's *Guided Tour of Campus Humor* contains numerous poems and short stories, including "Tears from One Who Didn't Realize How Good He Had It" and "Love Is a Fallacy."
> Ruth Benedict's "Synergy—Patterns of the Good Culture" appeared in the June, 1970, issue of *Psychology Today*.
> Stevenson's *Treasure Island* is divided into six parts, the last of which, called "Captain Silver," opens with a chapter entitled "In the Enemy's Camp."

Note: Quotation marks are sometimes used to enclose titles of books, periodicals, and newspapers, but italics are generally preferred: see **10a**.

16c

Words used in a special sense are sometimes enclosed in quotation marks.

> Such "prophecy" is intelligent guessing.
> The printer must see that quotation marks are "cleared"— that is, kept within the margins.
> "Puritanical" means "marked by stern morality." [OR *Puritanical* means "marked by stern morality." OR *Puritanical* means *marked by stern morality*. See also **10d**.]

16d

Do not overuse quotation marks.

Do not use quotation marks to enclose the title of your composition: see 8b(4). In general do not enclose in quotation marks common nicknames, bits of humor, technical terms, or trite or well-known expressions. Instead of using slang and colloquialisms within quotation marks, use more formal English. Do not use quotation marks for emphasis.

NEEDLESS PUNCTUATION "Hank" broke the silence.
BETTER Hank broke the silence.

INAPPROPRIATE USE OF SLANG In the end I "copped out."
APPROPRIATE In the end I refused to cooperate.

■ **Exercise 2** Add correctly placed quotation marks below.

1. In a poem entitled 2001, scientists turn one Einstein into three Einsteins.
2. Here, stoked means fantastically happy on a surfboard.
3. David enjoyed reading the short story A Circle in the Fire.
4. *Learning to Live Without Cigarettes* opens with a chapter entitled Sighting the Target.
5. The Beatles recorded Sergeant Pepper in 1967.

16e

When using various marks of punctuation with quoted words, phrases, or sentences, follow the conventions of American printers:

(1) Place the period and the comma always within the quotation marks.

"Gerald," he said, "let's organize."

(2) Place the colon and the semicolon always outside the quotation marks.

She spoke of "the protagonists"; yet I remembered only one in "The Tell-Tale Heart": the mad murderer.

(3) Place the dash, the question mark, and the exclamation point within the quotation marks when they apply only to the quoted matter; place them outside when they apply to the whole sentence.

Pilate asked, "What's truth?" [The question mark applies only to the quoted matter.]

What is the meaning of the term "half truth"? [The question mark applies to the whole sentence.]

Why did he ask, "What's truth?" [Both the quoted matter and the sentence as a whole are questions, but a second question mark does not follow the quotation marks.]

They chanted, "Hell no! We won't go!" [The exclamation points apply only to the quoted matter.]

Stop whistling "The Eyes of Texas"! [The whole sentence, not the song title, is an exclamation.]

■ **Exercise 3** Insert quotation marks where they are needed in the following sentences.

1. Helen's really out of it, I commented to Carl as we sat down to lunch in the cafeteria. Too bad she saw *The Rivals*. She's been acting like Mrs. Malaprop ever since.

2. Oh, cut it out about Helen! Carl snapped as he unrolled his napkin and sorted his silverware. I actually like Helen's bad jokes. Her word play—

3. Please pass the salt, I interrupted.

4. Ignoring my frown, Carl continued: I'll grant you that Helen's puns are usually as old as the joke ending with Squawbury Shortcake; but here she comes. Start talking about something else.

5. Clearing my throat noisily, I took his advice and said, Perhaps your parents should buy a perambulator.

6. A perambulator! Helen happily took up my cue as she plopped down in the chair near Carl. My parents bought me an eight-cup perambulator for my birthday. Just plug it in, and coffee is ready in four minutes!

7. Aren't you thinking of a percolator? I asked her in mock seriousness. An electric percolator heats quickly.

8. Sure, Helen replied, winking at Carl. It's the same thing as an incubator.

9. You don't mean *incubator!* I said sharply, and then I added a bit of my own nonsense: You mean *incinerator.* After a moment of silence, I yawned and said, Incinerator bombs are really fiery weapons. They cause much perturbation.

10. As though admitting defeat at her own game, Helen grinned and said, with a blasé sigh, Oh, let's forget this game. It's time we had a new aversion.

The Period and Other Marks

17

Use the period, the question mark, the exclamation point, the colon, the dash, parentheses, and brackets in accordance with standard practices. (For the use of the hyphen, see **18f.**)

End marks (periods, question marks, and exclamation points) signal intonation (pitch, stress, stops), which helps to reveal sentence meaning.

> Wilde defined a cynic. [Statement]
> Wilde defined a cynic? [Question]
> Wilde defined a cynic! [Exclamation]

Colons, dashes, parentheses, and brackets are signals for pauses or voice variations which usually indicate degrees of emphasis within a sentence.

> According to Oscar Wilde (1856–1900), a cynic always knows the price —never the value.
> Also in *Lady Windermere's Fan* is this witticism: "I [Lord Darlington] can resist everything except temptation."

The Period

17a

Use the period after declarative and mildly imperative sentences, after indirect questions, and after most abbreviations. Use the ellipsis mark (three spaced periods) to indicate omissions from quoted passages.

(1) Use the period to mark the end of a declarative sentence, a mildly imperative sentence, or an indirect question.

Everyone should drive defensively. [Declarative]
Learn how to drive defensively. [Mild imperative]
He asked *how drivers could cross the city without driving offensively.* [Indirect question]

(2) Use periods with most abbreviations.

Mr., Mrs., Dr., Jr., Ph.D., etc., B.C., A.D., C.O.D., A.M. OR a.m., P.M. OR p.m., r.s.v.p. OR R.S.V.P.

In current usage the period is frequently omitted after many abbreviations, especially for names of organizations and national or international agencies.

IBM, FM, ESP, TV, GI, CORE, AFL-CIO, FBI, USAF, UN, NATO, NAACP

When in doubt about the punctuation of an abbreviation, consult a good college dictionary. Dictionaries often list a range of choices (for example, *A.W.O.L., a.w.o.l., AWOL, awol*).

Caution: Do not use periods to indicate that such words as *I've, 2nd,* or *gym* are shortened.

(3) Use the ellipsis mark (three spaced periods) to indicate the omission of one or more words within a quoted passage.

If a complete sentence precedes the omission (whether or not it was a complete sentence in the original), use a period before the ellipsis mark. It is generally considered unnecessary to use an ellipsis mark at the beginning or the end of a quoted passage.

QUOTATION

No man is an island, entire of itself; every man is a piece of the continent, a part of the main. If a clod be washed away by the sea, Europe is the less, as well as if a promontory were, as well as if a manor of thy friend's or of thine own were. Any man's death diminishes me because I am involved in mankind, and therefore never send to know for whom the bell tolls; it tolls for thee.   —JOHN DONNE

QUOTATION WITH ELLIPSES

No man is an island . . . every man is a piece of the continent, a part of the main. . . . Any man's death diminishes me because I am involved in mankind.   —JOHN DONNE

Note 1: Especially in dialogue, three spaced periods are sometimes used to signal a pause or a deliberately unfinished statement:

"You watch your step," Wilson said, "and Mrs. Rolt . . ."
"What on earth has Mrs. Rolt got to do with it?"
                                        —GRAHAM GREENE

Note 2: A full line of spaced periods are used to mark the omission of a full paragraph or more in a prose quotation or the omission of a full line or more in a poetry quotation.

All I can say is—I saw it!

.   .   .   .

Impossible! Only—I saw it!
                    —from "Natural Magic" by ROBERT BROWNING

The Question Mark

17b

Use the question mark after direct (but not indirect) questions.

DIRECT QUESTIONS

Who started the riot?

Did he ask *who started the riot?* [The sentence as a whole is a direct question despite the indirect question at the end.]

Did you hear him say, "What right have you to ask about the riot?" [Double direct question followed by a single question mark]

Declarative sentences may contain direct questions:

"Who started the riot?" he asked. [No comma follows the question mark.]

He asked, "Who started the riot?" [No period follows the question mark.]

He told me—did I hear him correctly?—that he started the riot. [Interpolated question]

A declarative or an imperative sentence may be converted into a question:

He started the riot?

Start the riot?

Question marks may be used between the parts of a series:

Did he plan the riot? employ assistants? give the signal to begin? [Question marks cause full stops and emphasize each part. Compare "Did he plan the riot, employ assistants, and give the signal to begin?"]

Caution: Do not use a question mark to indicate the end of an indirect question. See also **17a(1)**.

He asked *what the cause of the riot was.*

To ask *why the riot started* is unnecessary.
How foolish it is to ask *what caused the riot!*

OTHER USES OF THE QUESTION MARK

A question mark within parentheses is used to express the writer's uncertainty as to the correctness of the preceding word, figure, or date: "Chaucer was born in 1340(?) and died in 1400." But the question mark is not a desirable means of expressing wit or sarcasm.

INEFFECTIVE   This kind (?) proposal caused Gulliver to take refuge in nearby Blefuscu. [Omit the question mark. If the context does not make the irony clear, revise the sentence (for example, try a straightforward approach, using a word like *unsettling* or *fiendish* instead of *kind*).]

Courtesy questions, which sometimes replace imperatives (especially in business writing), may be followed by question marks but are usually followed by periods.

Will you write me again if I can be of further service. [Here *will you* is equivalent to the word *please.*]

Caution: Do not use a comma or a period after a question mark.

"What is an acronym?" asked Marjorie.
Marjorie asked, "What is an acronym?"

The Exclamation Point

17c

Use the exclamation point after an emphatic interjection and after a phrase, clause, or sentence to express a high degree of surprise, incredulity, or other strong emotion.

Oh! A pox on them both!

What courage! How brave!
They are deceiving us!
Act! Enter the political arena!
   [Vigorous imperatives]

Caution 1: Avoid overuse of the exclamation point. Use a comma after mild interjections, and end mildly exclamatory sentences and mild imperatives with a period.

Oh, the ivory tower is crumbling.
Well, the college will survive.
How quiet the lake was.
Leave now.

Caution 2: Do not use a comma or a period after an exclamation point.

"Get off the road!" he yelled.
He yelled, "Get off the road!"

■ **Exercise 1** Illustrate the chief uses of the period, the question mark, and the exclamation point by composing and correctly punctuating brief sentences that meet the descriptions given in the items below.

EXAMPLE
a declarative sentence containing a quoted direct question
"What does fennel taste like?" she asked.

1. a direct question
2. a double direct question containing a quotation
3. a vigorous imperative
4. a mild imperative
5. a declarative sentence containing a quoted exclamation
6. a declarative sentence containing an indirect question
7. a declarative sentence converted into a direct question
8. an ellipsis in the middle of a quoted sentence
9. an ellipsis at the end of a complete quoted sentence
10. a declarative sentence containing an interpolated question

The Colon

17d

**Use the colon after a formal introductory statement
to direct attention to what follows. Avoid needless
colons.**

Although similar in name, the colon and the semicolon differ
greatly in use. The colon following a statement or a main
clause is a formal *introducer,* calling attention to something
that is to follow. The colon usually means "as follows." The
semicolon dividing main clauses is a strong *separator,* almost
equal to a period: see Section 14.

**(1) The colon may direct attention to a brief summary
or an appositive (or a series of appositives) at the
end of a sentence, to a formal list or explanation,
or to a quotation.**

All her thoughts were centered on one objective: liberation.
[A dash or a comma, which might be used instead of the
colon, would be less formal.]

Theories which try to explain the secret of fire walking fall
into three categories: physical, psychological, and religious.
—LEONARD FEINBERG

The sense of unity with nature is vividly shown in Zen
Buddhist paintings and poetry: "An old pine tree preaches
wisdom. And a wild bird is crying out truth."
—ANNE MORROW LINDBERGH

**(2) The colon may separate two main clauses when the
second clause explains or amplifies the first.**

The American conceives of fishing as more than a sport: it
is his personal contest against nature.   —JOHN STEINBECK

The scientific value of even the most recent contributions
to this literature, however, is seriously qualified: The sole
witness to the dream is the dreamer himself.
—SCIENTIFIC AMERICAN

Note: After the colon quoted sentences regularly begin with a capital, but other sentences (as the examples above show) may begin with either a capital or a small letter.

(3) Use the colon after the salutation of a business letter, between a title and a subtitle, and between figures indicating the chapter and verse of a Biblical reference or the hour and minute of a time reference.

Dear Sir:
Gluttons and Libertines : Human Problems of Being Natural
according to Matthew 6:10   at exactly 10:35 P.M.

(4) Avoid needless colons.

When there is no formal introduction or summarizing word, the colon is usually a needless interruption of the sentence.

NEEDLESS All her thoughts were centered on: liberation.
BETTER All her thoughts were centered on liberation.

NEEDLESS The one-way streets are: narrow, rough, and junky.
BETTER The one-way streets are narrow, rough, and junky.

■ **Exercise 2** Punctuate the following sentences by adding appropriate colons or semicolons. Between two main clauses, use the colon only when the second clause explains or amplifies the first. Put a checkmark after any sentence that needs no change.

1. Downtown businesses are suffering for another reason there is no place for customers to park.
2. It is one thing to secure a mortgage in a few days it is another thing to pay on a loan for thirty years.
3. Within two hours we had rain, hail, sleet, snow.
4. The meeting had only one purpose agreement upon a suitable location for the new fire station.
5. At social functions he enlarged on his favorite theme television is the opiate of the people.

6. Frequently I ask myself two important questions Where do I want to go? How shall I get there?

7. Professor Boaz suggested a variety of subjects for term papers "The Causes of the Arab-Israeli Conflict," "The Recession of 1969," "The Philosophy of Billy Graham."

8. Dr. Morrisey stopped at the newsstand to buy three magazines *U.S. News & World Report, The New Yorker,* and *Life.*

9. St. Paul's famous epistle on charity appears in I Corinthians 13 1–7.

10. In 1903 Shaw was forty-seven that very year his handbook for revolutionists carried this judgment "Every man over forty is a scoundrel."

The Dash

17e

Use the dash to mark a sudden break in thought, to set off a summary or an appositive, or to set off a parenthetical element that is very abrupt or that has commas within it.

On the typewriter the dash is indicated by two hyphens without spacing before, between, or after. In handwriting the dash is an unbroken line about the length of two or three hyphens.

Punctuation of Parenthetical Matter

Dashes, parentheses, commas—all are used to set off parenthetical matter. Dashes set off parenthetical elements sharply and therefore tend to emphasize them.

> Man's mind is indeed—as Luther said—a factory busy with making idols.   —HARVEY COX

Parentheses tend to minimize the importance of the elements they enclose.

> Man's mind is indeed (as Luther said) a factory busy with making idols.   [See **17f.**]

Commas are the mildest, most commonly used separators and tend to leave the elements they enclose more closely connected with the sentence.

> Man's mind is indeed, as Luther said, a factory busy with making idols. [See 12d.]

(1) Use the dash to mark a sudden break in thought, an interruption, or an abrupt change in tone.

> A hypocrite is a person who— but who isn't? —DON MARQUIS
>
> We are all alike— on the inside. —MARK TWAIN
>
> "It is hard to explain— " he said, and paused as they composed themselves. —LIONEL TRILLING
>
> Food and sex are different— almost any adult can tell them apart. —MARSTON BATES

(2) Use the dash to set off a brief summary or an appositive (or a series of appositives).

> Dirt and disease were the big sacraments here— outward and visible signs of an inward and spiritual disgrace.
> —SEAN O'CASEY [A colon, which might be used instead of the dash, would be more formal.]
>
> Mutual interest, mutual trust, mutual effort— these are the goals. —ROBERT S. McNAMARA

(3) Use the dash to set off a parenthetical element that is very abrupt or that has commas within it.

> A telltale suggestion of relief— or was it gratitude?— brightened their eyes. —JOHN MASON BROWN
>
> He stood up— small, frail, and tense— staring toward things in his homeland. —NORA WALN
>
> I was mediocre at drill, certainly— that is, until my senior year. —JAMES THURBER

Caution: Use the dash carefully in formal writing. Do not use dashes as awkward substitutes for commas, semicolons, or end marks.

Parentheses

17f

Use parentheses to set off parenthetical, supplementary, or illustrative matter and to enclose figures or letters when used for enumeration within a sentence.

We no longer blame everything on "the System" (the fifties) or "the Establishment" (the sixties). —JOSEPH WOOD KRUTCH

Some states (New York, for instance) outlaw the use of *any* electronic eavesdropping device by private individuals. —MYRON BRENTON [Dashes, which might be used instead of parentheses, would tend to emphasize the parenthetical matter.]

When confronted with ambiguities we are not certain as to how we should interpret (1) single words or phrases, (2) the sense of a sentence, (3) the emphases or accents desired by the writer or speaker, or (4) the significance of a statement. —LIONEL RUBY

Each entry will be judged on the basis of (*a*) its artistic value, (*b*) its technical competence, and (*c*) its originality.

When the sentence demands other marks of punctuation with the parenthetical matter, these marks are placed after the closing parenthesis.

According to Herbert J. Muller (1905–1967), instability is one of the conditions of life. [No comma before the first parenthesis]

Bliss Perry taught at Princeton (although he was there for only seven years).

If a whole sentence beginning with a capital is in parentheses, the period or other terminal mark is placed within the closing parenthesis.

She repeated the joke. (Ralph had heard it the first time.)

Is democracy possible in the South? (Is it possible anywhere?) —JONATHAN DANIELS

Brackets

17g

Use brackets to set off editorial corrections or interpolations in quoted matter and, when necessary, to replace parentheses within parentheses.

> Deems Taylor has written: "Not for a single moment did he [Richard Wagner] compromise with what he believed, with what he dreamed."

> The *Home Herald* printed the senator's letter, which was an appeal to his "dear fiends [*sic*] and fellow citizens." [A bracketed *sic*—meaning "thus"—tells the reader that the error appears in the original.]

> James Gould Cozzens' best-known novel deals with forty-nine hours of a man's life (*By Love Possessed* [New York: Harcourt, 1960]).

■ **Exercise 3** Correctly punctuate each of the following sentences by supplying commas, dashes, parentheses, or brackets. Be prepared to explain the reason for all marks you add, especially those you choose to set off parenthetical matter.

1. Gordon Gibbs or is it his twin brother? plays left tackle.
2. Joseph who is Gordon's brother is a guard on the second string.
3. "Dearest" he began, but his voice broke; he could say no more.
4. This organization needs more of everything more money, brains, initiative.
5. Some of my courses for example, French and biology demand a great deal of work outside the classroom.
6. A penalty clipping cost the Steers fifteen yards.
7. This ridiculous sentence appeared in the school paper: "Because of a personal fool *sic* the Cougars failed to cross the goal line during the last seconds of the game."
8. The word *Zipper* a trademark like Kodak is now used frequently without the initial capital as a common noun.
9. Rugged hills, rich valleys, beautiful lakes these things impress the tourist in Connecticut.

10. Our course embraced these projects: 1 the close reading of *Hamlet,* 2 the writing of critiques on various aspects of this tragedy, and 3 the formation of a tentative theory of tragedy.

■ **Exercise 4** Punctuate the following sentences (selected and adapted from the *Atlantic Monthly*) by supplying appropriate end marks, commas, colons, dashes, and parentheses. Do not use unnecessary punctuation. Be prepared to explain the reason for each mark you add, especially when you have a choice of correct marks (for example, commas, dashes, or parentheses).

1. Freeways in America are all the same aluminum guardrails green signs white lettering
2. "It's one thing for young people and blacks to complain but the easiest way to change a police department is to get in it" said Wesley Pomeroy associate administrator of the Law Enforcement Assistance Administration
3. I tell you again What is alive and young and throbbing with historic current in America is musical theater
4. Jim had enormous contempt for his municipal brothers-in-arms the firemen "What do you have to know to stand at the end of a hose" he said
5. "Judy" she exploded "Judy that's an awful thing to say" She raised an arm to slap her daughter but it wouldn't reach
6. Emily formerly Mrs Goyette caught McAndless' sleeve where no one could see and tugged it briefly but urgently
7. At last she had become what she had always wished to be a professional dancer
8. There are three essential qualities for vulture country a rich supply of unburied corpses high mountains a strong sun
9. As one man put it "Rose Bowl Sugar Bowl and Orange Bowl all are gravy bowls"
10. "Good and" can mean "very" "I am good and mad" and "a hot cup of coffee" means that the coffee not the cup is hot

SPELLING AND DICTION

Spelling and Hyphenation

18

Spell every word according to established usage as shown by a good dictionary. Hyphenate words in accordance with current usage.

Spelling

As you write, you use conventional combinations of letters to represent certain spoken sounds. Though pronunciation can serve as a guide to correct spelling, it can also be misleading: the written forms of many words (like *listen, whole*) do not reflect their exact pronunciation; some words that sound alike (*blew, blue*) have different spellings, different meanings; some spellings represent a number of different sounds (like *ough* in *rough, though, through*); and some sounds have various spellings (such as /sh/ in *ocean, ration, tissue*).

In spite of irregularities, there is consistency within the framework of our spelling system.[1] Compare, for example, the spelling and the pronunciation of the following words:

breath	breathe	diner	dinner
cloth	clothe	filing	filling
hug	huge	hoping	hopping
scar	scare	later	latter
writ	write	shining	shinning

---

[1] See Thomas Pyles and John Algeo, *English: An Introduction to Language* (New York: Harcourt, 1970), pp. 52–95.

In the following words "soft" *c*, representing /s/, and "soft" *g*, representing /j/, are followed by *e* or *i*. Before letters other than *e* or *i*, the *c* and *g* are "hard" and stand for /k/ and /g/ respectively.

/s/	/k/	/j/	/g/
decide	decade	angel	angle
innocent	significant	changeable	indefatigable
parcel	article	margin	bargain
participate	decorate	religious	analogous
pencil	political	sergeant	termagant

Notice in the following examples the relationship between *t* and *c*.

absent	absence	important	importance
accurate	accuracy	present	presence
different	difference	prophet	prophecy
existent	existence	significant	significance

Adding a suffix like *-ity, -ation,* or *-ic* can change pronunciation in such a way that the correct spelling of the base word becomes apparent.

moral	morality	condemn	condemnation
personal	personality	damn	damnation
practical	practicality	definite	definition
similar	similarity	narrative	narration

academy	academic
geography	geographic
symbol	symbolic
telepathy	telepathic

Spelling is a highly individual problem. You as an individual can improve your spelling by referring frequently to your dictionary, keeping a record of the words you misspell (see the model list on page 184), and studying your own list of problem words as well as the general rules and lists in this section.

18a

Do not allow mispronunciation to cause misspelling.

Mispronunciation often leads to the misspelling of such words as those listed below. To avoid difficulties resulting from mispronunciation, pronounce problem words aloud several times, clearly and distinctly, in accordance with the pronunciation shown by a dictionary. Be careful not to omit, add, or transpose any letter or syllable.

(1) Careless omission

Pronounce the following words distinctly, making it a point not to omit the sound represented by the letters in color.

candidate	quantity
everybody	recognize
library	surprise

Omitting the /ə/ can cause you to misspell such words as *literature, occasionally,* and *probably.*

(2) Careless addition

Pronounce the following words, being careful not to add any sound not represented by a letter or syllable.

athlete	hindrance
disastrous	lightning
drowned	mischievous
entrance	remembrance
grievous	umbrella

(3) Careless transposition

Pronounce the following words carefully. Correct pronunciation can help you to avoid careless transposition.

cavalry	irrelevant
children	prefer
hundred	prescription

Note: Even when such words as the following are pronounced correctly, letters may be carelessly transposed in writing.

doesn't   tragedy
prejudice   villain

18b

Distinguish between words of similar sound and spelling, and use the spelling required by the meaning.

Words such as *heroin* and *heroine* or *sole* and *soul* sound alike but have vastly different meanings. Always be sure to choose the right word for your context.

Words Frequently Confused

Following is a list of words that are frequently confused in writing. You may find it helpful to study the list in units of ten word groups at a time, using your dictionary to check the meaning of words not thoroughly familiar to you. Add any words you tend to misspell to your individual spelling list.

[I]
accent, ascent, assent
accept, except
advice, advise
affect, effect
all ready, already
all together, altogether
allusive, elusive, illusive
altar, alter
bare, bear
berth, birth

[II]
born, borne
capital, capitol
choose, chose
cite, sight, site
coarse, course
complement, compliment
conscience, conscious
consul, council, counsel
decent, descent, dissent
desert, dessert

[III]
device, devise
dual, duel
dyeing, dying
fair, fare
formally, formerly
forth, fourth
hear, here
holey, holy, wholly
instance, instants
irrelevant, irreverent

[IV]
its, it's
know, no
later, latter
lead, led
lessen, lesson
loose, lose
moral, morale
of, off
passed, past
peace, piece

[V]
personal, personnel
plain, plane
precede, proceed
presence, presents
principal, principle
prophecy, prophesy
quiet, quit, quite
respectfully, respectively
right, rite, -wright, write
sense, since

[VI]
shone, shown
stationary, stationery
than, then
their, there, they're
threw, through
to, too, two
weak, week
weather, whether
who's, whose
your, you're

18c

Distinguish between the prefix and the root. Apply the rules for spelling in adding suffixes.

The root is the base to which the prefix or the suffix is added.

PREFIXES

(1) Add the prefix to the root without doubling or dropping letters.

Take care not to double the last letter of the prefix when it is different from the first letter of the root (as in *disappear*)

or to drop the last letter of the prefix when the root begins
with the same letter (as in *immortal*).

dis-	+	appear	=	disappear
grand-	+	daughter	=	granddaughter
im-	+	mortal	=	immortal
un-	+	necessary	=	unnecessary

SUFFIXES

**(2) Drop final *e* before a suffix beginning with a vowel
but not before a suffix beginning with a consonant.**

Drop final *e* before a suffix beginning with a vowel.

combine	+	-ation	=	combination
come	+	-ing	=	coming
fame	+	-ous	=	famous
precede	+	-ence	=	precedence

Retain final *e* before a suffix beginning with a consonant.

care	+	-ful	=	careful
entire	+	-ly	=	entirely
manage	+	-ment	=	management
rude	+	-ness	=	rudeness

Exceptions: *argue, argument; awe, awful; due, duly; hoe,
hoeing; singe, singeing; true, truly.* After "soft" *c* or *g* a final
e is retained before suffixes beginning with *a* or *o*: *notice,
noticeable; courage, courageous.* Note that "hard" *c* and *g*
are not followed by *e* before *a* and *o*. Compare *noticeable*
and *despicable, courageous* and *analogous.*

**(3) Double a final single consonant before a suffix be-
ginning with a vowel (*a*) if the consonant ends an
accented syllable or a word of one syllable and (*b*)
if the consonant is preceded by a single vowel.
Otherwise, do not double the consonant.**

admit, admitted [Accented syllable with end consonant
preceded by a single vowel; BUT when syllable is un-
accented: *benefit, benefited*]

drop, dropping [A word of one syllable with end consonant preceded by a single vowel; BUT when preceded by a double vowel: *droop, drooping*]

(4) Except before *-ing,* final *y* is usually changed to *i*.

defy	+	-ance	=	defiance
happy	+	-ness	=	happiness
mercy	+	-ful	=	merciful
modify	+	-er	=	modifier
modify	+	-ing	=	modifying [No change before *-ing*]

Note: Verbs ending in *y* preceded by a vowel do not change the *y* to form the third person singular of the present tense or the past participle: *array, arrays, arrayed.* Exceptions: *lay, laid; pay, paid; say, said.*

18d

Apply the rules for spelling to avoid confusion of *ei* and *ie*.

When the sound is /ē/, write *ie* (except after *c*, in which case write *ei*).

				(After *c*)	
chief	grief	pierce	wield	ceiling	deceive
field	niece	relief	yield	conceit	perceive

When the sound is other than /ē/, usually write *ei*.

deign	feign	height	neighbor	sleigh	vein
eight	foreign	heir	reign	stein	weigh

Exceptions: *fiery, financier, seize, species, weird.*

■ **Exercise 1** Add the designated prefixes and suffixes in the following items, applying 18c.

1. weep + -ing
2. big + -est

3. occur $+$ -ence
4. profit $+$ -ed
5. definite $+$ -ly
6. plume $+$ -age
7. un- $+$ numbered
8. dis- $+$ satisfy
9. im- $+$ moral $+$ -ity
10. length $+$ -en $+$ -ing
11. care $+$ -less $+$ -ly
12. lone $+$ -ly $+$ -ness

■ **Exercise 2** Write out the following words, filling out the blanks with *ei* or *ie*.

(1) pr__st, (2) dec__t, (3) conc__ve, (4) fr__ght, (5) s__ve, (6) p__ce, (7) f__nd, (8) bes__ge, (9) r__gned, (10) th__f.

18e

Form the plural by adding *s* to the singular, but by adding *es* if the plural makes an extra syllable.

boy, boys; cap, caps; radio, radios
bush, bushes; match, matches [The plural
makes an extra syllable.]

Exceptions:

(1) If the noun ends in *y* preceded by a consonant, form the plural by changing the *y* to *i* and adding *es: comedy, comedies; sky, skies.* But after final *y* preceded by a vowel, *y* is retained and only *s* is added: *joy, joys.*

(2) If the noun ends in *fe*, change the *fe* to *ve* and add *s: knife, knives.*

(3) A few nouns ending in *o* take the *es* plural, although the plural does not make an extra syllable: *hero, heroes; potato, potatoes.*

(4) For plurals of compound words such as *father-in-law*, usually add *s* to the chief word, not the modifier: *fathers-in-law, maids of honor.*

For other plurals formed irregularly, consult your dictionary.

Note: Add *'s* or *s* alone to form the plurals of letters, abbreviations, figures, symbols, and words used as words: see **15d**.

■ **Exercise 3**   Supply plural forms for the following words, applying **18e**. (If a word is not covered by the rule, use your dictionary.)

(1) life, (2) leaf, (3) axis, (4) altar, (5) child, (6) theory, (7) crisis, (8) church, (9) belief, (10) tomato, (11) woman, (12) sheep, (13) valley, (14) height, (15) radius, (16) industry, (17) business, (18) fantasy, (19) schedule, (20) passer-by.

Words Frequently Misspelled

The following list of frequently misspelled words consists of 650 common words or word groups. The list is drawn by permission of Dean Thomas Clark Pollock from his study of 31,375 misspellings in the written work of college students.[2] Any word that is spelled the same as a part of a longer word is usually omitted. For example, the list includes *definitely* but not *definite, existence* but not *exist, performance* but not *perform*. Each of the first hundred words in the general list given here was misspelled more than forty-three times (or more than an *average* of forty-three times in the case of words grouped in Dean Pollock's report).

You may find it helpful to study the following list in units of fifty words at a time, using your dictionary to check the exact meaning of any words you are unsure of. Then, without the aid of your dictionary, test yourself by writing sentences in which each word is used and spelled correctly. Add to your individual spelling list any words that you misspell.

---

[2] From Thomas Clark Pollock and William D. Baker, *The University Spelling Book*, © 1955. Reprinted by permission of Prentice-Hall, Inc., Englewood Cliffs, New Jersey. See also Thomas Clark Pollock, "Spelling Report," *College English*, 16 (Nov. 1954), 102–09.

18e

The hundred words most frequently misspelled

In the list below an asterisk (*) indicates the most frequently misspelled words among the first hundred. The most troublesome letters for all words are in color.

[I]

1. accommodate
2. achievement
3. acquire
4. all right
5. among
6. apparent
7. argument
8. arguing
9. belief*
10. believe*
11. beneficial
12. benefited
13. category
14. coming
15. comparative
16. conscious
17. controversy
18. controversial
19. definitely
20. definition
21. define
22. describe
23. description
24. disastrous
25. effect
26. embarrass
27. environment
28. exaggerate
29. existence*
30. existent*

31. experience
32. explanation
33. fascinate
34. height
35. interest
36. its, it's
37. led
38. lose
39. losing
40. marriage
41. mere
42. necessary
43. occasion*
44. occurred
45. occurring
46. occurrence
47. opinion
48. opportunity
49. paid
50. particular

[II]

51. performance
52. personal
53. personnel
54. possession
55. possible
56. practical
57. precede*
58. prejudice

59. prepare
60. prevalent
61. principal
62. principle
63. privilege*
64. probably
65. proceed
66. procedure
67. professor
68. profession
69. prominent
70. pursue
71. quiet
72. receive*
73. receiving*
74. recommend
75. referring*
76. repetition
77. rhythm
78. sense
79. separate*
80. separation*
81. shining
82. similar*
83. studying
84. succeed
85. succession
86. surprise
87. technique
88. than

177

89. then	93. thorough	97. villain
90. their*	94. to,* too,* two*	98. woman
91. there*	95. transferred	99. write
92. they're*	96. unnecessary	100. writing

The next 550 words most frequently misspelled

[III]	129. actually	156. analysis
101. absence	130. adequately	157. analyze
102. abundance	131. admission	158. and
103. abundant	132. admittance	159. another
104. academic	133. adolescence	160. annually
105. academically	134. adolescent	161. anticipated
106. academy	135. advantageous	162. apologetically
107. acceptable	136. advertisement	163. apologized
108. acceptance	137. advertiser	164. apology
109. accepting	138. advertising	165. apparatus
110. accessible	139. advice, advise	166. appearance
111. accidental	140. affect	167. applies
112. accidentally	141. afraid	168. applying
113. acclaim	142. against	169. appreciate
114. accompanied	143. aggravate	170. appreciation
115. accompanies	144. aggressive	171. approaches
116. accompaniment	145. alleviate	172. appropriate
117. accompanying	146. allotted	173. approximate
118. accomplish	147. allotment	174. area
119. accuracy	148. allowed	175. arise
120. accurate	149. allows	176. arising
121. accurately	150. already	177. arouse
122. accuser		178. arousing
123. accuses	[IV]	179. arrangement
124. accusing	151. altar	180. article
125. accustom	152. all together	181. atheist
126. acquaintance	153. altogether	182. athlete
127. across	154. amateur	183. athletic
128. actuality	155. amount	184. attack

185. attempts	219. bury	253. compatible
186. attendance	220. business	254. competition
187. attendant	221. busy	255. competitive
188. attended	222. calendar	256. competitor
189. attitude	223. capitalism	257. completely
190. audience	224. career	258. concede
191. authoritative	225. careful	259. conceivable
192. authority	226. careless	260. conceive
193. available	227. carried	261. concentrate
194. bargain	228. carrier	262. concern
195. basically	229. carries	263. condemn
196. basis	230. carrying	264. confuse
197. beauteous	231. cemetery	265. confusion
198. beautified	232. certainly	266. connotation
199. beautiful	233. challenge	267. connote
200. beauty	234. changeable	268. conscience
	235. changing	269. conscientious
[V]	236. characteristic	270. consequently
201. become	237. characterized	271. considerably
202. becoming	238. chief	272. consistency
203. before	239. children	273. consistent
204. began	240. Christian	274. contemporary
205. beginner	241. Christianity	275. continuously
206. beginning	242. choice	276. controlled
207. behavior	243. choose	277. controlling
208. bigger	244. chose	278. convenience
209. biggest	245. cigarette	279. convenient
210. boundary	246. cite	280. correlate
211. breath	247. clothes	281. council
212. breathe	248. commercial	282. counselor
213. brilliance	249. commission	283. countries
214. brilliant	250. committee	284. create
215. Britain		285. criticism
216. Britannica	[VI]	286. criticize
217. burial	251. communist	287. cruelly
218. buried	252. companies	288. cruelty

289. curiosity	323. dropped	357. experiment
290. curious	324. due	358. extremely
291. curriculum	325. during	359. fallacy
292. dealt	326. eager	360. familiar
293. deceive	327. easily	361. families
294. decided	328. efficiency	362. fantasies
295. decision	329. efficient	363. fantasy
296. dependent	330. eighth	364. fashions
297. desirability	331. eliminate	365. favorite
298. desire	332. emperor	366. fictitious
299. despair	333. emphasize	367. field
300. destruction	334. encourage	368. finally
	335. endeavor	369. financially
[VII]	336. enjoy	370. financier
301. detriment	337. enough	371. foreigners
302. devastating	338. enterprise	372. forty
303. device, devise	339. entertain	373. forward
304. difference	340. entertainment	374. fourth
305. different	341. entirely	375. friendliness
306. difficult	342. entrance	376. fulfill
307. dilemma	343. equipment	377. fundamentally
308. diligence	344. equipped	378. further
309. dining	345. escapade	379. gaiety
310. disappoint	346. escape	380. generally
311. disciple	347. especially	381. genius
312. discipline	348. etc.	382. government
313. discrimination	349. everything	383. governor
314. discussion	350. evidently	384. grammar
315. disease		385. grammatically
316. disgusted	[VIII]	386. group
317. disillusioned	351. excellence	387. guaranteed
318. dissatisfied	352. excellent	388. guidance
319. divide	353. except	389. guiding
320. divine	354. excitable	390. handled
321. doesn't	355. exercise	391. happened
322. dominant	356. expense	392. happiness

393. hear	427. industries	461. livelihood
394. here	428. inevitable	462. liveliness
395. heroes	429. influence	463. lives
396. heroic	430. influential	464. loneliness
397. heroine	431. ingenious	465. lonely
398. hindrance	432. ingredient	466. loose
399. hopeless	433. initiative	467. loss
400. hoping	434. intellect	468. luxury
	435. intelligence	469. magazine
[IX]	436. intelligent	470. magnificence
401. hospitalization	437. interference	471. magnificent
402. huge	438. interpretation	472. maintenance
403. humorist	439. interrupt	473. management
404. humorous	440. involve	474. maneuver
405. hundred	441. irrelevant	475. manner
406. hunger	442. irresistible	476. manufacturers
407. hungrily	443. irritable	477. material
408. hungry	444. jealousy	478. mathematics
409. hypocrisy	445. knowledge	479. matter
410. hypocrite	446. laboratory	480. maybe
411. ideally	447. laborer	481. meant
412. ignorance	448. laboriously	482. mechanics
413. ignorant	449. laid	483. medical
414. imaginary	450. later	484. medicine
415. imagination		485. medieval
416. imagine	[X]	486. melancholy
417. immediately	451. leisurely	487. methods
418. immense	452. lengthening	488. miniature
419. importance	453. license	489. minutes
420. incidentally	454. likelihood	490. mischief
421. increase	455. likely	491. moral
422. indefinite	456. likeness	492. morale
423. independence	457. listener	493. morally
424. independent	458. literary	494. mysterious
425. indispensable	459. literature	495. narrative
426. individually	460. liveliest	496. naturally

181

497. Negroes
498. ninety
499. noble
500. noticeable

[XI]

501. noticing
502. numerous
503. obstacle
504. off
505. omit
506. operate
507. oppose
508. opponent
509. opposite
510. optimism
511. organization
512. original
513. pamphlets
514. parallel
515. parliament
516. paralyzed
517. passed
518. past
519. peace
520. peculiar
521. perceive
522. permanent
523. permit
524. persistent
525. persuade
526. pertain
527. phase
528. phenomenon
529. philosophy
530. physical

531. piece
532. planned
533. plausible
534. playwright
535. pleasant
536. politician
537. political
538. practice
539. predominant
540. preferred
541. presence
542. prestige
543. primitive
544. prisoners
545. propaganda
546. propagate
547. prophecy
548. psychoanalysis
549. psychology
550. psychopathic

[XII]

551. psychosomatic
552. quantity
553. really
554. realize
555. rebel
556. recognize
557. regard
558. relative
559. relieve
560. religion
561. remember
562. reminisce
563. represent
564. resources

565. response
566. revealed
567. ridicule
568. ridiculous
569. roommate
570. sacrifice
571. safety
572. satire
573. satisfied
574. satisfy
575. scene
576. schedule
577. seize
578. sentence
579. sergeant
580. several
581. shepherd
582. significance
583. simile
584. simple
585. simply
586. since
587. sincerely
588. sociology
589. sophomore
590. source
591. speaking
592. speech
593. sponsor
594. stabilization
595. stepped
596. stories
597. story
598. straight
599. strength
600. stretch

[XIII]

601. strict
602. stubborn
603. substantial
604. subtle
605. sufficient
606. summary
607. summed
608. suppose
609. suppress
610. surrounding
611. susceptible
612. suspense
613. swimming
614. symbol
615. synonymous
616. temperament

617. tendency
618. themselves
619. theories
620. theory
621. therefore
622. those
623. thought
624. together
625. tomorrow
626. tragedy
627. tremendous
628. tried
629. tries
630. tyranny
631. undoubtedly
632. unusually
633. useful

634. useless
635. using
636. vacuum
637. valuable
638. varies
639. various
640. view
641. vengeance
642. warrant
643. weather
644. weird
645. where
646. whether
647. whole
648. whose
649. yield
650. you're

Note 1: The preceding list gives American spellings only. British spellings often vary from the American, as in the following words: Am. *analyze*, Br. *analyse;* Am. *criticize*, Br. *criticise;* Am. *fulfill*, Br. *fulfil;* Am. *humor*, Br. *humour;* Am. *practice*, Br. *practise;* Am. *stabilization*, Br. *stabilisation.*

Note 2: Spellings that vary from the usual are called *variants.* For example, *advertize* is a variant spelling of *advertise*, *cigaret* of *cigarette.* Such variants may, in time, gain in popularity and replace the former spellings.

Individual Spelling Record

One of the best ways to improve your spelling is to keep a record of the words you tend to misspell. You may find it helpful to keep an individual spelling record like the one on the next page. Give the correct spelling for each problem word, write the same word in syllables, and make a note of the best means you have found to remember the correct spelling. (You might start your spelling list with the words misspelled in your written work and recorded in the spelling column of your "Record of Errors," as illustrated on page 91 at the end of Section **8**.) Study the words in your spelling list from time to time so that you will not make the same mistakes again.

SPELLING RECORD

Words	Syllabication	Notes
candidate	can-di-date	Pronounce the first _d_.
tragedy	trag-e-dy	Do not transpose _g_ and _d_.
its	its	No apostrophe in the possessive. _It's_ = _it is_ or _it has_.
recommend	rec-om-mend	_Re_ + _commend_ — one _c_
sincerely	sin-cere-ly	Keep _e_ before _-ly_
studying	stud-y-ing	Keep _y_ before _-ing_.
Machiavellian	Mach-i-a-vel-li-an	Add _-an_ to the name _Machiavelli_. Use _ch_ for /k/.

Hyphenation

18f

Hyphenate words chiefly to express the idea of a unit or to avoid ambiguity. For the division of words at the end of a line, see **8b(8)**.

A hyphenated word may be either two words still in the process of becoming one word or a compound form coined by the writer to fit the occasion. In the former case a recent dictionary will assist in determining current usage. Many compound forms now written as one word were originally separate words and then, in the transitional stage, were hyphenated. For example, *post man* first became *post-man* and then *postman*. More recently *basket ball* has passed through the transitional *basket-ball* to *basketball*. The use of the hyphen in compounding is in such a state of flux that authorities often disagree. Some of the more generally accepted usages are listed below.

(1) Use the hyphen to join two or more words serving as a single adjective before a noun.

> a bluish-green dress, a sleep-inducing hum, a well-known poem, chocolate-covered peanuts

But the hyphen is omitted when the first word of the compound is an adverb ending in *-ly* or when the adjectives (or adjectivals) follow the noun.

> a slightly elevated walk, a gently sloping terrace
> Her dress was bluish green.
> The hum was sleep inducing.
> The poem is well known.
> The peanuts were chocolate covered.

Phrases, clauses, or even sentences may be used as a single hyphenated unit modifying a noun.

> heat-and-serve products   a for-adults-only movie
> an after-you-have-eaten-too-much remedy
> a you-must-be-over-thirty look

Note 1: "Suspension" hyphens may be used in such series as the following:

> two-, three-, and four-line poems

Note 2: The hyphen is generally preferred (but not required) in units designating centuries when placed before the words modified:

> nineteenth-century fashions   twentieth-century language

(2) Use the hyphen with compound numbers from twenty-one to ninety-nine and with fractions.

twenty-two, forty-five, ninety-eight
one-half, two-thirds, nine-tenths

Note: Some writers omit the hyphen in fractions used as nouns.

Two thirds of the voters endorsed the amendment. [*Two thirds* is the subject, not an adjective. Compare "A *two-thirds* vote is needed."]

(3) Use the hyphen to avoid ambiguity or an awkward combination of letters or syllables between prefix and root or suffix and root.

His *re-creation* of the setting was perfect. [BUT Fishing is good *recreation*.]
He *re-covered* the leaky roof. [BUT He *recovered* his health.]
His father owns a toy-repair store. [Compare "His father owns a toy repair-store."]
micro-organism, re-enter, semi-independent, shell-like, thrill-less, sub-subcommittee [BUT microeconomics, rewrite, semisolid, faunlike, hatless, subterranean]

(4) The hyphen is generally used with such prefixes as *ex-* (meaning "former"), *self-, all-,* and *great-;* between a prefix and a proper name; and with the suffix *-elect.*

ex-judge, self-made, all-purpose, great-aunt, pro-French, mayor-elect

■ **Exercise 4** Convert the following word groups according to the pattern of the examples, applying **18f**.

EXAMPLES
an initiation lasting two months
a two-month initiation

186

ideas that shake the world
world-shaking ideas

1. an apartment with six rooms
2. examinations that exhaust the mind
3. fingers stained with nicotine
4. a voter who is eighteen years old
5. shoppers who are budget minded
6. tents costing a hundred dollars
7. peace talks that last all night
8. a program that trains teachers
9. a hitchhiker who was waving a flag
10. ponds covered with lilies

Good Use—Glossary

19

Use a good dictionary to help you select the words that express your ideas exactly.

A dictionary is a storehouse of words. A good dictionary brings together words used in the English language and gives reliable information about those words.

19a

Use a good dictionary intelligently.

A good English dictionary is based upon scientific examination of the writing and speaking habits of the English-speaking world; it records the origin, development, and changing use of words. Any dictionary is reliable only to the extent that it is soundly based on usage. But even the best dictionary cannot be perfect, as Dr. Johnson observed long ago.

The unabridged dictionaries—those that try to include the half million words in the language—must run to several thousand pages in a single volume or to a number of volumes. Among these large dictionaries, the following are especially useful.

The Random House Dictionary of the English Language. New York: Random, 1966.

New Standard Dictionary of the English Language. New York: Funk, 1966.

Webster's Third New International Dictionary. Springfield, Mass.: Merriam, 1961.

The Oxford English Dictionary (abbreviated *OED* or *NED*). 13 vols. Oxford: Oxford Univ. Press, 1933. (A corrected reissue of *A New English Dictionary on Historical Principles,* 10 vols. and Supplement, 1888–1933.)

From time to time you may need to consult one of these large dictionaries. But most of the time you can find the information you need in a good college dictionary such as the following:

The American College Dictionary (ACD). New York: Random, 1968.

The American Heritage Dictionary of the English Language (AHD). Boston: American Heritage and Houghton, 1969.

The Random House Dictionary of the English Language (RHD). College ed. New York: Random, 1968.

Standard College Dictionary (SCD). New York: Harcourt, 1963.

Webster's New World Dictionary of the American Language (NWD). 2nd College ed. New York: World, 1970.

Webster's Seventh New Collegiate Dictionary (NCD). Springfield, Mass.: Merriam, 1963.

Note: Dictionaries are usually kept up to date by frequent slight revisions, sometimes with supplementary pages for new words. The dates given above indicate the last thorough revision of each dictionary.

Intelligent use of a dictionary requires some knowledge of its plan and special abbreviations as given in the introductory matter. Following, for example, is a typical entry from the *AHD*.[1] Notice the various kinds of information supplied about the word *easy*.

Pronunciation Part of speech

Syllabication

Inflected forms

Spelling—**eas·y** (ē′zē) *adj.* **-ier, -iest.** **1.** Capable of being accomplished or acquired with ease; posing no difficulty: *"How easy is success to those who will only be true to themselves"* (Trollope). **2.** Free from worry, anxiety, trouble, or pain: *"Now as I was young and easy under the apple boughs"* (Dylan Thomas). **3.** Conducive to rest or comfort; pleasant and relaxing. **4.** Relaxed; easygoing; informal: *an easy, sociable manner.* **5.** Not strict or severe; lenient: *an easy teacher.* **6.** Readily persuaded or influenced; compliant. **7.** Not strained, hurried, or forced; moderate: *an easy walk around the block.* **8.** *Economics.* **a.** Small in demand and therefore readily obtainable: *Commodities are easier.* **b.** Plentiful and therefore obtainable at low interest rates: *easy money.* **9.** Evenly distributed between opponents. Said of cards: *easy aces.* **—adv.** In a cautious, restrained manner: *"She bid me take love easy, as the leaves grow on the tree"* (Yeats). See Usage note below. **—go easy on.** *Informal.* **1.** To use moderately or carefully: *go easy on the liquor.* **2.** To be indulgent or lenient with: *go easy on a tardy student.* **3.** To be delicate or tactful about: *go easy on the family scandal.* *Informal.* **1.** To refrain from exertion; relax. **2.** To refrain from anger or violence; stay calm. [Middle English *esy*, from Old French *aisie*, past participle of *aisier*, to put at ease, from *aise*, EASE.]

Synonyms: easy, simple, facile, effortless, smooth, light. These adjectives mean not requiring much effort or not reflecting effort or difficulty in performance. *Easy* applies both to tasks that require little effort and to persons who are not demanding. *Simple* describes tasks that are not complex and hence not demanding intellectually. *Facile* and *effortless* apply to performance and stress readiness and fluency of execution. *Facile*, however, sometimes has unfavorable connotations, as of haste or lack of care in action, glibness or lack of sincerity in speech, or superficiality of thought. *Effortless* can imply actual lack of effort but often refers to performance in which application of great strength or skill makes the execution seem easy. *Smooth* describes performance whose progress is even and unimpeded. *Light* refers to tasks or impositions that involve no taxing burdens or responsibilities.

Usage: Easy is used as an adverb principally in the constructions *easy come, easy go* and the informal *go easy on, take it easy,* and *easier said than done.* It is not customarily interchangeable with *easily.* Thus, *easy* and the comparative *easier* are not possible in such typical examples as these: *The handle turns easily. This is more easily recognized than the other.*

Definitions and examples of usage as an adjective

Special usage (technical)

Part of speech

Definitions and examples of usage as an adverb

Special usage (informal)

Origin

Synonyms: definitions and distinctions

Usage note

(1) Spelling, syllabication, and pronunciation As a writer, use a good dictionary not only to check spelling but also to find where words may be divided at the end of a line: see 8b(8). As a speaker, check the pronunciation of unfamiliar words in your dictionary. Keys to the sound symbols are at the bottom of the page as well as in the introductory matter at the front of the dictionary. A primary stress mark (′) normally follows the syllable that is most heavily accented. Secondary stress marks follow lightly accented syllables.

(2) Parts of speech and inflected forms Your dictionary provides labels indicating the possible uses of words in sentences—for instance, *adj.* (adjective), *adv.* (adverb), *v.t.* (verb, transitive). It also lists ways that given nouns, verbs, and modifiers change form to indicate number, tense, or comparison or to serve as another part of speech (for example, under *repress, v.t.,* may appear *repressible, adj.*).

(3) Definitions and examples of usage Dictionaries such as the *ACD,* the *AHD,* and the *SCD* give the most common meaning of a word first and list older, sometimes obsolete definitions later. For example, in defining *prevent,* these dictionaries give as the first definition "to keep from happening." Other dictionaries, however, arrange definitions in the historical order of development. For *prevent,* for instance, the *NCD* and the *NWD* begin with the original but obsolete meaning "to anticipate" and later give the present meaning "to keep from happening." The *OED,* the most detailed of all dictionaries of the English language, presents various quotations from English writers to show the exact meaning of a word at each stage of its history.

(4) Synonyms and antonyms Lists and discussions of synonyms in dictionaries often help to clarify the meaning of closely related words. By studying the connotations and denotations of words with similar meanings, you will find that you are able to choose your words more exactly and to convey more subtle shades of meaning. Lists of antonyms can help you to find a word that is the direct opposite of another in meaning. (For more complete lists of synonyms and antonyms, refer to a book of synonyms such as *Roget's International Thesaurus*, 3rd ed. [New York: T. Crowell, 1962], available in both paperbound and hardbound editions.)

(5) Origin: development of the language In college dictionaries the origin of the word—also called its *derivation* or *etymology*—is shown in square brackets. For example, after the entry *expel* in the *SCD* is this information: "[< L *expellere* < *ex*- out + *pellere* to drive, thrust]." This means that *expel* is derived from (<) the Latin (L) word *expellere*, which is made up of *ex*-, meaning "out," and the combining form *pellere*, meaning "to drive or thrust." Breaking up a word, when possible, into prefix (and also suffix, if any) and combining form, as in the case of *expel*, will often help to get at the basic meaning of a word.

	Prefix		*Combining form*		*Suffix*
dependent	*de-* down	+	*pendere* to hang	+	*-ent* one who
intercede	*inter-* between	+	*cedere* to pass		
preference	*pre-* before	+	*ferre* to carry	+	*-ence* state of
transmit	*trans-* across	+	*mittere* to send		

The bracketed information given by a good dictionary is especially rich in meaning when considered in relation to the historical development of our language. English is one of the Indo-European (IE)[2] languages, a group of languages apparently derived from a common source. Within this group of languages, many of the more familiar words are remarkably alike. Our word *mother,* for example, is *mater* in Latin (L), *meter* in Greek (Gk.), and *matar* in ancient Persian and in the Sanskrit (Skt.) of India. Words in different languages that apparently descend from a common parent language are called *cognates.* The large number of cognates and the many correspondences in sound and structure in most of the languages of Europe and some languages of Asia indicate that they are derived from the common language that linguists call Indo-European, which it is believed was spoken in parts of Europe about five thousand years ago. By the opening of the Christian era the speakers of this language had spread over most of Europe and as far east as India and had developed into eight or nine language groups. Of these, the chief groups that influenced English were the Greek (Hellenic) group on the eastern Mediterranean, the Latin (Italic) on the central and western Mediterranean, and the Germanic in northwestern Europe. English is descended from the Germanic.[3]

Two thousand years ago the Greek, the Latin, and the Germanic groups each comprised a more or less unified language group. After the fall of the Roman Empire in the fifth century, the several Latin-speaking divisions developed independently into the modern Romance languages, chief of which are Italian, French, and Spanish. Long before the fall of Rome the Germanic group was breaking up into three groups: (1) East Germanic, represented by the Goths, who were to play

---

[2] The parenthetical abbreviations for languages here and on the next few pages are those commonly used in bracketed derivations in dictionaries.

[3] See the inside back cover of the *NWD,* "Indo-European Roots" in the *AHD,* the entry *Indo-European* and "A Brief History of the English Language" in the *SCD,* or "Indo-European Languages" in the *NCD.*

a large part in the history of the last century of the Roman Empire before losing themselves in its ruins; (2) North Germanic, or Old Norse (ON), from which we have modern Danish (Dan.) and Swedish (Sw.), Norwegian (Norw.) and Icelandic (Icel.); and (3) West Germanic, the direct ancestor of English, Dutch (Du.), and German (Ger.).

The English language may be said to have begun about the middle of the fifth century, when the West Germanic Angles and Saxons began the conquest of what is now England and either absorbed or drove out the Celtic-speaking inhabitants. The next six or seven hundred years are known as the Old English (OE) or Anglo-Saxon (AS) period of the English language. The fifty or sixty thousand words then in the language were chiefly Anglo-Saxon, with a small mixture of Old Norse words as a result of the Danish (Viking) conquests of England beginning in the eighth century. But the Old Norse words were so much like the Anglo-Saxon that they cannot always be distinguished.

The transitional period from Old English to Modern English—about 1100 to 1500—is known as Middle English (ME). The Norman Conquest began in 1066. The Normans, or "Northmen," had settled in northern France during the Viking invasions and had adopted Old French (OF) in place of their native Old Norse. Then, crossing over to England by the thousands, they made French the language of the king's court in London and of the ruling classes, both French and English, throughout the land, while the masses continued to speak English. Only toward the end of the fifteenth century did English become once more the common language of all classes. But the language that emerged at that time had lost most of its Anglo-Saxon inflections and had taken on thousands of French words (derived originally from Latin). Nonetheless, it was still basically English, not French, in its structure.

The marked and steady development of the English language (until it was partly stabilized by printing, which was introduced in London in 1476) is suggested by the following passages, two from Old English and two from Middle English.

Hē ǣrst gescēop   eorðan bearnum
He first created   *for earth's children*

heofon tō hrōfe,   hālig scippend.
heaven as a roof,   *holy creator.*

From the "Hymn of Cædmon"
(middle of the Old English period)

Ēalā, hū lēas and hū unwrest is þysses middan-eardes wēla.
Alas! how false and how unstable is this midworld's weal!

Sē þe wæs ǣrur rīce cyng and maniges landes hlāford,
He that was before powerful king and of many lands lord,

hē næfde þā ealles landes būton seofon fōt mæl.
he had not then of all land but seven foot space.

From the *Anglo-Saxon Chronicle*, A.D. 1087
(end of the Old English period)

A knight ther was, and that a worthy man,
That fro the tyme that he first bigan
To ryden out, he loved chivalrye,
Trouthe and honour, fredom and curteisye.

From Chaucer's Prologue to the
Canterbury Tales, about 1385

Thenne within two yeres king Uther felle seke of a grete maladye. And in the meane whyle hys enemyes usurpped upon hym, and dyd a grete bataylle upon his men, and slewe many of his peple.

From Sir Thomas Malory's *Morte d'Arthur,*
printed 1485

A striking feature of Modern English (that is, English since 1500) is its immense vocabulary. As already noted, Old English used some fifty or sixty thousand words, very largely native Anglo-Saxon; Middle English used perhaps a hundred thousand words, many taken through the French from Latin and others taken directly from Latin; and unabridged dictionaries today list over four times as many. To make up this tremendous word hoard, we have borrowed most heavily from Latin, but we have drawn some words from almost every known language. English writers of the sixteenth century were especially eager to interlace their works with words from Latin authors. And, as Englishmen pushed out to colonize and to trade in many parts of the globe, they brought home new words as well as goods. Modern science and technology have drawn heavily from the Greek. As a result of all this borrowing, English has become the richest, most cosmopolitan of all languages.

In the process of enlarging our vocabulary we have lost most of our original Anglo-Saxon words. But those that are left make up the most familiar, most useful part of our vocabulary. Practically all our simple verbs, our articles, conjunctions, prepositions, and pronouns are native Anglo-Saxon; and so are many of our familiar nouns, adjectives, and adverbs. Every speaker and writer uses these native words over and over, much more frequently than the borrowed words. Indeed, if every word is counted every time it is used, the percentage of native words runs very high—usually between 70 and 90 percent. Milton's percentage was 81, Tennyson's 88, Shakespeare's about 90, and that of the King James Bible about 94. English has been enriched by its extensive borrowings without losing its individuality; it is still fundamentally the *English* language.

(6) **Special usage labels** Dictionaries ordinarily carry no usage labels for the bulk of English words. Unlabeled,

or general, words range from the very learned words appropriate in the most formal situations to the simple words used every day in both formal and informal situations.

Most dictionaries, however, provide a variety of special usage labels for words or for particular definitions of words. These labels indicate types or "levels" of usage that differ from the general. Below, for instance, is a sampling of labels from the *SCD*, together with typical word entries and definitions.

Archaic   **mete**   To measure.
Canadian   **growler**   In the Atlantic Provinces, a small iceberg.
Dialectal   **nohow**   In no way.
Illiterate and Dialectal   **ain't**   Am not: also used for *are not, is not, has not,* and *have not.*
Informal   **jam**   An embarrassing or dangerous predicament.
Obsolete   **peach**   To impeach, inform against.
Physics   **reradiation**   Secondary emission.
Rare   **yoke**   To bring into bondage.
Slang   **classy**   Stylish; elegant.

Other usage labels found in college dictionaries include *Colloquial, Humorous, Nonstandard, Regional, Substandard,* and *Vulgar.* A variety of labels are used to indicate that a word is in use in a specific country or a specific section of a country (for example, *British, United States, Western United States*) or to indicate that a word is a technical or professional term used only by a special group (for example, *Law, Medicine, Agriculture*).

Since language is constantly changing, the classification of words is often difficult. There are no clear-cut boundaries between the various classes, and even the best dictionaries do not always agree. Words that are labeled, however, should always be used with appropriate care: see **19b–i**.

(7) Usage notes   When a word presents a usage problem common to many people—such as the problem of when to use *among* or *between*—usage notes (or cross-references to them) ordinarily follow the dictionary entry. Because these explanations are specific and brief, they can be helpful timesavers for both speakers and writers.

■ **Exercise 1**   With the aid of your dictionary, write out the following words using sound symbols and stress marks to indicate the correct pronunciation.

(1) exquisite, (2) incongruous, (3) despicable, (4) physiognomy, (5) gargoyle, (6) interested, (7) reciprocity, (8) surveillance, (9) err, (10) impious.

■ **Exercise 2**   With the aid of your dictionary, classify each of the following words as a verb (transitive or intransitive), a noun, an adjective, an adverb, a preposition, or a conjunction. Give the principal parts of each verb, the plural (or plurals) of each noun, and the comparative and superlative of each adjective and adverb. (Note that some words are used as two or more parts of speech.)

(1) ski, (2) pay, (3) radio, (4) since, (5) bad, (6) often, (7) born, (8) like, (9) reprimand, (10) accidental.

■ **Exercise 3**   Study the following pairs of words in your dictionary (in the special usage notes, if any, that compare and contrast the pairs), and write sentences to illustrate the shades of difference in meaning.

1. irony—sarcasm
2. people—population
3. amiable—affable
4. sensual—sensuous
5. freedom—liberty
6. sound—noise
7. ambiguous—enigmatic
8. alien—foreigner
9. mercy—clemency
10. fluctuate—vacillate

■ **Exercise 4**   With the aid of your dictionary, list synonyms for each of the following words.

(1) fly, (2) smell, (3) awful, (4) fear, (5) anger, (6) attractive, (7) change, (8) fight.

■ **Exercise 5** With the aid of your dictionary, list antonyms for each of the following words.

(1) faithful, (2) correct, (3) impair, (4) freedom, (5) quicken, (6) clear, (7) smile, (8) danger.

■ **Exercise 6** With the aid of your dictionary, give the etymology of each of the following words.

(1) utopia, (2) credenza, (3) theology, (4) democracy, (5) OK, (6) oligarchy, (7) nasturtium, (8) namby-pamby, (9) onomatopoeia, (10) sputnik.

■ **Exercise 7** Classify the following words according to the usage labels in your dictionary. If a word has no special usage label, classify it as *General.*

(1) tote, (2) wino, (3) rookie, (4) osmosis, (5) unto, (6) swink, (7) slummy, (8) irregardless, (9) hushpuppy, (10) pooh-pooh.

19b

Avoid informal words in formal writing.

Words or expressions labeled *Informal* or *Colloquial* in college dictionaries are standard English and are used by speakers and writers every day. These words are thus appropriate in informal writing, especially in dialogue. But informal words or expressions are usually inappropriate in formal expository compositions. In formal writing, use instead the general English vocabulary, the unlabeled words in your dictionary.

INFORMAL   The repeated *phone* calls only *aggravated* me but made my sister *plenty mad.*

GENERAL   The repeated *telephone* calls only *annoyed* me but made my sister *very angry.*

As a rule, contractions are avoided in formal writing. Contracted forms like *won't, there's,* or *she'd* are normally written out: *will not, there is* or *there has, she would* or *she had.*

■ **Exercise 8** Consult your dictionary for informal meanings of the following words. For each word compose a sentence in which the word is used informally. Then in each sentence substitute a general (unlabeled) word with the same meaning.

(1) brass, (2) fizzle, (3) dig, (4) way.

19c

Use slang only when appropriate; avoid jargon in ordinary writing.

Slang is defined by the *SCD* as "language, words, or phrases of a vigorous, colorful, facetious, or taboo nature, invented for specific occasions or uses, or derived from the unconventional use of the standard vocabulary." On occasion, slang can be used effectively, even in formal writing. Below, for instance, is an example of the effective use of *spiels* and *hoopla,* both classified as *United States Slang.*

> Here comes election year. Here come the hopefuls, the conventions, the candidates, the spiels, the postures, the press releases, and the TV performances. Here comes the year of the hoopla.   —JOHN CIARDI

Slang words such as *spiel, hoopla, swinger,* or *up-tight* have a particularly vivid quality and may soon join former slang words such as *sham, mob,* and *banter* as standard words in the English language.

But much slang is trite, tasteless, and inexact. For instance, a person may describe everything he disapproves of as *lousy* when he could express himself more effectively with words such as *contemptible, unfair, mean,* or *worthless.* See also Section 20.

Like some slang words, trade language or professional jargon is confusing and sometimes meaningless outside the special group in which it originated. One type of confusing jargon is sometimes found in bureaucratic writing.

JARGON   All personnel functioning in the capacity of clerks will indicate that they have had opportunity to take due cognizance of this notice by transmitting signed acknowledgment of receipt of same.

GENERAL   All clerks will acknowledge in writing the receipt of this notice.

Note: Jargon in the sense of technical terms used by the learned professions can sometimes be very useful: see **19g**.

19d

Use regional words only when appropriate to the audience.

Regional, or *dialectal,* words (also called *localisms* or *provincialisms*) should normally be avoided in speaking and writing outside the region where they are current. Speakers and writers may, however, safely use regional words known to the audience they are addressing.

REGIONAL   Aunt Ella was *fixing* to go on a tour.
GENERAL   Aunt Ella was *getting ready* to go on a tour.

19e

Avoid nonstandard words and usages.

Words and expressions labeled by dictionaries as *Nonstandard* or *Illiterate* should be avoided in most writing and speaking. Many common illiteracies are not listed in college dictionaries at all.

NONSTANDARD The twins *ain't* going. *They's* no use asking them.

STANDARD   The twins *are not* going. *There's* no use asking them.

19f

Avoid archaic, obsolete, or obsolescent (rare) words.

All dictionaries list words (and meanings for words) that have long since passed out of general use. Such words as *ort* (fragment of food) and *yestreen* (last evening) are still found in dictionaries because these words, once the standard vocabulary of great authors, occur in our older literature and must be defined for the modern reader.

A number of modern "mistakes in grammar" are in reality archaic words still in use.

ARCHAIC   Yesterday I *drunk* blended asparagus.

STANDARD Yesterday I *drank* blended asparagus.

19g

Use technical words only when appropriate to the audience.

When you are writing for the general reader, avoid all unnecessary technical language. Since the ideal of the good writer is to make his thought clear to as many people as possible, he will not describe an apple tree as a *Malus pumila* or a high fever as *hyperpyrexia*. (Of course technical language, with its greater precision, is highly desirable when one is addressing an audience that can understand it, as when a physician addresses a group of physicians.)

Whenever technical terms come to be generally understood (as with *phosphate* and *autosuggestion,* for example), they may of course be used as freely as the unlabeled words in the dictionary.

19h

Avoid ornate or "fine" writing, "poetic" expressions, and unpleasing combinations of sounds (including overuse of alliteration).

(1) **"Fine" writing**   "Fine" writing is the unnecessary use of ornate words and expressions. It calls attention to words rather than to ideas, and it is generally fuzzy and repetitious. A simple, direct statement like "Since childhood I have looked forward to traveling abroad" can be transformed by fine writing into something like this: "Since the halcyon days of my early youth I have always anticipated with eagerness and pleasure the exciting vistas of distant climes and mysterious horizons."

(2) **"Poetic" expressions**   Genuine poetry has its very proper place, and the vivid language of simile and metaphor enriches even colloquial prose. But the sham poetry of faded imagery (*eye of night* for *moon*) and inappropriate expressions like *oft, eftsoons, 'twas,* and *'neath* are misplaced in most prose writing.

(3) **Unpleasing combinations of sounds (including overuse of alliteration)**   Good prose has rhythm, but it does not rhyme. In the sentence "In foreign *relations,* the Western *nations* are prone to *dictation,*" rhyme distracts the reader's attention from the meaning. Equally unpleasing to the average reader is the overuse of alliteration (repetition of the same consonant sound), as in "Some people *s*hun the *s*eashore."

■ **Exercise 9** With the aid of your dictionary, classify the following words as *Informal* or *Colloquial, Slang, Regional* or *Dialectal, Nonstandard, Archaic, Obsolete, Technical* (labels such as *Photography, Botany, Pathology, Nautical, Grammar*), *Poetic,* or *General.*

(1) his'n, (2) transitive, (3) manhandle, (4) hooligan, (5) betwixt, (6) nil, (7) e'en, (8) ballyhoo, (9) spunky, (10) goof.

■ **Exercise 10** Rewrite the following passages of bureaucratic, legal, or academic jargon in simple, formal, straightforward English.[4]

1. It is obvious from the difference in elevation with relation to the short depth of the property that the contour is such as to preclude any reasonable developmental potential for active recreation.
2. Verbal contact with Mr. Blank regarding the attached notification of promotion has elicited the attached representation intimating that he prefers to decline the assignment.
3. Voucherable expenditures necessary to provide adequate dental treatment required as adjunct to medical treatment being rendered a pay patient in in-patient status may be incurred as required at the expense of the Public Health Service.
4. I hereby give and convey to you, all and singular, my estate and interests, right, title, claim and advantages of and in said orange, together with all rind, juice, pulp and pits, and all rights and advantages therein.
5. I prefer an abbreviated phraseology, distinguished for its lucidity.
6. Realization has grown that the curriculum or the experiences of learners change and improve only as those who are most directly involved examine their goals, improve their understandings and increase their skill in performing the tasks necessary to reach newly defined goals.

[4]From *Power of Words* by Stuart Chase. Published by Harcourt Brace Jovanovich, Inc., and A. Watkins, Inc., 1953. Copyright 1953, 1954 Stuart Chase. Reprinted by permission.

Glossary of Usage

19i

Consult the following glossary to determine the standing of a word or phrase and its appropriateness to your purpose.

The entries in the following glossary are authoritative only to the extent that they describe current usage. They do not duplicate the descriptions in any one dictionary, but justification for each usage label can usually be found in at least two of the leading dictionaries.

For a discussion of the special usage labels used in dictionaries, see **19a(6)**. The following labels appear most frequently in this glossary:

General   Words in the standard English vocabulary, listed in dictionaries without special usage labels and appropriate in both formal and informal writing and speaking (for example, *acquaintance, associate, chum, friend*).

Informal   Words or expressions labeled *Informal* or *Colloquial* in dictionaries—words widely used by educated as well as uneducated writers and speakers but not appropriate in a formal context (for example, *buddy, pal*). See also **19b**.

Standard   All general and informal words or expressions (for example, *acquaintance, associate, buddy, chum, friend, pal*).

Nonstandard   Words or expressions labeled in dictionaries as *Archaic, Illiterate, Nonstandard, Obsolete, Slang,* or *Substandard*—words not considered a part of the standard English vocabulary (for example, *sidekick*). See also **19c, e**, and **f**.

Of course, the following glossary can include only a few of the words likely to cause difficulty. If the word you are looking for is not included, or if you need more information about any word in the list, consult a good college dictionary.

a, an   Use *a* before a consonant sound, *an* before a vowel sound.

> *a* heavy load, *a* nap, *a* uniform, *a* one-man show
> *an* honest boy, *an* ape, *an* umpire, *an* only child

about   *About* alone is preferable to *at about.* Avoid using *as to* as a substitute for *about.*

> WORDY   He arrived at about noon.
> BETTER   He arrived *about* noon.
> VAGUE   She spoke to me as to her plans.
> BETTER   She spoke to me *about* her plans.

accept, except   The verb *accept* means "to give an affirmative answer to" or "to receive." The verb *except,* seldom used, means "to exclude"; as a preposition, *except* means "with the exclusion of."

> Mary *accepted* the invitation to dinner.
> They *excepted* Mary from the invitation.
> All the boys *accept* John as their leader.
> All the boys *except* John are leaders.

accidentally, incidentally   When using these adverbs, remember that *-ly* is added to the adjective forms *accidental* and *incidental,* not to the noun forms *accident* and *incident.*

> NONSTANDARD   Mr. Kent accidently overheard the report.
> STANDARD   Mr. Kent *accidentally* overheard the report.

ad, exam, gym   Informal shortening of *advertisement, examination, gymnasium.* Formal writing requires the full word.

advice, advise   Pronounced and spelled differently, *advice* is a noun, *advise* a verb.

> Patients should follow their doctors' *advice.*
> Patients should do what their doctors *advise.*

affect, effect   *Affect,* meaning "to influence," is a verb only. *Effect* may function as a verb or a noun. The verb *effect* means "to bring about, to achieve"; the noun *effect* means "the result."

> The reforms *affected* many citizens.
> The citizens *effected* a few reforms.

He said that wars *affect* the economy.
He stressed the *effect* of wars on the economy.

aggravate Informally *aggravate* means "to provoke or exasperate, to arouse to anger." In general usage it means "to make worse" or "to intensify."

> INFORMAL Undisciplined children *aggravate* baby sitters.
> GENERAL Lack of water *aggravated* the suffering.

ain't A nonstandard contraction avoided by most writers, unless used for humorous effect.

alibi A legal term used informally for *excuse*. Inappropriate in general writing except in a legal context.

> INFORMAL He gave his usual *alibi*.
> GENERAL He gave his usual *excuse*.

all right, alright *Alright* is still a questionable spelling of *all right*.

all the farther, all the faster Nonstandard substitutes for *as far as, as fast as*.

> NONSTANDARD A mile is all the farther we can walk.
> STANDARD A mile is *as far as* we can walk.

allusion, illusion Do not confuse *allusion*, "an indirect reference," with *illusion*, "an unreal image or false impression."

> Timothy made an *allusion* to the Trojans.
> The Trojan Horse was no optical *illusion*.

almost, most *Most* is used informally as a substitute for *almost*.

> INFORMAL *Most* all referees strive to be fair.
> GENERAL *Almost* all referees strive to be fair.

a lot Sometimes misspelled as *alot*.

already, all ready *Already* means "before or by the time specified." *All ready* means "completely prepared."

> The theater was *already* full by seven o'clock.
> The cast was *all ready* for the curtain call.

altogether, all together   *Altogether* means "wholly, thoroughly." *All together* means "in a group."

> That type of rule is *altogether* unnecessary.
> They were *all together* in the lobby.

alumnus, alumna   An *alumnus* is a male graduate; *alumni,* two or more male graduates. An *alumna* is a female graduate; *alumnae,* two or more female graduates. *Alumni* also refers to male and female graduates grouped together.

A.M., P.M. (OR **a.m., p.m.**)   Use only with figures.

> The auction begins at *8:30* A.M. and ends at *4:00* P.M.
> The auction begins at *half-past eight in the morning* and ends at *four o'clock in the afternoon.*

among, between   *Among* always implies more than two, a group; *between* literally implies only two. *Between,* however, is now often used for three or more when each is regarded individually.

> What honor was there *among* the forty thieves?
> What is the difference *between* a thief and a robber?
> The difference *between* the three girls was so slight that they might have been triplets.

amount, number   *Amount* refers to things in bulk or mass; *number* refers to the countable.

> A large *amount* of rice is consumed annually.
> A large *number* of disgruntled men barred the entrance.

an, a   See **a, an**.

and etc.   See **etc**.

and/or   Usually considered inappropriate or distracting (except in legal or commercial writing).

anyone, any one   *Anyone* means "any person at all." *Any one* refers to a specific person or thing in a group. Similar forms are *everyone, every one; someone, some one.*

> *Anyone* can wax a floor.
> *Any one* of those men can wax a floor.

anyways, anywheres   Nonstandard for *anyway, anywhere.*

as In your formal writing avoid using *as* instead of *that* or *whether*. Do not use *as* as a substitute for *because, for, since, while, who,* or *which*.

INFORMAL	I do not know *as* I should go.
GENERAL	I do not know *whether* I should go.
AMBIGUOUS	As it was snowing, we played cards.
CLEAR	*While* it was snowing, we played cards.
	OR *Because* it was snowing, we played cards.

See also **like, as, as if**.

as to See **about**.

at Although *from* after *where* is standard, *at* after *where* is not standard.

NONSTANDARD	Where did the Brownings live at?
STANDARD	Where did the Brownings live?

at about See **about**.

awhile, a while Distinguish between the adverb *awhile* and the article and noun *a while*.

Rest *awhile* before you leave.
Rest for *a while* before you leave.

bad, badly The adverb *badly* is preferred after most verbs. But either *bad* or *badly* is now standard in the sense of "ill" or "sorry," and writers now usually prefer *bad* after such verbs as *feel* or *look*.

The organist plays *badly*.
Charles feels *bad*.

bank on Informal expression for *rely on*.

because See **reason . . . because**.

being as, being that Nonstandard for *since, because*.

beside, besides When meaning "except," *beside* and *besides* are interchangeable prepositions. Distinguish, however, between *beside* meaning "by the side of" and *besides* meaning "in addition to."

I sat *beside* the window.
Herbert has income *besides* his salary.

Notice the difference in meaning below:

He owns the car *beside* the house.
He owns the car *besides* the house.

better See **had better, had rather, would rather.**

between, among See **among, between.**

bug Informal for *germ* or *defect;* slang for *enthusiast.*

INFORMAL	The new car had a few *bugs.*
GENERAL	The new car had a few *defects.*
SLANG	He is a UFO bug.
GENERAL	He is a UFO *enthusiast.*

burst, bursted, bust, busted The principal parts of *burst* are *burst, burst, burst;* the archaic *bursted* is not standard usage. *Bust* and *busted* are slang.

but, hardly, scarcely *Can't help but* is now standard, both formally and informally, but such negatives as *can't hardly* and *don't scarcely* are still nonstandard.

NONSTANDARD	I couldn't hardly read his handwriting.
STANDARD	I *could hardly* read his handwriting.
STANDARD	I *couldn't help but* laugh. OR I *couldn't help* laughing.

but what Informal for *that* in negative expressions.

INFORMAL	Brad has no doubt *but what* the Lions will win.
GENERAL	Brad has no doubt *that* the Lions will win.

can, may Informal usage substitutes *can* for *may* in questions and negations. Formal usage still requires that *can* be used to denote ability to perform and *may* to denote permission to do.

INFORMAL	*Can* I use your class notes?
GENERAL	*May* I use your class notes?

can't hardly A double negative in implication. Use *can hardly.* See also **but, hardly, scarcely.**

case, line Often used in wordy expressions.

> WORDY   In the case of Jones there were good intentions.
> CONCISE Jones had good intentions.
> WORDY   Buy something in the line of fruit.
> CONCISE Buy some fruit.

complected Regional, or dialectal, for *complexioned*.

> REGIONAL They are light-complected children.
> GENERAL They are *light-complexioned* children. OR They are children *of light complexion*.

complementary, complimentary Do not confuse *complementary*, "completing" or "supplying needs," with *complimentary*, "expressing praise" or "given free."

> His talents and hers are *complementary*.
> He made several *complimentary* remarks.

considerable Used generally as an adjective, informally as a noun. Nonstandard as an adverb.

> NONSTANDARD Prices have dropped considerable.
> INFORMAL   *Considerable* has been donated to the civic fund.
> GENERAL   A *considerable* amount has been donated to the civic fund.

contact Frequently overused for more exact words or phrases such as *ask, consult, inform, query, talk with, telephone, write to*.

could of Nonstandard for *could have*.

credible, credulous *Credible* means "believable, reliable." *Credulous* means "disposed to believe on slight evidence" or "gullible."

> Her story was scarcely *credible*.
> The judge was not a *credulous* man.

data, criteria, phenomena The plurals of *datum* (rarely used), *criterion*, and *phenomenon. Criterion* and *phenomenon* have alternate plurals: *criterions, phenomenons*. The plural *data* is often construed as a collective noun: "This *data has* been verified."

deal Used informally to mean "business transaction." Frequently overworked in place of more exact words such as *sale, agreement, plan, secret agreement.*

different from In the United States the preferred preposition after *different* is *from.* But the more informal *different than* is accepted by many writers if the expression is followed by a clause.

> The Stoic philosophy is *different from* the Epicurean.
> The outcome was *different from* what I expected. OR The outcome was *different than* I had expected.

differ from, differ with *Differ from* means "to stand apart because of unlikeness." *Differ with* means "to disagree."

disinterested, uninterested Often used interchangeably. Some authorities, however, do not accept *disinterested* as a substitute for *uninterested,* meaning "indifferent."

done Standard as an adjective and as the past participle of the verb *do.* Nonstandard as an adverb and as a substitute for *did.*

NONSTANDARD	The bread is done sold.
STANDARD	The bread is *already* sold. The bread is *done.*
NONSTANDARD	Do the police know who done it?
STANDARD	Do they know who *did* it? Who *has done* it?

don't A contraction of *do not* rather than of *does not.*

NONSTANDARD	He don't smoke. (He do not smoke.)
STANDARD	He *doesn't* smoke. (He *does not* smoke.)
STANDARD	They *don't* smoke. (They *do not* smoke.)

each and every Redundant.

each other, one another Used interchangeably. Some writers prefer *each other* when referring to only two and *one another* when referring to more than two.

effect, affect See **affect, effect.**

either, neither Used to refer to one or the other of two. As subjects, both words are singular.

> *Either* a bicycle or a car will please him.
> *Neither* of the paintings *is* finished.

emigrate, immigrate *Emigrate* means "to leave a place of abode for residence in another country." *Immigrate* means "to come for permanent residence into a country of which one is not a native."

> Conrad *emigrated* from Poland.
> He *immigrated* to England.

eminent, imminent, immanent *Eminent* means "distinguished." *Imminent* means "about to happen, threatening." *Immanent* means "indwelling" or "invading all creation."

> He is an *eminent* scientist.
> Bankruptcy seemed *imminent*.
> We discussed Hardy's concept of the *Immanent* Will.

enthuse, enthused *Enthuse* is informal as a verb meaning "to show enthusiasm." *Enthused* is informal as a synonym for *enthusiastic*.

> INFORMAL   We were all *enthused* about the new club.
> GENERAL   We were all *enthusiastic* about the new club.

etc. An abbreviation of the Latin *et* (meaning "and") *cetera* (meaning "other things"). Use *etc.* sparingly. Do not place *and* before *etc.*, for then the *and* becomes redundant.

every so often, ever so often Do not confuse. *Ever so often* means "very often, frequently"; *every so often* means "occasionally, every now and then."

everyone, every one See **anyone, any one**.

everywheres Nonstandard for *everywhere*.

exam See **ad, exam, gym**.

except, accept See **accept, except**.

expect Informal when used for *suppose* or *think*.

> INFORMAL   I *expect* James voted yesterday.
> GENERAL   I *suppose* James voted yesterday.

fabulous Informal for *very good* or *pleasing*.

> INFORMAL   The pineapple salad was *fabulous*.
> GENERAL   The pineapple salad was *very good*.

farther, further These words are often used interchangeably to express geographic distance, though some writers prefer *farther*. *Further* is used to express additional time, degree, or quantity.

> Denver is *farther* north than Dallas.
> Will there be *further* improvements in city government?

fewer, less Informally used interchangeably. Formally *less* refers to value, degree, or amount; *fewer* refers to number, to the countable.

> Women now spend *less* time in kitchens.
> Women now spend *fewer* hours in kitchens.

fine Informal when used as an adverb meaning "well, excellently."

flunk Informal for *fail*.

folks Informal for *parents, relatives*.

former Refers to the first named of two. If three or more items are named, use *first* and *last* instead of *former* or *latter*.

> The Folger and the Huntington are two famous libraries; the *former* is in Washington, D.C., and the latter is in California.

get The verb *to get* is one of the most versatile words in standard English. It is common in such standard idioms as *get along with* (someone), *get the better of* (someone), *get at* (information), *get on* (a horse), or *get over* (an illness). Avoid, however, slang or very informal usages of *get* or *got*.

> SLANG   Their reactionary attitudes really *get* me.
> GENERAL Their reactionary attitudes *baffle* me.

good Nearly always used as an adjective. Generally considered informal when used as an adverb.

> INFORMAL Mrs. Nevins cooks *good*.
> GENERAL   She cooks *well*.   Mrs. Nevins cooks *good* meals.

got, gotten Past participles of *get*, the principal parts of which are *get, got, got* or *gotten*. In England *gotten* is now considered old-fashioned, but in the United States both *got* and *gotten* are in general use.

guy   Informal for *man* or *boy*.

gym   See **ad, exam, gym.**

had better, had rather, would rather   Standard idioms used to express advisability (with *better*) or preference (with *rather*). *Better* is an informal shortening of *had better*.

INFORMAL   Members *better* pay their dues.
GENERAL   Members *had better* pay their dues.

had of, had ought   Nonstandard for *had, ought*.

half a, a half, a half a   Use *half a* or *a half* (perhaps more formal), but avoid the redundant *a half a*.

REDUNDANT   He worked a half a day.
GENERAL   He worked *half a* day.
GENERAL   He worked *a half* day.

hanged, hung   Informally *hanged* and *hung* are often used interchangeably. Formal usage prefers *hanged* in referring to executions and *hung* in referring to objects.

The cattle thieves were *hanged*.
African trophies were *hung* in the hall of the lodge.

hardly   See **but, hardly, scarcely.**

have, of   See **of, have.**

healthful, healthy   Although both *healthful* and *healthy* are standard words meaning "conducive to health," *healthy* is most frequently used to mean "having health"; *healthful*, to mean "giving health."

STANDARD   That is a *healthful* climate.
STANDARD   That is a *healthy* climate.
RARE   *Healthful* pets are sold in that shop.
STANDARD   *Healthy* pets are sold in that shop.

himself   See **myself** (**himself**, etc.).

hisself Nonstandard for *himself.*

illusion, allusion See **allusion, illusion.**

immigrate, emigrate See **emigrate, immigrate.**

imminent, immanent See **eminent, imminent, immanent.**

imply, infer The writer or speaker *implies;* the reader or listener *infers. Imply* means "to suggest without stating"; *infer* means "to reach a conclusion based upon evidence." Often used interchangeably in informal English.

> His statement *implies* that he will resign.
> From his statement I *infer* that he will resign.

in, into *In* generally indicates "location within." Although *in* may be used for *into,* formal usage prefers *into* to indicate "motion or direction to a point within."

> GENERAL   A man came *in* the library to call the police.
> PREFERRED   A man came *into* the library to call the police.

Compare the meaning of these sentences:

> We flew *in* another jet.
> We flew *into* another jet.

in back of, in behind, in between Wordy for *behind* or *between.*

incidentally, accidentally See **accidentally, incidentally.**

incredible, incredulous *Incredible* means "too extraordinary to admit of belief." *Incredulous* means "inclined not to believe on slight evidence."

> The hunters told *incredible* stories.
> The hunters' stories made me *incredulous.*

individual, party, person *Individual* refers to a single thing, animal, or person. In legal writing *party* may refer to a group of people or to a single person, but in other formal writing *party* designates a group only. In general usage *person* is preferred for reference to a human being.

> INFORMAL   Paul is the only interested *party.*
> GENERAL   Paul is the only interested *person.*

infer, imply See **imply, infer.**

inferior than Nonstandard. Use *inferior to* or *worse than.*

ingenious, ingenuous *Ingenious* means "clever, resourceful"; *ingenuous* means "open, frank" or "artless."

> The electric can opener is an *ingenious* device.
> Don's *ingenuous* smile disarms the critics.

in regards to Nonstandard for *in regard to* or *as regards.*

inside of, outside of The *of* is often unnecessary. *Inside of* is informal for *within. Outside of* is informal for *except, besides.*

> INFORMAL   The job will be finished *inside of* ten days.
> GENERAL   The job will be finished *within* ten days.
> INFORMAL   He has no hobbies *outside of* golf.
> GENERAL   He has no hobbies *except* golf.

irregardless Nonstandard for *regardless.*

is when, is where Do not use *when* and *where* after *is* in giving definitions.

> AWKWARD   Steamrolling is when opposition is suppressed.
> BETTER   Steamrolling is the suppression of opposition.
> AWKWARD   "Future shock" is where extremely rapid change causes mental disturbance.
> BETTER   "Future shock" is mental disturbance caused by extremely rapid change.

its, it's *Its* is a possessive pronoun. *It's* is a contraction of *it is* or *it has.*

kind, sort Singular forms, which may be modified by *that* or *this.* Formally, use *those* or *these* to modify only plural forms.

> INFORMAL   Mr. Pratt prefers *these kind* to *those kind.*
> GENERAL   Mr. Pratt prefers *this kind* to *those kinds.*

kind of, sort of Informal when used as an adverb meaning "somewhat, rather, after a fashion."

> INFORMAL   The kitchen floor seems *kind of* uneven.
> GENERAL   The kitchen floor seems *somewhat* uneven.

kind of a   Omit the *a* in your formal writing.

later, latter   *Later,* referring to time, is the comparative form of *late. Latter* refers to the last named of two. If more than two items are named, use *last* instead of *latter.*

lay, lie   Do not confuse these verbs: see **7a(1)**.

learn, teach   *Learn* means "to acquire knowledge"; *teach* means "to impart knowledge."

> Miss Evans *taught* Earl only one week, but he *learned* how to study during that time.

leave, let   Do not use *leave* for *let. Leave* means "to depart from"; *let* means "to permit." But "Leave (OR Let) me alone" is a standard idiom.

> NONSTANDARD   I will not leave you go today.
> STANDARD   I will not *let* you go today.

less, fewer   See **fewer, less.**

let's us   Redundant for *let's,* which is a contraction of *let us.*

lie, lay   Do not confuse these verbs: see **7a(1).**

like, as, as if   In general usage, *like* functions as a preposition; *as* and *as if* (or *as though*) function as conjunctions. Although widely used in conversation and in public speaking, *like* as a conjunction is still controversial in a formal context.

> GENERAL   He drives *like* me.   [Prepositional function]
> CONTROVERSIAL   He drives *like* I do.   [Conjunction]
> GENERAL   He drives *as* a gentleman should.   [Conjunction]
> CONTROVERSIAL   He drives *like* he was angry.   [Conjunction]
> GENERAL   He drives *as if* he were angry.   [Conjunction]

In such elliptical constructions as the following, however, the conjunction *like* is appropriate, even in a formal context.

> He is attracted to blondes *like* a moth to lights.

likely, liable   Informally *liable* is sometimes substituted for *likely.* Formally *likely* means "probable" or "to be expected"; *liable* means "susceptible to something unpleasant" or "legally responsible."

> INFORMAL   My favorite program is *liable* to win an award.
> GENERAL   My favorite program is *likely* to win an award.
> GENERAL   John is *liable* to cut his foot with the power saw.

line, case   See **case, line.**

lose, loose   Do not confuse. *Lose* means "to cease having." The verb *loose* means "to set free"; the adjective *loose* means "free, not fastened."

> I was warned not to *lose* the keys.
> The keys are *loose* in my pocket.

mad   Still considered informal when used as a substitute for *angry* or *enthusiastic.*

may, can   See **can, may.**

may be, maybe   Distinguish between the verb form *may be* and the adverb *maybe,* meaning "perhaps."

> April *may be* the best time for a vacation.
> *Maybe* the family will take a vacation in April.

mighty   Informally used for *very, exceedingly.* The general meaning of *mighty* is "powerful, strong."

> INFORMAL   The Wards are *mighty* good neighbors.
> GENERAL   The Wards are *very* good neighbors.
> GENERAL   In Rhodes stood the *mighty* statue of Colossus.

moral, morale   The noun *moral* means "lesson, maxim"; the adjective *moral* means "pertaining to right conduct" or "ethical." *Morale,* a noun, means "a cheerful, confident state of mind."

> What is the *moral* of Thurber's fable?
> Has the *morale* of the team improved?

most, almost   See **almost, most.**

myself (**himself,** etc.)   Properly an intensive or reflexive pronoun: "I *myself* will go; I must see for *myself.*" In general *myself* is not a proper substitute for *I* or *me;* but it is informally substituted for *I* after comparisons with *than* or *as* and for *me* when used as the second member of a compound object.

> INFORMAL   Everyone worked as well as *myself.*
> GENERAL   Everyone worked as well as *I.*
> INFORMAL   He encouraged my brother and *myself.*
> GENERAL   He encouraged my brother and *me.*

neither, either   See **either, neither.**

nice   Overworked as a vague word of approval.

nohow   Nonstandard for *not at all.*

nowheres   Nonstandard for *nowhere.*

number, amount   See **amount, number.**

of, have   The preposition *of* is nonstandard when substituted in writing for the verb form *have.*

> NONSTANDARD   Mary could of (would of, may of, might of, must of, ought to of) done that last week.
> STANDARD   Mary could *have* (would *have*, may *have*, might *have*, must *have*, ought to *have*) done that last week.

off of   Omit the *of* in your formal writing.

OK, O.K., okay   All three are accepted as standard forms expressing general approval. A more specific word, however, usually replaces *OK* in a formal context.

one another, each other   See **each other, one another.**

outside of, inside of   See **inside of, outside of.**

party, person   See **individual, party, person.**

per   Careful writers generally avoid *per* except in business English or in Latin phrases.

phenomena   Plural of *phenomenon.* See **data, criteria, phenomena.**

phone   Informal for *telephone.* In your formal writing use the full word.

photo Informal for *photograph*. In your formal writing use the full word.

plenty Informal when used as an adverb meaning "very."

> INFORMAL The chemistry test was *plenty* hard.
> GENERAL The chemistry test was *very* hard.

P.M., A.M. See **A.M., P.M.**

practical, practicable *Practical* means "useful, sensible" or "not theoretical." *Practicable* means "feasible, capable of being put into practice."

> The sponsors are *practical*, and their plans are *practicable*.

principal, principle Distinguish between *principal*, an adjective or noun meaning "chief" or "chief official," and the noun *principle*, meaning "fundamental truth."

> A *principal* factor in his decision was his belief in the *principle* that men are born equal.

raise, rise See **rise, raise.**

real Informal when used as an adverb meaning "very, extremely."

> INFORMAL The victorious team was *real* tired.
> GENERAL The victorious team was *extremely* tired.

reason . . . because Informal redundancy. Use *that* instead of *because* or recast the sentence.

> INFORMAL The reason why he missed his class was *because* he overslept.
> GENERAL The reason why he missed his class was *that* he overslept. OR He missed his class *because* he overslept.

reckon Informal for *guess, think*.

respectfully, respectively *Respectfully* means "in a manner showing respect." *Respectively* means "each in the order given."

> Tom rose *respectfully* when Mrs. Hughes entered.
> The president commended the Army, Navy, and Air Force, *respectively*.

right along Used informally to mean "on without interruption, continuously."

> INFORMAL   Road construction moved *right along*.
> GENERAL   Road construction moved *on without interruption*.

rise, raise Do not confuse. *Rise* (*rose, risen*), an intransitive verb, means "to move upward." *Raise* (*raised, raised*), a transitive verb, means "to cause to move upward, to place erect."

> Franklin *rises* promptly at seven.
> Franklin *raises* his hand often in English class.

same, said, such Except in legal writing, questionable substitutes for *it, this, that, before-mentioned*.

says, said Not interchangeable. *Says* is present tense; *said*, past.

> NONSTANDARD   Allen dashed into the cafeteria and *says*, "Helen won the essay contest."
> STANDARD   Allen dashed into the cafeteria and *said*, "Helen won the essay contest."

scarcely See **but, hardly, scarcely**.

seldom ever Use *seldom, seldom if ever*, or *hardly ever*.

seldom or ever Use *seldom or never*.

shape up Informal for "to develop favorably" or "to behave properly."

sit, set Do not confuse these verbs: see **7a(1)**.

so, so that In clauses denoting purpose, *so that* is usually preferred to *so*.

> AMBIGUOUS   Ralph left so I could study.
> CLEAR   Ralph left *so that* I could study.

some Informal for *remarkable, striking, extraordinary*.

> INFORMAL   The St. Bernard is *some* dog!
> GENERAL   The St. Bernard is a *remarkable* dog!

someone, some one See **anyone, any one**.

somewheres Nonstandard for *somewhere*.

sort, kind   See **kind, sort.**

sort of, kind of   See **kind of, sort of.**

sort of a   Omit the *a* in your formal writing.

speak, speech   The verb *speak* means "to say aloud"; the noun *speech* is "the act of speaking" or "that which is spoken."

> Hamlet told the actors to "*speak* the *speech* trippingly on the tongue."

stationary, stationery   *Stationary* means "in a fixed position"; *stationery* means "writing paper and envelopes."

such   See **same, said, such.**

such that   When *such* is completed by a result clause, it should be followed by *that.*

> The rain was *such that* we had to stop on the freeway.

supposed to   See **used to, supposed to.**

sure   Informal for *surely* or *certainly.*

> INFORMAL   The sunrise *sure* was beautiful.
> GENERAL   The sunrise *surely* was beautiful.

sure and   Informal for *sure to.*

suspicion   Nonstandard when used as a verb in place of *suspect.*

> NONSTANDARD   I did not suspicion anything.
> STANDARD   I did not *suspect* anything.

take   In your formal writing avoid such informal expressions as *take it out on, take up with.* Use instead expressions such as *vent one's anger on, be friendly with.*

teach, learn   See **learn, teach.**

than, then   *Than* and *then* are not interchangeable. Do not confuse the conjunction *than* with the adverb or adverbial conjunction *then*, which relates to time.

> Nylon wears better *than* rayon.
> First it snowed; *then* it sleeted.

their, there, they're Do not confuse. *Their* is a possessive pronoun; *there* is an adverb or an expletive; *they're* is a contraction of *they are.*

> *There* is no explanation for *their* refusal.
> *They're* installing a traffic light *there.*

theirself, theirselves Nonstandard for *themselves.*

these kind, these sort, those kind, those sort See **kind, sort.**

this here, that there, these here, them there Nonstandard expressions. Use *this, that, these, those.*

to, too, two Distinguish the preposition *to* from the adverb *too* and the numeral *two.*

> If it isn't *too* cold, I will take my *two* poodles *to* the park.

try and Informal for *try to.*

type of Do not omit the *of* in expressions such as "that *type of* film" or "that *type of* hero."

undoubtably Nonstandard for *undoubtedly* or *without doubt.*

uninterested, disinterested See **disinterested, uninterested.**

used to, supposed to Be sure to add the *-d* to *use* and *suppose* when writing these expressions.

> Horses *used to* be indispensable.
> James was *supposed to* be in charge.

used to could Nonstandard or humorous for *used to be able.*

wait on Used generally to mean "to attend, to serve." Used informally to mean "to wait for."

> INFORMAL   At the station, Mike *waited on* his sister a full
>   hour.
> GENERAL   At the station, Mike *waited for* his sister a full
>   hour.
> GENERAL   She *waited on* her invalid father for years.

want in, out, down, up, off, through Informal or regional for *want to come* or *want to get in, out, down, up, off, through.*

want that Nonstandard when a *that* clause is the object of *want*.

> NONSTANDARD I want that he should have a chance.
> STANDARD I *want* him to have a chance.
> STANDARD I *want that*.

ways Informal for *way* when referring to distance.

> INFORMAL It's a long *ways* to Chicago.
> GENERAL It's a long *way* to Chicago.

where Informal for *that*.

> INFORMAL I saw in the newspaper *where* the strike had been settled.
> GENERAL I saw in the newspaper *that* the strike had been settled.

where . . . at Redundant. Omit the *at*.

which, who Use *who* or *that* instead of *which* to refer to persons.

while Do not overuse as a substitute for *and* or *but*. The conjunction *while* usually refers to time.

who, which See **which, who**.

worst way *In the worst way* is informal for *very much*.

> INFORMAL Mrs. Simmons wanted a color TV *in the worst way*.
> GENERAL Mrs. Simmons wanted a color TV *very much*.

would of Nonstandard for *would have*.

would rather See **had better, had rather, would rather**.

you Avoid the awkward use of *you* as an indefinite pronoun.

> AWKWARD When a person eats too much before bedtime, you may have nightmares.
> BETTER A person who eats too much before bedtime may have nightmares.

you was Nonstandard for *you were*.

Exactness

20

Select words that are exact, idiomatic, and fresh.

Especially when writing, you should strive to choose words that express your ideas exactly, precise words that convey the emotional suggestions you intend. Words that are effective in an informal composition may be inappropriate in a formal one: see **19b**. On certain occasions, slang or non-standard or archaic words can have power, persuasive force; on other occasions, these words can be weak, out of place: see **19c**, **19e**, and **19f**. Regional diction that is desirable inside a given geographical area may be humorous or confusing elsewhere: see **19d**. Similarly, technical words that make sense to a special group of listeners or readers may be wholly unintelligible to those outside the group: see **19g**. The choice of the right word will depend on your purpose, your point of view, and your reader.

If you can make effective use of the words you already know, you need not have a huge vocabulary. In fact, as shown by the following example, professional writers often choose short, familiar words.

> The ball was loose, rolling free near the line of scrimmage. I raced for the fumble, bent over, scooped up the ball on the dead run, and turned downfield. With a sudden burst of speed, I bolted past the line and past the linebackers. Only

two defensive backs stood between me and the goal line. One came up fast, and I gave him a hip feint, stuck out my left arm in a classic straight-arm, caught him on the helmet, and shoved him to the ground. The final defender moved toward me, and I cut to the sidelines, swung sharply back to the middle for three steps, braked again, and reversed my direction once more. The defender tripped over his own feet in confusion. I trotted into the end zone, having covered seventy-eight yards on my touchdown run, happily flipped the football into the stands, turned and loped casually toward the sidelines. Then I woke up.   —JERRY KRAMER[1]

Of course, as you gain experience in writing, you will become increasingly aware of the need to add to your vocabulary. When you discover a valuable new word, make it your own by mastering its spelling, its meaning, and its exact use.

20a

Consult a good dictionary for the exact word needed to express your idea.

(1) Make sure that the dictionary gives the exact meaning you have in mind.

WRONG WORD   I hope my mother will find the mountain air *enervating*. [*Enervating* means "weakening or destroying the vigor of."]

RIGHT WORD   I hope my mother will find the mountain air *invigorating*. [*Invigorating* means "animating or giving vigor to."]

INEXACT   A registration official *brainwashed* the freshmen for forty-five minutes. [*Brainwashing* is "the alteration of personal convictions, beliefs, habits, and attitudes by means of intensive, coercive indoctrination."]

---

[1] From *Jerry Kramer's Farewell to Football* by Jerry Kramer. Published by Bantam Books, Inc., 1969. Copyright 1969 by Jerry Kramer and Dick Schaap. Reprinted by permission.

EXACT   A registration official *briefed* the freshmen for forty-five minutes. [*To brief* is "to prepare in advance by instructing or advising."]

Be careful to use the right conjunction to express the exact relation between words, phrases, and clauses.

INEXACT   The halfback is clumsy *and* speedy. [*And* adds or continues.]

EXACT   The halfback is clumsy *but* speedy. [*But* contrasts.]

Caution: Do not confuse words that are similar in sound, spelling, or meaning. If necessary, review the list of frequently confused words in **18b** See also **19i.**

WRONG WORD   Early Christians stressed the *immorality* of the soul.

RIGHT WORD   Early Christians stressed the *immortality* of the soul.

■ **Exercise 1**   With the aid of your dictionary, give the exact meaning of each italicized word in the quotations below. (Italics have been added.)

1. The moon has become our *cosmic* Paris.

                  —WERNHER VON BRAUN

   Malcolm did not invent the new *cosmology*—black power, black is beautiful, think black—or the mystique of Africanism. —PETER SCHRAG

2. The capacity for rage, spite and aggression is part of our endowment as *human beings.* —KENNETH KENISTON

   Man, all down his history, has defended his uniqueness like a point of honor. —RUTH BENEDICT

3. Travel is no cure for melancholia; space-ships and time machines are no *escape* from the human condition.

                  —ARTHUR KOESTLER

   Well, Columbus was probably regarded as an *escapist* when he set forth for the New World. —ARTHUR C. CLARKE

4. Campus upheavals and union struggles are symptomatic of our times and of the general confusion and feeling of *estrangement.* —ALFRED A. MESSER

   Too many of the young—and the old—feel *disoriented* and dispensable. —PETER CLECAK

5. Once, a full high school education was the best achievement of a minority; today, it is the *barest minimum* for decent employment or self-respect. —ERIC SEVAREID

   Study and planning are an *absolute prerequisite* for any kind of intelligent action. —EDWARD BROOKE

■ **Exercise 2** Prepare for a class discussion of diction. After the first quotation below are several series of words that the author might have used but did not choose. Note the differences in meaning when an italicized word is substituted for the related word at the head of each series. Be prepared to supply your own alternatives for each of the words that follow the other four quotations.

1. With the corruption of language, humility—like charity—has become the name of a vice rather than a virtue.
   —KENNETH REXROTH
   a. corruption: *deterioration, decay, debasement*
   b. humility: *Uncle Tomism, modesty, meekness*
   c. charity: *generosity, philanthropy, beneficence*
   d. vice: *evil, transgression, blemish, sin*
   e. virtue: *goodness, grace, blessing, boon*

2. Since boyhood I have been charmed by the unexpected and the beautiful. —LOREN EISELEY
   a. charmed   b. unexpected   c. beautiful

3. Our plane rocked in a rain squall, bobbed about, then slipped into a patch of sun. —THEODORE H. WHITE
   a. rocked   b. bobbed   c. slipped   d. patch

4. The generation gap is now a moral chasm, across which the young stare at their elders with distrust, convinced that the values that make for success are fakes. —J. BRONOWSKI
   a. chasm   b. stare   c. distrust   d. values   e. fakes

5. The new sensibility is defiantly pluralistic; it is dedicated both to an excruciating seriousness and to fun and wit and nostalgia. —SUSAN SONTAG
   a. defiantly   b. dedicated   c. excruciating
   d. seriousness   e. fun   f. wit   g. nostalgia

(2) Select the word with the connotation, as well as the denotation, proper to the idea you wish to express.

The denotation of a word is what the word actually signifies. According to the dictionary, the word *hair* denotes "one of the fine, threadlike structures that grow from the skin of most mammals." The connotation of a word is what the word suggests or implies. *Hair,* for instance, may connote beauty, fertility, nudity, strength, uncleanliness, temptation, rebellion, or primitivism.

The connotation of a word includes the emotions or associations that surround it. For instance, *taxi, tin lizzie, limousine, convertible, station wagon, dump truck, hot rod*—all denote much the same thing. But to various readers, and in various contexts, each word may have a special connotation. *Taxi* may suggest a city rush hour; *tin lizzie,* a historical museum; *limousine,* an airport; *convertible,* a homecoming parade; *station wagon,* children and dogs; *dump truck,* highway construction; *hot rod,* noise and racing. Similarly, *jalopy, bus, sedan, bookmobile, moving van, ambulance, squad car*—all denote a means of transportation, but each word carries a variety of connotations.

A word may be right in one situation, wrong in another. *Female parent,* for instance, is a proper expression in a biology laboratory, but it would be very inappropriate to say "John wept because of the death of his female parent." *Female parent* used in this sense is literally correct, but the connotation is wrong. The more appropriate word, *mother,* conveys not only the meaning denoted by *female parent* but also the reason why John wept. The first expression simply implies a biological relationship; the second includes emotional suggestions.

■ **Exercise 3** Give one dictionary definition (denotation) and one connotation for each of the following words.

(1) red, (2) system, (3) astrology, (4) Chicago, (5) conservative, (6) law, (7) dog, (8) Africa, (9) technology, (10) idealism.

■ **Exercise 4** Be prepared to explain why the italicized words in the following sentences, although they may be literally correct, might be inappropriate because of their connotations.

1. At the sound of the organ, the professors, in full regalia, *scampered* down the aisle and *tramped* to their assigned seats.
2. We are building our new *abode* on the rim of a most delightful little *gulch.*
3. The soloist *tucked* his *fiddle* under his chin.
4. For the *enlightenment* of the other ladies, Mrs. Bromley measured upon her *belly* the area of her recent operation.
5. The conclusion of the Gettysburg Address indicates that President Lincoln *hankered* for a new *spurt* of freedom.

■ **Exercise 5** Be prepared to discuss the words below that because of their connotative value serve to intensify the author's meaning.

1. The country seemed to be dozing in an easy chair, belching intermittently to prove it was not quite asleep.
   —JACK NEWFIELD
2. Does not a mountain unintentionally evoke in us a sense of wonder? otters along a stream a sense of mirth? night in the woods a sense of fear? Do not rain falling and mists rising up suggest the love binding heaven and earth?
   —JOHN CAGE
3. Or am I bugged by my pointless affluence, my guilt about having fat on my hide at a time when sores of starvation are the rule for hundreds of millions elsewhere?
   —BENJAMIN DE MOTT

4. In all America, no one was so lucky as the Southerner who was a part of this social revolution, of this determination to reaffirm the principles of what we have called the American dream. —RALPH McGILL

5. A man with courage knows how to die standing up; he's got more guts than you could hang on a fence, gravel in his gizzard, and is as salty as Lot's wife and as gritty as fish eggs rolled in sand. —GEORGE D. HENDRICKS

(3) Select the specific and concrete word rather than the general and abstract.

A *general* word is all-inclusive, indefinite, sweeping in scope. A *specific* word is precise, definite, limited in scope.

General	Specific	More specific
food	dessert	apple pie
prose	fiction	short stories
people	Americans	Mr. and Mrs. Smith

An *abstract* word deals with concepts, with ideas, with what cannot be touched, heard, or seen. A *concrete* word has to do with particular objects, with the practical, with what can be touched, heard, or seen.

ABSTRACT WORDS   democracy, loyal, evil, hate, charity
CONCRETE WORDS   mosquito, spotted, crunch, wedding, car

All writers must sometimes use abstract words and must occasionally resort to generalizations, as in the sentence "Men through the ages have sought freedom from tyranny." Here abstractions and generalizations are vital to the communication of ideas and theories. To be effective, however, the use of these words must be based upon clearly understood and well-thought-out ideas.

Experienced writers may have little difficulty handling general and abstract words. Many inexperienced writers, however, tend to use too many such words, leaving their writing drab and lifeless due to the lack of specific, concrete words. In your writing be as specific as you can. For example, instead of the word *thin*, consider using *gaunt, slender, lanky,* or *frail.* When you are tempted to write *pretty,* think instead of words like *graceful, delicate, stunning,* or *becoming.*

To test whether or not a word is specific, ask one or more of these questions: Exactly who? Exactly what? Precisely when? Exactly where? Precisely how? As you study the examples below, notice what a difference specific, concrete words can make in the expression of an idea. Notice, too, how specific details expand or develop ideas.

DULL   All around us is a great deal of refuse.

SPECIFIC   We are burying ourselves under 7 million scrapped cars, 30 million tons of waste paper, 48 billion discarded cans and 28 billion bottles and jars a year.
—JACK SHEPHERD

DULL   I remember my pleasure at discovering new things about language.

SPECIFIC   I remember my real joy at discovering for the first time how language worked, at discovering, for example, that the central line of Joseph Conrad's *Heart of Darkness* was in parentheses.
—JOAN DIDION

DULL   The man who does not appreciate nature is missing something.

SPECIFIC   The man unaware or unmoved by the sea or the sky or the rock or the stream or the flower is not sophisticated; he is merely half-alive.
—MARYA MANNES

DULL   It was the home of a man in exile.

SPECIFIC   It was the cluttered temporary shelter of a black man in exile—where bags stay packed and all precious things are made portable.   —GORDON PARKS

■ **Exercise 6**   Expand the following ideas by adding details.

EXAMPLES

In rural America there are many euphemisms for the word "bull."

In rural America there are many euphemisms for the word "bull"; among them are "he cow," "cow critter," "male cow," "gentleman cow."   —S. I. HAYAKAWA

233

All over town automobile companies were holding revival meetings.

All over town automobile companies were holding revival meetings: hieratic salesmen preached to the converted and the hangers-back alike; lines at the loan companies stretched through the revolving doors and out onto the winter pavements. —HERBERT GOLD

1. In pawn shops there are frequently items of interest to collectors.
2. The crowded midway was a miniature battlefield.
3. A mechanical genius, my roommate can repair almost anything.
4. To many Europeans, New York City is America.
5. Many slang words and expressions are related to drugs and drug users.

■ **Exercise 7**   Using a regular dictionary or a dictionary of synonyms, choose five specific words or expressions that might be appropriately substituted for each of the following.

EXAMPLE
eat: *munch, nibble, bolt, gulp, feast on*

(1) see, (2) walk, (3) great, (4) bad, (5) happy, (6) man, (7) get, (8) nice, (9) think, (10) love.

■ **Exercise 8**   Study the italicized words below, first with the aid of a dictionary and then in the context of the sentences. Substitute a synonym for each italicized word and compare its effectiveness with that of the original.

1. Violence is a *threat,* not a solution.
                                —JOHN KENNETH GALBRAITH
2. That row of photographs we keep on the piano has been *maligned.* —WRIGHT MORRIS
3. It would be *sentimentality* to think that our society can be changed easily and without pain. —ROBERT PENN WARREN
4. With his magnifying lens, he discovered more organisms, each one *hugging* its grain of soil. —PETER FARB
5. What is disappearing is the *song* of the land.
                                —DONALD JACKSON

6. He *wandered back* in a heartbroken *daze,* his sensitive face *eloquent* with grief. —JOSEPH HELLER

7. Her moral indignation was always *on the boil.*
   —ALDOUS HUXLEY

8. *Discretion* is essential to survival on some campuses; *candor* to the point of sexual boasting is a must on others.
   —GAEL GREENE

9. Two girls went *skittering* by in short transparent raincoats, one green, one red, their heads *tucked* against the drive of the rain. —KATHERINE ANNE PORTER

10. Her beauty was *paralyzing*—beyond all words, all experience, all dream. —CONRAD AIKEN

■ **Exercise 9** Replace the general words or phrases in italics below with specific ones.

1. A police state *has certain characteristics.*
2. *A lot of people* are threatened by *pollution.*
3. *My relatives* gave me *two gifts.*
4. Every Monday he has *the same thing* in his lunch box.
5. Our history professor suggested that we subscribe to *some magazines.*
6. The mini-cars have *numerous disadvantages.*
7. The winning touchdown *was the result of luck.*
8. My father looked at my grade in science and said *what I least expected to hear.*
9. *Various aspects of the television show* were criticized *in the newspaper.*
10. *Students* are arrested for *the same violations again and again.*

(4) Use appropriate figurative language to create an imaginative or emotional impression.

A figure of speech is a word or words used in an imaginative rather than in a literal sense. The two chief figures of speech are the *simile* and the *metaphor.* A *simile* is an explicit comparison between two things of a different kind or quality, usually introduced by *like* or *as.* A *metaphor* is an implied comparison of dissimilar things. In a metaphor words of comparison, such as *like* and *as,* are not used.

SIMILES

My saliva became *like hot bitter glue.* —RALPH ELLISON

He was *as in love with life as an ant on a summer blade of grass.* —BEN HECHT

METAPHORS

The difficulty of *hunting down the rabbit truth in the thickets of experience* is apparent. —JAMES HEARST

A written constitution is *a life belt to which the exhausted can cling;* it is not, in itself, an aid to further progress.
—C. NORTHCOTE PARKINSON

Metaphors and similes are especially valuable because they are concrete and tend to point up essential relationships that cannot otherwise be communicated. (For faulty metaphors, however, see 23c.)

Two other frequently used figures of speech are *hyperbole* and *personification. Hyperbole* is deliberate overstatement or fanciful exaggeration. *Personification* is the attribution to the nonhuman (objects, animals, ideas) of characteristics possessed only by the human.

HYPERBOLE

I, for one, don't expect till I die to be so good a man as I am at this minute, for just now I'm *fifty thousand feet high—a tower with all the trumpets shouting.*
—G. K. CHESTERTON

PERSONIFICATION

Time talks. It speaks more plainly than words. . . . *It can shout* the truth where words lie. —EDWARD T. HALL

■ **Exercise 10** Complete each of the following by using a simile, a metaphor, hyperbole, or personification. Use vivid and effective figures of speech.

EXAMPLES

The grass rolls out to the bleachers like *a freshly brushed billiard table.* —JAY WRIGHT

The utopia of Karl Marx, like all utopias before or since, was *an image in a rearview mirror.* —MARSHALL McLUHAN

1. Sightseers flocked around the commune like _____.
2. A revolutionary idea in the 1970's, like a revolutionary idea in any age, is _____.
3. The mosquitoes in Texas _____.
4. The third hurricane of the season slashed through Louisiana swamps _____.
5. Death in a hovel or in a penthouse is _____.
6. Like _____, the class sat speechless.
7. The lecture was as _____.
8. Her feet looked like _____.
9. Surging forward, the defensive line _____.
10. The opinions of businessmen with vested interests are as predictable as _____.

20b

Select words that are idiomatic.

An idiomatic expression—such as *many a man, Sunday week,* or *hang fire*—means something beyond the simple combination of the definitions of its individual words. An idiom may be metaphorical: *He gets under my skin.* Such expressions cannot be sensibly translated word for word into another language. Used every day, they are at the very heart of the English language.

Be careful to use idiomatic English, not unidiomatic approximations. *Many a man* is idiomatic; *many the man* is not. Ordinarily native speakers use idiomatic English naturally and effectively, but once in a while they may have difficulty choosing idiomatic prepositions.

> UNIDIOMATIC comply to, superior than, buy off of
> IDIOMATIC comply *with*, superior *to*, buy *from*

When you are in doubt about what preposition to use after a given word, look up that word in the dictionary. In the *American College Dictionary,* for instance, the first definition of *angry* is followed by the helpful "*with* or *at* a person, *at* or *about* a thing."

Many idiomatic expressions are in general use. Others are labeled in dictionaries as *Informal* or *Colloquial; Humorous; Regional* or *Dialectal; Nonstandard, Illiterate,* or *Substandard; Vulgar;* or *Slang:* see **19a(6)**.

■ **Exercise 11** Using your dictionary, classify the following expressions as idiomatic or unidiomatic. Revise any expressions that are unidiomatic. Classify idiomatic expressions according to the usage labels in your dictionary, using *General* as the classification for unlabeled expressions.

> EXAMPLES
> similar with   *Unidiomatic—similar to*
> to let on   *Idiomatic, Informal*

1. oblivious about
2. to go at
3. to dress down
4. capable to
5. distaste for
6. to compare against
7. to break with
8. prior than
9. to drop in
10. to plug for

20c

Select fresh expressions instead of trite, worn-out ones.

Such trite expressions as *every inch a gentleman, to the bitter end,* and *rack his brain* were once striking and effective. Excessive use, however, has drained them of their original force and made them clichés. Euphemisms such as *laid to rest* (for *buried*) and *stretches the truth* (for *lies* or *exaggerates*) are not only trite but wordy. Such comparisons as *sticks out like a sore thumb* and *as plain as day* are also hackneyed expressions.

Good writers do not use trite, well-known phrases when simple, straightforward language and original expressions would be more effective. Compare the effectiveness of the following sentences.

TRITE	*It goes without saying* that it is time we stopped regarding Indians as *something out of the past* with no relevance to America *in this day and age*.
BETTER	Clearly, it is time we stopped regarding Indians as living museum pieces with no relevance to America today. —PETER FARB

To avoid trite phrases you must be aware of current usage, for catch phrases and slogans age quickly. Pat political phrases, such as *pulse of public opinion, popular choice,* and *the common man,* are notoriously short-lived. Similarly, expressions drawn from commercial advertising quickly become hackneyed. Owners of damaged freight might advertise that they "sell it like it is," or managers of high-rise apartments might use such slogans as "Your chance to live it up" or "Think tall." But slogans that are effective in advertising often become so familiar that they lose their force.

Nearly every writer uses clichés from time to time, when they suit his purposes.

> We feel free when we escape—even if it be but *from the frying pan into the fire.* —ERIC HOFFER

> Student claustrophobia makes any curricular requirement seem an unwarranted intrusion on the student's academic freedom to *do his own thing.* —DAVID RIESMAN

And nearly every writer uses familiar lines from literature or the Bible and quotes proverbs occasionally.

> Our lives are empty of belief. They are *lives of quiet desperation.* —ARTHUR M. SCHLESINGER, JR. [Compare Thoreau's *Walden:* "The mass of men lead lives of quiet desperation."]

> Slowly but steadily, in the following years, a new vision began gradually to replace the dream of political power—a powerful movement, the rise of another ideal to guide the unguided, another *pillar of fire by night* after a clouded day.
> —W. E. B. DUBOIS [Compare Exodus 13:21: "And the Lord went before them . . . by night in a pillar of fire, to give them light."]

It is not unusual for a professional writer to give a new twist to an old saying.

> He is every other inch a gentleman.   —REBECCA WEST
> If a thing is worth doing, it is worth doing badly.
> —G. K. CHESTERTON
> The victor belongs to the spoils.   —F. SCOTT FITZGERALD

Good writers, however, do not rely heavily on the phraseology of others; they choose their own words to communicate their own ideas.

■ **Exercise 12**   Substitute one carefully chosen word for each trite expression below.

> EXAMPLES
> stick to your guns   *persevere*
> the very picture of health   *robust*

1. white as a sheet	6. clear as crystal
2. a crying shame	7. over and done with
3. busy as a bee	8. at the crack of dawn
4. too cute for words	9. few and far between
5. really down to earth	10. follow in the footsteps of

■ **Exercise 13**   Make a list of ten hackneyed expressions that you often use; then rewrite each in exact, straightforward words of your own.

■ **Exercise 14**   Revise the following sentences, using original, specific diction in place of the trite and general words in italics.

> EXAMPLE
> Sometimes staying on the job until *the wee small hours of the morning,* the mechanic supports his large family *by the sweat of his brow.*
> *Sometimes staying on the job until 1 or 2* A.M.*, the mechanic works hard to support his large family.*

1. Despite the fact that he is in his *ripe old age,* Buckminster Fuller is *where the action is.*
2. After my talk with the professor, I thought I *had it made.*

3. The vocalist who accompanied the band on the tour never *really got with it.*

4. Knowing he was *doomed to disappointment,* he *sank to the depths of despair.*

5. Few writers have the ability to *tell it like it is.*

General Exercises on Exactness

■ **Exercise 15** First give the exact meaning in context of each italicized word below; then use each word appropriately in an original sentence. (Italics have been added.)

1. The scene is *apocalyptic*—afternoon *bedlam* in wild harsh sunlight and August heat.   —WILLIAM STYRON

2. There is nothing here of *nationalism* or riots or *apartheid.*
   —PHILIP ROTH

3. The *fissure* in the national *psyche* widened to the danger point.   —NORMAN MAILER

4. The atheist *existentialist* has my respect: he accepts his honest despair with *stoic* dignity.   —THOMAS MERTON

5. It is a terrible, an *inexorable,* law that one cannot deny the *humanity* of another without diminishing one's own: in the face of one's victim, one sees oneself.   —JAMES BALDWIN

■ **Exercise 16** Choose five of the ten items on the following page as the basis for five original sentences. Use language that is exact, idiomatic, and fresh.

EXAMPLES
the condition of her hair
Her hair poked through a broken net like stunted antlers.
   —J. F. POWERS

OR

Her dark hair was gathered up in a coil like a crown on her head.   —D. H. LAWRENCE

OR

She had been fussing with her hair, couldn't get it right; the brittle broken-off dyed yellow ends were curling the wrong way, breaking off on the brush, standing out from her head as if she were some strange aborigine preparing herself for the puberty rites.   —JEAN RIKHOFF

1. the look on his face
2. her response to fear
3. the way she walks
4. crime in the streets
5. spring in the air
6. the noises of the city
7. the appearance of the room
8. the scene of the accident
9. the final minutes of play
10. the approaching storm

■ **Exercise 17** Following are two descriptions, one of beauty, the other of terror. Read each selection carefully in preparation for a class discussion of the authors' choice of words, their use of concrete, specific language, and their use of figurative language.

[1] In the cold months there are few visitors, for northern Minnesota is not a winter playground. [2] And yet the intrepid traveler would be well rewarded by the natural beauty surrounding him. [3] The skies and the undulating fields merge as one; unreality assails the mind and the eye. [4] The sun swings in a low arc, and at sunrise and sunset it is not hard to imagine what the world may be like in many distant aeons when ice and snow envelop the earth, while the sun, cooled to the ruddy glow of bittersweet, lingeringly touches the clouds with warm colors of apricot, tangerine, lavender, and rose.

[5] Night skies may be indescribably clear. [6] The stars are sharp and brilliant, pricking perception; the northern constellations diagramed with utmost clarity upon the blackest of skies. [7] There is no illusion here that they are hung like lanterns just beyond reach. [8] The vast distances of space are as clear to see as the barbed points of light.

[9] When the aurora borealis sweeps in to dominate the night, it elicits a quite different and emotional reaction, not unlike the surging, impressive sight itself. [10] If the luminous, pulsing scarves of light were tangible streamers, certainly it would be possible to become entangled in and absorbed into the celestial kaleidoscope. —FRANCES GILLIS[2]

[1] The biblical story does not present the departure from Egypt as an everyday occurrence, but rather as an event accompanied by violent upheavals of nature.

[2] From "Winter North of the Mississippi" by Frances Gillis, *Atlantic Monthly*, March 1961. Copyright © 1960, by The Atlantic Monthly Company, Boston, Mass. Reprinted with permission.

² Grave and ominous signs preceded the Exodus: clouds of dust and smoke darkened the sky and colored the water they fell upon with a bloody hue. ³ The dust tore wounds in the skin of man and beast; in the torrid glow vermin and reptiles bred and filled air and earth; wild beasts, plagued by sand and ashes, came from the ravines of the wasteland to the abodes of men. ⁴ A terrible torrent of hailstones fell, and a wild fire ran upon the ground; a gust of wind brought swarms of locusts, which obscured the light; blasts of cinders blew in wave after wave, day and night, night and day, and the gloom grew to a prolonged night, and blackness extinguished every ray of light. ⁵ Then came the tenth and most mysterious plague: the Angel of the Lord "passed over the houses of the children of Israel . . . when he smote the Egyptians, and delivered our houses" (Exodus 12:27). ⁶ The slaves, spared by the angel of destruction, were implored amid groaning and weeping to leave the land the same night. ⁷ In the ash-gray dawn the multitude moved, leaving behind scorched fields and ruins where a few hours before had been urban and rural habitations.   —IMMANUEL VELIKOVSKY³

■ **Exercise 18**   Choose the word inside parentheses that best suits the context of each item below.

1. But the biology of today is molecular biology—life seen as the (hopping around, ballet) of the big molecules, the dance of the DNA.   —JAMES BONNER
2. A sports car (flattens, exterminates) the cocker spaniel.
   —CONRAD KNICKERBOCKER
3. To be an American and unable to play baseball is comparable to being a Polynesian unable to (swim, debate).
   —JOHN CHEEVER
4. Every evening at the rush hour the subway (unveils, disgorges) its millions.   —JACQUES BARZUN
5. There was a roaring in my ears like the rushing of (music, rivers).   —STEPHEN VINCENT BENÉT

³From *Ages in Chaos* by Immanuel Velikovsky. Published by Doubleday & Co., Inc., and Sidgwick & Jackson Ltd., 1952. Copyright, 1952, by Immanuel Velikovsky. Reprinted by permission.

243

Wordiness

21

Avoid wordiness. Repeat words only when needed for emphasis or clarity.

The best writers today make each word count, avoiding the telegraphic as well as the verbose style. As you write and revise your compositions, make sure that every word has a reason for being there, and eliminate all deadwood. Keep in mind George Orwell's advice: strike out "all stale or mixed images, all prefabricated phrases, needless repetitions, and humbug and vagueness"; get rid of every "lump of verbal refuse."

21a

Make every word count; omit words or phrases that add nothing to the meaning.

Notice below that the words in brackets contribute nothing to the meaning. Avoid such wordiness in your own writing.

> [each and] every man, all [of the] new styles
> cooperated [together], as a [usual] rule, [true] facts
> yellow [in color], small [in size], eleven [in number]

Bureaucratic jargon, sometimes called "gobbledygook," is often extremely wordy. See the example on page 201.

■ **Exercise 1** Substitute one or two words for each item below.

> EXAMPLES
> not very long after that   *soon*
> the candidate who is now serving out his time in office
>   *the incumbent*

1. on account of the fact that
2. the men who travel in outer space
3. down in the dumps
4. students who are in their first year at college
5. to make a long story short
6. to pay too much money in proportion to service rendered
7. at the present time
8. spoke in a very low tone of voice
9. glass that is easily broken
10. comments that more or less dodged the issues at hand

■ **Exercise 2** Without changing the meaning of the following sentences, strike out all unnecessary words. Put a checkmark after any sentence that needs no revision.

1. At that time we were then identifying with or feeling strong similarities to the characters in novels that were written by Hermann Hesse.
2. Architect James Hoban, the designer of the White House, was born in Dublin.
3. Never in a million years can an active American understand why the Chinese citizens in East Asia cannot leave their home towns that they live in unless they have a permit from the government giving them permission to leave town.
4. In the month of August, the year of 1971, my father was close to the point of bankruptcy.
5. The award-winning English playwright made ruthless murder and flagrant blackmail the absurd hobbies of his heroes.
6. One reason why Americans are well informed is because of the fact that books of all sorts on a great variety of subjects are available to them as inexpensive paperbacks.
7. There was a strong backlash that followed the Ecumenical Council.
8. About midnight Halloween evening, Lucille dropped in for a short, unexpected visit.

9. Los Angeles is very different in various ways from the city of San Francisco.
10. In this day and time, it is difficult today to find in the field of science a chemist who shows as much promise for the future as Joseph Blake shows.

21b

If necessary, restructure the sentence to avoid wordiness.

Notice in the following examples how changes in sentence structure reduce two sentences with a total of sixteen words to briefer sentences containing ten, nine, eight, and finally five words.

> There was a mist that hung like a veil. It obscured the top of the mountain.
> The mist hung like a veil and obscured the mountaintop.
> The mist, hanging like a veil, obscured the mountaintop.
> The mist, like a veil, obscured the mountaintop.
> The mist veiled the mountaintop.

Depending on the context, any one of these sentences may meet the special needs of the writer. By studying these examples, you can learn methods of restructuring your sentences to eliminate undesirable wordiness.

■ **Exercise 3**   Restructure the following sentences to eliminate wordiness.

1. There are some members of the sorority who work with mentally retarded children. These sorority members teach the children songs and games.
2. In junior high school it was like a circus that had three rings. The three rings were the classroom, the cafeteria, and the playground.
3. When the Indians made tools, they used flint and bone as materials.

4. Another thing is good health. It is one of our great blessings. It is the result of proper diet and exercise. Rest is also desirable.
5. My uncle was a tall man. He had a long nose. Over his right eye there was a deep scar.
6. If any workers were disgruntled, they made their complaints to the man who was in charge as manager.
7. Personally I believe it was the Spaniards rather than the Indians who first brought horses and ponies to America.
8. The grass was like a carpet. It covered the whole lawn. The color of the grass was a deep blue.
9. When anyone wants to start a garden, it is best to begin in the early part of the spring of the year.
10. Near the center of the campus of our university a new building has been erected. It is constructed of red brick.

21c

Avoid careless or needless repetition of words and ideas.

Unless you are repeating intentionally for emphasis or for clarity and smoothness of transition, be careful in your writing not to use the same word twice or to make the same statement twice in slightly different words.

AWKWARD	Since the committee has already made three reports, only one report remains to be reported on.
BETTER	Since the committee has already made three reports, only one remains to be presented.
REPETITIOUS	Julia delights in giving parties; entertaining guests is a real pleasure for her.
CONCISE	Julia delights in giving parties.

Use a pronoun instead of needlessly repeating a noun. As long as the reference remains clear, several pronouns in succession, even in successive sentences, may refer to the same antecedent noun.

NEEDLESS REPETITION

Salvation means many things in Dylan's songs. On one level salvation is the conquest of guilt, ambition, impatience, and all the other obsessive states of egotistic confusion in which we set ourselves apart from the natural flow of things. On another level salvation is the supremely free flight of the will. On still another level salvation is faith, an acceptance of a transcendent, omnipresent godhead without which we are lost. [The word *salvation* appears four times; *level,* three.]

BETTER

Salvation means many things in Dylan's songs. On one level it is the conquest of guilt, ambition, impatience, and all the other obsessive states of egotistic confusion in which we set ourselves apart from the natural flow of things. On another it is the supremely free flight of the will. On still another it is faith, an acceptance of a transcendent, omnipresent godhead without which we are lost. —STEVEN GOLDBERG[1] [The pronoun *it* is used for *salvation* three times, and *level* is used only once. The parallelism of the sentence beginnings contributes to clarity.]

■ **Exercise 4** Revise the following sentences to eliminate wordiness and useless repetition.

1. In the last act of the play there is the explanation of the title of the play.
2. In the decade from 1950 to 1960, enrollments at universities doubled; in 1960 there were twice as many students as in 1950.
3. That morning we went to Jones Beach so that we could enjoy all the pleasures and take advantage of the many opportunities for enjoyment that that famous beach affords.
4. The National Gallery of Art, which is in Washington, D.C., and which houses the Mellon, Kress, and Widener collections of paintings and sculpture, is one of the largest marble structures in the entire world.

---

[1]From "Bob Dylan and the Poetry of Salvation" by Steven Goldberg, *Saturday Review*, May 30, 1970. Copyright 1970 Saturday Review, Inc. Reprinted by permission.

5. The radio announcer repeatedly kept saying, "Buy Peterson's Perfect Prawns," over and over and over again.
6. There were fifty people in the hospital ward who were among those who received great benefit from the new drug.
7. I had an advantage over the other contestants because of the fact that I had just looked up the word myself in a dictionary.
8. I got busy and got my assignment finished.
9. He found the problem of discovering the legal status of the migrant workers an almost insoluble problem.
10. In order that an immigrant may apply to become a citizen of the United States he must make out an application stating his intention to become a citizen.

■ **Exercise 5** Restructure the sentences in the items below, following the patterns of the examples.

EXAMPLE
We felt safe and a little smug. We lived by old dogmas and creeds.
Safe, a little smug, we lived by old dogmas and creeds.
—PHYLLIS McGINLEY

1. He was tense and apparently apprehensive. He flinched each time the telephone rang.
2. The young doctor was crisp and a bit shy. He seemed to be clinically detached from personalities.

EXAMPLE
Men know how to sweat. And they also know how to endure.
Men know how to sweat and endure. —H. L. MENCKEN

3. Hunters know how to lure. And they also know how to trap.
4. They learned how to survive. They also learned how to exploit.

EXAMPLE
The eyes of Annabel were brimming again. They were responding to his sympathy.
Annabel's eyes were brimming again, responding to his sympathy. —MURIEL SPARK

5. The hands of the referee were waving again. They were indicating another costly penalty.
6. The wife of Bill was working then. She was supporting the entire family.

EXAMPLE
When people quarrel over the past, then they lose the future.
To quarrel over the past is to lose the future.

—NEWTON MINOW

7. When a person drops out of high school, then he forfeits a college education.
8. When a man has several children, then he has many responsibilities.

EXAMPLE
Not only was his family dissolving, but his marriage was disintegrating.
His family was dissolving, his marriage disintegrating.

—ROBERT COLES

9. Not only were taxes spiraling upward, but prices were skyrocketing.
10. Not only were my grades improving, but my interests were expanding.

Omission of Necessary Words

22

Do not omit a word or phrase necessary to the meaning of the sentence.

In many instances a word or a phrase is optional; a writer may use it or omit it without changing sentence meaning. In the examples below, optional words are italicized. Compare the alternate structures, noting any differences in meaning and emphasis.

> Landing was precise and, as usual, routine in dramatic fashion.   OR
>
> *The* landing was precise and, as usual, routine in *a* dramatic fashion.   —A. E. VAN VOGT
>
> It seems the poems and the songs of protest and liberation are always too late or too early: memory or dream.   OR
>
> It seems *that* the poems and the songs of protest and liberation are always too late or too early: memory or dream.
> —HERBERT MARCUSE
>
> In football, players are bought by the pound; *however,* in basketball, *they are bought* by the yard.   OR
>
> In football, players are bought by the pound; in basketball, by the yard.   —KENNETH EBLE

In other instances a given word or phrase is necessary rather than optional. Notice in the following alternate structures that the word *the* before *tame* and *wild* is optional and yet before *weakest* and *wall* it is necessary.

> All animals, both *the* tame and *the* wild, weaken in these circumstances, and the weakest go to the wall and die.
> OR
> All animals, both tame and wild, weaken in these circumstances, and the weakest go to the wall and die.
> —JOHN D. STEWART

"Weakest go to wall and die" might be appropriate as a caption, but it is not appropriate in a regular context.

If you omit necessary words in your compositions, your mind may be racing ahead of your pen, or your writing may reflect omissions in your spoken English.

> The analyst talked about the tax dollar goes.   [The writer thought "talked about where" but did not write *where*.]
> I been considering changing my major.   [The writer omits /v/ when saying *I've been,* and the error carried over to his writing.]
> Ted better be there on time!   [In speaking the writer omits *had* before *better.*]

To avoid omitting necessary words, proofread your compositions carefully and study **22a–c.**

22a

Do not omit a necessary article, pronoun, conjunction, or preposition.

(1) Omitted article or pronoun

> INCOMPLETE   Curiosity is at bottom of all sciences.
> COMPLETE   Curiosity is at *the* bottom of all sciences.
> —JOHN LEAR

> INCOMPLETE   The battle left him untouched: it was the peace undid him.
> COMPLETE   The battle left him untouched: it was the peace *that* undid him.   —VIRGINIA WOOLF

Note: When it is necessary to indicate plural number, repeat a pronoun or an article before the second part of a compound.

> My mother and father were there. [Clearly two persons— repetition of *my* before *father* not necessary]
>
> A friend and *a* helper stood nearby. [Two persons clearly indicated by repetition of *a*]

(2) Omitted conjunction

CONFUSING Quarrelling means trying to show the other man is in the wrong. [A reader may be momentarily confused by "to show the other man."]

BETTER Quarrelling means trying to show *that* the other man is in the wrong. —C. S. LEWIS

INCOMPLETE You think of peddling dope as a profession, then such terms as *fix, mainline, horse, junkie* are not slang but technical terms of business. [A comma splice in appearance]

COMPLETE *If* you think of peddling dope as a profession, then such terms as *fix, mainline, horse, junkie* are not slang but technical terms of business.
—PAUL ROBERTS

Note: The conjunction *that* may be omitted as an introduction to clauses when no confusion results. In the sentence below, for example, *that* is omitted after *all* but not after *is*.

> All I know about music is that not many people ever really hear it. —JAMES BALDWIN

(3) Omitted preposition

INFORMAL I had never seen that type movie before.
COMPLETE I had never seen that type *of* movie before.

INCOMPLETE Winter the Bakers ski at Chestnut Lodge.
COMPLETE *In* winter the Bakers ski at Chestnut Lodge.

Note: The preposition is regularly omitted in some idiomatic phrases indicating time or place.

The package was mailed Friday (*on* Friday).
Mrs. Melton stayed home (*at* home).

■ **Exercise 1** Fill in the blanks below with appropriate articles, pronouns, conjunctions, or prepositions.

1. _____ any member of a minority group is told long enough _____ he is unacceptable, _____ image sticks.
   —MARYA MANNES

2. _____ good are not always rewarded; _____ evil often prosper. Life is not _____ morality play.
   —MICHAEL NOVAK

3. It is like a maze _____ which almost all turnings are wrong turnings. —JULIAN HUXLEY

4. To me, there are two kinds of liberals: the type _____ fellow _____ would take off his coat in a snowstorm and put it around my shoulders, and the type _____ fellow _____ would caution me to wear a coat against the snow. —JAMES ALAN McPHERSON

22b

Avoid awkward omission of verbs and auxiliaries.

Usage is divided regarding the inclusion or the omission of verbs and auxiliaries in such sentences as the following.

> The Lions are overwhelming; the event is unavoidable.
> —E. B. WHITE [Plural *are* is used with *lions,* and singular *is* with *event.*]

> The sounds were angry, the manner violent.
> —A. E. VAN VOGT [Plural *were* is used with *sounds,* but singular *was* after *manner* is omitted.]

> Feeling without knowing never made a work of art and never will. —ARCHIBALD MacLEISH [*Make* is omitted after *will.*]

Be careful, however, not to cause awkwardness by omitting a necessary verb or auxiliary.

> AWKWARD The literature of the Orient has never and cannot be naturalized in the West.

BETTER   The literature of the Orient has never *been* and
cannot be naturalized in the West.

—KARL SHAPIRO

In parallel structures, verbs clearly understood may be
omitted to avoid repetition. See also **14c**.

Some approach life entirely with their eyes; others entirely
with their auditory apparatus. —ALFRED ADLER [Neither
approach nor its object *life* is repeated after the semicolon.]

22c

Do not omit words needed to complete comparisons.

INCOMPLETE	Ed's income is less than his wife.
COMPLETE	Ed's income is less than *that of* his wife. OR
	Ed's income is less than his wife's.
INCOMPLETE	Snow here is as scarce as Miami.
COMPLETE	Snow here is as scarce as *it is in* Miami.
CONFUSING	Bruce likes me more than Ann.
BETTER	Bruce likes me more than *he likes* Ann. OR
	Bruce likes me more than Ann *does*.
INCOMPLETE	Harry is as old, if not older than, Paul.
COMPLETE	Harry is as old *as*, if not older than, Paul. OR
	Harry is as old *as* Paul, if not older.
INFORMAL	Mr. Perkins is as shrewd as any man in the office.
COMPLETE	Mr. Perkins is as shrewd as any *other* man in the office.

Note 1: Some writers still prefer to avoid such intensives
as *so*, *such*, and *too* when used without a completing phrase
or clause.

GENERAL   Albert Einstein was thought to have so little
promise at graduation.

PREFERRED   Albert Einstein was thought to have so little
promise at graduation that no school or university
bothered to offer him a job. —MITCHELL WILSON

GENERAL	Many a man is praised for his reserve and so-called shyness when he is simply too proud.
PREFERRED	Many a man is praised for his reserve and so-called shyness when he is simply too proud to risk making a fool of himself. —J. B. PRIESTLEY

Note 2: Once a frame of reference has been established, an intelligible comparison may be made without explicit mention of the second term of the comparison.

> From here, it is forty miles to the nearest ranch. The nearest town is even farther.

■ **Exercise 2** Supply the words that have been omitted from the following sentences. Put a checkmark after any sentence that needs no revision.

1. In our state the winter is as mild as Louisiana.
2. The mystery of the stolen jewels reminds me of mysteries like Sherlock Holmes.
3. His wife and mother were standing beside him.
4. Mr. Carter paid me more than Jim.
5. The plains are used mostly for cattle raising, not farming.
6. If Jack goes into a profession which he is not trained, he will fail.
7. The lawyer had to prove whatever the witness said was false.

EFFECTIVE SENTENCES

Unity and Logical Thinking

Unity, coherence, emphasis, variety—these are fundamental qualities of effective prose. Unity and coherence in sentences help to make ideas logical and clear. Emphasis makes them forceful. Variety lends interest. All these are usually found in good writing.

23

Write unified, logical sentences.

A sentence is unified when all its parts contribute to making one clear idea or impression. The parts of an ideal sentence form a perfect whole, so that a clause, a phrase, or even a word cannot be changed without disturbing the clarity of the thought or the focus of the impression. A study of this section should help you to write unified, logical sentences, sentences that are not cluttered with obscurities, irrelevancies, or excessive details.

23a

Bring into a sentence only related thoughts; use two or more sentences for thoughts not closely related.

Make sure that the ideas in each sentence are related and that the relationship is immediately clear to the reader. Use two or more sentences to develop ideas that are too loosely linked to belong in one sentence.

UNRELATED	The ancient name for Paris, a city which in 1962 had about 2,800,000 inhabitants, was Lutetia.
BETTER	In 1962 Paris had about 2,800,000 inhabitants. The ancient name of the city was Lutetia. [The unrelated ideas are put into separate sentences, possibly in different parts of the composition.]
UNRELATED	Yesterday Ted sprained his ankle, and he could not find his chemistry notes anywhere.
RELATED	Accident-prone all day yesterday, Ted not only sprained his ankle but also lost his chemistry notes. [The relationship of the two ideas is made clear by the addition of the opening phrase.]

■ **Exercise 1** All the sentences below contain ideas that are apparently unrelated. Adding words when necessary, rewrite each of the sentences to indicate clearly a relationship between ideas. If you cannot establish a close relationship, put the ideas in separate sentences.

1. Although professional writers have their own versions of the idealism and the aims of youth, I went to the rally on September 9.
2. I hate strong windstorms, and pecans pelted my bedroom roof all night.
3. The fence and barn need repairs, and why are property taxes so high?
4. There are many types of bores at social gatherings, but personally I prefer a quiet evening at home.
5. A telephone lineman who works during heavy storms can prove a hero, and cowards can be found in any walk of life.
6. Jones was advised to hire a tutor in French immediately, but the long hours of work at a service station kept his grades low.
7. Macbeth was not the only man to succumb to ambition, and Professor Stetson, for example, likes to draw parallels between modern men and literary characters.

8. Brad sent his sister a dozen red roses, and she sang on a fifteen-minute program over KTUV.
9. The food in the cafeteria has been the subject of many jokes, and most college students do not look underfed.
10. Birds migrate to the warmer countries in the fall and in summer get food by eating worms and insects that are pests to the farmer.

23b

Do not allow excessive detail or excessive subordination to obscure the central thought of the sentence.

Bring into a sentence only pertinent details. Omit tedious minutiae and irrelevant side remarks. Avoid also clumsy, overlapping subordination, the house-that-Jack-built construction.

EXCESSIVE DETAIL In 1788, when Andrew Jackson, then a young man of twenty-one years who had been living in the Carolinas, still a virgin country, came into Tennessee, a turbulent place of unknown opportunities, to enforce the law as the new prosecuting attorney, he had the qualifications that would make him equal to the task.

BETTER In 1788, when Andrew Jackson came into Tennessee as the new prosecuting attorney, he had the necessary qualifications for the task.

EXCESSIVE SUBORDINATION Never before have I known a student who was so ready to help a friend who had gotten into trouble that involved money.

BETTER Never before have I known a student so ready to help a friend in financial trouble.

As you strive to eliminate irrelevant details, remember that length alone does not make a sentence ineffective. Good writers can compose very long sentences, sometimes of paragraph length, without loss of unity. Parallel structure, balance, rhythm, careful punctuation, and well-placed connectives can bind a sentence into perfect unity. Notice how many specific details John Steinbeck presents in the long second sentence below as he develops the key idea of the first sentence.

> Every summer morning about nine o'clock a stout and benign-looking lady came down the stairs from her flat to the pavement carrying the great outdoors in her arms. She set out a canvas deck chair, and over it mounted a beach umbrella—one of the kind which has a little cocktail table around it—and then, smiling happily, this benign and robust woman rolled out a little lawn made of green raffia in front of her chair, set out two pots of red geraniums and an artificial palm, brought a little cabinet with cold drinks—Coca-Cola, Pepsi-Cola—in a small icebox; she laid her folded copy of the *Daily News* on the table, arranged her equipment, and sank back into the chair—and she was in the country.
>
> —JOHN STEINBECK[1]

■ **Exercise 2**   Recast the following sentences to eliminate excessive subordination or detail.

1. During the first period last Monday in room 206 of the English building, we freshmen enjoyed discussing various aspects of civil disobedience.
2. The fan that Joan bought for her brother, who frets about any temperature that exceeds seventy and insists that he can't stand the heat, arrived today.
3. When I was only four, living in a house built during the colonial period, little of which remains today, I often walked alone the two miles between my house and the lake.
4. Four cars of various designs and makes piled up on the freeway, which was completed in 1971 at a cost of over a million dollars.
5. In a dark, pin-striped suit the senator advocated drastic reforms, occasionally taking time out for applause or for a sip of water.

---

6. The dilapidated boat, seaworthy ten years ago but badly in need of repairs now, moved out into the bay.

7. Flames from the gas heater that was given to us three years ago by friends who were moving to Canada licked at the chintz curtains.

8. After finishing breakfast, which consisted of oatmeal, toast, and coffee, Sigrid called the tree surgeon, a cheerful man approximately fifty years old.

9. At last I returned the book that I had used for the report which I made Tuesday to the library.

10. A course in business methods helps the undergraduate to get a job and in addition helps him to find out whether he is fitted for business and thus to avoid postponing the crucial test, as so many do, until it is too late.

23c

Avoid mixed or illogical constructions.

(1) Do not mix figures of speech by changing too rapidly from one to another.

> MIXED   Playing with fire can get a man into deep water.
> BETTER   Playing with fire can result in burned fingers.
>
> MIXED   Her plans to paint the town red were nipped in the bud.
> BETTER   Her plans to paint the town red were thwarted. OR Her plans for a gala evening were nipped in the bud.

(2) Do not mix constructions. Complete each construction logically.

> MIXED   When Howard plays the hypochondriac taxes his wife's patience. [An adverb clause, part of a complex sentence, is here combined with the predicate of a simple sentence.]
> CLEAR   When Howard plays the hypochondriac, he taxes his wife's patience. [Complex sentence] OR
>
>   Howard's playing the hypochondriac taxes his wife's patience. [Simple sentence]

Note: In defining words, careful writers tell *what* a thing is, not when it is or where it is.

AWKWARD   A sonnet is when a poem has fourteen lines.
BETTER   A sonnet is a poem of fourteen lines.

AWKWARD   Banishing a person is where he is driven out of his country.
BETTER   Banishing a person is driving him out of his country.

(3) Make each part of the sentence agree logically with the other parts.

Often a sentence is flawed by a confusion of singular and plural words.

CONFUSED   Hundreds who attended the convention drove their own car.
BETTER   Hundreds who attended the convention drove their own cars.

(4) Do not use a double negative.

NONSTANDARD   Dick did not like nothing about college life.
STANDARD   Dick did not like anything about college life.

See also **19i** under **but, hardly, scarcely**.

■ **Exercise 3** Revise the following sentences to eliminate mixed or illogical constructions.

1. For Don, money does grow on trees, and it also goes down the drain quickly.
2. Because his feet are not the same size explains the difficulty he has finding shoes that fit.
3. Friction is when one surface rubs against another.
4. Several of the delegates brought their wife with them.
5. I wouldn't take nothing for that experience!
6. Like a bat guided by radar, Hilda walks the straight and narrow.
7. To be discreet is where a person carefully avoids saying or doing something tactless.

8. Does anyone here know why Richard resigned or where did he find a better job?
9. Tourists are not permitted to bring their camera indoors.
10. When a child needs glasses causes him to make mistakes in reading and writing.

23d

Base your writing on sound logic.

Be sure that your sentences are well thought out and contain no slips or weaknesses of logic. The following principles of sound thinking may help you to avoid the most common errors.

(1) Be sure your generalizations are sufficiently supported.

FAULTY   None of the children in my family drink coffee; children do not like coffee. [The writer leaps to a conclusion without offering a sufficient number of examples in support of his belief.]

FAULTY   When an automobile accident occurs in this city, the police are never on hand. [Unless the writer has himself seen or read an authoritative account of every automobile accident in the city, he cannot sensibly make this assertion. By avoiding such words as *never* and *always,* using instead such qualifiers as *sometimes* or *often,* the writer can generalize more safely.]

(2) Be sure your evidence is objective and relevant to your assertion.

FAULTY   Henry is an honest boy; he will be successful in anything he tries. [Henry's honesty cannot possibly guarantee his success at every task. The writer's inference does not follow from the evidence.]

FAULTY   Donald is an atheist and a profligate; his arguments against a sales tax are worthless. [Donald might be an unbelieving and dissolute man and yet have excellent views on economic matters such as a sales tax. The evidence is not relevant to the assertion.]

Note: Try not to confuse fact and opinion. To support your opinions, choose your facts carefully.

FACT   Within forty-eight hours five airliners were hijacked, and eleven persons were killed in a plane crash.

OPINION   It is no longer safe to travel by air.

FACT   In August 1970 the women's liberation movement sponsored a nationwide strike.

OPINION   In the 1980's a woman will be president of the United States.

■ **Exercise 4**   Prepare for a class discussion of the faulty logic in the sentences below.

1. Everyone goes to Florida in the winter.
2. Breaking a mirror brings seven years of bad luck.
3. Do not elect my opponent to the Senate; his parents were not born in America.
4. Young people today do not obey their parents.
5. Joseph will be a good class president because all his classmates like him.
6. The other car was at fault, for the driver was a woman.
7. All Germans like opera; I have never met a German who did not.
8. I am sick today because I ate shrimp last night.
9. These razor blades give the smoothest shave; all the baseball players use them.
10. After the first atomic bomb was exploded, it rained for a week in my home town; scientists are wrong to maintain that atomic explosions do not affect the weather!

■ **Exercise 5**   Prepare for a class discussion of the evidence that might be used to reinforce or to discredit the following statements. Then choose one statement and support or refute it in a paragraph of approximately one hundred words. As you write, be careful to bring only related ideas and pertinent details into each sentence. Avoid mixed or obscure constructions, and present logical, convincing evidence in support of your point of view.

1. Painting is nothing more than the art of expressing the invisible through the visible.   —BERNARD MALAMUD

2. Our values and literary styles are as far from those of ancient Athens and Elizabethan England as neckties are from Spanish ruffs, or atom bombs from Greek fire.

—STANLEY HYMAN

3. In developing knowledge men must collaborate with their ancestors.   —WALTER LIPPMANN

4. Today Christmas is a major factor in our capitalist economy.

—ALDOUS HUXLEY

5. Religion is not for every man. It is a value, a skill, that can be acquired only at the expense of pain and blood.

—MICHAEL NOVAK

6. Not one of us who has thought about it expects man as we know him to be on this planet a million years from now.

—HARLOW SHAPLEY

7. The notion that advertising can somehow "manipulate" people into buying products which they should not buy is both arrogant and naive.   —MARTIN MAYER

8. All comedy is based on man's delight in man's inhumanity to man.   —AL CAPP

9. The learned think themselves superior to the common herd.

—W. T. STACE

10. A flood of goodwill has, in fact, eddied during the past two decades from the rich world to the poor, from men of sophistication to men of simplicity.   —JAMES MORRIS

Subordination

24

Use subordination to relate ideas concisely and effectively; use coordination only to give ideas equal emphasis.

In grammar, subordination relates ideas by combining dependent elements with independent ones. (See Section 1, pages 15–23.) The principle of subordination is of great importance in composition since it is one of the best means of achieving sentence unity.

One of the marks of a mature style is effective use of subordination, particularly of modifying phrases and clauses that give grammatical focus to main clauses. Inexperienced writers tend to use too many short simple sentences or stringy compound sentences. Compare the styles of the following groups of sentences.

> COORDINATION   Frank was listening to the radio. He heard the news then. One of his classmates was injured in an automobile accident. The accident had occurred at ten o'clock.

> SUBORDINATION   Listening to the radio, Frank heard that one of his classmates had been injured in an automobile accident at ten o'clock.   [One sentence containing a participial phrase, a noun clause, and a prepositional phrase replaces four simple sentences.]

267

COORDINATION In the future I might feel that I am losing my faith, but if so I would lie down, and then I would get over it, and I would get up again. [Four main clauses]

SUBORDINATION If I felt that I were losing my faith, I would lie down until I got over it. —WILLIAM F. BUCKLEY, JR. [Only one main clause: *I would lie down*]

As the subordinate clauses in the preceding examples indicate, grammatically subordinate structures may contain very important ideas.

24a

Use subordination to combine a related series of short sentences into longer, more effective units.

When combining a series of related sentences, first choose one complete idea for your sentence base; then use subordinate structures (such as modifiers, parenthetical elements, and appositives) to relate the ideas in the other simple sentences to the base.

CHOPPY The two boys objected. The girls knocked them down. The blows were of the karate variety.

EFFECTIVE When the two boys objected, the girls knocked them down with karate blows. —ROY BONGARTZ

CHOPPY Creative writing is a business. It is harrowing. It is a terrifying commitment. This commitment is to an absolute.

EFFECTIVE Creative writing is a harrowing business, a terrifying commitment to an absolute.

—WALTER KERR

Caution: Avoid excessive or clumsy, overlapping subordination: see **23b**.

■ **Exercise 1** Combine the following short sentences into longer sentences in which ideas are properly subordinated. (If you wish, keep one short sentence for emphasis: see **29h**.)

¹ I wrote a paper on the ideas of Thomas Carlyle. ² I tried to relate some of his ideas to contemporary thinking. ³ I was especially interested in Carlyle's analysis of the attributes of the great man. ⁴ His essays also treat the divinity in heroes. ⁵ I found it hard to relate his views to current thought. ⁶ I realized a basic difference between his time and ours. ⁷ His ideas fit the mood of the Victorian era. ⁸ Then many men agreed on a given set of values. ⁹ And their heroes could be measured by those values. ¹⁰ But today values are fluctuating. ¹¹ Our heroes are not stereotypes. ¹² They are not the products of an assembly line. ¹³ Today, one man's hero is another man's villain.

24b

Do not string main clauses together with *and, so,* or *but* when ideas should be subordinated. Use coordination only to give ideas equal emphasis.

AWKWARD   Faculty members came to speak, and they were friendly, but they were met with hostility, and this hostility was almost paranoid.

EFFECTIVE   Friendly faculty members who came to speak were met with an almost paranoid hostility.
                                                —WALTER P. METZGER

ACCEPTABLE   The offer was tempting, but I did not accept it. [Coordination used to stress equally the offer and the refusal]

OFTEN BETTER   Although the offer was tempting, I did not accept it. [Stress on one of the two—the refusal]

To express relationships between ideas, do not overwork such conjunctive adverbs as *however, then,* and *therefore.* Use subordinating conjunctions to indicate such relationships as cause (*because, since*), concession (*although, though*), time (*after, as, before, since, when, whenever, while, until*), place (*where, wherever*), condition (*if, unless*), or comparison (*as if*). Notice the differences in emphasis in the alternate structures that follow.

This news reached Wall Street; then there was a frenzied trading in tobacco shares. OR

When this news reached Wall Street, there was a frenzied trading in tobacco shares. —JAMES RIDGEWAY

The supply of time is totally inelastic; therefore, time is altogether unique. OR

Time is altogether unique because its supply is totally inelastic. —PETER F. DRUCKER

■ **Exercise 2** Revise the following sentences, using effective subordination to improve sentence unity.

1. Yesterday I was taking a shower, so I did not hear the telephone ring, but I got the message in time to go to the party.
2. Jean Henri Dunant was a citizen of Switzerland, and he felt sorry for Austrian soldiers wounded in the Napoleonic Wars; therefore, he started an organization, and it was later named the Red Cross.
3. First he selected a lancet and sterilized it, and then he gave his patient a local anesthetic and lanced the infected flesh.
4. Father Latour was at a friend's house, and he saw two fine horses, and he induced the owner to part with them.
5. I graduated from high school, and then I worked in a bank, and so I earned enough to go to college.
6. The president of the bank walked into his office promptly at nine, and just then he saw the morning paper, and the headlines startled him.
7. We had just reached the bend in the road, for we were on our way home, and we saw a truckload of laborers crowded off the highway by an oncoming bus.
8. The Spanish introduced the custom of branding cattle to America, and the Mexicans continued it, and Americans still brand cattle to show ownership.
9. Daniel Fahrenheit made a thermometer, and he used mercury in it; however, René Réaumur devised one too, but he used alcohol instead of mercury.
10. A wedding ring is worn on the third finger of the left hand, for a vein connects it to the heart, according to an old tale; therefore, the ring symbolizes the giving of the heart with the hand.

24c

Avoid illogical subordination.

In sentences such as the following, the writer decides which idea to subordinate; his decision depends upon what he wishes to emphasize.

> Although I sometimes parrot the rhetoric of newscasters, I do not always understand it.   OR
>
> Although I do not always understand the rhetoric of newscasters, I sometimes parrot it.

It is not always possible to choose which idea to subordinate, however. In the following sentence, for example, logic requires that one idea be subordinated rather than the other.

> COORDINATION   I struck the match, and at that moment the oven exploded.
>
> ABSURD SUBORDINATION   When the oven exploded, I struck the match.
>
> LOGICAL SUBORDINATION   When I struck the match, the oven exploded.   OR   The oven exploded when I struck the match.

■ **Exercise 3**   Revise the following sentences as necessary to eliminate illogical subordination. Put a checkmark after any sentence that needs no revision.

1. Although David slept soundly, the deafening noise continued.
2. As soon as we had a big turkey dinner, Thanksgiving arrived.
3. Even though I will not cut down the ragweed, I have hay fever.
4. While Susan watched television, Charlotte washed the dishes.
5. After he recognized Sylvia, he ran onto the airfield to meet her.

■ **Exercise 4**   Prepare to contribute to a class discussion of the subordination of ideas in the following paragraph.

[1] Very few people anywhere in the world were prepared for the first transplant of the human heart. [2] Even in the surgical profession, where the literature included many documented reports of successful transplantation of hearts in dogs by Dr. Norman Shumway and Richard Lower at Stanford University Medical School, there was little serious acceptance of Shumway's published prediction that the time for a human experiment was near. [3] Consequently, when news came from South Africa on December 3, 1967, that Dr. Christiaan Barnard had taken the heart of a young woman killed in a road accident and put it into a middle-aged grocer whose own heart was failing, the popular reaction everywhere was as to a miracle. —JOHN LEAR[1]

[1] From John Lear's review of *One Life*, by Christiaan Barnard and Curtis Bill Pepper, *Saturday Review*, May 23, 1970. Copyright 1970 Saturday Review, Inc. Reprinted by permission.

Coherence: Misplaced Parts, Dangling Modifiers

25

Avoid needless separation of related parts of the sentence. Avoid dangling modifiers.

Since the meaning of most English sentences depends largely on word order, the position of the parts of a sentence is especially important to clear communication.

MISPLACED   According to Sybil, the gypsies believe that any-one who eats honey and garlic every day will live a long time *in England.*

BETTER   According to Sybil, *the gypsies in England* be-lieve that anyone who eats honey and garlic every day will live a long time.

DANGLING   *When discussing creativity,* a person's ability to finish a pun is stressed by John E. Gibson.

BETTER   *When discussing creativity, John E. Gibson* stresses a person's ability to finish a pun.

The parts of a sentence should be placed to give just the emphasis or meaning desired. Note how the meaning of the following sentences changes according to the position of the modifier *only:*

He said that he loved *only* me. [He loved no one else.]
He said that *only* he loved me. [No one else loved me.]
He said *only* that he loved me. [He said nothing else.]
He *only* said that he loved me. [He did not mean it.]
Only he said that he loved me. [No one else said it.]
He said that he *only* loved me. [Even love has limitations.]

Normally the modifier should be placed as near the word modified as idiomatic English will permit.

Note: If you cannot distinguish readily the sentence parts and the various modifiers discussed in this section, review Section **1**, especially **1d**, and Section **4**.

Misplaced Parts

25a

Avoid needless separation of related parts of the sentence.

(1) In standard written English, adverbs such as *almost, only, just, even, hardly, nearly,* or *merely* are regularly placed immediately before the words they modify.

In spoken English, which tends to place these modifiers before the verb, ambiguity can be prevented by stressing the word to be modified. In written English, however, only correct placement of the adverb can ensure clarity.

AMBIGUOUS He is *just* asking for a trifle.
CLEAR He is asking for *just a trifle.*

INFORMAL The house *only* costs $12,500.
GENERAL The house costs *only $12,500.*

■ **Exercise 1** Revise the following sentences, placing the adverbs in correct relation to the words they modify.

1. The bomb of the guerrillas only killed one student.

2. Bruce polished his silver dollars almost until they looked like new.
3. The transistor nearly cost fifty dollars.
4. He even works during his vacation.
5. Some contemporary poets hardly show any interest in making their poems intelligible.

(2) The position of a modifying prepositional phrase should clearly indicate what the phrase modifies.

A prepositional phrase used as an adjective nearly always comes immediately after the word modified.

> MISPLACED Mother gave date muffins to my friends *with pecans in them.*
>
> BETTER Mother gave my friends *date muffins with pecans in them.*

The position of a prepositional phrase used as an adverb is ordinarily not so fixed as that of a prepositional phrase used as an adjective. Adverb phrases are usually placed near the word modified or at the beginning or end of a sentence. Sometimes, however, the usual placement can be awkward or unclear.

> MISPLACED One student said that such singing was not music but a throat ailment *in class.*
>
> BETTER *In class* one student *said* that such singing was not music but a throat ailment. OR One student *said in class* that such singing was not music but a throat ailment.

■ **Exercise 2** Recast the following sentences to correct undesirable separation of related parts.

1. Newspapers carried the story of the quarterback's fumbling in every part of the country.
2. At the age of two, my mother put me in a nursery school.
3. Students could not understand why Plato and Socrates were so widely admired in high school.

4. At the picnic Gertrude served sundaes to hungry guests in paper cups.

5. The professor made it clear why plagiarism is wrong on Monday.

(3) Adjective clauses should be placed near the words they modify.

MISPLACED   In Kansas, the applause of the students drowned out the jeers of the protesters *who agreed with what the president was saying.*

BETTER   In Kansas, the applause of the *students who agreed with what the president was saying* drowned out the jeers of the protesters.

MISPLACED   We bought gasoline in Arkansas at a small country store *which cost $3.12.*

BETTER   At a small country store in Arkansas, we bought *gasoline which cost $3.12.*

(4) Avoid "squinting" constructions—modifiers that may refer to either a preceding or a following word.

SQUINTING   I agreed *on the next day* to help him.
CLEAR   I agreed *to help him on the next day.*   OR
On the next day, I agreed to help him.

SQUINTING   The tug that was whistling *noisily* chugged up the river.
CLEAR   The whistling tug *chugged noisily* up the river.
OR   The tug *whistled noisily* as it chugged up the river.

(5) Avoid awkward separation of parts of verb phrases and awkward splitting of infinitives.

AWKWARD   There stood the old car that we *had* early last autumn *left* by our lake cottage.
BETTER   There stood the old car that we *had left* by our lake cottage early last autumn.

AWKWARD   You should now begin *to*, if you wish to succeed,
           hunt for a job.

BETTER   If you wish to succeed, you should now begin
           to hunt for a job.

Note: Although all split infinitives were once considered undesirable, those needed for smoothness or clarity are now acceptable.

Americans seem *to* always *be* searching for something new.
                                                    —NEWSWEEK

■ **Exercise 3**   Revise each sentence below to eliminate squinting modifiers or needless separation of related sentence parts.

1. An official warned the hunter not to carry a rifle in a car that was loaded.
2. Selby said in the evening he would go.
3. Marvin wanted to, even during the 6:15 P.M. sports news, finish our game of checkers.
4. Henry promised when he was on his way home to stop at the library.
5. The car was advertised in last night's paper which is only two years old and is in excellent condition.

Dangling Modifiers

25b

Avoid dangling modifiers.

Although any misplaced word, phrase, or clause can be said to dangle when it hangs loosely within a sentence, the term *dangling* is applied primarily to incoherent verbal phrases and elliptical clauses. A dangling modifier is one that does not refer clearly and logically to some word in the sentence.

When verbal phrases or elliptical clauses come before the main clause of a sentence, normal English word order requires that they immediately precede and clearly refer to the subject of the sentence.

PARTICIPIAL PHRASE *Taking our seats,* we watched the game. [We took our seats.]

GERUND PHRASE Instead of *watching the late show,* Nancy read a novel. [Nancy did not watch the late show.]

INFINITIVE PHRASE *To avoid the rush-hour traffic,* Mr. Clark left the office early. [Mr. Clark avoided the rush-hour traffic.]

ELLIPTICAL CLAUSE *When only sixteen,* my grandmother married my grandfather. [*She was* is implied in the elliptical clause.]

To correct a dangling modifier, (1) rearrange the words in the sentence to make the modifier clearly refer to the right word, or (2) add words to make the meaning clear and logical.

(1) Avoid dangling participial phrases.

DANGLING *Taking our seats,* the game started. [*Taking our seats* does not refer to the subject *game,* nor to any other word in the sentence.]

BETTER *Taking* (OR *Having taken*) *our seats, we* watched the opening of the game. [*Taking our seats* refers to *we,* the subject of the sentence.] OR

After we had taken our seats, the game started. [Participial phrase expanded into a clause]

DANGLING The evening passed very pleasantly, *eating candy* and *playing the radio.* [*Eating candy* and *playing the radio* refer to nothing in the sentence.]

BETTER *We* passed the evening very pleasantly, *eating candy* and *playing the radio.* [*Eating candy* and *playing the radio* refer to *we,* the subject of the main clause.]

Note 1: Notice in the last example above that the participial phrase at the end of the sentence modifies the subject at the beginning of the sentence. In sentences that conform to the patterns shown on the page opposite, the participial phrases do not dangle.

278

PATTERN   SUBJECT⌒VERB, PARTICIPIAL PHRASE.

Her *glasses* were on a little Donald Duck night table, *folded neatly and laid stems down.* —J. D. SALINGER

PATTERN
SUBJECT⌒VERB—OBJECT, PARTICIPIAL PHRASE.

Homer built the Iliad around contests, *stressing the humanity of both sides.* —WALTER KAUFMANN

Note 2: Participles do not dangle when they are used in an absolute phrase or when they are used to introduce or refer to a general truth.

> *Weather permitting,* we will have a cookout.
> *Generally speaking,* a pessimist is an unhappy man.

(2) Avoid dangling gerund phrases.

DANGLING   *By mowing the grass high and infrequently,* your lawn can be beautiful. [Who is to do the mowing?]

BETTER   *By mowing the grass high and infrequently, you* can have a beautiful lawn.

(3) Avoid dangling infinitive phrases.

DANGLING   *To write well*, good books must be read. [The understood subject of *to write* should be the same as the subject of the sentence.]

BETTER   *To write well*, a *student* must read good books. [*To write* refers to *student,* the subject of the sentence.]

DANGLING   *To run efficiently,* proper oiling is needed.

BETTER   *To run efficiently,* the *machine* must be properly oiled.

Note: Infinitive phrases do not dangle when they introduce a general truth instead of designating the action of a specific person or thing.

> *To be brief,* rats carry disease.
> *To judge from reports,* all must be going well.

(4) Avoid dangling elliptical clauses.

An elliptical clause—that is, a clause with an implied subject and verb—dangles unless the implied subject is the same as the subject of the main clause.

DANGLING   *When only a small boy,* my father took me with him to Denver. [*I was* is implied in the elliptical clause. *Father,* the subject of the main clause, is not the implied subject of the elliptical clause.]

BETTER   *When only a small boy,* I went with my father to Denver. [*I,* the subject of the main clause, is also the implied subject of the elliptical clause.]
OR
When I was only a small boy, my father took me with him to Denver. [Elliptical clause expanded so that meaning is clear]

DANGLING   Prepare to make an incision in the abdomen as soon as *completely anesthetized.*

BETTER   Prepare to make an incision in the abdomen as soon as *the patient is completely anesthetized.* [Elliptical clause expanded so that meaning is clear]

■ **Exercise 4**   Revise the following sentences to eliminate dangling modifiers. Put a checkmark after any sentence that needs no revision.

1. While wondering about this phenomenon, the sun sank from view.
2. By standing and repeating the pledge, the meeting came to an end.
3. Once made, you must execute the decision promptly.
4. To communicate effectively, eye contact between speaker and audience is needed.

5. After sitting there awhile, it began to snow, and we went indoors.
6. Darkness having come, we stopped for the night.
7. Having taken his seat, we began to question the witness.
8. To grow tomatoes successfully, be sure to provide stakes for the vines.
9. The slaves did not yield, thinking they could free themselves.
10. Keep stirring the water into the mixture until pale green.

■ **Exercise 5** Combine the two sentences in each item below into a single sentence. Use an appropriately placed verbal phrase or elliptical clause as an introductory parenthetical element.

EXAMPLES

We were in a hurry to leave Yellowstone. The dented fender was not noticed.

Being in a hurry to leave Yellowstone, we did not notice the dented fender.

A person may sometimes be confused. At such times he ought to ask questions.

When confused, a person ought to ask questions.

1. The statue has a broken arm and nose. I think it is an interesting antique.
2. James sometimes worried about the world situation. At such times joining the Peace Corps seemed to him a good idea.
3. I read the first three questions on the test. The test covered materials that I had not studied.
4. Larry was only twelve years old. His teachers noticed his inventive abilities.
5. I turned on the flashers and lifted the hood. A speeding motorist, I thought, might slow down, see my predicament, and offer me a ride.

Parallelism

26

Use parallel structure as an aid to coherence.

Words, phrases, clauses, or sentences are parallel when their
grammatical structure is balanced. According to Simeon
Potter, balanced sentences satisfy "a profound human desire
for equipoise and symmetry." Use parallel form, especially
with coordinating conjunctions, in order to express your ideas
simply and logically.

26a

**For parallel structure, balance a word with a word,
a phrase with a phrase, a clause with a clause, a
sentence with a sentence.**

As you study the following examples of parallelism, notice
that an adjective is balanced with an adjective, an active
verb with active verbs, a prepositional phrase with a prepositional phrase, an infinitive phrase with an infinitive phrase,
a noun clause with a noun clause, a main clause with a main
clause, and a complex sentence with a complex sentence.
Notice also that repetition of words can emphasize the
parallel structure. One item in a series may be expanded
without disturbing the total effect of the parallelism.

(1) Words

AWKWARD People begin to feel as though they have no faces and insignificant. [Adverb clause not parallel to adjective]

PARALLEL People begin to feel ‖ *faceless* and
          ‖ *insignificant.*
              —S. L. HALLECK

AWKWARD As the forest lives, decays, and is devoured by itself, it spawns exotic creatures. [Active verbs not parallel to passive verb]

PARALLEL As the forest ‖ *lives,*
         ‖ *decays,* and
         ‖ *devours* itself,
 it spawns exotic creatures.
           —NATIONAL GEOGRAPHIC

(2) Phrases

AWKWARD With the abolition of authority and when the individual is isolated, liberty becomes a universal fetish. [Prepositional phrase not parallel to adverb clause]

PARALLEL ‖ *With the abolition of authority* and
     ‖ *with the isolation of the individual,*
 liberty becomes a universal fetish.
            —ROBERT E. FITCH

AWKWARD It is easier to love humanity as a whole than loving one's neighbor. [Infinitive phrase not parallel to gerund phrase]

PARALLEL It is easier ‖ *to love humanity as a whole* than
       ‖ *to love one's neighbor.*
              —ERIC HOFFER

(3) Clauses

AWKWARD What we say and the things that we do somehow seem out of joint. [Noun clause not parallel to noun modified by adjective clause]

PARALLEL ‖ *What we say* and
     ‖ *what we do*
 somehow seem out of joint. —NORMAN COUSINS

283

| AWKWARD | The rights of creditors were studied deeply; in shallow style were the debtors' remedies passed by. |
| PARALLEL | ‖ *Creditors' rights were studied deeply;* ‖ *debtors' remedies were passed by shallowly.* |

—RALPH NADER

(4) Sentences

| AWKWARD | The danger of the past was that men became slaves. In the future, there is danger because men may become robots. |
| PARALLEL | ‖ *The danger of the past was that men became* ‖ *slaves.* ‖ *The danger of the future is that men may be-* ‖ *come robots.* —ERICH FROMM |

Note: Sentence structure after *and* or *or* is sometimes expanded for special emphasis and is not strictly parallel to the structure before the conjunction.

We are a country with billionaires and with, as we found recently, many thousands of people who do not have enough to eat. —ANTHONY LEWIS [Compare "We are a country with billionaires and with indigents."]

Caution: Do not use parallel structure for sentence elements not parallel in thought. Never use an awkward or unidiomatic expression for the sake of parallelism.

| AWKWARD | Our meetings were held on Friday afternoon, on Saturday morning, and on Saturday afternoon we started home. |
| EFFECTIVE | Our meetings were held on Friday afternoon and on Saturday morning. On Saturday afternoon we started home. |

| AWKWARD | The waves ebbed back into the Atlantic, rattled the stones together, made distinctive sounds, and reminded me of a cosmic dice game. [Parallel structure is used for ideas that could be related more effectively by means of subordination.] |
| EFFECTIVE | When the waves ebbed back into the Atlantic they rattled the stones together so that it sounded like a cosmic dice game. —JAMES K. FEIBLEMAN |

■ **Exercise 1** Underline parallel structures in the following sentences, and prepare to participate in a class discussion of the parallel grammatical constructions. (If necessary, review Section 1, especially 1c and 1d.)

1. In one collective thrust, the students of Columbia University had jumped from zero to infinity, from the anonymous to the historical.   —WALTER P. METZGER

2. Both absolute stillness and constant din tire our minds and spirits.   —ERNEST VAN DEN HAAG

3. Broadly speaking, human beings may be divided into three classes: those who are toiled to death, those who are worried to death, and those who are bored to death.
   —WINSTON CHURCHILL

4. Man is by nature free, and he is by nature social.
   —ROBERT M. HUTCHINS

5. Everybody knows how a rose feels and how a girl smells. Everybody knows how a feeling blooms and how red sings.
   —NANCY HALE

■ **Exercise 2** Revise the following sentences (selected and adapted from *National Geographic*) by recasting italicized words in a form parallel to that of other sentence elements.

EXAMPLE
The trees are magnificent—twisted by winds, hammered by storms, *and snows press them under.*
The trees are magnificent—twisted by winds, hammered by storms, pressed under snows.

1. The cameramen spent months in primitive areas, in African heat, in Alaskan blizzards, and *where there are jungles in South America.*

2. On the machinist's bench stood a variety of plastic birds, opening and closing their beaks, turning their heads, and *their tails flipped.*

3. During Divali festivals, the Indians like to paint their houses, to buy new clothes, *exchanging visits,* and *offering prayers for prosperity.*

4. They say in Arizona that men tear down nature's mountains, run them through mills and smelters, and *of the waste new mountains are built.*

5. The lake was only a small sapphire glinting behind a tiny wall; *there were the canals that looked as if they were only silver threads as they wound across a plain.*

26b

To make the parallel clear, repeat a preposition, an article, the sign of the infinitive, or the introductory word of a long phrase or clause. See also 22c.

OMISSION The reward rests not in the task but the pay.
COMPLETE The reward rests not ‖ *in* the task but
                     ‖ *in* the pay.
—JOHN K. GALBRAITH

OMISSION Life is a mystery and adventure which he shares with all living things.
COMPLETE Life is ‖ *a* mystery and
          ‖ *an* adventure
which he shares with all living things.
—JOSEPH WOOD KRUTCH

CONFUSING For the first time in all history, man possesses the tools and the knowledge to control nature—create a paradise on earth, or end all life on earth.
CLEAR For the first time in all history, man possesses the tools and the knowledge
‖ *to* control nature—
‖ *to* create a paradise on earth, or
‖ *to* end all life on earth. —DAVID SCHOENBRUN

CONFUSING We say that civilization cannot survive an atomic war, there can be no victory and no victors, nuclear weapons can annihilate all life on this planet.
CLEAR We say ‖ *that* civilization cannot survive an atomic war,
‖ *that* there can be no victory and no victors,
‖ *that* nuclear weapons can annihilate all life on this planet.
—ADLAI E. STEVENSON

286

■ **Exercise 3** Insert words needed to bring out the parallel structure in the following sentences.

1. They would lie on the battlefield without medical attention for an hour or day.
2. Two things I intend to do: to try and succeed.
3. I told him very politely that I could not attend and I had reasons.
4. I finally realized that one can learn much more by studying than worrying.
5. The sentences are difficult to understand, not because they are long but they are obscure.

26c

Correlatives (both . . . and, either . . . or, neither . . . nor, not only . . . but also, whether . . . or) usually connect parallel structures.

AWKWARD   History contains both what is past and the future.

PARALLEL   History contains ‖ *both the past* ‖ *and the future.* —JAN KOTT

AWKWARD   The censors can neither think that clearly, nor can they feel that acutely.

PARALLEL   The censors can ‖ *neither think that clearly* ‖ *nor feel that acutely.*

—BERNARD DE VOTO

26d

Be sure that a *who, whom,* or *which* clause precedes *and who, and whom,* or *and which.*

FAULTY   Inez Carter is a woman of great charm and who is seeking office. [A *who* clause does not precede the *and who;* the *of* phrase is not parallel to the *who* clause.]

BETTER   Inez Carter is a woman ‖ *who has great charm* and ‖ *who is seeking office.*

■ **Exercise 4** Revise the following sentences by using parallel structure to express parallel ideas. Put a checkmark after any sentence that needs no revision.

1. Not only liberals but also those who were conservatives wished to save the republic.
2. Our personalities are shaped by both heredity and what type of environment we have.
3. Someone has said that Americans cannot enjoy life without a TV set, an automobile, and a summer cottage.
4. My friend told me that the trip would be delayed but to be ready to start on Friday.
5. William is a boy with the best intentions and who has the highest principles.
6. A seal watches carefully the way his fellows act and how they obey their trainer.
7. He was quiet and in a serious mood after the talk.
8. I did not know whether I should go to some technical school or had better enter a liberal arts college.
9. The secretary must attend all meetings, call the roll, and keep the minutes.
10. People fall naturally into two classes: the workers and those who like to depend on others.

■ **Exercise 5** First study the parallelism in the sentence below. Then use Martin's sentence as a structural model for a sentence of your own.

Santiago is the loveliest city in the republic: double-spired church, ancient stores with massive mahogany doors swinging on iron hinges, narrow sidewalks forever thronged with people, narrow streets forever clogged with cars, trucks, bicycles, motor scooters, and horse-drawn carriages bearing ladies with parasols. —JOHN BARTLOW MARTIN

■ **Exercise 6** Carefully read the following paragraphs, noting all parallel constructions. Then write a similar composition of your own on a subject such as the importance of music, the value of travel, the beauty of friendship, the impact of automation, or the dangers of pollution.

¹ Man's greatest source of enlightenment lies in the printed word. ² No amount of persuasion can forever take away its imprint on the minds of a searching public. ³ Passing years cannot dilute its great truths nor still its gifts of laughter. ⁴ It alone passes from generation to generation the sum of mankind's knowledge and experience.

⁵ Through the medium of printing you can live a thousand lives in one. ⁶ You can discover America with Columbus, pray with Washington at Valley Forge, stand with Lincoln at Gettysburg, work in the laboratory with Franklin, Edison, Pasteur or Salk and walk the fields with St. Francis. ⁷ Through printing you can encompass in your imagination the full sweep of world history. ⁸ You can watch the rise and fall of civilizations, the ebb and flow of mighty battles and the changing pattern of life through the ages. ⁹ Through printing you can live a mental life of adventure. ¹⁰ You can roam with Marco Polo, sail the seas with Magellan, be a swashbuckling Musketeer, a member of Robin Hood's band of merry men, a Knight of King Arthur's Round Table or a conqueror of space.

¹¹ Printing lets you enrich your spirit with the Psalms, the Sermon on the Mount, the Beatitudes and all the other noble writings that are touched with divine fire. ¹² You can know the majesty of great poetry, the wisdom of great philosophers, the findings of the scientists.

¹³ You can start today where the great thinkers of yesterday left off because printing has immortalized man's knowledge. ¹⁴ Thinkers dead a thousand years are as alive in their works today as when they walked the earth. ¹⁵ Through printing you can orient your life to the world you live in, for printing links the past, the present and the future. ¹⁶ It is ever changing and immutably constant, as old as civilization and as new as this morning's newspaper.

¹⁷ It is man's enduring achievement.[1]

■ **Exercise 7** Prepare for a class discussion of the parallel structures in Lincoln's Gettysburg Address. See Section 1, Exercise 10.

---

[1] Reprinted by permission of the Padgett Printing Corporation, Dallas.

Point of View

27

Maintain a consistent point of view as an aid to coherence.

Sudden and illogical shifts in point of view tend to obscure meaning and thus to cause needless difficulty in reading.

27a

Avoid needless shifts in tense. See also 7d.

SHIFT   During their man-to-man talk Harvey *complained* about the idiocy of overkill while his father *discusses* the dangers of overlive.   [Shift from past to present tense]

BETTER   During their man-to-man talk Harvey *complained* about the idiocy of overkill while his father *discussed* the dangers of overlive.   [Both verbs in the past tense]

Note: When the historical present is used, as in summarizing plots of narratives, care will be needed to avoid slipping from the present tense into the past tense.

Romeo *goes* in disguise to a Capulet feast, *falls* in love with Juliet, and *marries* (NOT *married*) her secretly.

27b

Avoid needless shifts in mood. See also 7d.

SHIFT First *rise* to your feet and then you *should address* the chairman. [Shift from imperative to indicative mood]

BETTER First *rise* to your feet and then *address* the chairman. [Both verbs in the imperative mood]

27c

Avoid needless shifts in subject or voice.

A shift in subject often involves a shift in voice. A shift in voice nearly always involves a shift in subject.

SHIFT James liked fishing, but hunting was also enjoyed by him. [The subject shifts from *James* to *hunting*. The voice shifts from active to passive.]

BETTER James liked fishing, but he also enjoyed hunting. [The subject does not shift. Both verbs are active.]

SHIFT Mary took summer courses, and her leisure hours were devoted to tennis. [The subject shifts from *Mary* to *hours*. The voice shifts from active to passive.]

BETTER Mary took summer courses and devoted her leisure hours to tennis. [One subject only. Both verbs are active.]

27d

Avoid needless shifts in person.

SHIFT *We* have reached a point where *one* ought to face the possibility of a great and sudden change. [Shift from first to third person]

BETTER *We* have reached a point where *we* ought to face the possibility of a great and sudden change.

SHIFT *The student* will find the University Book Shop a great convenience. *You* need not leave the campus to purchase any school supplies *you* may need. [Shift from third to second person]

BETTER *The student* will find the University Book Shop a great convenience. *He* need not leave the campus to purchase any school supplies *he* may need.

■ **Exercise 1** In the following sentences, correct all needless shifts in tense, mood, subject, voice, or person.

1. Many Americans still considered the first landing on the moon a technological miracle; a few even believe it was all an entertaining hoax.
2. Take away phosphates in detergents, and housewives will be washing their clothes in hard water.
3. Mr. Marshall seems to speak off the cuff, but his comments are always written down, revised, and carefully rehearsed beforehand.
4. Robert followed the tracks up the mountain path, and soon the wounded bear was sighted.
5. I was told that billions of germs live on one's skin and that you should bathe often.

27e

Avoid needless shifts in number. See also **6b**, agreement of pronoun and antecedent.

SHIFT *Each student* in the Union Building *was* asked to sign *their name* on a master ditto sheet. [*Each, student, was,* and *name* are singular; *their* is plural.]

BETTER *Each student* in the Union Building *was* asked to sign *his name* on a master ditto sheet.

SHIFT The *United Nations deserves* encouragement. Indeed, *they deserve* much more than that. [Singular *deserves* indicates that *United Nations* is singular, but *they* and *deserve* are plural.]

BETTER   The *United Nations deserves* encouragement. Indeed, *it deserves* much more than that.

27f

Avoid needless shifts from indirect to direct discourse.

SHIFT   My friend asked *whether I knew* the coach and *will he be* with the team.   [Shift from indirect to direct discourse]

BETTER   My friend asked *whether I knew* the coach and *whether he would be* with the team.   [Indirect discourse]
OR
My friend asked, *"Do you know* the coach? *Will he be* with the team?"   [Direct discourse]

27g

Maintain the same tone or style throughout the sentence (as well as throughout the larger elements of discourse).

INAPPROPRIATE   Journalists who contend that the inefficiency of our courts makes legalized crime mandatory are *a bunch of kooks.*   [A shift from formal to colloquial style. Replace *a bunch of kooks* with a phrase such as *a group of eccentrics.*]

INAPPROPRIATE   After distributing the grass seed evenly over the lawn, rake the ground at least twice and then *gently bedew it with fine spray.*   [The italicized expression is too "poetic" in a sentence with a prosaic purpose. Substitute something like *water it lightly.*]

INAPPROPRIATE   It seemed to Juliet, as she gazed down from the balcony, that Romeo's face was as white as *the underside of a fish.*   [The italicized expression clashes with the romantic beginning of the sentence. Substitute something like *the petals of a gardenia.*]

27h

Maintain a consistent perspective throughout the sentence (as well as throughout the larger elements of discourse).

> FAULTY PERSPECTIVE   From the top of the Washington Monument, the government buildings seemed to be so many beehives, and the workers droned at their tasks behind long rows of desks. [The perspective shifts from the monument to the interior of the buildings.]
>
> CONSISTENT PERSPECTIVE   From the top of the Washington Monument, the government buildings seemed to be so many beehives, and it was easy to imagine the workers droning at their tasks behind long rows of desks.

■ **Exercise 2** In the following sentences, correct all needless shifts in tense, mood, subject, voice, person, number, type of discourse, tone, or perspective. Put a checkmark after any sentence that needs no revision. Prepare for a class discussion of the reason for each change you make.

1. One parapsychologist said that every thought we have was a living entity.
2. Standing before the house, he thought of the many happy years he had spent there and how quickly they are passing.
3. According to Helen Leath, Mr. Blake knows how to deal with annoying door-to-door salesmen; they are quickly frightened away by him.
4. Pretending to be a seller of knives, Mr. Blake waves a long butcher knife near the throat of the salesman. You can well imagine what they think.
5. A woman stepped forward, grabs the culprit by the collar, and demands that he apologize to the child.
6. He said he had a convertible model in the garage and would I like to try it out.
7. Janet likes to cook, but housecleaning is not a pleasant occupation.
8. A vacation is enjoyed by all because it refreshes the mind and the body.

9. Aunt Leila spent her summers in Wisconsin but flew to Arizona for the winters.
10. Jim wondered whether Jack had left and did he say when he would return?
11. Every citizen should do your duty as you see it.
12. You should get to the airport as soon as possible, and tell the taxi driver not to make any stops on the way.
13. The underwater scene was dark and mysterious; the branches of the willows lining the shores dipped gracefully into the water.
14. The darkness of the auditorium, the monotony of the ballet, and the strains of music drifting sleepily from the orchestra aroused in me a great desire to sack out.

■ **Exercise 3** Revise the following paragraph to eliminate all needless shifts. If necessary, expand the paragraph.

[1] He was a shrewd businessman, or so it had always seemed to me. [2] He has a deceptively open face, and his manner is that of an amiable farmer. [3] When questioned about his success, he tried to appear humble and says that "All I know is what I see on TV." [4] Nevertheless he will let it be known that he has considerable influence with important people. [5] Take these impressions for what they are worth; it may help one in your dealings with this cat.

Reference of Pronouns

28

Make a pronoun refer unmistakably to its antecedent. See also **6b**.

As a rule, place pronouns like *it, he, she, they, them, this, that, who, which,* and *such* as close as possible to their antecedents.

> There is very little joy left in modern intercollegiate football. It has become hard, specialized work.
>
> —PAUL GALLICO

> Languages are not invented; they grow with our need for expression.   —SUSANNE K. LANGER

As you proofread your compositions, check to see that the meaning of each pronoun is immediately obvious. If there is any chance of confusion, repeat the antecedent or use a synonym for it.

> AMBIGUOUS   Fear has power; this seeks to affirm itself by exertion. [Does *this* refer to *fear* or to *power?*]
>
> CLEAR   Fear has power; power seeks to affirm itself by exertion. —ROBERT COLES

If repetition proves awkward, recast your sentence.

28a

Avoid ambiguous reference either by making it clear which of two possible antecedents a pronoun refers to or by placing only one antecedent before a pronoun.

AMBIGUOUS   John told William that he had made a mistake. [Who made the mistake?]

CLEAR   John said to William, "You have made a mistake." OR John admitted to William that he had made a mistake.

AMBIGUOUS   Mary met Jane when she was handing out leaflets. [Who was handing out leaflets?]

CLEAR   When Mary was handing out leaflets, she met Jane. OR Jane was handing out leaflets when she met Mary.

28b

Avoid remote reference.

REMOTE   A freshman found herself the unanimously elected president of a group of enthusiastic reformers, mostly townspeople, *who* was not a joiner of organizations. [*Who* is too far removed from the antecedent *freshman*. See also 25a(3).]

BETTER   A *freshman who* was not a joiner of organizations found herself the unanimously elected president of a group of enthusiastic reformers, mostly townspeople.

VAGUE   He sat by the little window all day and worked steadily at his translating. *It* was too small to give much light. [Temporarily confusing: the antecedent of *it* is not clear until the reader finishes the sentence.]

BETTER   He sat by the little window all day and worked steadily at his translating. The *window* was too small to give much light.

| OBSCURE | When Johnson's club was organized, *he* asked Goldsmith to become a member. [Reference to antecedent in the possessive case] |
| BETTER | When *Johnson* organized his club, *he* asked Goldsmith to become a member. [See also 27c.] |

Caution: As a rule avoid pronoun reference to the title of a theme or to a word in the title.

Title: Is Work a Curse or a Blessing?

| AWKWARD | To a man who is harassed by a nagging wife and undisciplined children, *it* can be a great blessing, a welcome escape. |
| BETTER | To a man who is harassed by a nagging wife and undisciplined children, *work* can be a great blessing, a welcome escape. |

■ **Exercise 1** Revise each sentence below in order to eliminate ambiguous or remote reference.

1. Harold asked Mack what he had done wrong.
2. On the dashboard the various buttons and knobs seldom cause confusion on the part of the driver that are clearly labeled.
3. After Martin's advertising campaign was launched, he had more business than he could handle.
4. The lake covers many acres. Near the shore, water lilies grow in profusion, spreading out their green leaves and sending up white blossoms on slender stems. It is well stocked with fish.
5. Elaine waved to Mrs. Edwards as she was coming down the ramp.

28c

Use broad reference only with discretion.

Pronouns such as *it, this, that, which,* and *such* may refer to a specific word or phrase or to the general idea of a whole clause, sentence, or paragraph.

SPECIFIC REFERENCE His nose was absolutely covered with warts of different sizes; it looked like a sponge, or some other kind of marine growth. —DAN JACOBSEN [*It* refers to *nose.*]

BROAD REFERENCE This was One World now—and he owned a Volkswagen and a Japanese camera to prove it. —ARNOLD M. AUERBACH [*It* refers to *This was One World now.*]

When used carelessly, however, broad reference can interfere with clear communication. To ensure clarity, inexperienced writers may be advised to make each of their pronouns refer to a specific word.

(1) Avoid reference to the general idea of a preceding clause or sentence unless the meaning is clear and unmistakable.

VAGUE At the first performance William was absent, which caused much comment. [*Which* has no antecedent.]

CLEAR William's absence from the first performance caused much comment.

VAGUE The story referred to James, but Henry misapplied it to himself. This is true in real life. [*This* has no antecedent.]

CLEAR The story referred to James, but Henry misapplied it to himself. Similar mistakes occur in real life.

(2) As a rule do not refer to a word or idea not expressed but merely implied.

VAGUE He wanted his teachers to think he was above average, as he could have been if he had used it to advantage. [*It* has no expressed antecedent.]

CLEAR He wanted his teachers to think he was above average, as he could have been if he had used his ability to advantage.

VAGUE My mother is a music teacher, but I know nothing about this. [*This* has no expressed antecedent.]

CLEAR My mother is a music teacher, but I know nothing about the teaching of music.

(3) Avoid awkward use of the indefinite *you* or *it*.

AWKWARD   Often *a person* does not remember that what *you* do not do now *you* may not have the chance to do later. [Needless shift from third person to the indefinite, second-person *you*. See also **27d**.]

BETTER   Often *a person* does not remember that what *he* does not do now *he* may not have the chance to do later.

AWKWARD   In the book *it* says that many mushrooms are edible.

BETTER   The book says that many mushrooms are edible.

Note: Unless referring to a specific person or persons, some writers prefer not to use *you* in a formal context.

When *one* cannot swim, *he* fears deep, stormy waters. [Compare "When *you* cannot swim, *you* fear deep, stormy waters."]

28d

Avoid awkwardness arising from placing the pronoun *it* near the expletive *it*.

AWKWARD   Although it would be unwise for me to buy the new model, it is a beautiful machine. [The first *it* is an expletive; the second *it* is a pronoun referring to *model*.]

BETTER   Although it would be unwise for me to buy one now, the new model is a beautiful machine. OR For me to buy the new model would be unwise now, but it is a beautiful machine.

■ **Exercise 2** Revise the following sentences as necessary to correct faults in reference. Put a checkmark after any sentence that needs no revision.

1. It is a good idea to have every student voice his opinion of the curriculum, for it needs changing.

2. I devote an hour a day to exercising my body, for I feel that it improves my mind and my senses.
3. There was no confrontation erupting in violence, which made the administrators happy.
4. If one is guilty of violating a traffic law, the cost of your car insurance goes up.
5. Her sweet temperament was reflected in the graciousness of her manner. This was apparent from her every act.
6. In the book it states that Mrs. Garrett can see through her fingertips.
7. Our language is rich in connectives that express fine distinctions of meaning.
8. I did not even buy a season ticket, which was very disloyal to my school.
9. Mary told Ann that she had to read *Ecotactics.*
10. When building roads the Romans tried to detour around valleys as much as possible for fear that flood waters might cover them and make them useless.
11. The extra fees surprised many freshmen that seemed unreasonably high.
12. In Frank's suitcase he packs only wash-and-wear clothes.

Emphasis

29

Select words and arrange the parts of the sentence to give emphasis to important ideas.

Since ideas vary in importance, expression of them should vary in stress. Short, factual statements and routine description or narration cannot always be varied for emphasis without doing violence to the natural word order of the English language. For example, it would be absurd for a sportswriter to describe a football play by saying, "Short was the pass that Randy caught, and across the goal line raced he." But in most types of writing, word order may be changed to achieve emphasis without losing naturalness of expression.

You may emphasize ideas through the use of concrete words, especially verbs and nouns (see Section **20**); through economy of language (see Section **21**); and through subordination (see Section **24**). You may also gain emphasis—

a by placing important words at the beginning or end of the sentence;

b by changing loose sentences into periodic sentences;

c by arranging ideas in the order of climax;

d by using the active voice instead of the passive voice;

e by repeating important words;

f by putting a word or phrase out of its usual order;

g by using balanced sentence construction;

h by abruptly changing sentence length.

29a

Gain emphasis by placing important words at the beginning or end of the sentence—especially at the end.

UNEMPHATIC   Americans today have forgotten the meaning the United States once held for the world, if they ever knew. [The parenthetical qualifier placed in an important position weakens the sentence.]

EMPHATIC   Americans today have forgotten, if they ever knew, the meaning the United States once held for the world. —SEYMOUR MARTIN LIPSET

UNEMPHATIC

In my opinion, the spirit of science is the spirit of progress, above all. By that I mean that science does not seek a utopia or heaven that is static. Generally speaking, there are ever newer horizons and higher peaks for men to climb, mentally, spiritually, materially. [The most important words are not placed at the beginning or end of the sentences. Wordy phrases, such as *in my opinion* and *by that I mean that,* are unemphatic. In the last sentence, *materially* is the least important item in the series.]

EMPHATIC

Above all, the spirit of science is the spirit of progress. Science seeks no static utopia or heaven. It can afford men ever newer horizons and higher peaks to climb, materially, mentally, and spiritually. —HERMANN J. MULLER

Note: Since semicolons, sometimes called weak periods, are also strong punctuation marks, words placed before a semicolon also have an important position.

■ **Exercise 1**   Prepare for a class discussion of emphasis in the following paragraph, giving special attention to the choice of words at the beginning and end of each sentence.

[1] By a strange perversity in the cosmic plan, the biologically good die young. [2] Species are not destroyed for their short-

comings but for their achievements. [3] The tribes that slumber in the graveyards of the past were not the most simple and undistinguished of their day, but the most complicated and conspicuous. [4] The magnificent sharks of the Devonian period passed with the period, but certain contemporaneous genera of primitive shellfish are still on earth. [5] Similarly, the lizards of the Mesozoic era have long outlived the dinosaurs, who were immeasurably their biologic betters. [6] Illustrations such as these could be endlessly increased. [7] The price of distinction is death.

—JOHN H. BRADLEY[1]

■ **Exercise 2** Revise the following sentences to make them more emphatic. Change the word order when desirable, and delete unnecessary words and phrases.

1. In a sense, music has the power to hypnotize, or so it would seem.
2. There was, just outside the little town of Windermere, a sign directing the attention of tourists to a restaurant for vegetarians; the restaurant was about a mile away, more or less.
3. As I see it, Pat is another Don Quixote because of his incessant fighting for lost causes, however.
4. When risking her neck, a stunt woman who earns five thousand dollars for two hours of work is doing too much for too little, I am convinced.
5. They say that Lewisville decided to enforce the old ordinance one day; soon nearby towns revived similar laws and began clean-up campaigns also.

29b

Gain emphasis by changing loose sentences into periodic sentences.

A loose sentence is one that can be easily scanned, since the main idea comes toward the beginning and the reader can omit details, often parenthetical, placed later in the

[1]From "Is Man an Absurdity?" by John H. Bradley, *Harper's Magazine*, October 1936. Reprinted by permission.

sentence. To get the meaning of a periodic sentence, however, the reader cannot stop until he reaches the period.

LOOSE   Up it went, a great ball of fire about a mile in diameter, changing colors as it kept shooting upward, an elemental force freed from its bonds after being chained for billions of years.
—WILLIAM L. LAURENCE [The main idea—*up it went*—comes first; explanatory details follow.]

PERIODIC   Whether it is the legions of Herod trying to account for every child of Bethlehem, or a modern government attempting to count each of its citizens, no census is complete. —C. LORING BRACE [The main idea comes last, just before the period.]

Both types of sentences can be effective. The loose sentence is, and should be, the more commonly used. But the periodic sentence, by holding the reader in suspense, is more emphatic. Note the difference in tone in the following sentences.

LOOSE   There cannot be peace on earth as long as you see your fellow man as a being essentially to be feared, mistrusted, hated, and destroyed. [Main idea first—a good sentence]

PERIODIC   As long as you see your fellow man as a being essentially to be feared, mistrusted, hated, and destroyed, there cannot be peace on earth.
—THOMAS MERTON [Main idea last—a more emphatic sentence]

LOOSE   A humanly possible answer to the riddle of inequality can be found only in the unity of all beings in time and eternity. [Main idea first]

PERIODIC   Only in the unity of all beings in time and eternity can a humanly possible answer to the riddle of inequality be found.
—PAUL TILLICH [Main idea last]

Caution: Do not overuse the periodic sentence to the point of making your style unnatural. Variety is desirable: see Section 30.

■ **Exercise 3** Study the structure of the following sentences; then label each as either *loose* or *periodic*.

1. With every major and stubborn problem of the last half century—transportation, social security, welfare, education, housing, agricultural surplus, labor relations, race relations—we have seen the people turn to Washington for resolution. —RAMSEY CLARK

2. We perceive the outrageous only when we can perceive the possibility of reform. —GEORGE B. LEONARD

3. Out of this pain of loss, this bitter ecstasy of brief having, this fatal glory of the single moment, the tragic writer will therefore make a song for joy. —THOMAS WOLFE

4. Polyphemus continued to melt round the room, staring malignly at nothing. —ELIZABETH BOWEN

5. No one who has felt the fury of the fish charging like electric current through line and rod, who has heard the cacophonous screech of backing being ripped through guides, who has reeled with a madman's frenzy in the final seconds before boat and angler plunge into the Rogue's crashing, foaming white water, who has held on, bruised and shaken, until that sudden, inexplicable moment when the line goes slack and the contest is over as abruptly as it began—no one who has experienced such an encounter is ever the same again. —VIRGINIA KRAFT[2]

■ **Exercise 4** Convert the loose sentences in Exercise 3 to periodic sentences, and the periodic to loose. Notice how your revisions make for varying emphasis.

29c

Gain emphasis by arranging ideas in the order of climax.

Notice in the following examples that words, phrases, clauses, and sentences are arranged in the order of importance, with the strongest idea last.

---

[2]From "Steelheads on a Rough River" by Virginia Kraft, *Sports Illustrated*, November 15, 1965. © 1965 Time Inc. Reprinted by permission.

Mr. Raleigh fears poverty, illness, and death. [Words placed in order of importance]

We could hear the roar of artillery, the crash of falling timbers, the shrieks of the wounded. [Sentence climax reached with *shrieks of the wounded*]

Sometimes their anguish was my anguish; sometimes their cussedness was my fury; occasionally their pleasure was my despair. —RUSSELL LYNES [Clauses placed in order of importance]

In the language of screen comedians four of the main grades of laugh are the titter, the yowl, the belly laugh and the boffo. The titter is just a titter. The yowl is a runaway titter. Anyone who has ever had the pleasure knows all about a belly laugh. The boffo is the laugh that kills. —JAMES AGEE [First words and then sentences placed in climactic order]

Note: Arrangement of ideas in reverse order of climax, called anticlimax, is sometimes used for comic effect.

> To a distant cousin the rich old man willed his ranch, three
> oil wells, two tractors, and innumerable alley cats.

■ **Exercise 5** Arrange the ideas in the sentences below in what you consider to be the order of climax.

1. Franklin used the ant as a symbol of industry, wisdom, and efficiency.
2. Among the images in the poem are sun-drenched orchards, diamond-eyed children, and golden-flecked birds.
3. He left the city because his health was failing, his taxes were going up, and his pet dog was tired of the leash.
4. Something must be done at once. Unless we act now, the city will be bankrupt in five years. The commission is faced with a deficit.
5. The would-be governor shook hands with the man on the street, autographed books for teenagers, promised prosperity to all, and wrote letters to senior citizens.

■ **Exercise 6** Prepare for a class discussion of the effect of the arrangement of ideas on emphasis in the following paragraphs.

307

[1] I began to think about personal liability insurance the morning Mrs. Ehrlich, our cleaning woman, suddenly screamed down to me from her perch on the windowsill: "Mr. J., come help! I got another one of those dizzy spells!"

[2] I had asked Mrs. Ehrlich time and again to stop climbing around on the windowsills. [3] I had also asked her not to run so fast while carrying the big plate-glass top of the coffee table across the waxed floors, and to try not to pour quite so much water into the electrical outlets. [4] These restrictions may seem harsh, but I don't think I am what you could call a tyrannical employer. [5] I've left her plenty of room for fringe-benefit fun. [6] I've said nothing about blowing out the pilot light, sticking her fingers into the vacuum cleaner's turbo-jet engine, or tossing all the naphthalene, paint cans, and oil-soaked rags she pleases into the incinerator. —HAYES B. JACOBS[3]

29d

Gain emphasis by using the active voice instead of the passive voice.

UNEMPHATIC   Our picture window was punctured by hail, our garage was flattened by winds, and our basement was turned into a muddy swamp by the flood.

EMPHATIC   Hail punctured our picture window, winds flattened our garage, and the flood turned our basement into a muddy swamp.

Exception: If the receiver of the action is more important than the doer, the passive voice is more effective.

EMPHATIC

There in the tin factory, in the first moment of the atomic age, a human being was crushed by books. —JOHN HERSEY

Individual personalities cannot be mass produced (with happiness thrown in or your money back).

—ERNEST VAN DEN HAAG

[3] From "Accidental You, Fully Covered Me" by Hayes B. Jacobs, in Martin Levin's "Phoenix Nest," *Saturday Review*, May 15, 1965. Copyright 1965 Saturday Review, Inc. Reprinted by permission.

■ **Exercise 7**   Make each sentence below more emphatic by substituting the active for the passive voice.

1. A mink wrap was worn by the actress.
2. It is taken for granted by students in Dr. Boyer's class that they will have a weekly quiz.
3. Victorian literature is being reevaluated by modern British and American scholars.
4. When the play was brought to an end, the actors were greeted with a loud burst of applause by the audience.
5. It is greatly feared by the citizens that adequate punishment will not be meted out by the judge.

■ **Exercise 8**   Prepare for a class discussion of the effect of voice on emphasis in the following paragraph. Note the differences in emphasis that would result from converting the verbs *dislodged* and *sent* from active to passive voice.

[1] The earthquake dislodged about a million cubic yards of ice from a 2,600-foot cliff on the mountain.   [2] The ice crashed onto a glacier below the cliff and sent a wall of mud—30 million cubic yards of ice and water and 65 million cubic yards of earth—racing down the valley of the Rio Santa.   [3] The mudflow covered the nine miles in less than two and a half minutes, reaching the unglacial speed of more than 250 miles per hour. [4] It surged over a ridge and overwhelmed the city, covering it to an average depth of ten feet.   [5] Only a few dozen inhabitants survived.   —SCIENTIFIC AMERICAN[4]

29e

Gain emphasis by repeating important words.

Note the great difference between the careless repetition in **21c** and the effective repetition in the following passages. See also **31b(3)**.

---

[4] From "Science and the Citizen," *Scientific American,* August 1970. Copyright © 1970 by Scientific American, Inc. All rights reserved. Reprinted by permission.

EMPHATIC

No real revolt can be convenient for the privileged; no real revolt can be contained within comfortable bounds or be made respectable. —KENNETH CLARK

It seems that Herman Melville had a vision of evil in *Moby Dick,* that Nathaniel Hawthorne had a vision of evil in *The Scarlet Letter,* and that Henry James had a vision of evil in *The Turn of the Screw.* —HOWARD MUMFORD JONES

■ **Exercise 9** Prepare for a class discussion of the effect of repetition on emphasis in the following paragraph.

¹ The hatreds do not go one way: ghetto blacks hate policemen, and policemen hate upper-class radicals. ² One hates one class up as well as one class down, although the hatred downward is more violent and the hatred upward mixed with aspiration. ³ The natural alliance is between people a class apart who hate people in the middle for different reasons. ⁴ This suggests why elite intellectuals, for all their analyzed self-awareness, show immediate "understanding" for the ghetto black's hatred of the policeman yet find police violence directed at a partially upper-class political demonstration a sure sign of incipient fascism.
—MICHAEL LERNER[5]

29f

Gain emphasis by putting a word or phrase out of its usual order.

EMPHATIC

Crises there will continue to be. —DWIGHT D. EISENHOWER [Compare "There will continue to be crises."]

Faceless men they are, who doffed their native identities when they jettisoned their American names.
—ALBERT GOLDMAN [Compare "They are faceless men. . . ."]

[5]From "Respectable Bigotry" by Michael Lerner. Reprinted from *The American Scholar,* Volume 38, Number 4, Autumn, 1969. Copyright © 1969 by the United Chapters of Phi Beta Kappa. By permission of the publishers.

Caution: This method of gaining emphasis, if overused, will make the style distinctly artificial. And of course the order of the parts of the sentence should never be such as to cause ambiguity: see **25a**.

■ **Exercise 10** From your reading, copy five passages in which emphasis is secured by putting a word or phrase out of its usual order.

29g

Gain emphasis by using balanced sentence construction.

A sentence is balanced when identical or similar grammatical structure is used to express contrasted ideas. A balanced sentence uses parallel structure (see Section 26) and emphasizes the contrast between parts of similar length and movement.

BALANCED

Men who are unwilling to accept middle age are feminine. Women who easily accept theirs are masculine.

—THEODOR REIK

Love is positive; tolerance negative. Love involves passion; tolerance is humdrum and dull. —E. M. FORSTER

Caution: Do not overuse balance, which can lead to artificiality rather than emphasis. Lack of balance is preferable to awkwardness.

■ **Exercise 11** Use balanced, emphatic sentences to show the contrast between the following:

(1) men and women, (2) youth and age, (3) success and failure, (4) beauty and ugliness.

29h

Gain emphasis by abruptly changing sentence length.

> In the last two decades there has occurred a series of changes in American life, the extent, durability, and significance of which no one has yet measured. No one can. —IRVING HOWE
> [The short sentence, which abruptly follows a much longer one, is emphatic.]

■ **Exercise 12** Write a short, emphatic sentence to follow each long sentence below. Then write a similar pair of sentences—one long and one short—of your own.

1. According to a number of journalists, not to mention the references in the Condon Report, our astronauts have seen flying objects in outer space, objects that may have been clouds, satellites, or space debris.
2. For at least four hours, Charles worked with my hair; he painstakingly parted each segment, measured and cut each layer, carefully timed the waving lotion and the neutralizer; finally, after applying a dark rinse, setting and resetting each wave, shuttling me under and out from under a dryer, combing and recombing each curl, he handed me a mirror.

■ **Exercise 13** Revise the following sentences as necessary for greater emphasis.

1. At any rate, the gun fired when the fleeing youth tripped over the patrolman's foot.
2. The storm broke in all its fury at the close of a hot day.
3. A fast pass was caught by Milburn, and a thirty-yard gain was made by him before the whistle was blown by the referee.
4. Mr. Brown knew that he had made bad decisions, that he should apologize, that he had been guilty.
5. I asked her to marry me, two years ago, in a shop on Tremont Street, late in the fall.
6. The best article explains a game called "Body Talk," although interesting facets of both mind and internal organ control are featured in that issue of *Psychology Today*.
7. The zero hour had come. Already the armies were marching.

8. The art of the people was crude, but a great deal of originality was shown by some of them.
9. Members of the John Birch Society emphasize the differences between a republic and a democracy; those who support the Communist party are concerned with the links between democracy and socialism—according to Dr. Sun.
10. Edna Ferber's *The Giant* isolated and magnified the ugly features of Texas, unlike the usual tales highlighting only its beauties.

■ **Exercise 14** By citing specific principles given in this section, indicate the methods of gaining emphasis used below.

1. In advanced countries, a chief cause—perhaps the chief cause—of alienation of the young has been the school systems themselves. It is ironical. —PAUL GOODMAN
2. When the old pro is turned out to pasture, there are no picket lines. —DAN WAKEFIELD
3. Work is contemplation. Rite is contemplation. Yoga is contemplation. Learning is contemplation. All are prayer.
   —KENNETH REXROTH
4. Emotionally, Hemingway was adolescent all his life; intellectually, he was a Philistine on principle.
   —DWIGHT MacDONALD
5. The age of hallucination, of which Adolf Hitler was one of the earlier victims, has scarcely dawned.
   —C. NORTHCOTE PARKINSON
6. On rush the ships, pitching, rolling, throwing spray—white waves at their bows and white wakes reflecting the moon.
   —SAMUEL ELIOT MORISON
7. Why lands sink under the sea and rise again nobody knows. —WOLFGANG LANGEWIESCHE
8. A rhythm, a musical motif, a brush stroke, a color can be malicious. But the melody in a work, sonata, picture or poem cannot be malicious. —JACQUES MARITAIN
9. A social order based upon orgy would destroy its own effortless prosperity by failing to reproduce its technological genius. —MICHAEL HARRINGTON
10. And so, my fellow Americans, ask not what your country can do for you; ask what you can do for your country.
    —JOHN F. KENNEDY

Variety

30

Vary the structure and the length of your sentences to make your whole composition pleasing and effective.

The two descriptions below have the same content, but the structures of the first are monotonous. Notice how the variety in the second description makes it more effective than the first.

MONOTONOUS

The land is small, subdued. Its colors are low in key. The salt marshes and the low houses at their margins have a comforting dimension, and the woods beyond, the hidden ponds, and the suddenly revealed harbors do too. You should, however, look outward. The sea is always there. The sea is a great presence, for it is fraught with sublimity. You may in some places not actually see the ocean, but you can sense its proximity and catch whiffs of its tang. You hear or seem to hear its distant roar and rut. You may perhaps have the least bit of eschatological wonder. The Cape scene then may well tease you out of thought.   [Seven simple sentences and three compound ones, each beginning with the subject]

VARIED

The land is small, subdued; its colors are low in key. The salt marshes, the low houses at their margins, the woods beyond, the hidden ponds, the suddenly revealed harbors have a comforting dimension. But look outward and there is always the sea, a great presence fraught with sublimity. Even where you cannot actually see the ocean, you sense its proximity, catch whiffs of its tang, hear or think you hear its distant roar and rut. Thus, if you have the least eschatological wonder, the Cape scene may well tease you out of thought. —EDWARD B. GARSIDE[1] [Five sentences of varying length and structure: one simple, two compound, two complex. Sentences begin with subjects, a coordinating conjunction, an adverb, and a conjunctive adverb.]

Except for the loose, stringy sentences in 30c, this section deals only with *good* sentences. Throughout Section 30 you are cautioned against monotonous repetition of any one type of sentence, not because these sentences are not good ones, but because they do not combine to form a pleasing and effective pattern. Even the best sentence can be boring if it follows a long series of sentences similar in design.

Note: If you have difficulty distinguishing various types of structures, review the fundamentals of the sentence treated in Section 1, especially 1d.

30a

As a rule avoid a series of short simple sentences. Vary the length. See also 29h.

MONOTONOUS

She picked her way toward the garden chairs beside the front porch. She poured out a customary torrent of complaint. Her eyesight was failing. She found herself swatting raisins on the kitchen table. She thought they were flies. She brought her stick down on spiders. These turned out to be scurrying tufts of lint. Her hearing was going. She suffered from head noises. She imagined she heard drums beating. [Series of short, choppy sentences]

[1]From Edward B. Garside's review of *Cape Cod and the Offshore Islands*, by Walter Teller, *New York Times Magazine*, June 14, 1970. © 1970 by The New York Times Company. Reprinted by permission.

VARIED

As she picked her way toward the garden chairs beside the front porch, she poured out a customary torrent of complaint. Her eyesight was failing. She found herself swatting raisins on the kitchen table, thinking they were flies, and bringing her stick down on spiders that turned out to be scurrying tufts of lint. Her hearing was going, and she suffered from head noises. She imagined she heard drums beating.
—PETER DE VRIES[2] [Interspersed with longer sentences, the short sentences are emphatic.]

Rather than present your ideas in a series of choppy, ineffective sentences, learn how to relate your ideas precisely in a longer sentence.

CHOPPY	Customs vary. In some neighborhoods people compare notes on their dogs. In others they compare notes on their landlords.
EFFECTIVE	Customs vary: in some neighborhoods people compare notes on their dogs; in others they compare notes on their landlords. —JANE JACOBS [Use of the colon and the semicolon to relate ideas precisely]
CHOPPY	The sticky crowd was sluggish. It flowed up and down Broadway. He was swallowed up in this crowd.
EFFECTIVE	He was swallowed up in the sticky crowd flowing sluggishly up and down Broadway. —HARVEY SWADOS [Effective use of modifiers]
CHOPPY	Negro girls worked in kitchens. They did not work for wages. They worked for the toting privilege. This was the permission to take home leftovers.
EFFECTIVE	Negro girls worked in kitchens not for wages but for the toting privilege—permission to take home leftovers. —ARNA BONTEMPS [Use of parallel prepositional phrases and an appositive]

---

[2]From *The Vale of Laughter* by Peter De Vries. Published by Little, Brown & Co., 1967. Copyright © 1953, 1962, 1964, 1967 by Peter De Vries. Reprinted by permission.

CHOPPY	Events of the night rolled through her mind like sequences of an old movie. The plot was obscure. But the characters were stalking her as from ambush.
EFFECTIVE	Events of the night rolled through her mind like sequences of an old movie, the plot obscure but the characters stalking her as from ambush. —FLETCHER KNEBEL [Effective use of an absolute construction]
CHOPPY	He was a small boy. He had to drown three newborn puppies. The blind, tiny creatures struggled for life in the bucket. This conveyed to him a vivid sense. In everything there is an "I." This "I" deserves respect.
EFFECTIVE	When he was a small boy, he had to drown three newborn puppies, and the blind, tiny creatures struggling for life in the bucket conveyed to him a vivid sense that in everything there is an "I" which deserves respect. —PETER STANSKY [The conjunctions *when, and, that,* and *which* connect and relate ideas.]

Note: Not every series of short sentences is ineffective, as the following quotation illustrates.

I perceive something. I am sensible of something. I imagine something. I will something. I feel something. I think something. The life of human beings does not consist of all this and the like alone. —MARTIN BUBER [Effective use of balance and repetition in building toward a climax]

■ **Exercise 1** Study the structure of the sentences in the following paragraph, giving special attention to the variety of sentence lengths.

[1] Some people collect stamps or coins or antique cars. [2] I collect practically useless scraps of information without really wanting to. [3] Things that most people don't bother to remember accumulate in my mind like unused wire hangers in a coat closet. [4] For instance, hardly anybody except me remembers

the names of the four models of the Edsel (Pacer, Ranger, Corsair and Citation), or the name of the only New York newspaper that supported Harry Truman in 1948 (the now-defunct New York *Star*). [5] Do you know there's enough concrete in Boulder Dam to build a six-lane highway from Seattle to Miami? [6] I do. [7] I also know the origin of the word *hitchhike* (two people traveling with one horse), and that the Japanese word for first lieutenant (*chūi*) is the same as the Swahili word for leopard. [8] Just don't ask me why.   —WILLIAM ATWOOD[3]

■ **Exercise 2**   Convert each of the following series of short simple sentences to one long sentence in which ideas are carefully related.

1. There were thirty seconds of play left. Harrison intercepted the pass and raced downfield. He dropped the ball at the five-yard line.
2. The salesman's speech had an interesting thesis. A salesman should solve the existing problems of his customers. He should also point out new problems in order to solve them.
3. Bennett's Comet appeared in 1969. It disappeared again in 1970. It will not be visible again for thousands of years.
4. Mr. Dolan did not buy a second car. He bought a Piper. It is a cub plane. It flies at almost a hundred miles an hour.
5. J. Allen Boone is the author of *Kinship with All Life*. In his book Boone describes his ability to communicate with animals. He converses mentally with a dog. He orders ants to leave his home. They obey his orders. He even tames an ordinary housefly.

30b

Avoid a long series of sentences beginning with the subject. Vary the beginning.

Most writers begin about half their sentences with the subject—far more than the number of sentences begun in any

---

[3]From "The Birth of the Bikini" by William Atwood, *Look*, May 1970. Reprinted by permission.

other one way. But overuse of the subject-first beginning results in monotonous writing. If you tend to use this sentence pattern almost exclusively, make an effort to vary the word order of your sentences.

Basic Sentence Patterns	*Variations*
SUBJECT—VERB.	VERB—SUBJECT.

The professor walked in. A man lay beside the road.	In walked the professor. Beside the road lay a man.

SUBJECT—VERB—OBJECT.	OBJECT—SUBJECT—VERB.

Henry scorned honest men. I will not do that again.	Honest men Henry scorned. That I will not do again.

SUBJECT—LINKING VERB —COMPLEMENT.	COMPLEMENT—SUBJECT —LINKING VERB.

Bruce was a bungler then.
We shall never be completely
  secure.
	A bungler Bruce was then.
	Completely secure we shall
	  never be!

In addition to shifting the word order of basic patterns, you can vary the beginnings of sentences in the following ways.

(1) Begin with an adverb or an adverb clause.

> ADVERB   *Suddenly* the professor walked in.
> ADVERB CLAUSE   *Although Bruce has good manners now,* he was a bungler then.

(2) Begin with a prepositional phrase or a participial phrase.

> PREPOSITIONAL PHRASE   *At that moment* the professor walked in.
> PARTICIPIAL PHRASE   *Waiting patiently for help,* a man lay beside the road.

319

(3) Begin with a conjunction such as *and, but, or, nor, for,* **or** *yet.*

An effective sentence can often begin with a coordinating conjunction, but only when the conjunction shows the proper relation of the sentence to the preceding sentence: see **31b(4).**

> COORDINATING CONJUNCTION   The young woman wept and wrung her hands. *But* the injured man, lying beside the road, waited patiently for help.   [*But* contrasts.]

■ **Exercise 3**   Prepare for a class discussion of the types of sentence beginnings in the following two paragraphs.

¹ No longer do we Americans want to destroy wantonly, but our new-found sources of power—to take the burden of work from our shoulders, to warm us, and cool us, and give us light, to transport us quickly, and to make the things we use and wear and eat—these power sources spew pollution in our country, so that the rivers and streams are becoming poisonous and lifeless.   ² The birds die for the lack of food; a noxious cloud hangs over our cities that burns our lungs and reddens our eyes.   ³ Our ability to conserve has not grown with our power to create, but this slow and sullen poisoning is no longer ignored or justified.   ⁴ Almost daily, the pressure of outrage among Americans grows.   ⁵ We are no longer content to destroy our beloved country.   ⁶ We are slow to learn; but we learn.   ⁷ When a super-highway was proposed in California which would trample the redwood trees in its path, an outcry arose all over the land, so strident and fierce that the plan was put aside.   ⁸ And we no longer believe that a man, by owning a piece of America, is free to outrage it.   —JOHN STEINBECK⁴

¹ Mounting the spiraled staircase, he heard the voices roll in a steady wave, then leap to crescendo, only to die away, but always remaining audible.   ² Ahead of him glowed red letters: E—X—I—T.   ³ At the top of the steps he paused in front of

---

⁴From *America and Americans* by John Steinbeck. Copyright © 1966 by John Steinbeck. All rights reserved. Reprinted by permission of The Viking Press, Inc.

a black curtain that fluttered uncertainly. [4] He parted the folds and looked into a convex depth that gleamed with clusters of shimmering lights. [5] Sprawling below him was a stretch of human faces, tilted upward, chanting, whistling, screaming, laughing. [6] Dangling before the faces, high upon a screen of silver, were jerking shadows. [7] "A movie," he said with slow laughter breaking from his lips. —RICHARD WRIGHT[5]

■ **Exercise 4** Each of the sentences below begins with the subject. Recast each sentence twice to vary the beginnings, as shown in the following example.

EXAMPLE
Ten students invaded the registrar's office and demanded the immediate elimination of the grading system.
a. *Invading the registrar's office, ten students demanded the immediate elimination of the grading system.*
b. *In the registrar's office were ten student invaders demanding the immediate elimination of the grading system.*

1. We need better communication between the races now.
2. Reporters interviewed the newly appointed ambassador and asked him some sticky questions about world affairs.
3. Hundreds of students lined up in order to register in a floating university, the *Queen Elizabeth*.
4. Vernon enjoyed the course in Afro-American literature most of all.
5. The green fireballs traveled at great speed and fascinated sky watchers throughout the Southwest.

30c

Avoid the loose, stringy compound sentence. See also 24b.

To revise an ineffective compound sentence, try one of the following methods.

[5] From *Eight Men* by Richard Wright. Published by Paul R. Reynolds, Inc., 1944. Reprinted by permission.

(1) Convert it into a complex sentence.

COMPOUND   The Mississippi River is one of the longest rivers in the world, and in the springtime it often overflows its banks, and the lives of many people are endangered.

COMPLEX   The Mississippi River, which is one of the longest rivers in the world, often overflows its banks in the springtime, endangering the lives of many people.

(2) Use a compound predicate in a simple sentence.

COMPOUND   He put on his coat, and next he picked up his hat and cane, and then he hurried from the house.

SIMPLE   He put on his coat, picked up his hat and cane, and hurried from the house.

(3) Use a modifier or an appositive in a simple sentence.

COMPOUND   The town was north of the Red River, and a tornado struck it, and it was practically demolished.

SIMPLE   The town, located north of the Red River, was struck by a tornado and practically demolished.

COMPOUND   He was the mayor of the town, and he was a genial fellow, and he invited the four boys into his study.

SIMPLE   The mayor of the town, a genial fellow, invited the four boys into his study.

(4) Use phrases in a simple sentence.

COMPOUND   The streets were icy, and we could not drive the car.

SIMPLE   Because of the icy streets, we could not drive the car.

COMPOUND   You will reach your destination tomorrow, and then you can take a long rest.

SIMPLE   After reaching your destination tomorrow, you can take a long rest.

■ **Exercise 5** Using the methods illustrated in **30c**, revise the loose, stringy compound sentences below.

1. The small car hugs the road, and it is easy to drive in traffic, but it is not comfortable.
2. The Johnsons grew tired of city smog and noise pollution, so they moved to the country, but there they had no fire department or police protection.
3. Men at first traded their products, and then they began to use money and bank checks, and now they use the all-inclusive plastic credit card.
4. Harvey kept criticizing middle-class values, and he mentioned such things as marriage and two-car garages, but he did not define upper-class or lower-class values.

30d

Vary the conventional subject-verb sequence by occasionally separating subject and verb with words or phrases.

SUBJECT—VERB   The *auditorium is* across from the park, and *it is* a gift of the alumni.   [Compound sentence]

VARIED   The *auditorium,* across from the park, *is* a gift of the alumni.   [Simple sentence]

SUBJECT—VERB   The *crowd sympathized* with the visitors and *applauded* every good play.

VARIED   The *crowd,* sympathizing with the visitors, *applauded* every good play.

Caution: Avoid awkward or needless separation of subject and verb.

30e

Vary a series of declarative statements by using an occasional exclamation, command, or question.

VARIED

What if everyone did actually write his story, and what if everyone's story were Xeroxed? Imagine millions and millions of welterweight Norman Mailers, each making himself the center of existence and each describing his feelings as the only trustworthy view of the world's ways. Imagine it! What would all that writing, the whole of it, amount to? It might be life. It might be what no artist can conceive, bigger than the biggest visions of poets and madmen. That's it. That's what The Universal Xerox Life Compiler Machine could do for us, something "now" and "total," so to speak.

—WILLIAM JOVANOVICH[6]

■ **Exercise 6** The following sentences all have structures that make for variety in composition. By referring to specific parts of Section **30**, prepare for a class discussion of these structures. Then use five items of the seven as models for sentences of your own.

1. Of all our masculine machines the most intriguing is the hi-fi system. —HUBERT LAMB

2. But across the tracks of the Chicago and Illinois Western, in a little house just like his, waits the black man.
   —GENE MARINE

3. Interestingly enough, Ortega's definition of the "mass man" is identical with Plato's definition of the tyrant.
   —IRVING KRISTOL

4. Reading *The Penguin Book of Saints,* I am sorry to learn that St. Catherine of the catherine wheel never existed.
   —W. H. AUDEN

---

[6]Reprinted from *The Universal Xerox Life Compiler Machine* by William Jovanovich. © 1970 by William Jovanovich. Reprinted by permission of the author. (From *American Scholar,* Spring 1971.)

5. However virtuous the present radical movement may be, it has turned off somewhere between 60 and 90 percent of the American people. —ANDREW N. GREELEY

6. Now and then there is a house of brick. But what brick! When it is new it is the color of a fried egg.
—H. L. MENCKEN

7. The university, instead of reflecting misguided purposes and abandoned ideals, might fashion the mind of the new age.
—ROBERT M. HUTCHINS

■ **Exercise 7** Prepare for a class discussion of sentence variety in the following paragraphs.

[1] *Hamlet* has obsessed the Western mind for 369 years. [2] Why? [3] It is not because most people love great works of art. [4] On the contrary, most people find great works of art oppressive, since such works invariably center on the nature of human destiny, and that destiny is tragic. [5] Quite simply, *Hamlet* is a world, and like the world, it cannot be ignored. [6] Every man has lived some part of the play, and to be a man is to be inextricably involved in the play. [7] *Hamlet* probes and grips the profound themes of existence—death, love, time, fidelity, friendship, family, the relationships of a man and a woman, a son and father, a mother and son, murder and madness. [8] Above all, it probes the value of existence, man's most anguishing question put in the form that every man knows from the time he first hears and ponders it—to be or not to be.

[9] Far from being a surefire part, the role of Hamlet dwarfs most actors, for the magnitude of the role requires a corresponding size and scope in the actor who plays it. [10] Technique is not enough. [11] Verbal violin play, a graceful carriage, a handsome profile—these suffice for the ordinary Hamlet. [12] The great Hamlet is coached by life itself, schooled by life to think, listen, grow, love, hate, suffer and endure. [13] So rigorous is this demand that in these more than three and a half centuries there have been no more than a dozen great Hamlets.

—Editors of TIME[7]

---

[7] From "Elsinore of the Mind," *Time*, January 12, 1970. Reprinted by permission from *Time*, The Weekly Newsmagazine; Copyright Time Inc. 1970.

LARGER ELEMENTS

The Paragraph

31

Make paragraphs unified and coherent; develop them adequately.

A paragraph is a distinct unit of thought—usually a group of related sentences, though occasionally no more than one sentence—in a written or printed composition. The form of a paragraph is distinctive: the first line is indented. The content of a unified paragraph deals with one central idea. Each sentence fits into a logical pattern of organization and is therefore carefully related to other sentences in the paragraph.

Below is an example of a unified, coherent, adequately developed paragraph. As you read it, observe the clear statement of the controlling idea in the first sentence; the development of that idea in the sentences that follow; the orderly arrangement of the supporting facts; and the close relationship of the sentences to the central idea and to one another. (For easy reference, all forty-nine of the specimen paragraphs in this section are numbered.)

1   In voicing their demands, by the way, the blacks have developed at least three distinct accents or approaches, which have been too little noted. One might be called businesslike militancy; it is brisk, precise, eloquent, well informed, tough, often demagogic but not unrealistic. The best of the black leaders have

it, and at times one cannot help envying the joy and the certainty that comes with a single-minded struggle, with a clarity of goal. The only other people among whom this quality is readily found are the Israelis. The second accent might be called ritualized rage. It is irritating, infuriating, a deliberate shock tactic that also provides relief and release for those who use it. It can be turned on at will. This does not mean that it is phony, that much of the anger isn't real; but it is controlled, a game, and not without its dangers. The third accent is true despair—not tough, not raging, but steadily bitter, the result not of hopelessness but of insufficient hope. It is the third accent, of course, that is the most deeply disturbing.   —Editors of TIME[1]

The central idea of the above paragraph is stated in the first sentence; the key to the organization of the paragraph is the phrase *three distinct accents*. These accents are classified as *businesslike militancy, ritualized rage,* and *true despair.* The details of the paragraph are well organized. Transitional devices such as the words *one, the second,* and *the third* link the sentences within the paragraph and thus contribute to its coherence.

Since each paragraph in a composition is a distinct unit of thought, the beginning of a new paragraph is an important signal to the reader. It serves as a signpost marking an approaching curve in the avenue of thought; or it warns him that he must take a new avenue of thought. It announces a new time, place, person, or thing in the course of a narrative, a different point of view in description, a new step in exposition, or an advance in argument.

Length   Expository or argumentative paragraphs in current books and magazines are usually from 50 to 250 words in length, with the average perhaps 100 words. Paragraphs tend to run longer in books and shorter in the narrower

---

[1]From "Thoughts on a Troubled El Dorado," *Time,* June 22, 1970. Reprinted by permission from *Time,* The Weekly Newsmagazine; Copyright Time Inc. 1970.

columns of newspapers. Shorter paragraphs are more frequent in narrative writing, especially dialogue, in which each speech is paragraphed separately.

Indention   The first lines of paragraphs are indented uniformly, about one inch in longhand and five spaces in typewritten copy.

31a

Give unity to the paragraph by making each sentence contribute to the central thought.

A paragraph is said to have unity when each sentence contributes to the central thought. Any sentence that violates the unity of the paragraph should be deleted.

In expository writing, the main idea of a paragraph is most often stated in the first sentence. However, the statement of the controlling idea (often called the *topic sentence*) may appear anywhere in the paragraph—for example, after an introductory transitional sentence or at the end of the paragraph.

In each of the unified paragraphs below, the controlling idea is indicated by italics. As you read each paragraph, notice how every sentence develops the italicized topic.

2   Despite the fact that a sizable portion of the under-thirty crowd is trying to make its preoccupation with NOW the special mark of the late sixties and early seventies, *most of us* of whatever age *appear to be* more *concerned with the future.* The futures business is big business, according to a feature article in the August *Chemical and Engineering News;* there is even a World Futures Society with three thousand members and its own journal—the *Futurist.* Some of the most respectable people are staring into crystal balls, reading palms, consulting the numbers, or dropping hot wax into bowls of water; astrology is experiencing

a renaissance (there is even an astrological company that uses a computer to cast its horoscopes); the pentecostal movement, whether Catholic or Protestant, has revived interest in the charismatic gift of prophecy; biologists, picking up where science fiction left off, foresee the genetic engineering of slave animals and cybernetic organisms, as well as the control of mutation by genetic surgery or artificial wombs. Meanwhile, think-tanks such as the Rand Corporation, General Electric's TEMPO, the National Industrial Conference Board, the Institute for the Future, the Stanford Research Institute, and Herman Kahn's Hudson Institute continue to sophisticate their extrapolations and refine their scenarios in an effort to make the twenty-first century endurable, or at least possible—despite the fact that a man named Criswell has announced that the world as we know it will come to an end on August 18, 1999.   —JOHN P. SISK[2]

To achieve unity, you may find it helpful to make a plan for a paragraph, carefully listing points that support your central topic. Paragraph 2, for example, reveals the following plan:

CENTRAL TOPIC Concern with the future
DEVELOPMENT   1. the futures business
               2. a World Futures Society
               3. individual diviners
               4. popularity of astrology
               5. pentecostal interest in prophecy
               6. anticipation of genetic engineering
               7. forward-looking corporations, institutes
               8. Criswell's prediction

When the controlling idea is stated at or near the beginning of a paragraph, the concluding sentence may not only restate this idea—thus repeating key words or the main point—but also emphasize its importance.

---

[2]From "The Future of Prediction" by John P. Sisk, *Commentary*, March 1970.

3   *Everyone who makes money in the mechanized city uses the money that he makes there to escape,* as far and as frequently as he can, *from the inferno that is the source of his wealth.* As soon as he can afford it, he moves his home out from within the city-limits into suburbia; he takes his holidays in what is still left of genuinely rural country; and, when he retires, he withdraws to die on the French Riviera or in Southern California or at Montreux or Vevey. This is not surprising, considering that the mechanized city is as repulsively ugly as the mass-produced manufactures that it pours out. *It is,* however, *a spiritual misfortune for a worker to be alienated emotionally from the place in which he has done his work, has earned his living, and has made his mark,* for good or for evil, *on the history of the human race.*

—ARNOLD TOYNBEE[3]

Occasionally the central idea of a paragraph is stated in the last sentence only, especially when the writer progresses from particulars to a generalization:

4   When we watch a person walk away from us, his image shrinks in size. But since we know for a fact that he is not shrinking, we make an unconscious correcting and "see" him as retaining his full stature. Past experience tells us what his true stature is with respect to our own. Any sane and dependable expectation of the future requires that he have the same true stature when we next encounter him. *Our perception is thus a prediction; it embraces the past and the future as well as the present.*   —WARREN J. WITTREICH[4]

When not expressly stated, the controlling idea of a unified paragraph is distinctly implied:

5   San Francisco's Haight-Ashbury district degenerated into just another "Skid Row" after its brief heyday as the mecca of the "hippies." Campus radicals invaded buildings and hurled rocks at police—and now are beginning to find themselves ostracized on some campuses. In New York City and elsewhere, a few idealists have become revolutionaries who make and distribute bombs, sometimes blowing themselves up accidentally in the process. Radical girls are learning karate and other violent tactics to "liberate" themselves in a "male-dominated" society.

—U.S. NEWS & WORLD REPORT[5]

[Controlling idea: *A number of the activities of young rebels have led to degeneracy, isolation, and violence.*]

Caution: Do not make rambling statements that are only vaguely related to your topic. As you write a paragraph, hold to the main idea. For instance, if the controlling idea of a paragraph is "My roommate Bill Jones cannot keep a secret," irrelevant sentences about Bill Jones or about secrecy will disrupt the unity. Every statement should pertain to Bill Jones's inability to keep a secret.

If the paragraphs in your compositions tend to lack unity, use the following check list to help you in revision.

Check List for Revising a Faulty Paragraph

1. *Is the central idea of the paragraph clearly stated or implied?* If not, add a clear statement of the controlling idea.
2. *Does the subject of the paragraph shift one or more times?* If so, either develop each main point in a separate paragraph or restate the central idea so that it will closely relate all the points discussed.
3. *Are all sentences in the paragraph relevant to the central idea?* If not, cross out each irrelevant sentence. If any sentence is related to the central idea but not clearly so, revise it to make the relationship clear.

---

[5] From "Growing Concern over 'Crisis in Morality,'" *U.S. News & World Report*, June 29, 1970. Copyright © 1970 U.S. News & World Report.

Revision of a Faulty Paragraph

The very courtesy of a gentleman can make him a chronic late-comer. My friend Cliff, who is an excessively courteous [Controlling idea supplied]

gentleman, was late to his family dinner on Christmas

Eve. He had been delayed on a shopping trip. At the

entrance of a large bargain basement, he had stood

for a quarter of an hour holding doors open for last-

minute shoppers. Once inside, he lost more time

standing aside so that clerks could serve others

first. ~~Cliff bought a billfold for his brother.~~ [Irrelevant—deleted]

When Cliff at last left the store, he took time out

to carry some heavy packages for a woman whose car

was parked two blocks away. *When he finally arrived* ~~At~~ home, his family was [Relationship to central idea clarified]

eating dessert. The very next week, Cliff was late

for an important business conference. He had stood

outside a busy elevator and missed several cars by

letting everyone else on first; then he lost even

more time insisting that he be the last person off.

Once again, he was the last person to reach his

new ¶ destination.) Equally unpleasant side effects can [Subject shifts—new paragraph needed for development]

result from a gentleman's deference to ladies,

which often lifts the eyebrows of gossips.

■ **Exercise 1** Point out, or supply, the controlling idea for paragraphs 6, 7, and 8 on pages 336 and 337 and for any other paragraphs assigned by your instructor.

■ **Exercise 2** Revise the following faulty paragraph to improve unity. Be prepared to give the reasons for your revisions.

At my place last night, a tornadic wind played several mischievous pranks. Whistling loudly through the weather stripping, it sprayed dirty water all over the freshly mopped kitchen floor. Next, as though chiding me for my earlier complaints about stuffy air, it created enormous drafts by breaking half a dozen window panes. The moment an announcer on television started reading a special bulletin from the weather bureau, the wind knocked down my television antenna; just as I reached for the radio, it blacked out the whole house. Later I learned that a pilot flying above the turbulent weather had reported that he had never seen such a violent thunderstorm. The wind leveled a two-car garage belonging to Mr. Fulton, my neighbor. Traveling at ninety miles an hour, it also turned on an outdoor water faucet, flooding my flower bed; overturned the dog house, imprisoning my fox terrier; and dumped a stolen boat into the back yard, after ripping the motor off and breaking the oars. After that savage storm, my family and I are grateful to be alive and uninjured.

31b

Give coherence to the paragraph by so interlinking the sentences that the thought flows smoothly from one sentence to the next. Provide transitions between paragraphs as well as between sentences.

A paragraph is said to have coherence when the relationship between sentences is clear and when the transition from one sentence to the next is easy and natural. The reader should be able to follow the thought without difficulty. In order to secure coherence, the writer should rely on arrangement of the sentences in a clear, logical order; the use of pronouns referring to antecedents in the preceding sentences; repeated words or ideas; transitional expressions; and parallel structure. For the coherence of the whole composition, it is important for the writer to provide adequate transition between paragraphs.

ARRANGEMENT OF SENTENCES

(1) Arrange the sentences of the paragraph in a clear, logical order.

There are several common, logical ways to order the sentences in a paragraph. The choice of an appropriate order depends upon the writer's purpose and the nature of his material. Perhaps the simplest and most common order is *time order.* Narrative paragraphs, especially, lend themselves naturally to such arrangement.

6   Ed Wynn and Fields, as rival comedians, were constantly vying for laughs. During one performance, Wynn concealed himself beneath the pool table and tried to steal the scene by smirking and winking at the audience. Fields became uneasily aware that his laughs were coming at the wrong places, and his eye caught a suspicious movement under the table. He waited until Wynn, on all fours, carelessly stuck his head out too far. With a juggler's perfect timing, Fields swung the butt of his cue in a half-circle and lowered it into his rival's skull. Wynn sagged to the floor while Fields continued his game serenely amid boisterous applause. Every time that Wynn struggled back to consciousness and emitted a low moan, the audience laughed louder.
—COREY FORD[6]

Other types of paragraphs often have a time element that makes a chronological arrangement both possible and natural. For example, in explaining a process—how something

---

[6]From *The Time of Laughter* by Corey Ford. Published by Little, Brown and Company; reprinted in *Harper's Magazine,* October 1967. Copyright © 1967 by Corey Ford. Reprinted by permission.

is done or made—the writer can follow the process through, step by step, as in the following paragraph.

7 In *engraving*, the artist grooves out clean strips of metal from the plate with a steel instrument called a burin. The artist is actually drawing with the burin. After the picture is engraved, printing ink is rubbed over the entire plate. The surface is then wiped clean, leaving ink in the incised portions of the copper. A dampened sheet of paper is placed over the plate and together they are run through a roller press. The paper is dampened to retain the ink better and to avoid cracking or tearing, since a great deal of pressure must be exerted to force the paper into the incised areas.   —MARVIN ELKOFF[7]

Sentences that have no evident time order can sometimes be arranged in *space order,* in which the paragraph moves from east to west, from west to east, from the near to the distant, from the distant to the near, from the left to the right, and so on. This order is used especially in descriptive paragraphs. Note the movement from the warm, low coastal gardens to the cold, high areas in the following paragraph.

8 Late winter color heralds the approach of spring in all areas of the Southwest. In mild coastal gardens, this happens gradually as spring sneaks up without much fanfare. Farther inland, bulbs and flowering trees attract more attention. And in colder areas of the mountains and high desert, the appearance of the first buds on a deciduous shrub or tree is downright exciting after winter's snow.   —SUNSET[8]

Another good arrangement of sentences is in the *order of climax.* Here the least important idea is stated first, and the others are given in order of increasing importance, as in the following paragraph. See also **29c**.

---

[7] From "Collecting Original Art Prints" by Marvin Elkoff, *Holiday*, December 1965. Reprinted with permission from *Holiday*. © 1966 Curtis Publishing Co.

[8] From "The Earliest Color," *Sunset*, January 1959. Reprinted by permission.

9   An ant cannot purposefully try anything new, and any ant that accidentally did so would be murdered by his colleagues. It is the ant colony as a whole that slowly learns over the ages. In contrast, even an earthworm has enough flexibility of brain to enable it to be taught to turn toward the left or right for food. Though rats are not able to reason to any considerable degree, they can solve such problems as separating round objects from triangular ones when these have to do with health or appetite. Cats, with better brains, can be taught somewhat more, and young dogs a great deal. The higher apes can learn by insight as well as by trial and error.   —GEORGE R. HARRISON[9]

Sometimes the movement within the paragraph may be from the general to the particular, from the particular to the general, or from the familiar to the unfamiliar. A paragraph may begin with a general statement which is then supported by particular details, or, reversing the process, it may begin with a striking detail or series of details and conclude with a summarizing statement. Notice the movement from the general to the particular in paragraph 10 and from the particular to the general in paragraph 11.

10   In the ten years we have been married, I have yet to see Maurine act deviously. Although caginess is presumed to be a prerequisite for politics, she has marched to the top of the ballot by blurting out exactly what is in her mind. When she was asked to back a bill allocating a portion of dog-racing revenues for 4-H clubs, Maurine scolded her constituents for tying a worthy cause to pari-mutuel gambling. The special interests which she has offended would terrify most politicians—utility companies, dairy farmers, the Bar-Tenders' Union, the fairs in all thirty-six Oregon counties, slot-machine operators, the Farm Bureau Federation, even the American Legion.

—RICHARD L. NEUBERGER[10]

[9]From "How the Brain Works" by George R. Harrison, *Atlantic Monthly*, September 1956. Copyright © 1956 by The Atlantic Monthly Company, Boston, Mass. Reprinted with permission.

[10]From "My Wife Put Me in the Senate" by Richard L. Neuberger, *Harper's Magazine*, June 1955. Reprinted by permission.

[The first sentence states the topic: *Maurine never acts deviously.*
The second sentence begins the development with a general
statement about her positive action. The third sentence shows
specifically how she faced up to the 4-H clubs, and the fourth
lists other special interests defied in the same way.]

11   Many years ago a graduate student inconven-
ienced himself greatly to come a long distance to see me to ask
if I could help him secure some information about the term "poll
tax." He was preparing a doctor's thesis, he told me, and needed
to know how long this term had been in the language, what its
basic meaning was, and what other meanings it may have had
in the course of its use in English. He was most surprised when
I opened the *OED* to the appropriate place and showed him that
all he needed to know about this term had been available within
a few feet of his desk in the school where he was studying. It
is not at all likely that any but the exceptional student will ever
need all the information about words that the larger dictionaries
afford, but it is well worth the while of every student to become
acquainted with the fact that such information is available for
those who at any time need to make use of it.

—MITFORD M. MATHEWS[11]

[This paragraph explains how one particular graduate student
learned a lesson about dictionary usage and then suggests the
value of the lesson to all students.]

Paragraphs 6, 7, 8, 9, 10, and 11 above illustrate five of
many possible types of clear sentence arrangement within
the paragraph. Any order of sentences, or any combination
of orders, is satisfactory as long as it makes the sequence
of thought clear. Proper arrangement of the sentences is the
first, the basic, step to ensure good transitions from sentence
to sentence. All other steps presuppose that the sentences
have been arranged in the clearest possible order.

■ **Exercise 3**   Determine the type of sentence arrangement used
in paragraph 1, pages 328–29, and in paragraph 14, page 341.

[11]From "The Freshman and His Dictionary" by Mitford M. Mathews,
College Composition and Communication, December 1955. Reprinted by
permission.

TRANSITIONS BETWEEN SENTENCES

(2) Link sentences by means of pronouns referring to antecedents in the preceding sentences. See also Section **28**.

In the following paragraphs italics are used to indicate the pronouns serving as links between sentences. Such pronouns near the beginning of the sentence are often especially useful for paragraph coherence.

12   I was becoming conditioned by what I saw each day on Pahlavi Avenue as I walked to the university. I would pass a squatting merchant on a blanket, his wares before him, chanting to attract business. *He* had for sale thirty empty Carter's ink bottles; it was puzzling to imagine where *he* had gotten them. Farther along a man specializing in art objects was selling a page from an old copy of the *Saturday Evening Post. It* was a four-color advertisement for Hotpoint showing a father, mother, and two crisply dressed daughters smugly regarding the legend in needlework on the wall behind them: "Bless Our Happy Hotpoint Home." Now *it* was handsomely encased behind glass with a gold baroque frame.   —CURTIS HARNACK[12]

13   Amoebae are gray bits of jelly speckled with multitudes of grains and crystals. *They* have no particular form, although when *they*'re sleeping off a jag or just floating around passing the time of day, *they* assume a sort of star shape, like a splash of ink. Mostly *they* pour *themselves* along like a lava flow. Every once in a while *they* sit down on something and when *they* get up that something is inside *them*.   —ALFRED BESTER[13]

■ **Exercise 4**   Underline the pronouns used to link sentences in paragraphs 1 and 3 on pages 328–29 and 332, or in any other paragraphs assigned by your instructor. Check the antecedent (in a preceding sentence) to which each pronoun refers.

---

[12] From "The Wasteful Savers" by Curtis Harnack, *The Reporter,* September 29, 1960.

[13] From "The Compleat Hobbyist" by Alfred Bester, *Holiday,* December 1965. Reprinted with permission from *Holiday.* © 1965 Curtis Publishing Co.

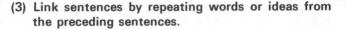

(3) Link sentences by repeating words or ideas from the preceding sentences.

Notice in the next paragraph the repetition of the key words—*liberal, radical, leftist, left, conservative, rightist, right*—and the repetition of key ideas—*labels, distinction, classifications, ideological positions, system of classifying philosophies.* Notice also that the repetition of *world* and the use of *French* and *France's* link sentences within the paragraph.

14 The *liberal-conservative labels* parallel the *left-right distinction* that grew out of the *French* Revolution. In *France's* National Assembly of 1789, the *conservatives* sat to the *right* of the speaker, and became known as *rightists,* and the *radicals* sat at the *left* and became known as *leftists.* From then on, it was commonly assumed that you could place *ideological positions* somewhere on a list ranging from the *left* to the *right.* This *system of classifying* political *philosophies* is attractive because it seems so tidy. But it is woefully inadequate, since it is one-dimensional, whereas the *world* is three-dimensional. The *world* today is much too complex to hold still for the *left* versus *right* and the *liberal* versus *conservative classifications.*

—BOB SENSER[14]

■ **Exercise 5** Link the sentences in each of the following pairs by revising the second sentence to repeat a word or an idea in the first sentence. Follow the pattern of the examples below and at the top of the next page.

EXAMPLES
Radio and television perpetuated myths. The majority was not silent in the 1960's.
Radio and television perpetuated myths. One myth spread by the media was that the majority was silent in the 1960's.

---

[14] From "Don't Get Obsessed with Labels" by Bob Senser, *Our Sunday Visitor,* May 7, 1961. Reprinted by permission.

A family reunion makes my parents happy. I have a sudden yearning to travel overseas.

A family reunion makes my parents happy. The mere thought of dozens of relatives in our house makes me suddenly yearn to travel overseas.

1. William likes to read the editorials in the *Greenview Herald*. His roommate prefers original advertisements.
2. Living in a high-rise apartment house can be boring. There is no lawn to keep.
3. Marian attends only pro football games. She can boo with a clear conscience.
4. Enrollment in colleges suddenly began to drop. The values of the young shifted.

(4) Link sentences by using such transitional expressions as the following.

Transitional Expressions

1. *Addition:* moreover, further, furthermore, besides, and, and then, likewise, also, nor, too, again, in addition, equally important, next, first, second, third, in the first place, in the second place, finally, last
2. *Comparison:* similarly, likewise, in like manner
3. *Contrast:* but, yet, and yet, however, still, nevertheless, on the other hand, on the contrary, after all, notwithstanding, for all that, in contrast to this, at the same time, although this may be true, otherwise
4. *Place:* here, beyond, nearby, opposite to, adjacent to, on the opposite side
5. *Purpose:* to this end, for this purpose, with this object
6. *Result:* hence, therefore, accordingly, consequently, thus, thereupon, as a result, then
7. *Summary, repetition, exemplification, intensification:* to sum up, in brief, on the whole, in sum, in short, as I have said, in other words, that is, to be sure, as has been noted, for example, for instance, in fact, indeed, to tell the truth, in any event

8. *Time:* meanwhile, at length, immediately, soon, after a few days, in the meantime, afterward, later

Note the transitional expressions in the paragraph below.

15 Since the major cost of advanced education, if the student is away from home, is board and lodging, one can argue that as far as possible the expansion of public education beyond high school should be arranged locally. *Otherwise* in order to offer equal opportunities we should have to envisage using public funds to provide years of free board and room for a considerable fraction of our high school graduates. *But* there are various types of professional and vocational education which can be given at only a few centers in even a very populous state. It is literally impossible, *for example,* to give adequate instruction in clinical medicine except in cities of sufficient size to support large hospitals. *Similarly,* advanced work in the arts, sciences, and letters can be done only where adequate libraries and laboratories are at hand. It is clearly in the national interest to find all the latent talent available for the lengthy training that research careers demand. *Yet* to establish research centers at every point in the United States where general education beyond the high school is desired would be not merely uneconomical, but impossible.

—JAMES BRYANT CONANT[15]

■ **Exercise 6** Insert an appropriate transitional expression in the second sentence of each item below.

1. The students were elected to the senate by majority vote. The speeches of the elected senators did not reflect the thinking of the majority of the students.
2. Some comic books provide a painless education for the young. Many adults could profit from reading educational comic books.
3. Over a thousand policemen were injured or killed. Hundreds of policemen went to Washington to protest.
4. It was a year of natural disasters. Earthquakes shook Peru.

---

[15] From *Education in a Divided World* by James Bryant Conant. Published by Harvard University Press. Reprinted by permission.

(5) Link sentences by means of parallel structure—that is, by repetition of the sentence pattern.

A paragraph—especially one presenting a comparison or contrast—may be made coherent by the use of parallel structure in all sentences that develop the central idea:

16   There are two Americas. One is the America of Lincoln and Adlai Stevenson; the other is the America of Teddy Roosevelt and the modern superpatriots. One is generous and humane, the other narrowly egotistical; one is self-critical, the other self-righteous; one is sensible, the other romantic; one is good-humored, the other solemn; one is inquiring, the other pontificating; one is moderate, the other filled with passionate intensity; one is judicious and the other arrogant in the use of great power.   —J. WILLIAM FULBRIGHT[16]

Or parallelism may be used for only some of the sentences that develop the central idea, as in the second, third, and fourth sentences of the following paragraph:

17   Insofar as men are ever the "product" of education, the Founding Fathers and those who supported them were the product of an education that was traditionalist, classical, and—certainly in our eyes—antiquarian. When they thought about wars—and fought them—it was the wars of the Greeks and the Persians or of the Romans and the Carthagenians. When they thought about constitutions—and wrote them—it was in terms of the constitutional principles of Greece and Rome and seventeenth-century England. When they pondered the problems of federalism—and created a federal system—it was to the confederations of ancient Greece, of the Italian city states, and of the Swiss and the Dutch that they turned, if not for relevant provisions then for inspiration. In some areas there were no classical antecedents: popular education, for example, or the new colonial system, or penal reform. Even here their approach was

---

[16]From *The Arrogance of Power* by J. William Fulbright. Published by Random House, Inc., and Jonathan Cape Ltd., 1966. Reprinted by permission.

philosophical rather than technical; that is no doubt why we still turn to what they wrote for guidance today.

—HENRY STEELE COMMAGER[17]

■ **Exercise 7** Prepare to develop the following topics orally in class; use parallel structure to link ideas. In parentheses after each topic is a suggested point of departure.

1. There are two types of students, the conformists and the nonconformists. (*One* _____; *the other* _____.)
2. Men fear the unknown. (*When* _____, *then* _____.)

We have observed that easy transition from sentence to sentence within the paragraph depends on clear arrangement of the sentences and then on the use of linking devices such as pronouns, repeated words or ideas, transitional expressions, and parallel structure. Usually several of these aids to coherence are found in a single paragraph. In the following paragraph the linking devices are underlined and are explained in the margins.

18   It would seem that the

great virtue of <u>writing</u> is its power

Repetition of word

to arrest the swift process of thought

for steady contemplation and analysis.

Parallel structure

<u>Writing</u> is the translation of the audible

into the visual. In large measure <u>it</u> is

Pronoun (referring to *writing*)

Transitional word

the spatialization of thought. Yet writing

Repetition of word

---

[17] By Henry Steele Commager, *Phi Delta Kappan,* January 1970. Reprinted by permission.

Repetition of idea (*process of thought*)

on papyrus and parchment fostered a very different set of <u>mental habits</u> from those we associate with print and books.

<u>In the first place</u>, silent reading was un-known until the macadamized, stream-lined surfaces of the printed page arrived to permit <u>the swift traverse of the eye alone</u>. <u>In the second place</u>, difficulty of access of manuscripts impelled students to memorize so far as possible everything they read. <u>This</u> led to encyclopedism, but also to having on tap in oral discourse one's entire erudition.

Transitional expression

Parallel structure

Repetition of idea (*silent reading*)

Transitional expression

Pronoun (referring to *memorize . . . everything they read*)

—MARSHALL McLUHAN[18]

■ **Exercise 8** As is done in the margins of paragraph 18, label specifically the linking devices used in the following paragraph.

19   As probably the best-known scientist in the field of ESP, Dr. Rhine has noted a decline in the interest in survival after death since the scholarly days of William James, and he blames it on several factors. He attributes this in part to the loss

[18] From "Sight, Sound and Fury" by Marshall McLuhan, *Commonweal*, April 9, 1954. Reprinted by permission.

of such persuasive influences as that of Sir Arthur Conan Doyle, whose efforts to communicate with the living after death were monumental, and considered by some to be rather startlingly convincing. But for the most part, he considers the progress made in ESP research itself to have diverted the interest in survival to that of telepathy and clairvoyance and the other aspects of nonphysical communication. Telepathy and clairvoyance were easier and simpler to accept than communication from the dead, and therefore would be preferable to the inquiring mind. Later, when both of these phenomena became widely accepted, principally because of Dr. Rhine's cold-turkey laboratory work at Duke University, the more reflective researchers had to admit that the survival-after-death theory became ambiguous. The honest medium's powers *had* to be acknowledged by those who were open-minded enough to study the evidence, but the powers could just as well be those of telepathy as those of communicating with those who had died. The reliable mediums could offer no clear-cut solution, because they themselves had no conscious idea of where their most remarkable observations were coming from. In other words, they were as amazed about what their trances were turning up as the subjects who heard from them information that was so factually correct that it could not be disputed.

—JOHN G. FULLER[19]

■ **Exercise 9**   Revise the sentences in the following paragraph so that the thought flows smoothly from one sentence to the next. Use a variety of linking devices as necessary.

Perhaps Quarterback Norris should retire from pro football. Four passes out of fifteen were completed, and three were intercepted. The defensive line charged through and dropped the quarterback for a loss twice. A weak knee might account for a pickup of only eighteen yards rushing, although the crucial fumbles are difficult to excuse. The team won by two points, a safety. Norris was not on the field to take credit for the victory.

---

[19]From *The Great Soul Trial* by John G. Fuller. Published by Macmillan and Co. Reprinted by permission of International Famous Agency. Copyright © 1969 by John G. Fuller.

TRANSITIONS BETWEEN PARAGRAPHS

(6) Provide clear transitions between paragraphs.

Transitions from one paragraph to the next are even more necessary than those between sentences within the paragraph. The reader takes it for granted that all sentences in one paragraph are on the same topic. But the paragraph break signals a new topic or a new phase of the preceding one, and the reader wants to know at once what the new one is to be. In the three connected paragraphs below, notice how each opening sentence ties in with the preceding paragraph and also indicates the direction in which the new paragraph is to go.

20   In Philadelphia, the advantage of a small car was recently illustrated in a court of law. A baffled policeman had brought before a magistrate the owners of two MGs which had both been parked in the motor space designed for a single vehicle. It was the view of the officer that this arrangement resulted in an illicit mulcting of the city at the rate of a dime an hour. The magistrate disagreed; he commended the drivers for their ingenuity.

21   Another and no less precious asset arises not so much from size as from lighter and differently distributed weight. A small car is supremely handy in icy weather. It is almost never trapped by snow or mud, and it will almost never lose traction on a slippery grade. Its skids are rare and gentle. And its driver can enjoy the soul-satisfying experience of wending his way up a steep and snowy hill at an even speed among big cars which have skidded into the gutter or which lie helplessly athwart the highway.

22   For many of the more than a million Americans who own two or more cars, these and other advantages have dictated the choice of a small car as a supplement to the basic big car. The combination of, say, a station wagon and an MG provides a nice balance between capacity and chic and provides an escape from the status of a two-car family with all the financial and social implications it involves. A small car doesn't seem to be *exactly* a car; its sheepish owner can treat it as a gadget and explain that it costs next to nothing to operate.

—LAURENCE LAFORE, R. W. LAFORE, and R. W. LAFORE, JR.[20]

The topics of the three paragraphs may be stated thus: (20) *Ease of parking small cars was recently illustrated in Philadelphia.* (21) *The light weight of small cars is especially advantageous in icy weather.* (22) *The small car is an ideal second car.* The opening sentence of paragraph 20 refers, by the word *advantage,* to the previously discussed ease of parking small cars and also leads up to the illustration to be used in the paragraph. The next paragraph begins with *another . . . asset,* showing at once that an additional advantage of small cars is to be pointed out. (At the same time, *another* calls attention to the advantage just discussed.) And *these and other advantages* in the opening sentence of paragraph 22 both ties in with what has preceded and leads up to what is to follow.

Sometimes a paragraph is used to make a transition. Paragraph 24 in the series of paragraphs below is an example of a transitional paragraph.

23 I am overwhelmed by our material and materialistic culture—and its accomplishments. We have developed manufacturing and marketing techniques unsurpassed by any other country. The editors of *Fortune* magazine have observed, "The foreign visitor is drenched with sights and sounds and smells emanating from a man-made environment to which almost all Americans appear to give all their energies."

24 What are some of the factors that make us different from the rest of the world?

25 Our *standard of living* is considerably higher than that of any other nation. In fact, the American way of living is

---

[20]From "The Small Cars: Fun on Wheels" by Laurence Lafore, R. W. Lafore, and R. W. Lafore, Jr., *Harper's Magazine,* March 1955. Reprinted by permission.

one in which an ever-increasing standard of living is considered our birthright. And with a high standard of living, we have not only great physical and material well-being but also an opportunity to expand our economy still further, especially in the last part of the twentieth century.   —STEUART HENDERSON BRITT[21]

Notice how paragraph 24 links paragraph 23, which stresses our difference from the rest of the world, with paragraph 25, which discusses one factor that makes us different. (The paragraphs after 25 develop other differentiating factors.)

■ **Exercise 10** Prepare for a class discussion of all the transitions in the four paragraphs below—not only those between the sentences within a paragraph but also those between paragraphs.

26   The fact that languages differ from one another in the way they relate to the world about us suggests an intriguing question: Do all men think in the same patterns, regardless of their native language, or do those who speak different languages think in different ways? Clearly this question involves another: Does the way we think depend on the way we talk? With regard to these questions there are two extreme positions that can be described by different metaphors.

27   First, we might say that language is like a suit of clothes that covers the body of thought. This metaphor implies that language and thought are relatively independent—just as the same body can be dressed in different clothes, so the same thought can be expressed in different languages or different words. Indeed, in this view language is no more than a superficial adornment. A naked thought, like a naked body, can be so draped with words that we must infer it from the surface form of the language, yet it is still the thought that gives shape to the language.

28   Second, we may say that language is like a mold that gives shape to whatever plastic thought is poured into it. The implications here are that thought is dependent on language

[21]From *The Spenders* by Steuart Henderson Britt. Copyright 1960 McGraw-Hill Book Co., Inc. Used with permission of McGraw-Hill Book Company.

for the form it assumes, that the "same" thought, expressed in different words, is not the same at all. Before it has been formed into a distinctive shape by the mold of language, thought is amorphous—indeed, hardly worthy of the name. Whatever deserves to be called thought is simply unspoken language.

29 Each of these positions has something to be said for it. The feeling that all of us have from time to time that we know just what we mean but cannot find the right words for it suggests that language is merely a clothing for thought. On the other hand, there is the common experience of talking to oneself, which may be practically without visible sign or may involve a good deal of silent lip movement and facial contortion. The fact that everybody talks to himself—and many find it distinctly easier to solve problems when they do so—suggests that thinking is a matter of language. E. M. Forster tells of an old lady whose complaint "How can I tell what I think till I see what I say?" shows that for her thought and language are identical.

—THOMAS PYLES and JOHN ALGEO[22]

31c

Develop the paragraph adequately. Supply enough information to satisfy the reader but avoid excessively long paragraphs.

(1) Supply enough information to satisfy the reader.

Many short paragraphs are adequately developed. In expository writing, a short paragraph may be used for transition (see paragraph 24) or for emphasis. Even a one-sentence paragraph sometimes provides enough information to satisfy the reader, as the following two paragraphs demonstrate.

30 When some future historian shall sit down to summarize what the present generation of Americans has accom-

---

[22] From *English: An Introduction to Language* by Thomas Pyles and John Algeo. Published by Harcourt Brace Jovanovich, Inc., 1970. Reprinted by permission.

plished, his climactic sentence could read, "Of the waters, they made a cesspool; of the air, a depository for poisons; and of the good earth itself, a dump where rats nuzzled in piles of refuse."

—GEORGE R. STEWART[23]

31   If environment refers to what's around us, then our environment also includes the awesome coast of Oregon, the sparkling desert nights in southern Arizona, the Everglades glowing red in the summer dawn, the waltzing wheatfields of Kansas, the New York City skyline at dusk, the luxurious cabin of a jet airliner, air-conditioned autos and broad turnpikes and winding parkways, the pretty clothes of American women, and the laughter of children. —EDWIN A. ROBERTS, JR.[24]

But a series of paragraphs each less than fifty words in length (except in dialogue and other special types of writing) suggests inadequate development of the thought. If such choppy paragraphs deal with the same topic, they should be combined into one or more longer paragraphs. If they deal with different topics, each paragraph should be expanded to the point where the thought is adequately developed.

PARAGRAPHS THAT SHOULD BE COMBINED

The line of demarcation between capitalism and socialism is sharp and clear.

Capitalism is that form of organization in which the means of production—and by that is meant the machine and the funds required to utilize the machine—are controlled by private individuals or by privately owned organizations.

Under a socialistic regime the control of the means of production, the control of capital—for even socialists concede the need for capital—is by the group. Under capitalism the profits accrue to the private individual; under socialism, to the group.

---

[23] From *Not So Rich as You Think* by George R. Stewart. Published by Houghton Mifflin Company, 1970. Reprinted by permission.

[24] From "Struggling to Control Growing Trash Heaps" by Edwin A. Roberts, Jr., *National Observer*, August 18, 1969. Reprinted by permission.

These three short paragraphs, when read together, actually make one unified paragraph of ninety words and should be so written. Taken separately, the paragraphs are short and choppy; together they form a paragraph of average length developing a clearly stated central idea: *The line of demarcation between capitalism and socialism is sharp and clear.*

PARAGRAPHS THAT SHOULD BE EXPANDED

During his first term of office President Roosevelt introduced many laws to promote national recovery. These laws covered all phases of the national life.
[The reader should be told specifically what some of these laws were.]

Forestry work is healthful, educational, and financially rewarding. A forester, for example, soon learns how to prevent and to fight forest fires.
[The reader expects to find out about three aspects of forestry work, but the writer comments briefly on only one. How is the work healthful? What else does a forester learn? What are the financial rewards?]

The football game was much more like a movie than like real life. The most improbable things happened.
[Some of the improbable happenings should be mentioned, and the implied contrast between the movies and real life should be elaborated.]

Each of these short paragraphs begins with a promising statement of the controlling idea and then stops before supplying enough information to satisfy the reader. In other words, the paragraphs are not adequately developed. If the paragraphs in your compositions tend to be inadequately developed, study the seven methods of paragraph development described and illustrated in **31d**, pages 355–71.

(2) Avoid excessively long paragraphs.

In current writing, paragraphs seldom run to more than 200 or 300 words, and the average is much shorter, perhaps not more than 100 words. Whenever a writer finds that he needs more than 250 words to develop his central thought, he should, if possible, divide his material into two or more paragraphs. Let us examine, for example, the possible divisions in the following long paragraph, which Richard Steele wrote more than two hundred years ago, when readers were less hurried than those of our time.

¹ When a good artist would express any remarkable character in sculpture, he endeavors to work up his figure into all the perfections his imagination can form, and to imitate not so much what is, as what may or ought to be. ² I shall follow their example, in the idea I am going to trace out of a fine gentleman, by assembling together such qualifications as seem requisite to make the character complete. ³ In order to do this I shall premise in general, that by a fine gentleman I mean a man completely qualified as well for the service and good as for the ornament and delight of society. ⁴ When I consider the frame of mind peculiar to a gentleman, I suppose it graced with all the dignity and elevation of spirit that human nature is capable of. ⁵ To this I would have joined a clear understanding, a reason free from prejudice, a steady judgment, and an extensive knowledge. ⁶ When I think of the heart of a gentleman, I imagine it firm and intrepid, void of all inordinate passions, and full of tenderness, compassion, and benevolence. ⁷ When I view the fine gentleman with regard to his manners, methinks I see him modest without bashfulness, frank and affable without impertinence, obliging and complaisant without servility, cheerful and in good humor without noise. ⁸ These amiable qualities are not easily obtained; neither are there many men that have a genius to excel this way. ⁹ A finished gentleman is perhaps the most uncommon of all the great characters in life. ¹⁰ Besides the natural endowments with which this distinguished man is to be born, he must run through a long series of education. ¹¹ Before he makes his appearance and shines in the world, he must be principled in religion, instructed in all the moral virtues, and led through the whole course of the polite arts and sciences. ¹² He should be no stranger to courts and to camps; he must travel to open his mind, to enlarge his views, to learn the policies and interests of foreign states, as well as to fashion and polish himself, and to get clear of national prejudices,

of which every country has its share.   [13] To all these more essential improvements he must not forget to add the fashionable ornaments of life, such as are the languages and the bodily exercises most in vogue; neither would I have him think even dress itself beneath his notice.   —RICHARD STEELE

A careful reading shows that this whole paragraph of 404 words develops Steele's concept of the ideal gentleman. The paragraph has unity; except for the excessive length, there would be no reason for dividing it. Fortunately it can, like most overlong paragraphs, be divided into shorter paragraphs, each developing a specific part of the general topic. Steele's long paragraph can be divided, without any rewriting, into three good paragraphs, as follows:

First paragraph (sentences 1–3): The method to be used in depicting the ideal gentleman and a general definition of such a man.

Second paragraph (sentences 4–7): The ideal gentleman's specific qualities of mind, heart, and manners.

Third paragraph (sentences 8–13): The education needed to develop these qualities.

If the long paragraph were thus divided into three shorter ones, each paragraph would be well unified, and there would be good transitions from one to the other. Note especially the excellent transition at the beginning of the third paragraph: "These amiable qualities are not easily obtained; neither are there many men that have a genius to excel this way."

31d

Master various methods of paragraph development.

You can learn to write good paragraphs by studying the various techniques that professional writers use to develop ideas. The more you read, the more you will find that no one method, or no one combination of methods, is better than another except as it fits the needs of a given paragraph. As you analyze the following illustrations of good paragraph development, notice how the controlling ideas (indicated by italics) are developed by each of the other sentences in the paragraph.

(1) Supply relevant specific details to develop the controlling idea.

The controlling idea of a paragraph often brings specific details to mind. Take, for example, "She was a living advertisement for the products she sold." This statement raises such questions as "How exactly did she resemble an advertisement?" and "What products did she sell?" By answering these questions and choosing his details with care (remembering to omit irrelevant details, no matter how interesting they are in themselves), the writer can develop the central idea effectively.

32 *Thyra was a living poster for the virtues and effects of the products she promoted across her sweet-smelling counter.* Her hair was a fiery dark orange. As it slowly grew out it would reveal another color—greying white, and she would vigorously apply a preparation from a fancy bottle at the Beauty Bar to restore its solid color. Her face was white and the skin was tightly drawn over her forehead and cheekbones until it shone. She painted her eyelids with an Egyptian blue and put something over that to make them shine as she turned her glance. Her eyes were pale grey, folded about by a system of tiny wrinkles which you could not see from a little distance. Her natural eyebrows were removed and she pencilled in their substitutes high on the polished bone of her forehead. For her cheeks she chose a thick dusty rouge called *Rose Geranium.* Her nose was large, spatulate at the end, with nostrils flaring open to take an extra abundance of life through the sense of smell. This hint of appetite was emphasized by her mouth, which was small, and painted smaller, as if to represent a kiss which she was keeping for the world at large. Women understood and hated her on sight.

—PAUL HORGAN[25]

[Carefully selected details bring Thyra clearly into focus.]

33 When it was over and I escaped through the ropes, shaking, bleeding a little from the mouth, with rosin dust on my pants and a vicious throbbing in my head, *I knew all there was to know about being hit in the prize-ring.* It seems that I had gone to an expert for tuition. I knew the sensation of being stalked and pursued by a relentless, truculent professional destroyer whose trade and business it was to injure men. I saw the quick flash of the brown forearm that precedes the stunning shock as a bony, leather-bound fist lands on cheek or mouth. I learned more (partly from photographs of the lesson, viewed afterwards, one of which shows me ducked under a vicious left hook, an act of which I never had the slightest recollection) about instinctive ducking and blocking than I could have in ten years of looking at prizefights, and I learned, too, that as the soldier never hears the bullet that kills him, so does the fighter rarely, if ever, see the punch that tumbles blackness over him like a mantle, with a tearing rip as though the roof of his skull were exploding, and robs him of his senses.   —PAUL GALLICO[26]

[The details of this paragraph describe how the author learned what it is to be a prizefighter. Notice that in this paragraph and in paragraph 32, the order of development is from the general to the particular.]

■ **Exercise 11** Write a paragraph in which you develop one of the following topics by using carefully selected specific details.

1. The photograph of the man suggested his character.
2. I know now what it means to be an outsider.

---

[25] From *Whitewater* by Paul Horgan. Published by Farrar, Straus & Giroux, Inc., and The Bodley Head Ltd., 1970. Reprinted by permission of Virginia Rice. Copyright © 1970 by Paul Horgan.

[26] From *Farewell to Sport* by Paul Gallico. Published by Alfred A. Knopf, Inc. Reprinted by permission of Harold Ober Associates Incorporated. Copyright 1937, 1938 by Paul Gallico.

3. Television sets can be excellent babysitters.
4. Western man has no monopoly on violence.

(2) Use several closely related examples or one striking example to illustrate the controlling idea.

Examples are especially useful for developing a generalization that a reader might question or might not understand. Take, for instance, the statement "Experts nearly always greet the new with negative arguments." A skeptical reader might challenge this statement unless two or three convincing specific instances are given. To be convincing, the examples given in support of a generalization must be truly representative.

34 *It is unlikely that any major enterprise was ever undertaken without an expert arguing conclusively that it would not succeed.* At the behest of King Ferdinand and Queen Isabella, a panel of Spanish sages looked at Columbus' plan for a voyage to the Indies, and in 1490 came up with six good reasons why it was impossible. So many centuries after the creation, they concluded triumphantly, it was unlikely that anyone could find hitherto unknown lands of any value. This negative reaction was similar to the learned argument that greeted Galileo when he reported that Jupiter had moons. "Jupiter's moons are invisible to the naked eye," said a group of Aristotelian professors, "and therefore can have no influence on the earth, and therefore would be useless, and therefore do not exist." —Editors of TIME[27]

[Two closely related examples illustrate the negative reactions of experts.]

35 *The day may arrive soon when there is little or no difference between advanced art and a disturbance.* Already we have avant-garde types who don't play pianos but hack and bash them to pieces in what they believe to be a meaningful

---

[27] From "Putting the Prophets in Their Place," *Time,* February 15, 1971. Reprinted by permission from *Time,* The Weekly Newsmagazine; Copyright Time Inc. 1971.

fashion. Soon there may be plays in which stinkbombs are hurled
into the audience at the end of the first act and nobody sees the
final scene of the second act because of the tear gas. There may
be novels that will explode as page 193 is turned. We want to be
disturbed, do we? Well, the arts will be right in there with us.
—J. B. PRIESTLEY[28]

[The second, third, and fourth sentences present separate examples of the potential similarity between art and disturbance.]

36   *The belief in punishment at a distance was strik-
ingly illustrated by a report from South Africa last April.* It seems
that the caning of offenders was being carried out in a magistrates'
court located near the center of Cape Town. Sentences of up
to ten cuts were inflicted on malefactors, beginning with eight-
year-old boys, in that particular jurisdiction. The matter became
newsworthy when the public began to object to the practice. The
objection, however, was not to the punishment itself but to the
uncomfortable circumstance that it was administered in the business district of the city. One citizen complained, "We can clearly
hear the swish and smack of the cane and the pleadings and
screams of the people being beaten." It appears that this noise
was upsetting women office workers. Not only the women were
disturbed. One man said "that his conversations with important
clients had been interrupted by the 'howling of somebody being
thrashed.'" The problem was solved by police assurances that the
beatings would thereafter be administered in the basement, where
they would not disturb the public.   —DAVID L. BAZELON[29]

[The controlling idea is developed by one striking example. Notice
that the example of the citizens' reactions to *nearby* punishment
makes immediately clear what the author means by the rather
abstract idea "the belief in punishment at a distance."]

■ **Exercise 12**   Write a paragraph using either several examples
or one striking example to develop one of the following topics.

[28] From *Essays of Five Decades* by J. B. Priestley. Published by Little,
Brown and Company, 1968. Reprinted by permission.

[29] From "The Imperative to Punish" by David L. Bazelon, *Atlantic
Monthly,* July 1960. Copyright © 1960 by The Atlantic Monthly Company,
Boston, Mass. Reprinted with permission.

1. Almost anything can be a symbol.
2. Bumper stickers give a clear indication of the American mood.
3. Even the rich have serious problems.
4. It is easy to be a coach (OR a judge OR the president) at a distance.
5. We are living in a decade of crises.

(3) Formulate and develop a definition.

A formal definition has two parts: first the thing being defined is put into a class of similar things; then it is differentiated from all other things in that class. Notice in the following paragraph that Kenneth Rexroth first classifies the ballad as a narrative folk song and then points out its distinguishing characteristics—its brevity, dramatic situation, rhetoric, measure, and so on.

37 *The ballad has been defined as a folk song which tells a story, concentrating on the dramatic situation of the climax, rather than a long narrative unfolding action and reaction.* The tale is presented directly in act and speech with little or no comment by the narrator. Although the most violent passions may be shown by the characters, the maker of the ballad remains austerely unmoved. So does the performer. Emotional comment, where it occurs, comes through a special kind of rhetoric peculiar to the ballad, often, especially in some of the refrains, dependent upon the use of rather remote metaphors to intensify the psychological situation. Most ballads are in "ballad measure," four lines of alternating eight and six syllables—really fourteen syllables or seven stressed syllables with a strong pause after the eighth—rhyming usually at the end of each fourteen syllables. However this pattern varies constantly even within the same song. What varies it is the fluency of the music clustered around a simple melodic pattern, which a good ballad singer seldom, stanza for stanza, repeats exactly.   —KENNETH REXROTH[30]

---

[30] From "The English and Scottish Ballad" by Kenneth Rexroth, *Saturday Review*, December 14, 1968, p. 26. Copyright 1968 Saturday Review, Inc. Reprinted by permission.

38 *Rioting is a spontaneous outburst of group violence characterized by excitement mixed with rage.* The outburst is usually directed against alleged perpetrators of injustice or gross misusers of political power. The typical rioter has no premeditated purpose, plan or direction, although systematic looting, arson and attack on persons may occur once the riot is under way. Also, criminals and conspirators may expand their routine activities in the wake of the riot chaos. While it is quite clear that riots are unpremeditated outbursts, they are not as a rule *senseless* outbursts. The rage behind riots is a shared rage growing out of specific rage-inducing experiences. In the United States, the rage felt by Negroes (increasingly manifested in ghetto riots) is based on centuries of oppression, and in latter times on discriminatory practices that frustrate equal opportunity to social, economic and political goals. While all riots stem from conflicts in society similar to those that inspire civil disobedience, they ordinarily do not develop directly from specific acts of civil disobedience. Yet repeated failures of civil disobedience to achieve sought-after goals can and often do result in frustrations that provide fertile ground for the violent outbursts we call riots.   —RALPH W. CONANT[31]

[Notice how rioting is differentiated from other types of group violence, such as mutiny and revolt. An example—the rage of Negroes in the United States—is used to clarify one aspect of rioting.]

■ **Exercise 13**   Write a paragraph presenting a definition of (1) *pop art,* (2) *liberating,* (3) *reactionary,* (4) *materialism,* or (5) *peace.*

(4) Use classification to relate ideas.

To classify is to divide into categories. Some classifications are based on similarities: for instance, such trees as the black oak, the sycamore, and the cottonwood may all be classified as *deciduous.* Other classifications are based on differences: such trees as the black oak, the sycamore, and the cotton-

---

[31]From "Rioting, Insurrection and Civil Disobedience" by Ralph W. Conant, *American Scholar,* Summer 1968. Reprinted by permission.

wood may be differentiated from the cedar, the fir, and the pine by the labels *deciduous* and *evergreen*. A classification relates ideas by listing and characterizing the members of a group.

39 *There are three kinds of book owners.* The first has all the standard sets and best-sellers—unread, untouched. (This deluded individual owns woodpulp and ink, not books.) The second has a great many books—a few of them read through, most of them dipped into, but all of them as clean and shiny as the day they were bought. (This person would probably like to make books his own, but is restrained by a false respect for their physical appearance.) The third has a few books or many—every one of them dog-eared and dilapidated, shaken and loosened by continual use, marked and scribbled in from front to back. (This man owns books.)   —MORTIMER J. ADLER[32]

[Adler divides book owners into three main categories and then lists and describes each type.]

40 *The alienated groups consist of two sorts: the estranged and the excluded.* The estranged are those who in the past have formed part of the national community—the intellectuals, the young, the lower-middle-class whites, for example—and are disaffected on recent and particular grounds: the intellectuals and the young because of the Vietnam war; the lower-middle-class whites because of the Negro revolution. For them one can speak of the "restoration" of social ties. The excluded are those—the traditionally poor, the blacks, the Indians, the Puerto Ricans, the Mexican-Americans—who have never been full members of this nation. For them the issue is not the restoration but the achievement of national status.   —ARTHUR M. SCHLESINGER, JR.[33]

[Schlesinger divides the alienated into two classes: the estranged and the excluded. He then uses details to point out differences between the two classes.]

---

[32] From "How to Mark a Book" by Mortimer J. Adler, *Saturday Review*, July 6, 1940. Copyright 1940 The Saturday Review Company, Inc.; renewed 1967 Saturday Review, Inc. Reprinted by permission.

[33] From *The Crisis of Confidence* by Arthur M. Schlesinger, Jr. Published by Houghton Mifflin Company, 1969. Reprinted by permission.

■ **Exercise 14** Write a paragraph on one of the following topics in which you use classification to relate ideas.

1. There are various kinds of home owners (OR automobile mechanics, airline hostesses, campus lecturers).
2. As the controversy raged, letters to the editor fell into two (OR three OR four) categories.

(5) Use a contrast or a comparison to develop the controlling idea.

To contrast is to point out differences between members of the same class—for example, differences between rival philosophers such as the sophists and Socrates. Frequently, the very basis of a contrast or a comparison is the common class to which the persons or things discussed belong.

41 To some of his contemporaries Socrates looked like a sophist. But *he distrusted and opposed the sophists wherever possible.* They toured the whole Greek world: Socrates stayed in Athens, talking to his fellow-citizens. They made carefully prepared continuous speeches; he only asked questions. They took rich fees for their teaching; he refused regular payment, living and dying poor. They were elegantly dressed, turned out like filmstars on a personal-appearance tour, with secretaries and personal servants and elaborate advertising. Socrates wore the workingman's clothes, bare feet and a smock; in fact, he had been a stonemason and carver by trade, and came from a working-class family. They spoke in specially prepared lecture-halls; he talked to people at street-corners and in the gymnasium (like public baths and bathing beaches nowadays), where every afternoon the young men exercised, and the old men talked, while they all sun bathed. He fitted in so well there that he sometimes compared himself to the athletic coach, who does not run or wrestle, but teaches others how to run and wrestle better: Socrates said he trained people to think. Lastly, the sophists said they knew everything and were ready to explain it. Socrates said he knew nothing and was trying to find out.   —GILBERT HIGHET[34]

---

[34] From *The Art of Teaching* by Gilbert Highet, pp. 156–57. Published by Alfred A. Knopf, Inc., and Methuen & Co. Ltd., 1950. Reprinted by permission.

[The first sentence is transitional, linking this paragraph with the author's foregoing one. The second sentence states the controlling idea, which is developed by contrasting the sophists with Socrates. Socrates and the sophists both belong to the class *philosopher-teachers.* This common class provides the basis of the contrast, for it permits Highet to contrast the two kinds of philosophers not only in their methods and their personal habits but, most important, in the ideas or theories of knowledge they taught.]

■ **Exercise 15** Write a paragraph in which you develop by contrast one of the following topics.

1. the service at a soda fountain and in a hotel dining room
2. the dialogue of a motion picture and that of Shakespeare
3. the architecture of the Washington Monument and that of the Lincoln Memorial
4. the relative effectiveness of radio and television

42   *The living language is like a cowpath:* it is the creation of the cows themselves, who, having created it, follow it or depart from it according to their whims or needs. From daily use, the path undergoes change. A cow is under no obligation to stay in the narrow path she helped make, following the contour of the land, but she often profits by staying with it and she would be handicapped if she didn't know where it was and where it led to. Children obviously do not depend for communication on a knowledge of grammar; they rely on their ear, mostly, which is sharp and quick. But we have yet to see the child who hasn't profited from coming face to face with a relative pronoun at an early age, and from reading books, which follow the paths of centuries.   —E. B. WHITE[35]

[White compares the living language to a cowpath and the children who speak the language to the cows that use the path. In the process he points out similarities regarding creation, usage, change, and profitable knowledge and conformity. Notice that, unlike the literal contrast in paragraph 41, the figurative comparison here is between members of two different classes.]

---

[35] By E. B. White in "Notes and Comment," *New Yorker,* February 23, 1957. Reprinted by permission.

As paragraphs 41 and 42 demonstrate, there are two different ways of developing a contrast or a comparison. In paragraph 41, both sides of the contrast are given in almost every sentence; in paragraph 42, first one side of the comparison is completely developed and then the other. Either type of development is effective, and so is a combination of the two.

■ **Exercise 16** Write a paragraph in which you develop by comparison one of the following topics.

1. exploring outer space and crossing unknown seas
2. our first childhood and our second childhood
3. compulsive smokers and compulsive eaters
4. conservative Democrats and liberal Republicans

(6) Show cause or effect to develop the controlling idea.

A paragraph developed by causal analysis must not only raise the question *why* but answer it to the satisfaction of the reader. The cause or causes must satisfactorily explain the result. Notice that paragraphs 43 and 44 below are developed by explaining why the opening statement is true.

43   *Tragedy was a Greek creation because in Greece thought was free.* Men were thinking more and more deeply about human life, and beginning to perceive more and more clearly that it was bound up with evil and that injustice was of the nature of things. And then, one day, this knowledge of something irremediably wrong in the world came to a poet with his poet's power to see beauty in the truth of human life, and the first tragedy was written. As the author of a most distinguished book on the subject says: "The spirit of inquiry meets the spirit of poetry and tragedy is born." Make it concrete: early Greece with her godlike heroes and hero-gods fighting far on the ringing plains of windy Troy; with her lyric world, where every common thing is touched with beauty—her twofold world of poetic creation. Then a new age dawns, not satisfied with beauty of song and story, an age that must try to know and to explain. And for the first time tragedy appears. A poet of surpassing magnitude, not content with the

365

old sacred conventions, and of a soul great enough to bear new and intolerable truth—that is Aeschylus, the first writer of tragedy. —EDITH HAMILTON[36]

[Miss Hamilton holds that tragedy began when the ancient Greeks discovered, through free inquiry, that evil is an inevitable part of human life. This discovery was, then, the *cause* of the writing of tragedy. But before this cause could result in the creation of tragic plays, a great poet had to come along—Aeschylus.]

44 *One might wonder why, after the Norman Conquest, French did not become the national language, replacing English entirely.* The reason is that the Conquest was not a national migration, as the earlier Anglo-Saxon invasion had been. Great numbers of Normans came to England, but they came as rulers and landlords. French became the language of the court, the language of the nobility, the language of polite society, the language of literature. But it did not replace English as the language of the people. There must always have been hundreds of towns and villages in which French was never heard except when visitors of high station passed through. —PAUL ROBERTS[37]

[The opening sentence raises the question of why the Norman Conquest did not, as might have been expected, make England a French-speaking country. This sentence thus states an *effect* or *result* of the Conquest. The sentences that follow develop the controlling idea by showing *causes* to account for the result.]

■ **Exercise 17** Write a paragraph that begins with one of the following statements. Develop the paragraph by showing why the opening statement is true.

1. One might wonder how such a small percentage of American students created such a major national problem.

---

[36] Reprinted from *The Greek Way* by Edith Hamilton. By permission of W. W. Norton & Company, Inc. Copyright 1930, 1943 by W. W. Norton & Company, Inc. Copyright renewed 1958 by Edith Hamilton, 1971 by Dorian Reid.

[37] From *Understanding English* by Paul Roberts. Published by Harper & Row, Publishers, Inc. Reprinted by permission.

2. In the past few years, higher education has become less important to young people than it was previously.
3. Childhood experiences shape personality.
4. Men of the twenty-first century may have to live underground.

(7) Use a combination of methods to develop the controlling idea.

Many good paragraphs are developed not by any one specific method but by a combination of methods. Some good paragraphs almost defy analysis. The important consideration is not the specific method used but the adequacy of the development.

45 *I wonder why American towns look so much alike that I sometimes mix them up in my memory.* The reference to the standard influence of mass production whose agents are the traveling salesman, the mail-order houses, the five-and-ten cent stores, the chain stores, the movies, is not sufficient. If you stay two days in Bologna and in Ferrara, or in Arles and in Avignon, you will never mix them up in all your life. But it may well happen that after you spend two days in St. Louis and in Kansas City the images of these towns soon merge into one. I think the real reason for this is that these towns have not yet had time enough to individualize and to crystallize visible local traditions of their own. Physiognomically speaking, children are much less differentiated from each other than grown people.   —PAUL SCHRECKER[38]

[Notice how this effective paragraph combines both cause and effect and comparison and contrast.]

46 I have heard rumors of visitors who were disappointed. The same people will be disappointed at the Day of Judgment. In fact, the Grand Canyon is a sort of landscape Day of Judgment. It is not a show place, a beauty spot, but a revelation. The Colorado River, which is powerful, turbulent, and so thick

---

[38] From "American Diary" by Paul Schrecker, *Harper's Magazine*, July 1944. Reprinted by permission.

with silt that it is like a saw, made it with the help of the erosive forces of rain, frost, and wind, and some strange geological accidents; and all these together have been hard at work on it for the last seven or eight million years. It is the largest of the eighteen canyons of the Colorado River, is over two hundred miles long, has an average width of twelve miles, and is a good mile deep. It is the world's supreme example of erosion. But this is not what it really is. It is, I repeat, a revelation. The Colorado River made it, but you feel when you are there that God gave the Colorado River its instructions. It is all Beethoven's nine symphonies in stone and magic light. Even to remember that it is still there lifts up the heart. If I were an American, I should make my remembrance of it the final test of men, art, and policies. I should ask myself: Is this good enough to exist in the same country as the Canyon? How would I feel about this man, this kind of art, these political measures, if I were near that Rim? Every member or officer of the Federal Government ought to remind himself, with triumphant pride, that he is on the staff of the Grand Canyon.

—J. B. PRIESTLEY[39]

■ **Exercise 18** Pick out the statement of the controlling idea in paragraph 46. Show how Priestley effectively develops this idea. What specific methods or combination of methods of development does he use?

■ **Exercise 19** Prepare for a class discussion of the following paragraphs. Be able to point out controlling ideas, methods of development, types of organization or arrangement of sentences, and devices used for transition.

47 Father's elevation and dignity had a silencing effect on our home. The words Managing Director put him in a trance. He told us that we now had many privileges; first, we were the children of a Managing Director, living in a refined neighborhood among neighbors who would study our manners. We also had the privilege of living within a couple of hundred

[39] From *Midnight on the Desert* by J. B. Priestley. Published by A. D. Peters and Company and Harper & Row, Publishers, Inc., 1937. Reprinted by permission of A. D. Peters and Company.

yards of a remarkable family and an even more remarkable woman, the secretary to the company, whose brother, high in financial circles, played tennis at a most exclusive club. My father doubted if this family would feel able to know us immediately, but if by some generous condescension they did, we would remember to have our hands and shoes clean, brush our hair, raise our caps and never sit down until told to do so. Father's face had lost its roundness. It had become square, naked and authoritative. It also looked pained, as if he were feeling a strange, imposed constraint.   —V. S. PRITCHETT[40]

48   Young Americans at the ages of seventeen or eighteen are not completely babes in the woods. Most of those who go to college have seen the inside of middle-class American homes—their own and their friends'. They know what goes on there and vicariously, if not through direct experience, they've made some pretty extensive observations of life—of marriage and divorce, sex, liquor, money, dope, and politics. If they are city people, they've probably been on the streets. At eighteen the American male—out of self-interest if nothing else—begins to worry about war and peace; and the American female, about marriage and children. The American teenager has many other peepholes through which he may look at the way things seem to be. There are television and printed things and always, of course, automobiles. He undoubtedly has a lot to learn. On the other hand, it should not be assumed that his mind is a blank slate just waiting for some eager college to write on. It's a mind containing some very definite ideas at a time in life which is exploratory.   —WILLIAM BIRENBAUM[41]

49   The fact that the women are now complaining about "tokenism" indicates that they are lagging about five to

---

[40] From *A Cab at the Door* by V. S. Pritchett. Published by Random House, Inc., and Harold Matson Company, Inc., 1968. Copyright 1968 by V. S. Pritchett, reprinted by permission of the Harold Matson Company, Inc., and Random House, Inc.

[41] From *Overlive: Power, Poverty and the University* by William Birenbaum. Published by Delacorte Press and Curtis Brown, Ltd., 1969. Reprinted by permission of Curtis Brown, Ltd., and Delacorte Press. Copyright © 1969 by William Birenbaum.

eight years behind the Negro revolution. If they follow the stages of the Negro minority in its own struggle for equal rights, it may be that in a decade or even less the militant women's organizations will have scorned the male population altogether and become primarily concerned with "Female Power." The most radical of their leaders will advocate complete separation of the sexes, arguing that living together was tried and never worked because males always secretly regarded them as inferior, an attitude ingrained by the many years in which the male population held them in slavery. Those women who still feel some accommodation can be made with the men will be scorned as "Aunt Jemimas." There may be an attempt at some sort of political coalition with the militant females and the most liberal males (those who will do anything to please them), but if such a coalition convention is held the women will demand more votes than the men, some of the men will walk out of the convention in a huff, and the militant women will say gleefully that it only proved that those men who left never understood the true aspirations of their revolution anyway.   —DAN WAKEFIELD[42]

■ **Exercise 20**   Using paragraph 47 as a model, write a paragraph based upon a personal experience.

■ **Exercise 21**   Using paragraph 48 as a model, write a paragraph setting forth and developing a personal opinion.

■ **Exercise 22**   Using paragraph 49 as a model, write a paragraph presenting your speculations about the future of a current movement or interest.

■ **Exercise 23**   Indicate an appropriate method or combination of methods for developing each of the following statements.

1. Public schools may soon be extinct.
2. There are three major threats to the privacy of Americans.
3. The development of an international language has disadvantages as well as advantages.

---

[42] From *Supernation at Peace and War* by Dan Wakefield. Published by Little, Brown and Company, 1968. Reprinted by permission.

4. Irony is harder to define than to illustrate.
5. Before talking about democracy one should at least say what democracy is not.
6. Some men think our great cities are monuments of progress; others say they are symptoms of social disease.
7. At college I have discovered two kinds of friends.
8. A self-reliant person must know his predominant weaknesses as well as his predominant strengths.
9. Computers are revolutionizing American business.
10. The right of a nation to self-determination means one thing in Havana and another in Washington.

Planning and Writing the Whole Composition

32

Arrange and express your ideas effectively.

The four units of composition, in an ascending order, are the word (Sections 19–22), the sentence (Sections 23–30), the paragraph (Section 31), and the whole composition (Section 32). Words make up the sentence, sentences make up the paragraph, and paragraphs make up the whole composition.

A paragraph is usually a series of sentences developing one topic. A composition is usually a series of paragraphs developing several topics that are closely related. Just as a unified paragraph has a stated or implied topic to which each sentence contributes, a unified composition has a central idea to which each paragraph contributes. Therefore, many of the techniques used to write paragraphs (for example, developing a central idea, arranging supporting details logically and effectively, making appropriate transitions) are applicable to the composition as a whole: see Section 31.

In fact, sometimes the major difference between a paragraph and a composition is merely a matter of scale. For example, the topic sentence of paragraph 1 on pages 328–29 could easily be converted to the central idea of a composition. The three points made in paragraph 1 could then be topic sentences for separate paragraphs. Of course, more specific details would be necessary to develop each paragraph adequately. An introductory and a concluding paragraph might also be added.

32a

Choose an appropriate subject and limit it properly.

Be sure to select a topic that will enable you to say something interesting about what you know well. Limit the topic you choose so that you can develop it adequately and specifically.

A subject is appropriate—
1. if it appeals to you, or if you can develop an interest in it as you work on it.
2. if it is acceptable to the intended reader.

A subject is properly limited—
1. if you know enough about it or can learn enough in a reasonable period. (Subjects that require extensive reading should be reserved for the library paper: see Section **33**.)
2. if the topic is not too broad to treat in the time or space at your disposal. ("Amateur Photography" might be a satisfactory title for a paper of several thousand words; but if you must limit yourself to several hundred words, you will do better with a topic such as "Developing a Film" or "The Growth of My Interest in Photography.")

Let us suppose that you have chosen (or have been assigned) "Sports" as the general subject for a paper of five hundred words. Obviously, you cannot cover everything to be said about sports in five hundred words. You must therefore find a more limited topic. You may be particularly interested in one sport, but "Football" or "Baseball" is still too broad a topic for your short paper. Therefore you should concentrate on a narrow phase of the sport chosen, such as "The Importance of Fumbles in Saturday's Game" or "The Characteristics of a Good Shortstop."

PURPOSE

Before making a final decision regarding the specific topic, you should consider your purpose in writing the composition. If your purpose is to inform the reader, either "The Importance of Fumbles in Saturday's Game" or "The Characteristics of a Good Shortstop" would be appropriate. If, however, you decide that you want to argue about the merits of watching football or baseball on television as compared with attending the games in person, you might choose a title such as "Zooming in on the Action" or "The Superiority of a Bird's Eye View." If you decide to write a narrative account of the exciting ending of a game, a good title might be "With Only Seconds to Go." Or if your primary aim is to describe your feelings as you watched a particularly heart-breaking defeat, you might choose a title such as "A Cold Day at Memorial Stadium."

Each of the purposes you might select corresponds to one of the four main types of writing as they are conventionally classified in rhetoric—exposition or explanation (the giving of information), argument (or persuasion), narration, and description. *Exposition* is the most common kind of non-fiction writing and the kind most frequently written by college students. *Argument* is similar to exposition but is written with the intention of convincing rather than simply explaining. In *narration,* events are presented in a time sequence. And in *description,* a sensory impression of an object or feeling is conveyed. Very seldom is description written independently. Usually it is only part of a composition in which one of the other types of discourse dominates. In fact, few compositions are a single form of discourse. Most are mixtures in which one form predominates. Thus, a paper on "How to Drive a Car" would be primarily exposition but would also contain bits of description (perhaps of the steering mechanism) and bits of narration (perhaps an anecdote about the author's first drive).

Whatever form of discourse a paper may take, it does not fall into order by chance. *Order is the result of careful planning.*

CENTRAL IDEA

After deciding upon your purpose, you will find it helpful to set down, in a single sentence, the central or controlling idea for your paper. If your purpose is to inform, your sentence may read, "A good shortstop thinks and acts quickly." This thesis statement helps to limit the subject and especially helps to determine the items to be included in the outline. In fact, if in the beginning you can set down a central idea containing logically arranged main points (see the first example below), you will already have the main headings of your outline. If you do not give the main points in your thesis statement (see the second through the fifth examples below), you may later wish to reword the statement in order to show its close relation to the items in your outline. In dealing with some subjects, you may need to list your ideas and then find and consider more evidence before you can decide upon an appropriate thesis. If not determined in the process of limiting the subject, the controlling idea for your composition should be written out before the outline is completed and then used to test the contents of the outline.

1. *Purpose:* To inform by pointing out ways to appraise a used car   [Exposition]
    Title: How to Buy a Good Used Car
    Central Idea: Before selecting a used car, a wise buyer will carefully inspect the car himself, talk to the former owner of the car, and engage a good mechanic to examine its motor.

2. *Purpose:* To convince the reader of a need for change in the examination system   [Argument]
    Title: Why Have Final Examinations?
    Central Idea: Final examinations should be abolished.

3. *Purpose:* To tell a story about a true experience
   [Narration]
   Title: Dangerous Waters
   Central Idea: Looking for dolphin twenty miles out, I
   steered my light fishing boat into dangerous waters and
   spent hours battling high winds before being rescued.

4. *Purpose:* To describe Rushville and its surroundings
   [Description]
   Title: Rushville: A Beautiful City in the Mountains
   Central Idea: Rushville is a beautiful city in the mountains.

5. *Purpose:* To describe Old Tony and show that he is a
   colorful individual [Exposition, description, narration]
   Title: Old Tony
   Central Idea: Old Tony is the most colorful individual I
   know.

Each of the suggestions listed below is a suitable subject
for a student paper. Some of the suggestions, as worded, may
provide the exact title you need for your paper. In all likelihood, however, you will wish to limit the subject to the scope
of your experience and to sharpen the wording to suit your
purpose. (For the proper capitalization of titles, see **9c**.)

Suggestions for Written Work

Home and the individual

1. Living in a mobile home
2. The commune versus the family unit
3. Who is head of the household today?
4. Computers in the home
5. Our vanishing family traditions
6. Seeking an identity
7. I am the victim of my own prejudices
8. Ideals I live by
9. How I please (OR displease) my peers
10. Our fight against dehumanization

College life

1. What is student power?
2. Students in the news
3. The free university
4. Campus politics

5. Cheating related to the grading system
6. Types of campus turmoil
7. Underground newspapers

Economics, history, sociology

1. The causes of inflation (OR recession)
2. Our monetary system
3. The blue-collar voters
4. What our taxes buy
5. War and the economy
6. Why status symbols change
7. The effect of advertising on society
8. Welfare or socialism?
9. The Peace Corps (OR the United Nations)
10. The relationship of crime to environment

8. Drugs and the student
9. Self-education at college
10. If I were on decision-making committees

11. The mass media and mind control
12. The rights of criminals (OR of the police)
13. Types of personalities
14. The loss of privacy
15. Overpopulation—fact or fiction?
16. When industry is nationalized
17. The war on poverty
18. Racism defined
19. Middle-class values
20. Our continuing search for Utopia

Science and medicine

1. Is death necessary?
2. Brain transplants
3. Discoveries in space
4. Experiments with animals
5. Controlling the weather (OR a specific disease)

6. The implications of cloning
7. Chemical warfare
8. Underwater explorations
9. The dangers of drug use
10. Does science face facts?

Miscellaneous

1. The advantages of a different life style
2. Exploring the occult
3. How motion pictures are rated
4. Football for women
5. Persistent UFOs
6. Predictions for the Age of Aquarius

7. Nonverbal communication
8. The language of dissent
9. Fads in dress (OR music)
10. Our merchant-sponsored holidays
11. Types of short-wave radio programs
12. Religion in America in the 1970's

377

■ **Exercise 1** Select five subjects from the preceding list of suggestions for written work; then limit each one to an appropriate composition topic and decide what your purpose would be in writing a composition on each topic. Write (1) your purpose, (2) an appropriate title, and (3) the central idea for each topic that you choose. (You may find it helpful to refer to the examples on pages 375–76.)

32b

Develop a working plan or an outline before writing a composition. See also 33c.

Although a formal outline may not be required for every paper, learning to make and use a good outline is important to inexperienced writers because an outline is a working plan that can make the actual writing of a composition easier.

The outline is the blueprint of the composition. Just as the carpenter or the engineer follows his blueprint to the letter in order to avoid costly structural blunders, so the writer—especially the student writer—follows his outline carefully so that he may arrange his ideas effectively.

But blueprints can be changed and improved, and so can outlines. The writer should make the outline his helpful tool; he should not become its slave. He should keep the outline a growing, developing plan which he will not hesitate to change at any stage of his composition whenever he hits upon a way to improve it. He will naturally try to perfect his outline before he starts to write the paper, but the actual writing will almost certainly suggest a few desirable changes in the arrangement of details.

The first step in the preparation of an outline is the jotting down of ideas on the topic. Keeping the purpose of the composition firmly in mind, the student should jot down as many ideas as occur to him; and he should do it rapidly, without much concern for the proper order.

Suppose, for example, that a student has chosen to write a composition on the language of dissent. He has strong opinions on the subject and decides to argue that the current language of dissent is ineffective and ought to be changed. The purpose of his paper will be to convince the reader of the truth of his argument. He next chooses a tentative title for his composition: "Needed: A New Language of Dissent." Then he jots down ideas related to his central idea and to his tentative title.

List of Ideas for a Composition on the Language of Dissent

What is:	*What ought to be:*
shouting of obscenities	meaningful words and ideas
weak verbal attacks	strong verbal arguments
emotional outbursts	emphasis on reason
defiance of the law	respect for the legal process
inexact vocabulary	exact vocabulary
crudeness, lack of dignity	dignity
dramatic acts	challenging speech
rhetoric of violence	rhetoric of peaceful change
"body talk"	verbal communication
trite slogans	original expressions
rocks and bombs	words and good ideas
debasement of the language	elevation of the language

Ideas on a list such as this often overlap; some are general, and some are specific. As the student looks over his list, he singles out the ideas that seem most important to him—for example, the weakness of many verbal attacks, the current rhetoric of violence, and the resulting debasement of language. He then uses these key points to formulate a statement of the central idea of his paper:

> *Central idea:* By using weak verbal attacks and the rhetoric of physical violence, modern protesters debase language, which can be the most powerful expression of dissent.

Next the student arranges the main headings suggested by his central idea in a logical order (see **31b** and **32e**):

I. The weakness of the protesters' verbal attacks
II. The crudeness of the protesters' rhetoric of physical violence
III. The power of language as an expression of dissent

Any idea on the list which does not clearly support or clarify one of these main headings—for example, defiance of the law as opposed to respect for the legal process—should be discarded.

After the student decides how he wishes to develop each main heading, he adds subheadings. These may list specific details, give examples, develop a definition or a classification, and so on: see 31d.

Only one decision remains in planning the composition—whether or not to include introductory and concluding paragraphs: see 32g(2). If these paragraphs are deemed desirable or necessary, the writer should add to his plan an explanation of each. In a topic outline or a sentence outline, these statements need not be numbered: see 32c.

Once the writer has thought his subject through, he may wish to select a more appropriate or more interesting title. He may also want to change the wording of his central idea.

32c

Use an outline of the type specified by your instructor.

The types of outlines most commonly used are the topic outline, the sentence outline, and the paragraph outline. Topic outlines and sentence outlines have the same parts and the same groupings; they differ only in the fullness of expression employed. In a paragraph outline no effort is made to classify the material into major headings and subheadings: the topic of each paragraph is simply listed in the order in which it is to come. Paragraph outlines are especially helpful in writing short papers. Topic or sentence outlines may be adapted to papers of any length.

TOPIC OUTLINE

Violent Protest: A Debased Language

Central idea: By using weak verbal attacks and the rhetoric of physical violence, modern protesters debase language, which can be the most powerful expression of dissent.

Introduction: The change in the meaning of *dissent* from challenging speech to "body rhetoric"

  I. The weakness of the protesters' verbal attacks
     A. Their emphasis on feeling
     B. Their inexactness
 II. The crudeness of the protesters' rhetoric of physical violence
III. The power of language as an expression of dissent
     A. French Revolution made important by effectively expressed principles
     B. American Revolution revived by brilliant words

Conclusion: The need in our nation for a healing and elevating language of dissent

SENTENCE OUTLINE

Violent Protest: A Debased Language

Central idea: By using weak verbal attacks and the rhetoric of physical violence, modern protesters debase language, which can be the most powerful expression of dissent.

Introduction: The meaning of *dissent* has changed from challenging speech to "body rhetoric."

  I. The protesters' verbal attacks are weak.
     A. They emphasize feeling.
     B. They are inexact.
 II. The protesters' rhetoric of physical violence is crude.
III. Language as an expression of dissent can be powerful.
     A. Effectively expressed principles made the French Revolution important.
     B. Brilliant words revived the American Revolution.

Conclusion: Our nation needs a healing and elevating language of dissent.

PARAGRAPH OUTLINE

Violent Protest: A Debased Language

Central idea: By using weak verbal attacks and the rhetoric of physical violence, modern protesters debase language, which can be the most powerful expression of dissent.

1. The meaning of *dissent* has changed from challenging speech to "body rhetoric."
2. The protesters' verbal attacks are weak because they emphasize feeling.
3. The rhetoric of the protesters is inexact.
4. Violence is a crude and inarticulate way to attempt to communicate.
5. Words are more effective than weapons as a means of expressing dissent.
6. Our nation needs a healing and elevating language of dissent.

32d

Make sure that the outline covers the subject.

An adequate outline is essential to a successful composition. The major headings (I, II, III, and so on) must be sufficient in number and in scope to satisfy the expectations aroused by the title. Just as the central idea must be covered by the major headings, each of these headings must in turn be covered by its subheadings. The subheadings, however, should not be unduly detailed. They should include only basic points to be made in the composition.

INADEQUATE COVERAGE OF SUBJECT

Characteristics of Ideal Parents

  I. A father's sense of humor
 II. His generosity
III. His understanding

The Grading System

 I. What a *B* means
II. What a *C* means

ADEQUATE COVERAGE OF SUBJECT

Characteristics of Ideal Parents

I. Their sense of humor
II. Their generosity
III. Their understanding

The Grading System

I. Differences between an *A* and a *B*
II. Differences between a *C* and a *D*
III. Meaning of *F*

Note that the main headings in the former examples could be left unchanged if the titles were altered to agree—for example, "Characteristics of an Ideal Father" and "The Meaning of *B* and *C* in the Grading System."

In reality, making an outline is a process of thinking through the paper. Ordinarily, if your outline does not fit the rules for an outline, there is something awry with the plan for the paper itself—a missing element, a misstated title, or an inadequate purpose. Thus an outline can help you give focus to your paper and can sometimes show the need for further limitation of your topic.

32e

Make sure that the parts of the outline are logically arranged.

Logical arrangement is second in importance only to adequacy of coverage. If the outline is disorganized and ineffective, the paper that follows it will also be disorganized and ineffective. See also **31b**.

(1) Group related ideas.

Although you may begin your outline by hastily jotting down as many ideas on your topic as possible, without regard to order, you should later bring related ideas together, grouping them under major headings. Compare the first list of ideas for a composition on the language of dissent (page 379) with the groupings in the finished outlines (pages 381–82).

(2) Arrange the parts in a natural, logical order.

The problem of arrangement within the paper as a whole is much the same as that of arrangement within each separate paragraph: see pages 336–39. The nature of the subject will suggest an appropriate arrangement, such as time order, space order, or order of climax.

TIME ORDER	ORDER OF CLIMAX
Building a Storm Cellar	Types of Wars
I. Choosing the site	I. Civil
II. Digging the hole	II. International
III. Pouring the cement	III. Interplanetary
IV. Adding the door	

■ **Exercise 2** Make a list of three, four, or five main points closely related to one of the following subjects; then arrange the items in a natural, logical order. (In parentheses are suggestions for appropriate arrangements.)

1. an encounter with the law   (*time order*)
2. ways to influence legislation (*order of climax*)
3. a walk across the campus   (*space order*)
4. a successful experiment   (*time order*)
5. the trials of being a college freshman   (*order of climax*)

(3) Do not allow headings to overlap.

Overlapping often occurs when a writer attempts an arrangement based on more than one principle.

MIXED ARRANGEMENT

Advertising on Television

I. Since the advent of color   [Arrangement by time]
II. Its effect on sales   [Arrangement by cause and effect]
III. Pain relievers   [Arrangement by classification]

UNMIXED ARRANGEMENT

Advertising on Television

Time	Cause and Effect	Classification
I. Before color	I. Creates demand	I. Detergents
II. After color	II. Influences sales	II. Household appliances
	III. Affects economy	III. Pain relievers

(4) Do not coordinate any heading that should be subordinated. Do not subordinate any heading that should be coordinated.

ILLOGICAL   Wonder Products in TV Advertisements

     I. Detergents
        A. Household appliances
     II. Washing machines
     III. Remedies for headaches
        A. Pain relievers
        B. Cures for upset stomachs

LOGICAL   Wonder Products in TV Advertisements

     I. Detergents
     II. Household appliances
        A. Washing machines
        B. Refrigerators
     III. Pain relievers
        A. For headaches
        B. For upset stomachs

(5) Do not use single headings or subheadings anywhere in the outline.

Headings and subheadings stand for divisions, and a division denotes at least two parts. Therefore, to be logical, each outline should have at least two main headings, I and II.

If it has a subheading marked A, it should also have a subheading marked B; if it has a 1, it should also have a 2.

INCOMPLETE   II. Household appliances
                   A. Washing machines
              III. Pain relievers

Unless another subheading is added under the main heading II in the example above, the main heading itself should be revised to read simply "Washing machines." The third main heading in the outline would then be revised to name another specific type of product.

32f

Check the outline for the formal details of notation and indention and for parallel structure.

(1) In the outline use one system of notation consistently, and indent subheadings to indicate degrees of subordination.

Any intelligible system of notation is acceptable. The one used for both the topic outline and the sentence outline in 32c is in common use and may well be adopted. This system, expanded to show subheadings of the second and third degrees, is as follows:

I. . . . .   [Used for major headings]
    A. . . . .   [Used for subheadings
    B. . . . .   of the first degree]
        1. . . . .   [Used for subheadings
        2. . . . .   of the second degree]
            a. . . . .   [Used for subheadings
            b. . . . .   of the third degree]
II. . . . .

Seldom, however, will a short outline—or even a longer one—need subordination beyond the first or second degree.

The indention, as well as the notation, should indicate the degree of subordination. Major headings (I, II, III, and so on) should be aligned, subheadings of the first degree (A, B, C, and so on) should be indented equally, subheadings of the second degree (1, 2, 3, and so on) should be indented more, and subheadings of the third degree (a, b, c, and so on) should be indented still more. If a heading or subheading runs beyond the end of the line, it is given "hanging" indention, as shown in the topic and sentence outlines on page 381.

(2) Use parallel structure for parallel parts of the topic outline to clarify the coordination of parts. For a full discussion of parallel structure, see Section **26**.

PARALLEL STRUCTURES

  I. The weakness of the protesters' verbal attacks
 II. The crudeness of the protesters' rhetoric of physical violence
                     [Nouns and prepositional phrases]
    A. French Revolution made important by effectively expressed principles
    B. American Revolution revived by brilliant words
                    [Nouns and participial phrases]

In topic outlines, the major headings (I, II, III, and so on) should be expressed in parallel structure, as should each group of subheadings. But it is unnecessary to strive for parallel structure between different groups of subheadings—for example, between A, B, and C under I and A, B, and C under II. (Parallel structure is not a concern in either the sentence outline or the paragraph outline.)

■ **Exercise 3** Make an outline (of the type specified by your instructor) on one of the subjects you used for Exercise 1 on page 378. Then check your outline against the principles set forth in 32d–f.

32g
Write the paper from the outline.

Once you have checked your outline to make sure that it covers the subject (see **32d**), that it is logically arranged (see **32e**), and that it has proper notation, indention, and parallel structure (see **32f**), you are ready to write the paper. Simply write a series of effective paragraphs (with good transitions between them: see **31b(6)**) to cover all items in the outline, taking up each item in the order in which it appears in the outline. The actual writing of the paper may very well suggest a better arrangement for some of the details covered by the outline.

Notice how the following essay is related to the sample outlines on pages 381–82.

Violent Protest: A Debased Language

1   Words, like trees, bend with the prevailing winds. In the climate of opinion of the past few years, the word *dissent* has undergone a decided transformation. For most of our history, it clearly meant speech—the unorthodox opinion, the challenging idea. Then, during the 1960s, civil rights protesters took to the streets to fight segregation, and the word became associated with demonstrations as much as with speech. As protests have continued to broaden and increase, *dissent* has come to be used to describe and defend a wide variety of physical acts, including violence toward property and even toward people. The explanation many protesters offer for their switch from verbal to physical dissent is that no one pays attention to words alone any longer. However eloquent it has been, however imaginative its uses, language has not succeeded in eliminating racial discrimination or ending the war in Indochina. So the protesters have resorted to what Franklyn Haiman of Northwestern University calls "body rhetoric"—sit-ins, lie-ins, marches—and more and more bodies have started colliding. Such public confrontations are an expression of gathering frustration over a society that no longer seems to respond to more traditional forms of dissent.

2   This argument contains a measure of truth. It is also true that in many cases the massed forces of dissent—as at most rallies mourning the Kent State four—have demonstrated a commendable restraint in not letting verbal protest build into violence. The fact remains, however, that all too often these days dissent is a matter of arson and rock throwing. The reason may be that protesters have despaired of the efficacy of words before they have really mastered them. It is significant that this generation of dissenters has failed to produce a literature, or even a polemic that is likely to endure. On the contrary, it has been persistently, even proudly, nonverbal. It has emphasized a communication of feeling rather than of words. The vocabulary of protest, often weighted down with an outmoded Marxism, is relentlessly conventional and conformist. The same phrases—"up against the wall," "get the pigs," "tell it like it is"—are endlessly repeated, less for their intrinsic eloquence than for their emotive and symbolic value. And that sort of thing gets tiresome; to borrow from the jargon, it "turns people off." Even the most outrageous obscenities lose their impact when they are used ad nauseam.

3   There is often a disconcerting inexactness about today's rhetoric of dissent. To denounce the Establishment in blanket terms makes little sense in a society composed of several establishments, each with its own ideology and set of mores—many of them surprisingly competitive. "Power to the people" is an admirable democratic slogan—except that, as used presently, what it really seems to mean is power to the leftist radicals who seek to control any revolution in America. It is verbal overkill to describe every mild demurral by whites against the most bluntly radical of black-militant demands as nothing but "racism." And the case for political dissent is weakened when almost any attempts, however peaceful, by college authorities to restore law and order on campus are automatically condemned by militant radicals as proof that the United States is a "fascist Amerika." Taken at face value, many protest slogans suggest that the dissenters have seriously misestimated our society and its possibility for evolutionary change.

4   The ultimate debasement of language, of course, is violence. Except for protesters who simply want to destroy—and there are more than a few—most dissenters turn to violence in a desperate effort to communicate their profound feelings of grievance. Yet surely this is too crude a way to get their message across. A bomb, for example, lacks specificity; its meaning is as scattered as its debris. Some people may interpret such an act as a signal to pay more attention to the protester and his cause; many more are likely to read into it a need to make life a lot tougher for the protester. Violence is, essentially, a confession of ultimate in-articulateness.

5 Throughout history, dissent has been more effectively expressed by the word than by the weapon. The French Revolution was betrayed by the ruthless masters of the Terror who silenced all opposition with the guillotine. The enduring importance of the revolution lies, rather, in the principles enunciated on its behalf by the philosophers of the Enlightenment, who bequeathed the notion of human equality to the modern world. During its bleakest hours, the American Revolution was resuscitated not so much by brilliant military strategy as by brilliant words—those of Tom Paine in the "times that try men's souls." Even less persuasive and more recondite words can have an impact that dramatic acts do not. Wrote Lord Keynes: "Madmen in authority, who hear voices in the air, are distilling their frenzy from some academic scribbler of a few years back. I am sure that the power of vested interests is vastly exaggerated compared with the gradual encroachment of ideas."

6 Reactionary as the thought may seem, words are still as powerful a force as ever, when they are cogently used. During a period of national turmoil and self-doubt, it is all the more imperative for protesters to put down their rocks and find their voices again. Today the nation is in considerable need of healing, as well as elevating, language; often in the past that need has been filled by protesters whose perspective on society matched their passionate commitment to its improvement. Now is the time for dissenters to assert their own dignity and maintain their tradition by upholding the ultimate value of the word.

—Editors of TIME[1]

---

[1]From "Violent Protest: A Debased Language," *Time*, May 18, 1970. Extracted from *Time*, The Weekly Newsmagazine; Copyright Time Inc. 1970. Reprinted by permission.

(1) The paragraphs in relation to the outline

Although the paragraphs must develop the headings (including the subheadings) of the outline in the exact order in which they appear in the outline, there is no rule regarding the number of these headings that a paragraph may cover. In a general way, however, the writer is limited by the need to make each paragraph a unit and to keep it from being too short or too long. Let us notice, for example, how the six paragraphs of "Violent Protest: A Debased Language" are related to the topic outline on page 381.

Paragraphs	Relation to outline
1	Introduction
2	I and subheading A
3	Subheading B
4	II
5	III and subheadings A and B
6	Conclusion

Since each paragraph in the body of a composition (such as paragraphs 2 through 5 above) should be easily identified with a main heading or subheading in the outline, the writer may wish to revise his outline to make it correspond more exactly with his organization into paragraphs.

■ **Exercise 4** Carefully read the essay on pages 388–90 in preparation for a class discussion of (1) the selection and limitation of the subject, (2) the purpose of the writer, (3) the choice of the title, (4) the development of the central idea, (5) the arrangement of main points, and (6) the transitions between ideas.

■ **Exercise 5** First make an outline; then write a brief essay on one of the following topics (or on any other topic assigned by your instructor).

1. the language of music (OR of animals)
2. the change in the meaning of the word *democracy* (OR of the word *hero*)

3. the need for new words on campus
4. what habits of language reveal about a speaker
5. the rhetoric of evangelists (OR of politicians)

(2) Effective beginnings and endings

Although formal introductions and conclusions are often not necessary for short papers, every composition should have an effective beginning and ending.

Beginnings   There are two ways to begin a composition effectively. One way is to begin with a sentence that not only arouses the reader's interest but also starts the development of the topic by discussing the first main point in the outline. The second way is to begin with a formal introduction (often only one paragraph). This arouses the reader's interest and introduces the central idea of the paper but does not start the development of the topic. Sometimes the limitations of the subject are defined in a formal introduction. The choice of the type of beginning depends upon the nature of the topic and the length of the composition.

Whichever method you use, remember that an effective beginning gains the reader's interest. One of the easiest and best ways to gain interest is to use specific facts and details instead of generalizations: see **20a(2)** and **31d**. Compare the effectiveness of the following two introductions:

Topic: A solution for the overpopulation problem

GENERAL

I have a solution for the overpopulation problem. The usual methods of controlling population have disadvantages of one kind or another. My solution is not only different from but also better than the familiar solutions.

SPECIFIC

I have a solution for the overpopulation problem. Unlike the Pill, it has no side effects. Unlike abortion, it does not offend anyone with religious scruples. Unlike war, it requires no bloodshed. It is painless, humane, and eminently sensible.

—RICHARD ARMOUR[2]

Another way to arouse interest is to refer to some common experience (such as shyness on a first date, an encounter with an eccentric door-to-door salesman, a clumsy slip of the tongue on an important occasion, the joy of winning a game or a special honor)—an experience that the reader will probably associate with himself.

Title: Cable Television: Birth of a New Giant?

Every investor dreams of getting rich by discovering relatively small companies that later mature into flourishing giants. Some investment experts believe they have found such a group of corporate sprouts in the CATV—the community antenna or cable television—industry.   —CHANGING TIMES[3]

A third way to gain the interest of the reader is to point out one or more striking facts.

Title: The Zoo Story

There are eight times as many known paintings by Rembrandt as there are whooping cranes and California condors together, and it is safe to say that more living Americans have seen the work of this seventeenth-century Dutch painter than one of these spectacular native birds. But rarities aside, how many people living in Chicago or New York have ever seen a wild otter, a fox, or an American elk? How many have seen a bullfrog, a box turtle, or a ruby-throated hummingbird?

[2]From "A Small Solution" by Richard Armour, in Martin Levin's "Phoenix Nest," *Saturday Review,* November 14, 1970. Copyright 1970 Saturday Review, Inc. Reprinted by permission.

[3]From "Cable Television: Birth of a New Giant?" Reprinted by permission from *Changing Times,* the Kiplinger Magazine (November 1970 issue). Copyright 1970 by The Kiplinger Washington Editors, Inc., 1729 H. Street, N.W., Washington, D.C. 20006.

A proportionately decreasing number of Americans will ever see any wild animals outside of zoos. This is a bleak, unpleasant prospect. But it is difficult to dispute and has many implications; one is that the role and development of zoos are worth a new look. —WILLIAM G. CONWAY[4]

Another method of capturing interest is to begin with an interesting incident or anecdote that is closely related to the topic.

Title: The Elusive Dr. Szilard

At a party in a university community a few weeks ago the guests amused themselves by drawing up a list of men who have played unique roles in recent history. They finally agreed upon five who had done things which could not have been accomplished, in their times, by anybody else. The first four are familiar to everybody—Lincoln, Gandhi, Hitler, and Churchill. But the fifth might puzzle even many well-informed people. It was Leo Szilard. —ALICE KIMBALL[5]

Still another method is to refute an opinion that is commonly held.

Title: The Lunar Soil

The lunar landscape is not dominated by jagged rocky ridges, as were so often depicted in the illustrations accompanying articles and science fiction of past decades. Indeed, barren rock is all but absent from the surface of the moon; the observations of both manned and unmanned missions have revealed everywhere a rolling, hummocky terrain of plowed-up "soil"—more properly a loose, unconsolidated material mechanically similar to terrestrial soil. The lunar landscape resembles nothing so much as a World War I battlefield after intensive artillery bombardment, and for good

---

[4] From "The Zoo Story" by William G. Conway, *Natural History,* December 1968. Reprinted by permission.

[5] From "The Elusive Dr. Szilard" by Alice Kimball, *Harper's Magazine,* July 1960. Reprinted by permission.

reason: both kinds of terrain have been tortured by a rain of explosive projectiles. —JOHN A. WOOD[6]

Closely related to this approach is the "straw man" technique: someone else's views are set up to be knocked down.

Title: Freedom: Who Needs It?

"Individuality is the aim of political liberty," James Fenimore Cooper wrote in 1838, in *The American Democrat,* and a decade later, in his *Civil Disobedience,* Henry David Thoreau insisted that "there will never be a really free and enlightened state until the state comes to recognize the individual as a higher and independent power, from which all its power and authority are derived, and treats him accordingly."

How wrong—how mistaken in prophecy—our American moralists have been! . . . —RICHARD ROVERE[7]

An effective beginning introduces a subject and is therefore directly related to it. As you read the following paragraph (written by a student), notice the repetition of the key words of the title: *Carousel, new, experience.* In the last sentence the controlling idea of the composition is given. Such an introduction is closely related to the topic and contributes to the unity of the whole composition.

Title: Carousel—A New Experience

All of us enjoy wearing a new pair of shoes, eating a dish we have not had before, seeing a movie with an unusual plot, or touring in a new section of the country; in other words, we like experiences which are novel, different. I happen to be one of those people who enjoy discovering an unfamiliar

---

[6] From "The Lunar Soil" by John A. Wood, *Scientific American,* August 1970. Copyright © 1970 by Scientific American, Inc. All rights reserved. Reprinted by permission.

[7] From "Freedom: Who Needs It?" by Richard Rovere, *Atlantic Monthly,* May 1968. Copyright © 1968 by The Atlantic Monthly Company, Boston, Mass. Reprinted with permission.

poem by a famous poet, reading a good book, or attending a choral or band concert. I like new and different cultural outlets, and a few weeks ago my English assignment brought me face to face with just such an experience: Carousel, theater-in-the-round. The play which I attended was an Irish drama by Paul Vincent Carroll, entitled *Shadow and Substance*, and I should like to use it as the vehicle in my description of Carousel itself—the interior of the theater, the actors, the techniques used.

Caution: Do not write aimless, dull introductions. If you have difficulty writing an interesting and pertinent introductory paragraph that contributes to the effectiveness of your whole composition, then begin immediately with a discussion of your first main point.

Title: Characteristics of a Nonconformist

One of the distinguishing characteristics of a nonconformist is his great respect for the freedom of the individual. For example, ...

■ **Exercise 6** Evaluate the effectiveness of the following beginnings of student papers.

1. *Title:* Protest in the 1970's

In "The Hollow Men," T. S. Eliot said that the world would end with a whimper, not a bang. In the noisy 1970's only a deaf man could agree with Eliot. It is possible that pollution will suffocate us, that guerrilla warfare will mutilate us, that our enemies will try to exterminate us. If so, we will protest. We will fight, kick, shriek. No matter how our world ends, we will not go down with a whimper.

2. *Title:* Justice in *The Unvanquished*

Justice is a word with many applications and definitions. This point is well illustrated in *The Unvanquished*, a novel of Civil War times by William Faulkner. Justice, as practiced by Faulkner's characters, takes on many forms; indeed, the meaning of the word is warped to suit any occasion that may arise. Applications of justice may range all the way from mouth soaping to murder; many different situations call for different forms of justice.

Loosh, the old Negro slave, felt that he was justified in tearing down Bayard's and Ringo's model of the city of Vicksburg. . . .

Endings   A composition should end; it should not merely stop. Two ways to end a composition effectively are to stress the final point of the main discussion by using an emphatic last sentence and to write a strong concluding paragraph. Often a concluding paragraph clinches, restates, or stresses the importance of the central idea or thesis of the composition: see the concluding paragraph of "Violent Protest: A Debased Language," pages 388–90. When the body of a composition describes an experiment or presents evidence, the conclusion often presents a discovery or a theory.

Topic: The nature of dreams

These and other findings suggest that our dream experiences do in fact reflect our personalities. If, as I believe, dreams serve as mirrors of the self, then the use of dream-content analysis offers a fascinating look at the structure of the psyche.   —R. L. VAN DE CASTLE[8]

If the title of an essay poses a question, the conclusion may give a direct answer or may indicate that there is no pat answer.

Title: Are Teachers Fair to Boys?

Unhappily, in too many of the nation's female-oriented schools we are still planting the seeds which may be making millions of Johnnies low-achievers, dropouts, truants, delinquents, and maladjusted members of society.

—JACK HARRISON POLLACK[9]

---

[8] From "His, Hers and the Children's" by R. L. Van de Castle, *Psychology Today*, June 1970. Copyright © Communications/Research/Machines, Inc. Reprinted by permission.

[9] From "Are Teachers Fair to Boys?" by Jack Harrison Pollack, *Today's Health*, April 1968. Published by the American Medical Association.

Title: New York: Dream or Nightmare?

And so the dream struggles against the nightmare, Fun City against Fear City. Neither label is real, but people do not necessarily live and act on facts. What counts is what people believe, and New York's crisis has become one of crumbling faith in the city.   —GERALD ASTOR[10]

Effective endings often consist of relevant incidents or anecdotes that the reader is likely to remember.

Topic: The extermination of the prairie dog

The men poured grain from the sacks into bags, slung these over their shoulders, and moved into the meadow. Small earthen craters were scattered over the hillside, and here and there prairie dogs could be seen running through the grass to their holes. Their warning calls sounded from all sides as the men approached. An owl rose, battling the wind. Lemm and McDaniel walked through the nodding heads of grass, ankle-high and dotted with blue flowers. The sky was beautifully clear, the sun benevolent and warm. The wind pressed the grass into silver waves ahead of the work crew, who were now walking from crater to crater on a methodical course, dropping poisoned oats from long-handled spoons as though they were leaving a tiny gift on each doorstep. The prairie dogs had disappeared. "They don't come out and eat right away," McDaniel said. "But if you come back later and watch, you'll see 'em feeding. Then, all of a sudden, you'll hear that little ol' dog scream, and see him head for his hole."   —FAITH McNULTY[11]

Often a concluding paragraph summarizes the main points of the discussion.

---

[10] From "New York: Dream or Nightmare?" by Gerald Astor, *Look*, April 1, 1969. Reprinted by permission.

[11] From "The Prairie Dog and the Black-Footed Ferret," copyright © 1970 by Faith McNulty, originally published in the *New Yorker* magazine from the book *Must They Die?* by Faith McNulty. Reprinted by permission of Doubleday & Company, Inc., and McIntosh and Otis, Inc.

Topic: The role of the machine

One is confronted, then, by the fact that the machine is ambivalent. It is both an instrument of liberation and one of repression. It has economized human energy and it has misdirected it. It has created a wide framework of order and it has produced muddle and chaos. It has nobly served human purposes and it has distorted and denied them.

—LEWIS MUMFORD[12.]

An effective ending may also present a pertinent and thought-provoking question or quotation, a timely suggestion or challenge.

Topic: Euthanasia as a human necessity

Euthanasia has been called "pagan" and "indecent." One may well ask, which is better—pagan mercifulness, indecent compassion, or devout inhumanity?   —HARRY BENJAMIN[13]

Topic: Consumers and deceptive packaging

Efforts at industry self-government directed toward higher ethical standards are, of course, laudable and welcome. But consumers probably would do well to continue to hope, and to urge, that all existing Governmental agencies which exercise regulatory powers in this area—including the FTC, the FDA, certain divisions of the Department of Agriculture, and the Treasury's alcohol-control agency—will, in the future, act with more vigor and with a greater awareness of consumer needs.   —CONSUMER REPORTS[14]

Or an ending may present a solution to a problem.

---

[12] From *Technics and Civilization* by Lewis Mumford. Published by Harcourt Brace Jovanovich, Inc., and Martin Secker & Warburg Limited, 1934. Reprinted by permission.

[13] From "Euthanasia—A Human Necessity" by Harry Benjamin, *The Nation,* January 28, 1950.

[14] From *Consumer Reports,* January 1961. By permission of Consumers Union, Mount Vernon, New York, a non-profit organization.

Topic: American doctors who are barred from hospitals

What will help to solve the complicated and disturbing problem, he [John G. Steinle, management consultant to hospitals] says, is a greater public awareness of the role of the hospital as a community institution and a willingness on the part of the public to become involved in the management of its community affairs. Such a force of informed public opinion can right more wrongs than any laws devised.
—ROLAND H. BERG[15]

Caution: Do not devote too much space to introductions and conclusions. A short paper often has only one paragraph for a beginning or an ending; frequently one sentence for each is adequate. Remember that the bulk of your composition should be the development of the central idea, the discussion of the main headings and subheadings in your outline.

■ **Exercise 7**   In a magazine recommended by your instructor, find and copy a good short conclusion to an article. Be prepared to explain why the conclusion is effective and how it is related to the central idea of the article.

■ **Exercise 8**   Giving special attention to the beginning and ending, write a composition based on the outline you prepared for Exercise 3 on page 387.

■ **Exercise 9**   Proofread and revise the composition you wrote for Exercise 5 on pages 391–92, using the Proofreader's Check List on pages 86–87.

■ **Exercise 10**   Prepare for a class discussion of the following outline and composition, which were written by a college freshman. Be prepared to support your comments by referring to parts of this section (**32a–g**).

---

[15]From "Why Hospitals Lock Out Doctors" by Roland H. Berg, *Look*, January 17, 1961. Reprinted by permission.

Mayville

Central idea: Visiting such familiar landmarks as Dr. Weaver's drugstore, the old fire hall, and Mel Tanner's service station proved to me that Mayville was still the same quiet, sleepy little town I had left.

Introduction: Mayville as seen from a train window

I. Weaver's Drugs
   A. Characteristics sixteen years ago
   B. Characteristics at time of visit
II. Mayville Fire Hall
III. Tanner's Gulf Service
   A. Building and property
   B. Action going on at station

Conclusion: The small, quiet town, almost extinct

1   The trip from Lenox City had been a long and tiring one. As I peered through the blackened train window, Mayville came into view. From a distance it seemed even smaller than it actually is: it appeared only as a few boxes scattered beside the thin black line that is the railroad track. Then the conductor cried, "Mayville, all out for Mayville!" As the train huffed and lurched to a halt in front of the station, I took my single bag and stepped out onto the wooden platform in front of the train station; then, draping my coat over my arm, I walked toward town.

2   There were few cars on the Mayville streets and no noise or clamor to break the stillness of the air. (It was the same quiet, sleepy little town I had left sixteen years before.) On the right stood Dr. Weaver's corner drugstore, its white plaster face cracked with wrinkles of age. The drugstore was always a place to go after school for a milkshake or a Coke. It would be so crowded with school children that Dr. Weaver could hardly get around to take orders and to speak to his young friends. When the children left, the drugstore fell into a deep silence broken only by the clinking of glasses as Dr. Weaver cleaned off the counter and the two small tables by the window. The drugstore

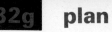

was just as it had been then. The black tile floor was as spotless as ever, and the black countertop shone like a mirror, reflecting the stacks of clean glasses on the shelf above. The wooden stools in front of the counter were worn from many pairs of blue jeans, and the brass rail was scuffed by countless shoes. The door hinges creaked as I left, just as I knew they would.

3   Across the street from the drugstore stood the Mayville Fire Hall. The old red brick building stood tall and erect as if indifferent to age, and the two doors facing the street were open. The antiquated fire engine had seen very little action and was covered with dust. On the pale green plaster wall hung buckets, axes, and hoses, all waiting in readiness. Everyone must have been out to lunch, for beside the fire engine stood a small table on which lay an unfinished checker game. The glass in the side window that Billy Joe Jacobs and I had broken when we were about twelve had not been replaced, and Chief Hansen's office door still lacked a doorknob. Brushing aside the cobwebs, I walked on out the back door.

4   Across the corner was Mel Tanner's Gulf Station, where I worked for three summers pumping gas and being an all-around junior grease monkey. High on the high building were orange metal letters spelling Tanner's Gulf Service. But the *V* in "service" had blown away during a storm one summer (before I ever worked there) and had never been replaced. Two stark gas pumps stood alone, projecting from the sea of concrete in front of the station. The often malfunctioning cold drink machine was creased and scarred from the kicks of disgruntled or persistent customers. Mel, unexpectedly aged, was leaning against the wall in a chair and smoking his pipe. A few cans of oil and one or two headlamps were stacked haphazardly on the metal shelves behind him, and a new set of tires for the old Ford service truck lay on the green concrete floor in front of his desk. Monte was in the back washing Mrs. Gillian's old Mercury and singing happily to himself. The grease-covered service rack was empty, and the tools from the open box were scattered on the wooden counter. Jumbled inside a rusted oil drum were discarded oil filter boxes, used paper towels, and a chamois, now beyond further use.

5   Saying good-by to Mel and Monte, I walked to the hotel and rented a room. The few restful days I spent in Mayville seemed more an escape than a vacation. With the world in a constant rush and everyone struggling to industrialize and urbanize all the Mayvilles in the world, it occurred to me that before many years the peace and quiet will vanish with the death of the small town. And there will no longer be any asylum for a homesick and tired assistant vice-president.   —BAYARD TARPLEY[16]

---

[16]By Bayard Tarpley. Reprinted by permission of the Department of English, The University of Tennessee.

Library Paper

33

Learn how to prepare a library paper.

A library paper (sometimes called a research or term paper) is usually a formal, well-documented composition based for the most part on outside readings. These readings may be from various books in the library or from a collection of essays on a specific subject, a collection commonly called a *sourcebook*. The usual steps in writing a library paper are as follows:

a   Select and limit a subject.
b   Prepare a bibliography.
c   Develop an outline.
d   Take notes on readings.
e   Write a properly documented paper.

33a
Select and limit a subject.

If you do not know how to select an appropriate subject and to limit it properly, review **32a**. How much you limit a subject for a library paper depends not only upon the assigned length but also upon the materials available in your library or sourcebook.

GENERAL   Symbols in literature
LIMITED   Symbols in Romantic poetry
MORE LIMITED   Symbols in *The Rime of the Ancient Mariner*
EVEN MORE LIMITED   The albatross as a symbol in *The Rime of the Ancient Mariner*

Report or thesis   The type of library paper you write will depend upon your purpose. Suppose, for example, that you have chosen the subject "The Meaning of Dreams." If you develop your subject by an organized presentation of the opinions of experts, like Jung and Adler, you will be writing a *report* paper. You may, however, wish to prove or disprove an opinion or theory. If you wish to convince your reader that dreams are significantly related to conscious behavior, that they are not merely mirrors of subconscious fears or wishes, you will be writing a *thesis* paper. Although with either purpose you should be able to write an effective paper, the purpose you select will influence your collecting of facts and should therefore be determined as soon as possible.

■ **Exercise 1**   List three general fields in which you have some interest. Then by the process of limitation derive three topics (1) that are suitable for library papers of from one to three thousand words each and (2) that especially interest you. The subject headings and the cross references in the library card catalog or the *Readers' Guide* (see 33b below) may suggest subjects and possible ways of limiting them. Determine, if possible, whether each topic lends itself to development as a report or as a thesis.

33b

Prepare a bibliography in acceptable form.

The bibliography lists sources of information—such as books, pamphlets, and articles—from which you will draw the material for your paper. Use the card catalog, indexes to periodicals, and reference books (as explained on the following pages) to make a preliminary bibliography by writing down the most promising titles you can find. Copy each title on a separate card (generally 3 × 5 inches) in an acceptable form: see page 417. You should keep these cards in alphabetical order until you complete your paper, adding useful titles as you find them and discarding those that prove useless. The final bibliography, to be typed at the end of your paper, will most often include only the works that help in the actual writing—usually those cited in the footnotes.

(1) Use the card catalog.

The card catalog is the index to the whole library. It lists all books and all bound magazines, whether they are housed in the stacks, on the open shelves of the reference room, or in any other part of the building. In many libraries one general card catalog lists all books owned by the university and shows whether the book is in the general library or in a special collection in another building.

Usually the card catalog consists of cards arranged alphabetically in drawers. These may be "author" cards, "title" cards, or "subject" cards, for in most libraries each book is listed alphabetically, once according to its author, again according to its title, and again according to its subject or subjects. These cards (usually printed) are identical except that the title card and the subject card have extra, typewritten headings.

(2) Use indexes to periodicals.

When preparing your bibliography, remember that the periodical indexes do for articles what the card catalog does for books in the library. You will probably find the *Readers' Guide* (an index to over one hundred periodicals) the most useful of these indexes. You may have occasion, however, to use others from the following list.

SAMPLE CATALOG CARDS

```
QH          Since Silent spring.                                    ———————TITLE CARD
75     Graham, Frank, 1925–
.G68        Since Silent spring.  Boston, Houghton-Mifflin, 1970.
```

```
            PESTICIDES AND THE ENVIRONMENT                          ———SUBJECT CARDS
QH
75     Graham, Frank, 1925–
.G68        Since Silent spring.  Boston, Houghton-Mifflin, 1970.
```

```
            CARSON, RACHEL LOUISE
                 SILENT SPRING
QH
75     Graham, Frank, 1925–                                         ———AUTHOR CARD
.G68        Since Silent spring.  Boston, Houghton-Mifflin, 1970.
```

```
                                                                    ——Call number
QH
75     Graham, Frank, 1925–                                         ——Author's name and
.G68        Since Silent spring.  Boston, Houghton-Mifflin, 1970.       date of birth
            xvi, 388 p.  22 cm.  6.95                                 Title, with
            Includes bibliographical references.                         publication data
                                                                      Description of book

            1. Pesticides and the environment.  2. Carson, Rachel Louise.   ——Headings under
       Silent spring.   I. Title.                                              which the book
            QH75.G68            ( )        632′.95        77-82948              is cataloged
                                                          MARC
            Library of Congress        70 ₍30-2₎
```

Indexes to Periodicals

General

Poole's Index. 1802–1906. (Subject index only)
Nineteenth Century Readers' Guide. 1890–99. (Author, subject)
Readers' Guide. 1900—. (Author, title, subject)
Book Review Digest. 1905—. (Author, title, subject)
International Index. 1907–65. Succeeded by *Social Sciences and Humanities Index.* 1965—. (Author, subject)
New York Times Index. 1913—. (A useful guide for finding the dates of important events, which can then be looked up in all other newspapers)

Special

Agricultural Index. 1916–64. Succeeded by *Biological and Agricultural Index.* 1964—. (Subject)

Art Index. 1929—. (Author, subject)
Bibliographic Index. 1937—. (Subject)
Biography Index. 1946—. (Subject)
Book Review Index. 1965—. (Title)
Catholic Periodical Index. 1930—. (Subject)
Education Index. 1929—. (Author, subject)
Engineering Index. 1884—. (Subject)
Index Medicus. 1879–1926. Succeeded by *Quarterly Cumulative Index Medicus.* 1927—. (Author, subject)
Index to Book Reviews in the Humanities. 1960—. (Title)
Index to Legal Periodicals. 1908—. (Author, subject)
Industrial Arts Index. 1913–57. Succeeded by *Applied Science and Technology Index.* 1958—. *Business Periodicals Index.* 1958—. (Subject)
Music Index. 1949—. (Subject)
Public Affairs Information Service. 1915—. (Subject)
Technical Book Review Index. 1917–29; 1935—. (Title)

See also the various abstracts, such as *Biological Abstracts,* 1926—; *Chemical Abstracts,* 1907—; *Psychological Abstracts,* 1927—.

(3) Use reference books.

Dictionaries, encyclopedias, atlases, and other books especially helpful for reference are usually kept on the open shelves of the reference room, where students may use them directly without having to request that they be brought from the stacks. Each of these books is listed in the card catalog, and the call number will often help you to find the book. You should learn the general location of the chief classes of reference books in order that you may turn to them without loss of time. For a detailed list of such books, with a short description of each, consult Constance M. Winchell's *Guide to Reference Books* (8th ed.; Supplements, 1966–68). Since many reference books, especially some of the encyclopedias, are kept up to date by frequent revisions, you should remember to cite the latest copyright date of the edition you are using. A few of the more important reference books are listed on the following pages (with abbreviated bibliographical information).

Reference Books

General dictionaries (unabridged)

A *Dictionary of American English on Historical Principles.* 4 vols.
  1938–44.
Century Dictionary and Cyclopedia. 12 vols. 1911. 3 vols. 1927–33.
New Standard Dictionary of the English Language. 1947, 1952,
  1966.
The Oxford English Dictionary. 13 vols. 1933. Originally issued
  as *A New English Dictionary on Historical Principles.* 10 vols.
  and Supplement. 1888–1933.
The Random House Dictionary of the English Language. 1966.
Webster's Third New International Dictionary. 1961.

Special dictionaries

Evans, Bergen and Cornelia. *A Dictionary of Contemporary
  American Usage.* 1957.
Fowler, H. W. *Dictionary of Modern American Usage.* 2nd ed.
  Rev. Sir Ernest Gowers. 1965.
Hayakawa, S. I., and the Funk & Wagnalls dictionary staff. *Modern
  Guide to Synonyms and Related Words.* 1968.
Lewis, Norman. *The New Roget's Thesaurus.* 1965.
Major, Clarence. *Dictionary of Afro-American Slang.* 1970.
Nicholson, Margaret. *A Dictionary of American-English Usage.*
  1957. (Based on Fowler)
Partridge, Eric. *Dictionary of Slang and Unconventional English.*
  5th ed. 1961.
Roget's International Thesaurus. 3rd ed. 1962.
Webster's Dictionary of Synonyms. 1942.
Wright, Joseph. *English Dialect Dictionary.* 6 vols. 1961.

General encyclopedias

Chambers's Encyclopædia. 15 vols.
Collier's Encyclopedia. 23 vols.
Encyclopedia Americana. 30 vols.
Encyclopædia Britannica. 24 vols.
Encyclopedia International. 20 vols.

Special encyclopedias

Adams, J. T. *Dictionary of American History.* 6 vols. 1940—. Concise version. 1962.

Buttrick, George Arthur. *Interpreter's Dictionary of the Bible.* 4 vols. 1962.

Edwards, Paul. *Encyclopedia of Philosophy.* 8 vols. 1967.

Encyclopædia of the Social Sciences. 15 vols. in 8. 1967.

Encyclopedia of World Art. 1959—.

Graham, Irvin. *Encyclopedia of Advertising.* 2nd ed. 1969.

Grove's Dictionary of Music and Musicians. 9 vols. 1954. Supplement. 1961.

Harris, Chester W. *Encyclopedia of Educational Research.* 1960.

Hastings, James. *Encyclopædia of Religion and Ethics.* 13 vols. 1908–27.

Langer, William L. *An Encyclopedia of World History.* 4th ed. 1968.

McGraw-Hill Encyclopedia of Science and Technology. 15 vols. 1966.

McGraw-Hill Encyclopedia of Space. 1968.

McLaughlin, A. C., and A. B. Hart. *Cyclopedia of American Government.* 3 vols. 1914; rpt. 1949.

Meetham, A. R. *Encyclopædia of Linguistics, Information, and Control.* 1969.

Munn, Glenn G. *Encyclopedia of Banking and Finance.* 6th ed. 1962.

New Catholic Encyclopedia. 14 vols. 1967.

Thompson, O. *International Cyclopedia of Music and Musicians.* 9th ed. 1964.

Werblowsky, Raphael Jehudah Zwi, and Geoffrey Wigoder. *Encyclopedia of the Jewish Religion.* 1966.

Worldmark Encyclopedia of the Nations. 5 vols. 1963.

Atlases and gazetteers

Collier's New World Atlas and Gazetteer. 1953.

Columbia Lippincott Gazetteer of the World. 1952.

Encyclopædia Britannica World Atlas. 1962.

Hammond's Ambassador World Atlas. 1954.

Rand-McNally Commercial Atlas. 1962. (Revised annually)

Times (London) *Atlas of the World.* Comprehensive ed. 1967.

Webster's Geographical Dictionary. Rev. ed. 1962.
Urban Atlas: 20 American Cities. 1966.

Yearbooks—current events

Americana Annual. 1923—.
Annual Register. 1758—.
Britannica Book of the Year. 1938—.
Economic Almanac. 1940—.
Facts on File. 1940—.
Information Please Almanac. 1947—.
New International Year Book. 1907—.
Statesman's Year-Book. 1864—.
Statistical Abstract of the United States. 1878—.
Whitaker's Almanack. 1869—.
World Almanac. 1868—.

Biography

Contemporary Authors. 1963—. (Published semiannually)
Current Biography. 1940—.
Dictionary of American Biography. 20 vols. and Index. 1928–43. (Supplements to date)
Dictionary of International Biography. 1963—.
Dictionary of National Biography (British). 22 vols. 1908–09. (Indexes and supplements to date)
International Who's Who. 1935—.
Kunitz, S. J., and Howard Haycraft. *American Authors, 1600–1900.* 1938.
Two Thousand Women of Achievement. 1969—. (Published annually)
Who's Who. 1848—.
Who's Who in America. 1899—.
Who's Who of American Women. 1958—.
Who Was Who in America. 3 vols. 1897–1960.

Literature—mythology

Aken, Andreas R. *The Encyclopedia of Classical Mythology.* 1965.
Bartlett's Familiar Quotations. 14th ed. 1968.

Bateson, F. W. *Cambridge Bibliography of English Literature.*
 5 vols. 1941–57.
Benét, William Rose. *The Reader's Encyclopedia.* 2nd ed. 1965.
Brewer's Dictionary of Phrase and Fable. 1953.
Cambridge History of American Literature. 3 vols. in 1. 1943.
Cambridge History of English Literature. 15 vols. 1932.
Evans, Bergen. *Dictionary of Quotations.* 1968.
Fiction Catalog. 7th ed. 1960. (Supplements)
Frazer, Sir James G. *The Golden Bough.* 3rd ed. 13 vols. 1955.
Gayley, C. M. *Classic Myths in English Literature and in Art.*
 1939.
Granger, Edith. *Index to Poetry.* 5th ed. 1962. (Supplements)
Hart, James D. *Oxford Companion to American Literature.* 4th
 ed. 1965.
Harvey, Sir Paul. *Oxford Companion to Classical Literature.* 1937.
———. *Oxford Companion to English Literature.* 4th ed. 1967.
Modern Humanities Research Association. *Annual Bibliography
 of English Language and Literature.* 1920—.
Mythology of All Races. 13 vols. 1916–32.
Oxford Classical Dictionary. 1949.
Sears, Minnie Earl, and Marian Shaw. *Essay and General Litera-
 ture Index.* 1900—.
Short Story Index. 1953. (Supplements)
Spender, Stephen. *Concise Encyclopedia of English and American
 Poets and Poetry.* 1963.
Spiller, Robert E., et al. *Literary History of the United States.*
 3rd ed. 2 vols. 1963. (Useful bibliographies)
Thrall, William Flint, Addison Hibbard, and C. Hugh Holman.
 A Handbook to Literature. 1960.
Zimmerman, John Edward. *Dictionary of Classical Mythology.*
 1964.

(4) Use a standard bibliographical form.

Put each item of your bibliography on a separate card (3 × 5
or 4 × 6 inches in size) so that you can readily drop or add
a card and can arrange the list alphabetically without re-
copying it. Write in ink and follow exactly and consistently
the bibliographical form you are instructed to use. The form
shown by the following models closely follows the second

edition of *The MLA Style Sheet,* published in May, 1970, by the Modern Language Association of America.

Bibliographical entries often consist of only three units, which are separated by periods:

1. *Name of the author.* Give the last name first to make alphabetization easy.
2. *Title of the book.* Underline (italicize) the title, and capitalize it in accordance with **9c.** Always include the book's subtitle.
3. *Publication data.* Include the place of publication, the publisher, and the latest copyright date as shown on the copyright page. You may give a shortened form of the publisher's name as long as it is clear.

```
Graham, James J.  The Enemies of the Poor.  New York:
    Random, 1970.

Rosa, Joseph G.  The Gunfighter: Man or Myth?  Norman:
    Univ. of Oklahoma Press, 1969.
```

Some entries, however, require more than three units. These must be given special treatment. As you study the following model bibliographical entries, which cover most of the special problems you are likely to encounter, observe both the arrangement of information and the punctuation. See also page 424 for a list of abbreviations that are permissible in bibliographies, footnotes, and tables.

Model Bibliographical Entries

Books

```
Aiken, Michael, Lewis A. Ferman, and Harold L. Sheppard.
    Economic Failure, Alienation, and Extremism.  Ann
    Arbor: Univ. of Michigan Press, 1968.
```

[A book by three authors. Notice that the name of the first author is inverted, but the names of the other two authors are given in the normal order.]

413

Baron, Salo Wittmayer. <u>A Social and Religious History of the Jews</u>. 2nd ed. 14 vols. New York: Columbia Univ. Press, 1952-69.

[A multivolume work published over a seventeen-year period]

Bebout, John E., and Ronald J. Grele. <u>Where Cities Meet: The Urbanization of New Jersey</u>. New Jersey Historical Series, Vol. 22. Princeton: Van Nostrand, 1964.

[A book by two authors; also a book in a series. Notice that the volume number of a book in a series is given in Arabic rather than Roman numerals.]

Brown, Milton P., et al. <u>Problems in Marketing</u>. New York: McGraw-Hill, 1968.

[A book by more than three authors]

Commission on English. <u>Freedom and Discipline in English</u>. New York: College Entrance Examination Board, 1965.

[A book with corporate authorship]

Pratt, Robert A., et al., eds. <u>Masters of British Literature</u>. 2 vols. Boston: Houghton, 1958.

[A work with more than three editors]

Sartre, Jean Paul. <u>Literary Essays</u>. Trans. Annette Michelson. New York: Philosophical Library, 1957.

[A translation]

Trilling, Diana. "The Image of Women in Contemporary Literature." <u>The Woman in America</u>. Ed. Robert Jay Lifton. Boston: Houghton, 1965.

[A specific article from an edited anthology]

Undset, Sigrid, et al. <u>The Achievement of D. H. Lawrence</u>. Ed. Frederick J. Hoffman and Harry T. Moore. Norman: Univ. of Oklahoma Press, 1953.

[A work with more than three authors and two editors]

Zimmern, Alfred. <u>America</u> <u>and</u> <u>Europe</u> <u>and</u> <u>Other</u> <u>Essays</u>.
   1920; rpt. Freeport, N.Y.: Books for Libraries
   Press, 1969.

[A reprint of a book first published in 1920. Notice that the state in which the book was published is given along with the city to avoid confusion with Freeport, Ill.]

Magazines and newspapers

"African Riviera." <u>Ebony</u>, Dec. 1970, pp. 83-87.

[An unsigned article in a monthly magazine]

Gray, Ralph. "How Do You Move the Mountain into the
   Classroom?" <u>NEA</u> <u>Journal</u>, 55, No. 3 (1966), 34-36.

[An article from a journal in which pages are numbered separately for each issue. Notice that both *Vol.* and *pp.* are omitted when both volume and page numbers are given. The issue number follows the volume number when the month or season of publication is not specified on the title page.]

Hunt, George P. "Education of a Wanderer." <u>Life</u>, 25 April
   1969, p. 3.

[A signed article in a weekly magazine]

Peterle, Tony J. "Characteristics of Some Ohio Hunters."
   <u>The</u> <u>Journal</u> <u>of</u> <u>Wildlife</u> <u>Management</u>, 31 (1967), 375-89.

[An article from a journal in which pages are numbered continuously through each year]

Schonberg, Harold C. "Modern Literalism and Repeats."
   <u>New</u> <u>York</u> <u>Times</u>, 20 March 1966, p. 11, cols. 1-2.

[A signed article from a newspaper. Notice that column numbers may be supplied for ease of reference.]

<u>Wyoming</u> <u>State</u> <u>Tribune</u>, 29 Nov. 1970, p. 3, cols. 2-3.

[An unsigned, untitled news story]

Encyclopedias

"Jenkins, Robert." Encyclopaedia Britannica, 1967, XII, 998.

[An unsigned article. Notice that it is unnecessary to give full publication information for familiar reference works.]

Thomson, Irving L. "Great Seal of the United States."
    Encyclopedia Americana, 1968, XIII, 365–66.

[A signed article]

Bulletins and pamphlets

Standards of Practice for Radio Broadcasters of the United
    States of America. Washington, D.C.: National Assn. of
    Radio and Television Broadcasters, 1954.

Velvetbean Caterpillar, The. Dept. of Agriculture, Bureau
    of Entomology and Plant Quarantine Leaflet No. 348.
    Washington, D.C.: Government Printing Office, 1953.

[Notice that titles beginning with *a, an,* or *the* are alphabetized under the first word following the article.]

Unpublished dissertations

Woodall, Guy Ramon. "Robert Walsh, Jr., as an Editor
    and Literary Critic: 1797-1836." Diss. Univ. of
    Tennessee, 1966.

Note: If you use two or more works by the same author in your paper, list each work separately in your bibliography, but do not repeat the author's name. To indicate the omission of the name, use seven hyphens (or a straight line) followed by a period. Notice that entries of this type are alphabetized by title.

Erikson, Erik H. Childhood and Society. Rev. ed. New
    York: Norton, 1964.

-------. Gandhi's Truth. New York: Norton, 1969.

The preceding model entries are single-spaced with hanging indention (but with double-spacing between entries). This is a proper form for the entries in the final bibliography, which is submitted as a part of the library paper (see page 456). On the separate cards used in compiling the bibliography, you may use the same form; or you may write the author, title, and facts of publication on separate lines:

BIBLIOGRAPHY CARD

```
                                    PR
                                    4581
        Wilson, Angus.             .W52

   The World of Charles Dickens.

   New York: Viking, 1970.
```

Whatever bibliographical form you adopt, you should be consistent, each time using commas, periods, underlining (italics), and quotation marks exactly as called for by your model. This model will usually be suggested by the department, the periodical, or the organization for which the paper is being written. If your instructor does not specify a different form, you may use the one described in this handbook.

■ **Exercise 2** Choose a topic for a library paper from the three topics you selected for Exercise 1 on page 405. Then prepare a preliminary bibliography on your topic. Use at least ten of the most promising references (books, bulletins, articles in periodicals or reference books) you can find. (Often you will find helpful bibliographies in the books that you consult, especially at the ends of articles in encyclopedias and other reference works.)

33c

Develop an outline.

After completing a preliminary bibliography and a minimum of general reading on your subject (an encyclopedia article and parts of one or·two other works may suffice), make a preliminary outline that will give direction to your investigation. This tentative outline will enable you to discard irrelevant material from your bibliography and to begin spotting valuable passages on which you will want to take notes. If you attempt to take notes without first knowing what you are looking for, your efforts will lead only to frustration.

Be careful, however, not to adhere too rigidly to your preliminary outline. For although the outline will direct your reading, your reading will almost certainly suggest ways in which the outline may be improved. No outline should be regarded as complete until the research paper has been finished. As you take notes, you will probably revise your original outline frequently, adding subheadings to it, changing subheadings to major headings, perhaps dropping some headings entirely.

Follow the general directions for outlining given in **32b–f**. Make either a topic outline or a sentence outline. (A paragraph outline would be less satisfactory for a paper as long as a library paper.)

33d

Take notes on readings (after evaluating the sources).

As you take notes on your readings, learn how to find and evaluate useful passages with a minimum of time and effort. Seldom will a whole book, or even a whole article, be of use as subject matter for any given research paper. To get what is needed for your paper, you will find that you must turn to many books and articles, rejecting most of them altogether and using from others only a section here and there. You cannot take the time to read each book carefully. Use the table of contents and the index of a book, and learn to scan the pages rapidly until you find the passages you need.

One important consideration always is the reliability of the source. Does the author seem to know his subject? Does he have an official position that implies competence? Do others speak of him as an authority? Is he prejudiced in any way? Is the work recent enough to provide up-to-date information? Is the edition being used the latest one available? Use your best judgment to determine the most dependable sources for your paper. You may find in the *Book Review Digest* convenient summaries of critical opinion on a book in your bibliography.

Usually the best way to take notes is on cards or paper sheets of uniform size, commonly 3×5 or 4×6 inches. (The smaller card may be used for the bibliography and the larger for notes.) Each card should contain a single note with a heading keyed to a significant word or phrase in the preliminary outline—not to the notation (IA, II, IIIC, and so on), which is especially subject to change. If the paper is to have the customary footnotes, each card must also show the source of the note, including the exact page or pages from which it is drawn.

Compare the source material below with the note card that follows. Then turn to page 447 to see how the information is used in the finished library paper; notice the documentation in footnote 9.

SOURCE

The blessing under moonlight is the critical turning-point of the poem. Just as the Albatross was not a mere bird, so these are not mere water-snakes—they stand for all "happy living things." The first phase of redemption, the recovery of love and the recovery of the power of prayer, depends on the Mariner's recognition of his kinship again with other natural creatures: it is an assertion and recognition of the other central principle in the letter to Sotheby:

> that everything has a life of its own, and that we are all *One Life*.

And at that point the reminder of the sin against this principle is gone— [From Humphry House, *Coleridge: The Clark Lectures, 1951–52* (1962; rpt. London: Hart-Davis, 1969), p. 102][1]

NOTE CARD

Unity in nature

Both albatross + snakes are symbols of all "happy living things." Mariner can love & pray because of his "recognition of his kinship again with other natural creatures." A repetition of the idea in the letter to Sotheby: "everything has a life of its own ... we are all _One Life_."

House, p. 102

The note card above is a concise summary or précis. Carefully observe that copied words are inside quotation marks and that words omitted from a quotation are indicated by an ellipsis mark: see **17a(3)**.

---

[1] Reprinted by permission of Rupert Hart-Davis Ltd.

Direct quotations   Any quotations that you use in your
paper should be telling and important ones. When you
discover such a passage in your reading, you should take
it down verbatim—that is, copy every word, every capital
letter, and every mark of punctuation exactly as in the
original. Be sure to enclose the quoted passage in quotation
marks. When you are quoting, quote accurately. When you
are not quoting, use your own sentence structure and phraseology, not a slightly altered version of your source.

Plagiarism   If you fail to acknowledge borrowed material,
then you are plagiarizing. Plagiarism is literary theft. When
you copy the words of another, be sure to put those words
inside quotation marks and to acknowledge the source with
a footnote. When you paraphrase the words of another, use
your own words and your own sentence structure, and be
sure to give a footnote citing the source of the idea. A
plagiarist often merely changes a few words or rearranges
the words in the source. As you take notes and as you write
your paper, be especially careful to avoid plagiarism.

■ **Exercise 3**   Read paragraphs 37 (page 360) and 41 (page
363) in Section **31**. Then write a précis of each paragraph, using
as your model the specimen note card on the opposite page. Unless
you are quoting directly, avoid entirely the sentence patterns of the
source. Choose your words carefully to convey the ideas in the
source exactly.

33e

**Using the outline, the bibliography, and the notes,
write a properly documented library paper.**

After you have made your outline as complete as possible
and have taken a number of notes on every major heading
and every subheading of the outline, you are ready to begin

writing. Arrange your notes in the order of the outline, and then use them as the basis of your paper. Naturally you will need to expand some parts and to cut others, and you will need to provide transitional sentences—sometimes even transitional paragraphs. Write the material in the best way you can—in your own style, in your own words. Follow the suggestions for writing given in **32g**.

(1) Footnotes and footnote form Since you will get your material for the library paper largely from the published work of others, you will need to give proper credit in the paper itself. To do so, use footnotes numbered consecutively throughout the paper and placed at the bottoms of the appropriate pages (see the library paper on pages 433–57) or in one list at the end of the paper, if your instructor so directs. Footnote numerals in the text should come immediately after the part of the sentence to which the footnote refers and should come *after* all punctuation except the dash. The number of footnotes needed will vary with the paper. Every quotation must have its footnote, and so must all the chief facts and opinions drawn from the work of others. From one to four footnotes for each page will be needed for proper documentation of the average library paper.

As the following model forms show, the first footnote reference to a source is similar to, but not identical with, the bibliographical entry. Notice differences in indention and punctuation. Notice also that the author's name is inverted in the bibliographical entry but not in the footnote reference, and that the subtitle of the book is included in the bibliography but may be omitted in the footnote.

Note: If you type your paper, single-space each footnote and each bibliographical entry but double-space between them. If you write your paper by hand, do not skip lines between footnotes or between bibliographical entries: see page 457.

BIBLIOGRAPHICAL ENTRIES

```
Gardiner, John A.  The Politics of Corruption: Organized
     Crime in an American City.  New York: Russell Sage
     Foundation, 1970.
```

```
Lear, John.  "Thor Heyerdahl's Next Voyage."  Saturday
     Review, 3 May 1969, pp. 49-56.
```

FIRST FOOTNOTE REFERENCES

```
    1 John A. Gardiner, The Politics of Corruption (New
York: Russell Sage Foundation, 1970), pp. 47-48.
```

```
    2 John Lear, "Thor Heyerdahl's Next Voyage,"
Saturday Review, 3 May 1969, p. 52.
```

Points to Remember about First Footnote References

1. The first line is indented five spaces. (Normal paragraph indention is used instead of the hanging indention used to make each entry stand out in a bibliography.)
2. Footnote numbers are typed slightly above the line, followed by a space.
3. The names of authors and editors are given in the normal order, first names first. (Since footnotes are never alphabetized, there is no need to give the last name first.)
4. Commas are used between the main items (but not before parentheses).
5. In references to books, parentheses enclose the publication data. In references to journals, parentheses enclose the month and year of publication (except when the day of month is given).
6. Each footnote ends with a period.
7. Such abbreviations as the following may be used. (These abbreviations are also appropriate in bibliographies and

423

in tables, but they are inappropriate in the text of a library paper.)

Assn.	Association
bk., bks.	book, books
cf.	compare
ch., chs.	chapter, chapters
col., cols.	column, columns
Dept.	Department
Diss.	Dissertation
ed.	edition OR edited by, editor
eds.	editions OR edited by, editors
et al.	and others
f., ff.	and the following page, pages (Inclusive page numbers are preferred: "pp. 5–13" instead of "pp. 5 ff.")
ibid.	in the same place; in the source cited in the immediately preceding footnote
l., ll.	line, lines
MS, MSS	manuscript, manuscripts
n.d.	no date (of publication)
n., nn.	(foot)note, (foot)notes (e.g., "p. 6, n. 2")
No., Nos.	Number (of issue), Numbers
n.p.	no place (of publication)
p., pp.	page, pages
pt., pts.	part, parts
rev.	revision OR revised, revised by
rpt.	reprinted, reprint
sec., secs.	section, sections
trans.	translated by, translator
Univ.	University
vol., vols.	volume, volumes

Standard abbreviations for months of publication and for names of states and countries (sometimes given to prevent confusion of cities such as Cambridge, Mass., and Cambridge, Eng.)

Compare the following model footnotes to the sample bibliographical entries on pages 413–16 to see exactly how the treatment differs.

Model Footnotes—First References

Books

¹ James J. Graham, <u>The Enemies of the Poor</u> (New York: Random, 1970), p. 73.

² <u>The Gunfighter</u> (Norman: Univ. of Oklahoma Press, 1969), pp. 14-15.

[The author's name may be omitted if it appears in full in the text of the paper. Notice that the subtitle *Man or Myth?* is also omitted.]

³ Michael Aiken, Lewis A. Ferman, and Harold L. Sheppard, <u>Economic Failure, Alienation, and Extremism</u> (Ann Arbor: Univ. of Michigan Press, 1968), pp. 184-86.

[A book by three authors]

⁴ Salo Wittmayer Baron, <u>A Social and Religious History of the Jews</u>, 2nd ed., XIV (New York: Columbia Univ. Press, 1969), 281-85.

[The number of volumes in a multivolume work is not given in a reference to a specific passage. Notice that the volume number precedes the publishing information when the various volumes of the work have been published in different years. Notice also that both *Vol.* and *pp.* are omitted when both volume and page numbers are given.]

⁵ John E. Bebout and Ronald J. Grele, <u>Where Cities Meet</u>, New Jersey Historical Series, Vol. 22 (Princeton: Van Nostrand, 1964), pp. 61-62.

[A book by two authors; also a book in a series. Notice that the volume number of a book in a series is given in Arabic rather than Roman numerals.]

⁶ Milton P. Brown et al., <u>Problems in Marketing</u> (New York: McGraw-Hill, 1968), p. 43.

[A book by more than three authors]

[7] Commission on English, _Freedom and Discipline in English_ (New York: College Entrance Examination Board, 1965), p. 124.

[A book with corporate authorship]

[8] Robert A. Pratt et al., eds., _Masters of British Literature_ (Boston: Houghton, 1958), I, 15.

[A work with more than three editors. Notice that the volume number follows the publishing information when the various volumes of a multivolume work were published in the same year.]

[9] Jean Paul Sartre, _Literary Essays_, trans. Annette Michelson (New York: Philosophical Library, 1957), p. 29.

[A translation]

[10] Diana Trilling, "The Image of Women in Contemporary Literature," in _The Woman in America_, ed. Robert Jay Lifton (Boston: Houghton, 1965), pp. 70–71.

[A specific article from an edited anthology]

[11] Sigrid Undset et al., _The Achievement of D. H. Lawrence_, ed. Frederick J. Hoffman and Harry T. Moore (Norman: Univ. of Oklahoma Press, 1953), p. 7.

[A work with more than three authors and two editors]

[12] Alfred Zimmern, _America and Europe and Other Essays_ (1920; rpt. Freeport, N.Y.: Books for Libraries Press, 1969), p. 23.

[A reprint of a book first published in 1920. Modern paperback books that are reprints of previously published works are footnoted in this way.]

Magazines and newspapers

[13] "African Riviera," _Ebony_ (Dec. 1970), pp. 85 and 87.

[An unsigned article in a monthly magazine]

¹⁴ Ralph Gray, "How Do You Move the Mountain into the Classroom?" NEA Journal, 55, No. 3 (1966), 35.

[An article from a journal in which pages are numbered separately for each issue. Notice that both *Vol.* and *pp.* are omitted when both volume and page numbers are given. The issue number follows the volume number when the month or season of publication is not specified on the title page.]

¹⁵ George P. Hunt, "Education of a Wanderer," Life, 25 April 1969, p. 3.

[A signed article in a weekly magazine]

¹⁶ Tony J. Peterle, "Characteristics of Some Ohio Hunters," The Journal of Wildlife Management, 31 (1967), 384-85.

[An article from a journal in which pages are numbered continuously through each year]

¹⁷ Harold C. Schonberg, "Modern Literalism and Repeats," New York Times, 20 March 1966, p. 11, col. 2.

[A signed article from a newspaper. Notice that column numbers may be supplied for ease of reference.]

¹⁸ Wyoming State Tribune, 29 Nov. 1970, p. 3, cols. 2-3.

[An unsigned, untitled news story]

Encyclopedias

¹⁹ "Jenkins, Robert," Encyclopaedia Britannica, 1967, XII, 998.

[An unsigned article. The title is given here as ''Jenkins, Robert'' because it is listed under *J* in the encyclopedia.]

²⁰ Irving L. Thomson, "Great Seal of the United States," Encyclopedia Americana, 1968, XIII, 365.

[A signed article]

Bulletins and pamphlets

²¹ <u>Standards</u> <u>of</u> <u>Practice</u> <u>for</u> <u>Radio</u> <u>Broadcasters</u> <u>of</u> <u>the</u> <u>United</u> <u>States</u> <u>of</u> <u>America</u> (Washington, D.C.: National Assn. of Radio and Television Broadcasters, 1954), p. 18.

²² <u>The</u> <u>Velvetbean</u> <u>Caterpillar</u>, Dept. of Agriculture, Bureau of Entomology and Plant Quarantine Leaflet No. 348 (Washington, D.C.: Government Printing Office, 1953), p. 3.

Unpublished dissertations

²³ Guy Ramon Woodall, "Robert Walsh, Jr., as an Editor and Literary Critic: 1797–1836," Diss. Univ. of Tennessee, 1966, p. 186.

The models below show second (or later) footnote references in an appropriately abbreviated form. Compare them with the first footnote references to see exactly how they have been shortened. Pay special attention to the use of *ibid.*, which means "in the same place" or "in the source just cited." Notice that two or more short footnotes may be given on the same line.

Model Footnotes—Second References

Books

²⁴ Graham, p. 27.   ²⁵ Sartre, pp. 14–15.

²⁶ Aiken, Ferman, and Sheppard, p. 188.

²⁷ Bebout and Grele, p. 65.

²⁸ Ibid.

[Exactly the same source as the immediately preceding footnote]

²⁹ Pratt et al., I, 14.

³⁰ Bebout and Grele, p. 67.

[*Ibid.* here would refer to the work by Pratt et al.]

31 Baron, XIV, 290.

32 Ibid., p. 150.

[Baron's work, also Vol. XIV, but a different page]

33 Ibid., IX, 112–13.

[Baron's work, but a different volume and page. When the various volumes of a work have been published in different years, be sure that the first reference to each new volume cited is a complete reference, giving the specific date of publication of that particular volume.]

Magazines and newspapers

34 Gray, pp. 36–37.   35 Schonberg, p. 11.

36 "African Riviera," p. 86.

37 <u>Wyoming State Tribune</u>, p. 3.

[Note, however, that if more than one article from the same newspaper is used, the full reference must be repeated.]

Encyclopedias

38 "Jenkins, Robert," XII, 998.

39 Thomson, XIII, 365.

Bulletins and pamphlets

40 <u>Standards of Practice for Radio Broadcasters</u>, p. 17.

[Notice that a title may be shortened as long as it is easily identified.]

41 <u>Velvetbean Caterpillar</u>, p. 3.

[Notice that the initial *The* is omitted.]

Unpublished dissertations

⁴² Woodall, p. 135.

If you refer in your paper to two or more works by the same author, include titles (in shortened form if the title is long) in your second footnote references.

⁴³ Sartre, <u>Literary Essays</u>, pp. 102–04.

⁴⁴ Sartre, <u>Essays in Aesthetics</u>, p. 14.

If you refer to works by two authors with the same last name, repeat the full name of the author in second references.

⁴⁵ James J. Graham, p. 68.

⁴⁶ Ian C. Graham, p. 98.

If you use articles with the same title from two or more encyclopedias, include the name of the encyclopedia in your footnote.

⁴⁷ "Jenkins, Robert," <u>Encyclopaedia Britannica</u>, XII, 998.

⁴⁸ "Jenkins, Robert," <u>Encyclopedia Americana</u>, XIII, 355.

Note: Information related to the central idea of the paper but not directly supporting it may be presented in a footnote: see footnote 3 of the library paper, page 439.

Whatever footnote form you adopt, use it consistently. Unless your instructor directs you to use a different style, you may adopt the one that is described in this handbook, which closely follows the second edition of *The MLA Style*

Sheet, published in May, 1970, by the Modern Language Association of America.

(2) Final outline and paper After writing the first draft of your paper, complete with footnotes, read it over carefully, correcting all errors in spelling, mechanics, and grammar. Check to be sure that the arrangement is logical and that the writing is as clear, concise, and pleasing in style as you can possibly make it. You will probably rewrite some sentences, strike out others, and add still others. Your outline, which should have developed steadily throughout the note-taking and the first draft of the paper, will now be in its final form. It serves primarily, of course, as a guide to the writing of the paper; but it can also serve, if copied in its final stage, as a guide to the contents of the paper.

After you have proofread and revised your first draft, and after you have put your outline in final form, write the final draft of your paper. Use a typewriter if possible. If not, use pen and ink, writing legibly and neatly.

(3) Final bibliography You should have assembled a preliminary bibliography early in your research. As you pursued your investigation, you probably eliminated some items and added others. Not until you have completed your paper can you know which items should make up your final bibliography. Once your paper is complete, look through your footnotes. Every book or article appearing even once in a footnote belongs in the bibliography. (Your instructor may ask you to include everything that you have examined, whether you have actually used it in your writing or not. In that case your bibliography may have, instead of a dozen items, as many as fifty.) Once you have determined which items should be included, you can easily arrange the bibliography cards in alphabetical order and copy them, either in one alphabetical list or in a list classified according to your instructor's directions.

Students are often asked to submit, along with the completed paper, both the final and the preliminary outlines; the notes, on cards; and the rough draft of the paper, with footnotes.

Library Paper

On the following pages is a completed library paper. For purposes of comparison, the pages facing those of the library paper contain not only selected passages from the sources but also note cards used in preparing the paper. Comments on form are also provided. Notice, as you read the paper, how the student credits the other authors whose work he has used.

■ **Exercise 4** Prepare for a class discussion of the strengths and the weaknesses of the following library paper. Give special attention to content and form, organization, and documentation.

THE ALBATROSS AS A SYMBOL

IN <u>THE</u> <u>RIME</u> <u>OF</u> <u>THE</u> <u>ANCIENT</u> <u>MARINER</u>

by

Gavin Shafer

COMMENTS

This library paper consists of four units:

1. *Title page.* The title page gives the title of the paper in capital letters and the full name of the student writer. This information is centered on the page and is attractively spaced. (Follow the directions of your instructor regarding the placement of any additional information—such as the name and section number of the course, the date of writing, and so on.) Notice that the title page is not numbered.

2. *Final outline.* The final outline serves as a table of contents. Since the outline occupies only one page, it is not numbered. (In outlines occupying more than one page, all pages after the first are numbered with small Roman numerals in the upper right-hand corner of the page.)

3. *Text of the paper, with footnotes at the bottom of each page.* The first page of the text of the paper is not numbered. All pages after the first are numbered with Arabic numerals in the upper right-hand corner of the page. Notice that no period follows the page numbers. (When footnotes are listed on a separate page or pages, they come immediately after the text of the paper, before the bibliography, and are numbered with the text.)

4. *Bibliography.* The bibliography begins on a new page and is numbered with the text of the paper.

OUTLINE

<u>Central idea</u>: The mysterious role of the albatross in
<u>The Rime of the Ancient Mariner</u> has led to various
interpretations of the bird as a symbol.

<u>Introduction</u>: Coleridge's concept of a symbol and the
variety of interpretations of the albatross

I. The mysterious role of the albatross

    A. Its appearance

    B. Its death

    C. Its impact on the life of the mariner

II. The various interpretations of the albatross as
    a symbol

    A. As the unity in nature

        1. Coleridge's view of the universe

        2. The mariner's recognition of his kinship
           with other creatures

        3. Warren's theory of "One Life"

    B. As the creative imagination

        1. Symbolic association with the moon

        2. Symbolic association with the wind

    C. As the human father

    D. As a totem-animal

<u>Conclusion</u>: The difficulty of interpreting a symbol like
the albatross and the poetic power of such a symbol

lib

SOURCE

[**p. 100**]

An IDEA, in the *highest* sense of that word, cannot be conveyed but by a *symbol;* and, except in geometry, all symbols of necessity involve an apparent contradiction. [From Coleridge, *Biographia Literaria,* I]

COMMENTS

For the arrangement of the material on the page, see **8b**.

Since the quotation in the first sentence is a complete sentence in itself, the semicolon in the original is dropped and a period is used instead: see **17a(3)**. Notice that the capital letters and the italics in the source are reproduced in the paper.

In the last sentence of the first paragraph, the introductory *he wrote that* makes it unnecessary to use an ellipsis mark to show the omission before *all.*

Notice that the footnotes are separated from the text by triple spacing.

Footnote 1: Since Coleridge's full name is given in the text, it is not repeated in the footnote. Because both volume and page numbers are given, the abbreviations *Vol.* and *p.* are not used.

Footnote 2: A period follows the abbreviation *Ibid.*, which is not underlined (italicized) in a footnote. The page number given in the preceding note is not repeated.

436

The Albatross as a Symbol

in The Rime of the Ancient Mariner

Samuel Taylor Coleridge once wrote: "An IDEA, in
the highest sense of that word, cannot be conveyed but by
a symbol."[1] Coleridge's ideas are conveyed by many
powerful symbols in The Rime of the Ancient Mariner, the
tale of an old man's terrifying journey through sin and
expiation to redemption. The senseless killing of an
albatross, a huge sea bird of the southern hemisphere,
is the pivotal symbolic experience of the poem. Yet the
question of exactly what the albatross symbolizes is one
that has baffled and divided literary critics for almost
two hundred years. Perhaps Coleridge had the albatross
in mind when he wrote that "all symbols of necessity
involve an apparent contradiction."[2]

This paper reports on four of the most interesting
and varied critical interpretations of the meaning of

[1] Biographia Literaria, ed. J. Shawcross (Oxford:
Clarendon, 1907), I, 100.

[2] Ibid.

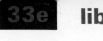

SOURCE

[p. 189]

> The ice was here, the ice was there,
> The ice was all around: 60
> It cracked and growled, and roared and howled,
> Like noises in a swound!

Till a great sea-bird, called the Albatross, came through the snow-fog, and was received with great joy and hospitality.

> At length did cross an Albatross,
> Thorough the fog it came;
> As if it had been a Christian soul, 65
> We hailed it in God's name.

[From *The Rime of the Ancient Mariner,* in *The Poems of Samuel Taylor Coleridge*]

COMMENTS

The quoted lines of poetry are set off by indention and single-spacing: see **16a(2)**. Compare the lines in the paper with those of the source: note the spelling of *Thorough*, the capitalization of *Albatross*.

Footnote 3: The information supplied here is related to but does not support the central idea of the library paper.

NOTE CARD

> Symbolism in Coleridge's poetry
> Symbolists like R. P. Warren & Kenneth Burke
> don't seem to understand Coleridge's inten-
> tions & statements. A lot has been said
> about <u>Ancient Mariner</u> — its moral, its symbols.
> But the poem ought to be appreciated as a
> traditional ballad, a beautiful poem telling
> a good story — as a tale with some super-
> natural & some superstitious elements.
> Stoll, pp. 102-18

438

the albatross as a symbol.[3] First, the bird has been
seen as a symbol of the unity in all nature. Second,
it has been called a symbol of the creative imagination.
Third, it has been seen as representing the human
father. And, finally, it has been seen as a sacred
"totem-animal," the select emissary of the gods. No
one of these interpretations can answer all the
questions a reader may have about the meaning of the
albatross. Yet each of them illuminates one aspect
of the bird's role as a primary symbol in the poem.

The albatross first appears in the poem when the
mariner and his shipmates have been driven southward
into the polar sea by a storm:

> At length did cross an Albatross,
> Thorough the fog it came;

[3] Not every reader considers the albatross as
a symbol. Elmer Edgar Stoll, for example, disagrees
with the opinions of symbolists like Robert Penn
Warren. See "Symbolism in Coleridge," in British
Romantic Poets, ed. Shiv K. Kumar (New York: New
York Univ. Press, 1966), pp. 102-18.

SOURCE

[p. 189]

> It ate the food it ne'er had eat,
> And round and round it flew.
> The ice did split with a thunder-fit;
> The helmsman steered us through!   70

And lo! the Albatross proveth a bird of good omen, and followeth the ship as it returned northward through fog and floating ice.

> And a good south wind sprung up behind;
> The Albatross did follow,
> And every day, for food or play,
> Came to the mariner's hollo!
>
> In mist or cloud, on mast or shroud,   75
> It perched for vespers nine;
> Whiles all the night, through fog-smoke white,
> Glimmered the white Moon-shine.'

The ancient Mariner inhospitably killeth the pious bird of good omen.

> 'God save thee, ancient Mariner!
> From the fiends, that plague thee thus!—   80
> Why look'st thou so?'—With my cross-bow
> I shot the ALBATROSS.

[From *The Rime of the Ancient Mariner,* in *The Poems of Samuel Taylor Coleridge*]

COMMENTS

Notice the selection of lines quoted from the source.

Notice also that the present tense is used for the summary of the action in the poem.

Footnote 4: The source was first published in 1912 and was reprinted in 1961. Because the footnote states that the edition it cites is the edition used throughout the paper, other footnote references are not needed for subsequent quotations from the poem.

3

> As if it had been a Christian soul,
> We hailed it in God's name. (lines 63-66)[4]

With the bird comes a wind from the south, and the ship
moves northward once again. The joyful men regard the
albatross as a good omen, and they playfully call to it
and feed it as it follows the ship. Then, with no
apparent motive, the mariner kills the friendly bird.

> 'God save thee, ancient Mariner!
> From the fiends, that plague thee thus!--
> Why look'st thou so?'--With my cross-bow
> I shot the ALBATROSS. (lines 79-82)

At first his shipmates blame the mariner for shooting
the bird that brought good fortune; but when the sun
reappears, they begin to praise him, thinking the bird
had brought the mist and fog. Powered by supernatural
forces, the ship speeds on to the equator. But there
it comes to a sudden halt, and drought begins to
plague the stranded crew. The bewildered men, holding
the mariner responsible, hang the dead albatross around
his neck as a sign of guilt.

[4] Samuel Taylor Coleridge, The Poems of Samuel
Taylor Coleridge, ed. Ernest Hartley Coleridge (1912;
rpt. London: Oxford Univ. Press, 1961), p. 189. In
this paper, all quotations from The Rime of the
Ancient Mariner are taken from this edition.

SOURCES

[**p. 198**]

Their beauty and their happiness.	O happy living things! no tongue Their beauty might declare: A spring of love gushed from my heart,
He blesseth them in his heart.	And I blessed them unaware: 285 Sure my kind saint took pity on me, And I blessed them unaware.
The spell begins to break.	The self-same moment I could pray; And from my neck so free The Albatross fell off, and sank 290 Like lead into the sea.

[**p. 208**]

And ever and anon throughout his future life an agony constraineth him to travel from land to land;	Since then, at an uncertain hour, That agony returns: And till my ghastly tale is told, This heart within me burns. 585
	I pass, like night, from land to land; I have strange power of speech; That moment that his face I see, I know the man that must hear me: To him my tale I teach. 590

[From *The Rime of the Ancient Mariner*, in *The Poems of Samuel Taylor Coleridge*]

Then begins the long exile and the dreadful penance of the ancient mariner. Alone on a rotting ship, he despises the creatures of the sea and yearns to die; he finds himself unable to pray. Finally, after many days and nights of penance, he is blessed with a vision of the beauty of the water-snakes, and he realizes that his heart is filled with love. He exclaims,

> The self-same moment I could pray;
> And from my neck so free
> The Albatross fell off, and sank
> Like lead into the sea. (lines 288-91)

The mariner is briefly comforted by sleep and rain. But his sin is not yet expiated, and his penance soon begins anew. When at last he is absolved of his guilt and is conveyed by an angelic host to his native country, his whole being has been transformed by his experience. He becomes a seer who travels from land to land, compelled by some awful but redemptive force to tell others the strange tale of his journey.

Those who have seen the albatross as symbolic of the unity in nature have found support for their interpretation in Coleridge's own concept of the universe. As David P. Calleo writes,

SOURCES

[**p. 39**]
When Coleridge imagined the universe, he saw not a dead heap of uniform particles governed by simple, invariable, and mechanical laws. His universe was a vast arena filled with squirming, individual particulars, each with a vitality and purpose of its own. Yet there is a divine energy—a shaping spirit that coaxes individual inclination into general purpose. Nature is not like a machine, but an organism made up of many individual parts, each with its own character and function, and yet all participating in a larger unity. Like an organism, Nature is governed by a balance of opposite forces—an equilibrium that must itself reflect the progressive growth of the whole. When man applies his mind to the study of Nature, he must be careful to lose sight neither of the general laws nor of the particular parts. He must employ, in short, both his Reason and his Understanding. [From Calleo, *Coleridge and the Idea of the Modern State*][2]

[**p. 118**]
Natural, supernatural, human, and divine, "the pious bird" is versatile enough to be symbolic as well. The same Coleridge who sought love in the empyrean, who gave love wings in "The Destiny of Nations," adumbrates the mystery while the Ancient Mariner is "in a swound": the Polar Spirit "loved the bird that loved the man / Who shot him with his bow." Even in the farthest and loneliest reaches of the sea, love wings its way to the ship and is willfully rejected by [**p. 119**] the Mariner, who sacrilegiously cuts himself off from nature, the unity of life, and love. [From Parsons, "The Mariner and the Albatross"][3]

COMMENTS

Notice the treatment of the long prose quotation: see **16a(1)**. Also notice the difference in the treatment of the two omissions: see **17a(3)**.

[2] From *Coleridge and the Idea of the Modern State* by David P. Calleo. Published by Yale University Press, 1966. Reprinted by permission.

[3] From "The Mariner and the Albatross" by Coleman O. Parsons, *Virginia Quarterly Review,* Winter 1950. Reprinted by permission.

> When Coleridge imagined the universe,
> he saw not a dead heap of uniform particles
> governed by simple, invariable, and mechani-
> cal laws. His universe was a vast arena
> filled with squirming, individual particu-
> lars, each with a vitality and purpose of
> its own. Yet there is a divine energy—a
> shaping spirit that coaxes individual
> inclination into general purpose. Nature
> is not like a machine, but an organism
> made up of many individual parts . . . all
> participating in a larger unity. . . . When
> man applies his mind to the study of Nature,
> he must be careful to lose sight neither of
> the general laws nor of the particular parts.[5]

As a creature with its own vitality and purpose, the
albatross thus participates in the larger unity of the
natural world. In a world viewed pantheistically, it
can be argued that the mariner, by shooting the albatross,
"cuts himself off from nature, the unity of life, and
love."[6]

In his analysis of The Rime of the Ancient Mariner,
Max F. Schulz emphasizes the passages that reflect
Coleridge's "reverence for life"[7] and his consciousness

[5] Coleridge and the Idea of the Modern State, Yale
Studies in Political Science, No. 18 (New Haven, Conn.:
Yale Univ. Press, 1966), p. 39.

[6] Coleman O. Parsons, "The Mariner and the
Albatross," Virginia Quarterly Review, 26 (1950), 119.

[7] The Poetic Voices of Coleridge (Detroit: Wayne
State Univ. Press, 1963), p. 57.

NOTE CARDS

Unity in nature

p. 57 – On the "unified portions" of <u>Ancient
Mariner</u>, "with their evocation of a world
in which moral order and reverence for
life obtain, we hear ... Coleridge's real ...
voice."

p. 64 – C.'s "awareness of good and evil and man's
oneness with the external world adds
moral and metaphysical dimensions" to
awful events in poem.

Schulz

Unity in nature

Both albatross & snakes are symbols of
all "happy living things." Mariner can love
& pray because of his "recognition of
his kinship again with other natural
creatures." A repetition of the idea in
the letter to Sotheby: "everything has a
life of its own ... we are all <u>One Life</u>."

House, p. 102

Shooting of albatross = symbolic murder

p. 398 – Because of mariner's lack of
motive in killing albatross, the act is
much like the Fall. Mariner really
guilty of murder.

p. 402 – "One Life" = primary theme
"theme of the imagination" = secondary
theme

Warren

---

of "man's oneness with the external world."[8] When the mariner kills the albatross, he destroys a beautiful and happy living creature; later, when he realizes the beauty of the water-snakes, he blesses and loves "happy living things." At this moment, the spell that has bound him begins to break, and the dead albatross falls symbolically from his neck. The redemption of the mariner begins with his recognition of his own close relationship to other creatures.[9]

Robert Penn Warren, who considers the motiveless shooting of the albatross symbolic murder and who relates the mariner's crime to the Fall of Man, believes that the theme of "One Life"--of one being shared by all the creatures of the universe--is the primary motif of The Rime of the Ancient Mariner. Thus, in killing the albatross, the mariner commits a crime against nature. But Warren also points to a secondary theme in the poem: a linking of the albatross with the imagination.[10]

---

[8] Ibid., p. 64.

[9] Humphry House, Coleridge (1962; rpt. London: Hart-Davis, 1969), p. 102.

[10] "A Poem of Pure Imagination (Reconsiderations VI)," Kenyon Review, 8 (1946), 398 and 402.

SOURCES

[p. 189]

> In mist or cloud, on mast or shroud,   75
> It perched for vespers nine;
> Whiles all the night, through fog-smoke white,
> Glimmered the white Moon-shine.'

The ancient Mariner
inhospitably killeth
the pious bird of
good omen.

> 'God save thee, ancient Mariner!
> From the fiends, that plague thee thus!—   80
> Why look'st thou so?'—With my cross-bow
> I shot the ALBATROSS.

PART II

> The Sun now rose, upon the right:
> Out of the sea came he,

[From *The Rime of the Ancient Mariner,* in *The Poems of Samuel
Taylor Coleridge*]

NOTE CARD

> Albatross = creative imagination
> p. 407 – Albatross = "moon-bird." It & moon
> appear in poem at same time.
> "Luminous haze" = "symbolic
> equivalent of moonlight." "Creative"
> wind is linked to bird too. The
> wind + "friendly bird "+ "moonlight
> of imagination" are "one symbolic
> cluster."
> p. 408 – Mariner is guilty of "crime against
> the imagination."
> Warren

COMMENT

Notice that the student's insertion in the quoted lines of poetry
is enclosed in brackets: see **17g.**

According to Warren, the albatross may be
considered as a kind of "moon-bird." When it first
appears, it is associated with mist and fog, with snowy
haze, which Warren calls the "symbolic equivalent
of moonlight."[11] The moon first appears in the poem
almost immediately after the albatross:

> In mist or cloud, on mast or shroud,
> It [the albatross] perched for vespers nine;
> Whiles all the night, through fog-smoke white,
> Glimmered the white Moon-shine.' (lines 75-78)

In the poem, the killing of the albatross is followed
immediately by the rising of the sun (lines 82 and 83),
the prevailing image through the subsequent period of
torture and drought that constitutes the mariner's
first penance. With the death of the albatross, in
effect, the moon disappears from the poem for 128 lines.

Similarly, as Warren shows, the albatross is closely
associated with the wind. In the poem, the south wind
begins to blow immediately after the albatross arrives
at the ship, and the crew link the bird with the welcome
breezes. Warren sees the wind as symbolic of creativity
and the moonlight as symbolic of the imagination.
Because the albatross is associated with both, the bird

[11] Ibid., p. 407.

SOURCES

[p. 191]

The shipmates, in their sore distress, would fain throw the whole guilt on the ancient Mariner: in sign whereof they hang the dead sea-bird round his neck.

And every tongue, through utter drought,   135
Was withered at the root;
We could not speak, no more than if
We had been choked with soot.

Ah! well a-day! what evil looks
Had I from old and young!   140
Instead of the cross, the Albatross
About my neck was hung.

[From *The Rime of the Ancient Mariner,* in *The Poems of Samuel Taylor Coleridge*]

[p. 721]

At the end of Part IV the Mariner breathes forth unawares a blessing upon the creatures of the deep and immediately the guilty weight of the Albatross falls from him and sinks "Like lead into the sea."

Students are often tempted to interpret this action as symbolizing the Mariner's forgiveness and release from pain. But to accept this interpretation is to ignore the words of the spirit at the end of Part V: "The man hath penance done, / And penance more will do." The Mariner suffers when the Albatross is about his neck, and he continues to suffer when he is released from its weight. [From Ciardi, *How Does a Poem Mean?*][4]

---

[4] From *How Does a Poem Mean?* by John Ciardi, Part 3 of *An Introduction to Literature,* edited by Gordon N. Ray et al. Published by Houghton Mifflin Company. Reprinted by permission.

is part of what Warren calls a "symbolic cluster" representing the creative imagination. Thus, when the mariner shoots the albatross, he also commits a "crime against the imagination."[12]

Whether considered as a symbol of the unity of nature, or as a symbol of the creative imagination, or as both, the albatross is clearly a symbol of guilt. (Indeed, this meaning of the albatross is made clear by Coleridge himself, who explains in a marginal note that the shipmates hang the dead bird around the mariner's neck as a sign of his guilt.) As John Ciardi points out, however, the mariner's release from the "guilty weight of the Albatross" is not a sign of his forgiveness: further penance must be undergone.[13] Such prolonged and terrible penance has suggested to some critics that the mariner must be guilty of a crime of the greatest magnitude--the murder of his own father, or the slaying of a sacred totem-animal.

[12] Ibid., pp. 407-08.

[13] How Does a Poem Mean? Pt. 3 of An Introduction to Literature, ed. Gordon N. Ray et al. (Boston: Houghton, 1959), p. 721.

NOTE CARDS

Albatross = human father
p. 150 – Coleridge had an "Oedipal struggle."
p. 151 – According to Eli Marcovitz, poet was
  unconsciously hostile toward father and
  repressed his desires for his mother.
p. 153 – Like Oedipus, mariner kills bird
  because he acts from "primeval instinct."
  His "Oedipal crime... is part of the unconscious
  heritage of man, of Sophocles as well
  as Coleridge."

Lupton

Shooting of albatross

"The shooting of the Albatross comes quite
suddenly and unexplained; superficially
it is unmotivated and wanton."
House, p. 95

Albatross = totem-animal

It's a disaster, bringing excommunication,
to shoot "totem-animal" without gods' approval.
According to Sir James G. Frazer, such killers
are cast out of society and can't return
till they "undergo rites of purification."
A sacred animal has a soul.

Lupton, p. 155

COMMENTS

Notice that the reference to footnote 15 comes immediately after
the part of the sentence to which it refers and is typed *after* the
colon.

Some who have studied the life of Coleridge contend that the poet suffered from an "Oedipal struggle"-- repressed desire for his mother and unconscious hostility toward his father.[14] Coleridge's own Oedipal complex could then be reflected in the mariner's crime, which is only superficially motiveless:[15] the albatross symbolizes the human father, and the mariner, in killing it, is motivated by a "primeval instinct" that is a "part of the unconscious heritage of man, of Sophocles as well as Coleridge."[16]

Others, drawing on the work of Sir James G. Frazer, have seen the albatross as a "totem-animal," a sacred bird with a soul. Among many primitive peoples, the killing of a totem-animal against the gods' will is considered an extremely serious offense and is punished by exile and excommunication.[17] The killer--like the

[14] Mary Jane Lupton, "'The Rime of the Ancient Mariner': The Agony of Thirst," American Imago, 27 (1970), 150-51.

[15] House, p. 95. [16] Lupton, p. 153.

[17] Ibid., p. 155.

SOURCES

[p. 68]

He is able to pray again and the burden of sin is lightened:

> The Albatross fell off, and sank
> Like lead into the sea.

This certainly marks a turning point in the poem and could be taken as the beginning of Christian redemption or as renewed reconciliation with the living world he had outraged. . . . Yet, as *The Ancient Mariner* progresses, the redemption seems only partial and doubtful, nor is the Mariner's return home brought about by natural forces. We must beware of oversimplifying the poem to make a neat moral pattern, since we have seen from Coleridge's notebooks and letters at the time that no solution entirely satisfied him. [From Adair, *The Waking Dream*][5]

[p. 10]

A good poem resists to the death its reduction to a flat statement; and verse which is made up of such flat statements is already dead as poetry. Yet since the climate of our age demands headline certainties and packaged information, the best hope (and not a large hope) for the public is that it will read more poetry, and more imaginative prose when it is of the nature of poetry. Only through long familiarity and practice can the reader respond easily to symbolic thinking. It will repay him many times over, for it is the most spacious, and may be the truest, activity of the human mind: it minimizes neither the particularities of experience nor the large informing ideas which give that experience its significance. [From Stauffer, "Poetry as Symbolic Thinking"][6]

---

[5] Adapted from: Patricia M. Adair: *The Waking Dream: A Study of Coleridge's Poetry*. Published by Edward Arnold (Publishers) Ltd. and Barnes & Noble, New York, N.Y., 1967. Reprinted by permission.

[6] From "Poetry as Symbolic Thinking" by Donald A. Stauffer, *Saturday Review of Literature*, March 22, 1947. Copyright 1947 The Saturday Review Associates, Inc. Reprinted by permission.

ancient mariner--cannot return to society until he has undergone long and severe rituals of penance.

All these interpretations of the albatross, although sometimes overlapping and often contradictory, can be justified in some measure through a close reading of the poem. What _does_ the albatross symbolize? There is no simple answer to the question, and to insist on one would be to underestimate the complexity of Coleridge's own moral view of the world.[18] Moreover, as Donald A. Stauffer has written, "A good poem resists to the death its reduction to a flat statement; and verse which is made up of such flat statements is already dead as poetry."[19] Perhaps, indeed, it is precisely because of the stubborn suggestive power of images like the albatross that _The Rime of the Ancient Mariner_ has so steadfastly refused to die.

[18] Patricia M. Adair, _The Waking Dream_ (London: Arnold, 1967), p. 68.

[19] "Poetry as Symbolic Thinking," _Saturday Review_, 22 March 1947, p. 10.

BIBLIOGRAPHY

Adair, Patricia M. The Waking Dream: A Study of
    Coleridge's Poetry. London: Arnold, 1967.

Calleo, David P. Coleridge and the Idea of the Modern
    State. New Haven, Conn.: Yale Univ. Press, 1966.

Ciardi, John. How Does a Poem Mean? Pt. 3 of An
    Introduction to Literature. Ed. Gordon N. Ray et
    al. Boston: Houghton, 1959.

Coleridge, Samuel Taylor. Biographia Literaria. 2 vols.
    Ed. J. Shawcross. Oxford: Clarendon, 1907.

-------. The Poems of Samuel Taylor Coleridge. Ed.
    Ernest Hartley Coleridge. 1912; rpt. London:
    Oxford Univ. Press, 1961.

House, Humphry. Coleridge: The Clark Lectures, 1951-52.
    1962; rpt. London: Hart-Davis, 1969.

Lupton, Mary Jane. "'The Rime of the Ancient Mariner':
    The Agony of Thirst." American Imago, 27 (1970),
    140-59.

Parsons, Coleman O. "The Mariner and the Albatross."
    Virginia Quarterly Review, 26 (1950), 102-23.

Schulz, Max F. The Poetic Voices of Coleridge: A Study
    of His Desire for Spontaneity and Passion for Order.
    Detroit: Wayne State Univ. Press, 1963.

Stauffer, Donald A. "Poetry as Symbolic Thinking."
    Saturday Review, 22 March 1947, pp. 9-10.

Stoll, Elmer Edgar. "Symbolism in Coleridge." British
    Romantic Poets: Recent Evaluations. Ed. Shiv K.
    Kumar. New York: New York Univ. Press, 1966.

Warren, Robert Penn. "A Poem of Pure Imagination
    (Reconsiderations VI)." Kenyon Review, 8 (1946),
    391-427.

Note: Some instructors prefer to receive handwritten rather than typewritten papers. Below is a sample page from a handwritten library paper.

But Warren also points to a secondary theme in the poem: a linking of the albatross with the imagination.[10]

According to Warren, the albatross may be considered as a kind of "moon-bird." When it first appears, it is associated with mist and fog, with snowy haze, which Warren calls the "symbolic equivalent of moonlight."[11] The moon first appears in the poem almost immediately after the albatross:

> In mist or cloud, on mast or shroud,
> It [the albatross] perched for vespers nine;
> Whiles all the night, through fog-smoke white,
> Glimmered the white Moon-shine.' (lines 75-78)

In the poem, the killing of the albatross is followed immediately by the rising of the sun (lines 82 and 83),

---

[10] "A Poem of Pure Imagination (Reconsiderations VI)," <u>Kenyon Review</u>, 8 (1946), 398 and 402.

[11] Ibid., p. 407.

Letters

34

Letters should follow conventional forms.

All the principles of good writing set forth in this handbook apply to letters and should be used by the student whenever he is called upon to write them. In addition, certain conventional forms should be observed.

Business letters are preferably typewritten on one side only of white sheets $8\frac{1}{2} \times 11$ inches in size. They are mailed in standard business envelopes, either about $3\frac{1}{2} \times 6\frac{1}{2}$ inches or about 4×10 inches in size. Personal letters and social notes are commonly written by hand on note paper, which can be bought in a wide variety of colors and styles. Both sides of the sheet may be used.

34a
Business letters should conform to standard practices.

A business letter has six essential parts:

(1) the heading;
(2) the inside address;
(3) the salutation (or greeting);
(4) the body of the letter;
(5) the complimentary close;
(6) the signature.

Model Business Letter

(1) 1288 Catawba Street
Columbia, Missouri 65201
April 24, 1971

(2) Mr. J. W. Rice
Editor, Rushville News
122 East Market Street
Rushville, Missouri 64484

(3) Dear Mr. Rice:

(4) Mr. Erskine Freeman, of your City Room, has mentioned to me your regular practice of employing two student reporters every summer. I am now majoring in journalism at the University of Missouri, and I should like, therefore, to apply for one of those positions for this next summer.

By the end of this college year I shall have completed three quarters of the university program in journalism. Included in this work are two courses in reporting and one in copyreading. Before I began my college work, I had served four years as sports editor of my high school newspaper, where I learned some of the fundamentals of page make-up. Last year I was awarded the Missouri Press Association Scholarship for journalism.

I have permission to refer you to my employer of the last three summers:

> Mr. George Armour
> Armour Drug Store
> Rushville, Missouri 64484

and to the professors under whom I have taken courses in journalism:

> Dr. James D. Turner
> Professor of Journalism
> University of Missouri
> Columbia, Missouri 65201

> Dr. John M. Cain
> Assistant Professor of Journalism
> University of Missouri
> Columbia, Missouri 65201

I shall be in Rushville after June 6 and should appreciate an opportunity to call at your office for an interview at your convenience.

(5) Very truly yours,

(6) *Donald Burke*

Donald Burke

Model Addressed Envelope

```
Donald Burke
1288 Catawba Street
Columbia, Missouri 65201



            Mr. J. W. Rice
            Editor, Rushville News
            122 East Market Street
            Rushville, Missouri 64484
```

Note: With a zip code, special abbreviations not followed by a period may be used for names of states:

```
Rushville, MO 64484

Otter, MT 59062
```

(1) The heading should give the full address of the writer and the date of the letter.

The heading is blocked as in the model, with no end punctuation.

```
860 Fremont Street
Bessemer, Alabama 35020
February 3, 1971
```

If letterhead paper (which supplies the address) is used, the date may be centered, begun at center, or written flush with the right margin.

(2) The inside address (identical to the address that appears on the envelope) should give the name and the full address of the person to whom the letter is written.

The inside address should be consistent in form with the heading. The inside address is typed flush with the left margin about six spaces lower than the heading.

(3) The salutation (or greeting) should be consistent with the tone of the letter, the first line of the inside address, and the complimentary close.

The salutation is written flush with the left margin two spaces below the inside address and is followed by a colon. The following salutations are used:

For men	*For women*
Dear Sir:	Dear Madam:
Dear Mr. Smith:	Dear Mrs. Smith:
Gentlemen:	Ladies:

Note: The masculine salutation is used to address an organization (*Gentlemen*) or an individual whose name the writer does not know (*Dear Sir*).

In some instances a business letter is addressed to a company or a department of a company but is marked for the attention of a particular person. In such letters, the "attention line" is placed two lines above the salutation, thus:

Attention: Mr. L. W. Jones

Gentlemen:

For the proper forms of addresses and salutations in letters to government officials, ecclesiastical dignitaries, and so on, see "Forms of Address," pp. 51a–54a in *Webster's Third New International Dictionary*.

Standard abbreviations used in salutations and addresses include *Mr.* (plural, *Messrs.*), *Mrs.* (plural, *Mmes.*), *Ms.* (for *Mrs.* or *Miss*), and *Dr.*

(4) The body of the letter should follow the principles of good writing.

Typewritten business letters are usually single-spaced, with double spacing between paragraphs. All paragraphs should begin flush with the left-hand margin, as in the model business letter on page 459, or should begin with an equal indention (usually five spaces). The subject matter should be well organized and well paragraphed, but the paragraphs will frequently be shorter than in ordinary writing. The style should be clear and direct. Indirect, abbreviated, or outdated phrasing should be avoided.

INDIRECT

I beg to inform you that we have . . .   I beg to send . . .
Permit us to report that we now supply . . .

BETTER

We have . . .   I am sending . . .   We now supply . . .

ABBREVIATED

Hope to have . . .   Enclose check for six dollars.

BETTER

We hope to have . . .   I enclose a check for six dollars.

Note: If the letter continues to a second page, the sender's address (whether on the letterhead or in a typed heading) should not be repeated. The full name of the recipient of the letter, the page number, and the date should be given, arranged on separate lines at the upper left margin of the page.

```
Mr. J. W. Rice
Page 2
April 24, 1971

Before I began my college work . . .
```

(5) The complimentary close should be consistent with the tone of the letter and with the salutation.

Ordinary business letters addressed to strangers should close with *Yours truly, Yours very truly,* or *Very truly yours.* Professional letters, or business letters addressed to an individual and having an opening such as *Dear Mr. White,* may well close with *Yours sincerely, Sincerely yours, Sincerely,* or *Cordially yours.*

(6) The signature should be written by hand directly below the complimentary close.

If the writer's name does not appear in the letterhead, it may be typed just below the signature. Ordinarily, neither professional titles nor degrees should be used with the signature, but the writer's official capacity should be indicated:

```
INAPPROPRIATE    James M. Smith, M.A.

APPROPRIATE      James M. Smith
                 President
```

A married woman should sign her own name: *Mary Hughes Black* or *Mary H. Black* (NOT *Mrs. John K. Black*). In business letters single or married status may be indicated by the use of parentheses as follows:

```
(Miss) Eleanor Morgan

Mary Hughes Black
(Mrs. John K. Black)
OR
(Mrs.) Mary Hughes Black
```

463

(7) The letter should be folded to fit the envelope.

Below are the steps for folding a business letter to fit the long standard envelope (about 8 × 10 inches in size) and for placing it inside the envelope.

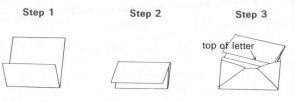

Step 1   Step 2   Step 3

Fold bottom up   Fold top down, leaving
                  about ¼ inch

Fold the standard-sized paper to fit a small business envelope (about 3½ × 6½ inches in size) as follows:

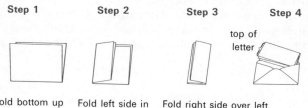

Step 1   Step 2   Step 3   Step 4

Fold bottom up   Fold left side in   Fold right side over left,
                                      leaving about ¼ inch

34b

Personal letters and informal social notes should conform to standard practices.

Friendly letters usually omit the inside address. Often only the date is given in the heading when the recipient of the letter is thoroughly familiar with the sender's address.

The salutation is usually followed by a comma instead of the more formal colon. As in the business letter, the salutation and the complimentary close should be in keeping with the tone of the letter. An appropriate complimentary close for a letter beginning with *Dear Martha* or *Dear Mrs. Anderson* may range from the casual (such as *As always, Fondly, Yours*) to the formal (such as *Sincerely yours* or *Yours truly*).

The tone, style, and content of the letter will vary greatly with the occasion and with the personality of the writer. An easy, informal style is best.

34c

Formal social notes—announcements, invitations, answers to invitations—should conform to very definite conventions.

For the rare occasions when formal notes are required, engraving or handwriting (not typing) is the rule. Formal notes are always written in the third person. They have no heading, no inside address, no salutation, no complimentary close, and no signature. (The writer's street address and the month and the date may be placed beneath the body of the note at the left.) Every word (except the street number and the abbreviations *Mr.*, *Mrs.*, and *Dr.*) is spelled out in full. Acceptances and regrets follow the form of the invitation closely, repeating the hour and the date to ensure understanding.

■ **Exercise 1** Write a business letter in which you apply for a position that you are competent to fill. Be sure to include the following: (1) a brief description of the job desired—be specific; (2) your qualifications, including age, schooling, and experience; (3) at least three references—people who know you well and are able to evaluate your ability; (4) a request for an interview. (See the model business letter on page 459.)

■ **Exercise 2** Write a business letter in which you do one of the following:

1. Request the circulation manager of a newspaper to send your paper to a new address.
2. Ask the manager of a New York City hotel to reserve a room for you.
3. Call the attention of your representative in the city government to some needed repairs in a street near your home.
4. Explain to your employer why you must resign from your position at the end of the year.
5. Request the permission of a former employer to use his name as a reference in applying for a new position.

■ **Exercise 3** Write a personal letter in which you do one of the following:

1. Accept an invitation to spend a weekend with a friend.
2. Answer a friend's inquiry about the course in dramatics (OR chemical engineering astonomy, political science, and so on) given at your college.
3. Congratulate a friend in another college on his election to some class office (OR on any other honor).
4. Introduce a friend to one of your former classmates who lives in a distant city.
5. Express your sympathy to a friend suffering from pain or grief.

466

Glossary of Grammatical Terms

The following glossary presents brief explanations of grammatical terms frequently used by students of the language. References to further treatment of most of the terms in this glossary, as well as to a number of terms not listed, may be found in the index.

absolute construction   A parenthetical word group which qualifies the rest of the sentence or a main clause and is not linked to it by a subordinating conjunction or by the preposition *with*. The construction consists of a noun or a noun substitute followed by an adjective or by a participle (with any objects, complements, or modifiers).

> *His face and clothes white with dust,* the man looked like a ghost.   [Compare *"Because his face and clothes were white with dust,* the man looked like a ghost."]
>
> Macbeth stood there, *his hands dripping blood.*   [Compare *"*Macbeth stood there, *with his hands dripping blood.*"]
>
> *The expressway jammed with rush-hour traffic,* we were delayed two hours.   [Compare *"Because the expressway was jammed with rush-hour traffic,* we were delayed two hours."]

The term *nominative absolute* is also used to describe this structure, because the nominative case is always used for the word or words heading the construction.

> *Frank and he obviously bored,* Anna changed the subject.

See also **12d(3)**.

467

abstract noun See **noun.**

active voice See **voice.**

adjectival Like an adjective. A word which is used as an adjective but which regularly functions as another part of speech is called an adjectival.

> The *rinse* water was clean. [Here *rinse,* regularly used as a verb or a noun, modifies the noun *water* and functions as an adjective. Compare the adjective *rinsable.*]

Nouns in the possessive case—as well as such pronouns as *my, his, our,* and *their*—may be classified as adjectivals.

> *Their* search for *Noah's* ark continued.

Phrases and clauses which function as adjectives are also called adjectivals.

> The man *on third base* stumbled. [A phrase modifying *man*]
> The dog *that barks* may bite. [A clause modifying *dog*]

adjective A part of speech regularly used to modify (qualify, describe, or limit) a noun or a pronoun. An adjective may also modify a gerund.

Descriptive adjectives

cloudy sky, *good* acting, *greatest* work, *reasonable* prices
a *Christlike* figure, a *Byronic* hero [Proper adjectives]
They seem *happier* now. Were your neighbors *friendly?*

Limiting adjectives

ARTICLE	*a* plum, *an* outburst, *the* large desk
DEMONSTRATIVE	*this* one, *that* map, *these* rods, *those* keys
INDEFINITE	*some* milk, *more* cans, *many* feet, *few* pets
INTERROGATIVE	*Whose* cap is it? *What* bill? *Which* one?
NUMERICAL	*one* pear, *three* plums, *third* base, *tenth* year
POSSESSIVE	*my* opinion, *its* nest, *their* homes, *our* right
RELATIVE	The boy *whose* dog had died was silent.

Limiting adjectives—especially the articles *a, an,* and *the*—are often called *noun markers* or *determiners,* because they indicate that a noun is to follow. See also **marker.**

A *predicate adjective* is used with a linking verb and modifies the subject.

The shirts were *inexpensive.*   How *busy* is he?

See also Section 4.

adjective clause A subordinate clause used adjectivally.

Velasquez, *whose work influenced the French Impressionists,* was a famous Spanish realist.   [The adjective clause modifies the noun *Velasquez.*]

See also pages 20–21.

adverb A part of speech regularly used to modify a word or word group other than a noun or a pronoun. An adverb may restrict, qualify, or limit a verb, an adjective, another adverb, an infinitive, a gerund, a participle, a phrase, a clause, or even the rest of the sentence in which it appears. An adverb often indicates time ("are *now* fighting"), place ("stayed *there*"), manner ("acting *quickly*"), or degree ("*very* eager").

Mildred owns an *extremely* old clock, which runs *very quietly.* [*Extremely* modifies the adjective *old; quietly* modifies the verb *runs; very* modifies the adverb *quietly.*]
Naturally, the villain succeeds at first by *completely* outwitting the hero. [*Naturally* modifies the rest of the sentence, and *completely* modifies the gerund *outwitting.*]

See also Section 4.

adverb clause A subordinate clause used adverbially. According to meaning, it may be classified as an adverb clause of time, place, manner, cause, purpose, condition, concession, comparison, or result.

The common mole is valuable *because it eats insects.*
Although George Mason is not famous, his ideas were used in our Bill of Rights.
Cartoonists make at least eighteen drawings *so that Woody Woodpecker can laugh victoriously.*

See also pages 20 and 21.

grt

adverbial Like an adverb. A word which is used as an adverb but which regularly functions as another part of speech is called an adverbial.

> Gerard left *home Monday.* [Here *home* and *Monday,* regularly used as nouns, modify the verb *left* and function as adverbs.]

Phrases and clauses which function as adverbs may also be classified as adverbials.

> The stores close *at five o'clock.*
> He moved to Oregon *after he had sold his home.*

agreement The correspondence in form of one word with another (for example, a verb with its subject or a pronoun with its antecedent) to indicate number: see Section **6.**

antecedent The name given to a word or group of words to which a pronoun refers.

> This is the *man who* came to the house. [*Man* is the antecedent of the relative pronoun *who.*]
> When *John* and *Mary* came, *they* told us the facts in the case. [*John* and *Mary* are the antecedents of the personal pronoun *they.*]

appositive A noun or noun substitute set beside another noun or noun substitute and identifying or explaining it.

> I met Ron, an *actor.* [*Actor* is in apposition with *Ron.*]

See also **12d(2).**

article See **adjective.**

auxiliary A verb helper in a verb phrase. An auxiliary precedes the main verb (though other words may intervene) and is often called a *verb marker,* because it indicates that a verb is to follow. See also **marker.**

> *are* talking, *have* succeeded, *had* always paid

When functioning as an auxiliary before a past participle, a form of *be* indicates the passive voice.

> may *be* put, *were* promoted, has *been* raised

470

Modal auxiliaries are verb helpers that do not change form to indicate a third-person singular subject: *will, would, shall, should, may, might, must, can, could, ought to,* and *used to.*

See also **1a** and Section **7**.

case   The inflectional form of a noun or a pronoun which shows the function of the word in a sentence. A subject is in the *subjective,* or *nominative,* case (*man, he*). A possessive noun or pronoun is in the *possessive,* or *genitive,* case (*man's, his*). And an object is in the *objective* case (*man, him*). See also **inflection** and Section **5**.

clause   A group of related words that contains both a subject and a predicate and that functions as a part of a sentence. A clause may be *main* (*independent, principal*) or *subordinate* (*dependent*). A main clause can stand by itself as a simple sentence; a subordinate clause cannot. Subordinate clauses are used as nouns, adjectives, or adverbs: see **1d(3)** and **1d(4)**.

MAIN	*The moon rose,* and *the stars came out.* [Two main clauses, either of which can stand by itself as a sentence]
SUBORDINATE	*That he will run for office* is doubtful. [Noun clause: a subordinate clause used as subject of the sentence]

collective noun   See **noun**.

colloquial   Appropriate for conversation and informal writing but usually inappropriate for formal writing.

common noun   See **noun**.

comparison   The change in the form of an adjective or adverb to indicate degrees in quality, quantity, or manner. There are three degrees: *positive, comparative,* and *superlative.*

Positive	*Comparative*	*Superlative*
good, well	better	best
high	higher	highest
quickly	more quickly	most quickly
slowly	less slowly	least slowly

See also **inflection** and **4c**.

grt

complement A word or words used to complete the sense of the verb (*direct* and *indirect objects*), the subject (*subject complements*), or the object (*object complements*).

OBJECTS (with transitive verbs)

William lent *Susan* his *book*. [*Book* is the direct object; *Susan* is the indirect object.]

SUBJECT COMPLEMENTS (with linking verbs)

The boy is *obedient*. [*Obedient,* a predicate adjective, modifies the subject *boy*.]

Samuel is a good *child*. [*Child,* a predicate noun, refers to the subject *Samuel.*]

The keys are *here*. [*Here,* an adverb of place, refers to the subject *keys*.]

OBJECT COMPLEMENTS

He called the man a *hero*. [The noun *hero* refers to *man,* which is the direct object.]

Jack painted his garage *blue*. [The adjective *blue* modifies the direct object *garage*.]

complete predicate See **predicate**.

complete subject See **subject**.

complex sentence See **sentence**.

compound A word or word group with two or more parts that function as a unit.

COMPOUND NOUNS dropout, hunger strike, sister-in-law

COMPOUND SUBJECT *Republicans, Young Democrats,* and *Independents* are working together.

COMPOUND PREDICATE Kate *has tried* but *has* not *succeeded.*

See also **sentence**.

compound-complex sentence See **sentence**.

compound sentence See **sentence**.

concrete noun See **noun**.

conjugation A list of the inflected forms of a verb that indicate
tense, person, number, voice, and mood, as follows:

CONJUGATION OF THE VERB *SEE*

Principal Parts
see, saw, seen

Active Voice	*Passive Voice*

INDICATIVE MOOD

PRESENT TENSE

I (you, we, they) *see* he (OR she OR it) *sees*	I *am seen*, he (OR she OR it) *is seen* you (we, they) *are seen*

PAST TENSE

I (he, you, we, they) *saw*	I (he) *was seen* you (we, they) *were seen*

FUTURE TENSE

I (he, you, we, they) *will* (OR *shall*) *see*	I (he, you, we, they) *will* (OR *shall*) *be seen*

PRESENT PERFECT TENSE

I (you, we, they) *have seen* he *has seen*	I (you, we, they) *have been seen* he *has been seen*

PAST PERFECT TENSE

I (he, you, we, they) *had seen*	I (he, you, we, they) *had been seen*

FUTURE PERFECT TENSE (seldom used)

I (he, you, we, they) *will* (OR *shall*) *have seen*	I (he, you, we, they) *will* (OR *shall*) *have been seen*

SUBJUNCTIVE MOOD

PRESENT TENSE

that he (I, you, we, they) *see*   that he (I, you, we, they) *be seen*

PAST TENSE

that he (I, you, we, they) *saw*   that he (I, you, we, they) *were seen*

PRESENT PERFECT TENSE

that he (I, you, we, they) *have seen*   that he (I, you, we, they) *have been seen*

PAST PERFECT TENSE

(same as the indicative)

IMPERATIVE MOOD

PRESENT TENSE

see   be seen

See also Section **7**.

conjunction   A part of speech (often called a *function word*) used to connect words, phrases, or clauses. There are two kinds of conjunctions: coordinating conjunctions and subordinating conjunctions.

Coordinating conjunctions connect words, phrases, and clauses of equal rank: *and, but, or, nor, for,* and sometimes *so* and *yet.* See also **correlatives.**

Subordinating conjunctions connect subordinate clauses with main clauses: *after, although, as, as if, because, before, if, since, though, till, unless, until, when, whenever, where, wherever, while,* and so forth. Subordinating conjunctions are sometimes called *subordinate-clause markers,* because they indicate that a subordinate clause is to follow. See also **marker.**

conjunctive adverb   An adverb used to connect or relate main clauses: *accordingly, also, anyhow, besides, consequently, further-*

more, hence, henceforth, however, indeed, instead, likewise, mean-
while, moreover, nevertheless, otherwise, still, then, therefore, thus,
and so on.

construction See **syntax.**

correlatives Coordinating conjunctions used in pairs: *both . . .*
and, either . . . or, neither . . . nor, not only . . . but also, whether
. . . or. See also **26c.**

declension A list of the inflected forms of a noun or a pronoun:
see **inflection.**

dependent clause A subordinate clause: see **clause.**

descriptive adjective See **adjective.**

determiner A word such as *a, an,* or *the* which signals the
approach of a noun. See also **marker.**

diagraming A graphic means of showing relationships within
the sentence. Various forms are used; any form is serviceable if
it helps the student to understand the sentence. (A diagram is
only a means to an end, not an end in itself.)

Illustrations of both a traditional diagram and a tree diagram
are given below and on the following page.

TRADITIONAL DIAGRAM

> SENTENCE PATTERN   **SUBJECT—PREDICATE.**

The dark clouds on the horizon had appeared suddenly.

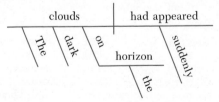

The lines and the placement of words not only show the sentence
pattern but also indicate the function of words and the relationship between them. A key to the diagram follows:

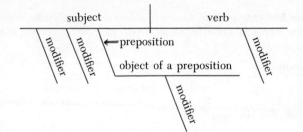

TREE DIAGRAM

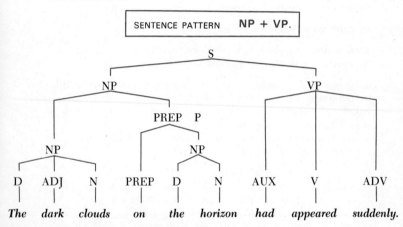

SENTENCE PATTERN	NP + VP.

The lines and the placement of abbreviations not only show the sentence pattern but also indicate parts of speech and the relationship between them. A key to the abbreviations follows:

ADJ	Adjective	PREP	Preposition
ADV	Adverb	PREP P	Prepositional Phrase
AUX	Auxiliary	S	Sentence
D	Determiner	V	Verb
N	Noun	VP	Verb Phrase
NP	Noun Phrase		

Note: In the pattern NP + VP = S, the term *noun phrase* refers to the complete subject, *verb phrase* to the complete predicate.

476

direct address   A noun or pronoun used parenthetically to direct a speech to a definite person.

I hope, *Mary,* that you will go.   *Mary,* close the door.

direct object   See **object**.

direct quotation   The exact oral or written words of others.

DIRECT QUOTATION   John asked, "Why haven't you joined the group, Martha?"
INDIRECT QUOTATION   John asked Martha why she had not joined the group.

See also **16a**.

elliptical construction   A construction in which words are omitted but clearly understood.

Mary is prettier than Helen [is pretty].
When [it is] possible, get a full night's sleep.
His hair is black; his face [is] deeply tanned.

embedding   The incorporation of an otherwise independent idea as a subordinated idea in the sentence.

He thinks *that it is going to snow.*   [Compare "It is going to snow."]
She gave us a *what-do-you-want* look.   [Compare "What do you want?"]
Father wanted *me to marry Helen.*   [Compare "I may marry Helen."]

expletive   The word *it* or *there* used merely as an introductory word or filler.

It is true that he is not coming.
There were few men present.

finite verb   The principal verb of a sentence or a clause. A finite verb can serve as the only verb of a sentence. Participles, gerunds, and infinitives are not finite verbs.

One prisoner *escaped.*   Clyde *will read* the book.

form change   See **inflection**.

function words Words (such as prepositions, conjunctions, aux-iliaries, and articles) that indicate the functions of other words (*vocabulary words*) in a sentence and the grammatical rela-tionships between them. See also **vocabulary words.**

genitive See **case.**

gerund A nonfinite verb that ends in *-ing* and functions as a noun. Gerunds may take objects, complements, or modifiers.

> He escaped by *swimming rapidly.* [The gerund *swimming* is the object of the preposition *by* and is modified by the adverb *rapidly.*]
> *Borrowing money* is a mistake. [The gerund phrase—the gerund *borrowing* and its object, *money*— serves as the subject of the sentence.]

A possessive noun or pronoun before a gerund may be classified either as a modifier of the gerund or as the subject of the gerund.

> *His borrowing* money is a mistake. [Compare "*his* action" and "*He borrowed* the money."]

idiom An expression in good use that is characteristic of or peculiar to a language. Perfectly acceptable idioms may seem illogical if taken literally or may violate established rules of grammar.

> He *gave himself away* by smiling.
> I have known him for *many a year.*

imperative See **mood.**

indefinite See **adjective** and **pronoun.**

independent clause A main clause: see **clause.**

indicative See **mood.**

indirect object See **complement** and **object.**

indirect quotation See **direct quotation.**

infinitive A nonfinite verb used chiefly as a noun, less frequently as an adjective or an adverb. The infinitive is usually made up of the word *to* plus the present form of a verb (called the *stem* of the infinitive), but the *to* may be omitted after such verbs as *let, make,* and *dare.* Infinitives may have subjects, objects, complements, or modifiers.

> Hal wanted *to open* the present. [*Present* is the object of the infinitive *to open;* the whole infinitive phrase is the object of the verb *wanted.*]
> The noise made *the baby cry.* [*Baby* is the subject of the infinitive (*to*) *cry;* the infinitive phrase is the object of the verb *made.*]
> I have work *to do.* [The infinitive *to do* is used adjectivally to modify the noun *work.*]
> *To tell* the truth, our team almost lost. [The infinitive phrase is used adverbially to modify the rest of the sentence.]

inflection A change in the form of a word to show a specific meaning or grammatical relationship to some other word or group of words. The inflection of nouns and pronouns is called *declension;* the inflection of verbs, *conjugation;* that of adjectives and adverbs, *comparison.*

> INFLECTIONS OF VERBS (indicating tense, person, number, mood)
>
> look, looks, looking, looked
> drink, drinks, drinking, drank, drunk
> know, knows, knowing, knew, known
> be, am, is, are, being, was, were, been
>
> INFLECTIONS OF NOUNS (indicating number, case)
>
> dog, dogs; dog's, dogs'
> child, children; child's, children's
>
> INFLECTIONS OF PRONOUNS (indicating person, case, number)
>
> I, me, my, mine   we, us, our, ours
> who, whom, whose   someone, someone's
> *This* is old. *These* are old. *That* is older than *those.*
>
> INFLECTIONS OF MODIFIERS (indicating comparison, number)
>
> fast, faster, fastest   bad, worse, worst
> attractive, more attractive, most attractive
> *this* letter, *these* letters, *that* letter, *those* letters

See also **conjugation.**

intensive pronoun See **pronoun**.

interjection A part of speech used for simple exclamations: *Oh! Ouch! Whew!* When used in sentences, mild interjections are set off by commas.

interrogative See **adjective** and **pronoun**.

intransitive See **verb**.

irregular verb A verb that does not form its past tense and past participle in the standard way—that is, by the addition of *-d* or *-ed* to the stem of the infinitive (as with the regular verbs *hope, hoped; look, looked*). The principal parts of five common types of irregular verbs are given below.

> swim, swam, swum [Vowels changed]
> beat, beat, beaten [*-en* added]
> feel, felt, felt [Vowel changed to consonant and *-t* added]
> send, sent, sent [*-d* changed to *-t*]
> set, set, set [No change]

limiting adjective See **adjective**.

linking verb A verb which relates the subject to the subject complement. Words commonly used as linking verbs are *become, seem, appear, feel, look, taste, smell, sound,* and the forms of the verb *be.*

> The tires *look* good. The surface *feels* rough.
> *Did* she *become* a nurse? What *could* that *be?*

main clause An independent clause: see **clause**.

marker A word (such as *a, an,* and *the; has, will, did,* and *may; very* and *too; who, which,* and *that;* or *although, because,* and *when*) that signals the approach of a noun, a verb, a modifier, or a subordinate clause.

> *a* penny, *an* exciting speech, *the* war [Articles—noun markers]
> *has* won, *will* never quit, *did* promise, *may* not work [Auxiliaries—verb markers]
> *too* wordy, *very* happily [Adverbs—adjective or adverb markers]

I know *who* he is.   I wonder *which* he will choose.   [Relative pronouns—subordinate-clause markers]

When she sews, she likes to be alone.   [Subordinating conjunction—subordinate-clause marker]

Note that words such as *has, very, who,* and *when* are not always markers:

He has a large family.   [*Has* is the only verb in the sentence.]

The very idea!   [*Very* is an adjective modifying the noun *idea.*]

Who will go?   [*Who* is an interrogative pronoun used as the subject of the sentence.]

When will he paint it?   [*When* is an adverb modifying the verb *paint.*]

modal auxiliary   See **auxiliary**.

mode   See **mood**.

modifier   Any word or word group functioning as an adjective or an adverb.

modify   To describe or qualify the meaning of a word or group of words.

Very old men hobbled *slowly along the road.*   [*Old* modifies *men; very* modifies *old; slowly* and *along the road* modify *hobbled; the* modifies *road.*]

mood (mode)   The form of the verb which indicates the manner in which the action or state is conceived. English has the indicative, imperative, and subjunctive moods.

The *indicative mood* is used in making a statement or asking a question.

You *have* a good mind.   *Have* you any ideas?

Mother *is* here.   *Is* mother here?

The *imperative mood* is used in giving a command, making a request, or giving directions.

Be careful.   *Watch* your step, please.

Take the next street on the right.

The *subjunctive mood* is used in *that* clauses of motion, resolution, recommendation, command, or demand; in the expression of contrary-to-fact condition in formal writing; and in certain idiomatic expressions.

> They demanded that he *be* there.
> I wish his mother *were* here.   [Preferred in formal writing]
> *Come* what may, he will persevere.   [Idiomatic]

See also Section **7**.

nominal   Like a noun. A noun substitute or a substantive.

nominative   See **case**.

nominative absolute   See **absolute construction**.

nonfinite verb (verbal)   A participle, a gerund, or an infinitive. Nonfinite verbs serve as nouns, adjectives, or adverbs. See also **gerund, infinitive,** and **participle**.

nonrestrictive   Nonessential to sentence meaning. A phrase or clause is nonrestrictive (parenthetical) when it is not necessary to the meaning of the main clause and may be omitted: see **12d**.

> The old horse, *slow but confident,* plodded on.   [Phrase]
> The airplane, *now being manufactured in large numbers,* is of immense commercial value.   [Phrase]
> The airplane, *which is now being manufactured in large numbers,* is of immense commercial value.   [Clause]

See also **restrictive**.

noun   A part of speech that names a person, place, thing, idea, animal, quality, or action: *Mary, America, apples, justice, goose, strength, departure.* A noun usually changes form to indicate the plural and the possessive case, as in *man, men; man's, men's.* See also **inflection**.

Types of nouns

COMMON	a *man,* the *cities,* some *trout* [General classes]
PROPER	*Mr. Ford,* in *Boston,* the *Forum* [Capitalized, specific names]

COLLECTIVE	a *flock*, the *jury*, my *family* [Groups—singular in form but singular or plural in meaning, depending on the context]
CONCRETE	an *egg*, the *bus*, his *ear*, two *trees* [Tangibles]
ABSTRACT	*ambition, jealousy, pity, hatred* [Ideas, qualities]

Functions of nouns

SUBJECT OF FINITE VERB   *Dogs* barked.

OBJECT OF FINITE VERB OR OF PREPOSITION   He gave *Jane* the *key* to the *house*.

SUBJECT COMPLEMENT (PREDICATE NOUN)   She is a *nurse*.

OBJECT COMPLEMENT   They named him *Jonathan*.

SUBJECT OF NONFINITE VERB   I want *Ed* to be here.

OBJECT OF NONFINITE VERB   I prefer to drive a *truck*.

APPOSITIVE   Moses, a *prophet*, saw the promised land.

DIRECT ADDRESS   What do you think, *Angela*?

noun clause   A subordinate clause used as a noun.

> *Whoever comes* will be welcome.   [Subject]
> I hope *that he will recover*.   [Direct object]
> I will give *whoever comes first* the best seat.   [Indirect object]
> Spend it for *whatever seems best*.   [Object of a preposition]
> This is *what you need*.   [Subject complement]
> I loved it, *whatever it was*.   [Appositive]
> *Whoever you are*, show yourself!   [Direct address]

noun phrase   See **phrase**.

noun substitute   A pronoun or any group of words (especially a gerund phrase, an infinitive phrase, or a noun clause) functioning as a noun. See also **substantive**.

number   The inflectional form of a noun, a pronoun, a demonstrative adjective, or a verb which indicates number, either singular or plural.

> book, man, I, one, this, that   [Singular]
> books, men, we, ones, these, those   [Plural]

Verbs change form to indicate a third-person singular subject: see **6a**.

483

object A noun or noun substitute governed by a transitive active verb, by a nonfinite verb, or by a preposition.

A *direct object,* or the *object of a finite verb,* is any noun or noun substitute that answers the question *What?* or *Whom?* after a transitive active verb. A direct object frequently receives, or is in some way affected by, the action of the verb.

> William raked *leaves.*   *What* did he say?
> The Andersons do not know *where we live.*

As a rule, a direct object may be converted into a subject with a passive verb: see **voice**.

An *object of a nonfinite verb* is any noun or its equivalent that follows and completes the meaning of a participle, a gerund, or an infinitive.

> Washing a *car* takes time.   He likes to wear a *tie.*
> Following the *truck,* a bus rounded the bend.

An *indirect object* is any noun or noun substitute that states *to whom* or *for whom* (or *to what* or *for what*) something is done. An indirect object ordinarily precedes a direct object.

> He bought *her* a watch.
> I gave the *floor* a second coat of varnish.

It is usually possible to substitute a prepositional phrase beginning with *to* or *for* for the indirect object.

> He bought a watch for her.

An *object of a preposition* is any noun or noun substitute which a preposition relates to another word or word group.

> Cedars grow tall in these *hills.*   [*Hills* is the object of *in.*]
> *What* am I responsible for?   [*What* is the object of *for.*]

object complement See **complement**.

objective See **case**.

participle A nonfinite verb that functions as an adjective. Endings of participles vary—for instance, *-ing, -ed, -t, -en.* Participles may take modifiers, objects, or complements.

My friends ***traveling*** *in Italy* feared earthquakes. [The participle *traveling* is modified by the prepositional phrase *in Italy,* and the whole participial phrase modifies *friends.*]

*Very **confused**,* they lost their way and stopped at a motel. [The participle *confused* is modified by the adverb *very,* and the participial phrase modifies *they.*]

Losing *her balance,* she toppled forward. [*Balance* is the object of the participle *losing,* and the participial phrase modifies *she.*]

particle   A word such as *across, after, in, up, off, on, down, over,* or *out* that is not inflected. A particle may be used with a verb to form a single unit of meaning.

    She picked *out* a purse.   I cut him *off.*

parts of speech   The eight classes into which most grammarians group words according to their form changes and their position, meaning, and use in the sentence: *verbs, nouns, pronouns, adjectives, adverbs, prepositions, conjunctions,* and *interjections.* Each of these is discussed separately in this glossary. It is important to note that part of speech is determined by function. The same word is often used as several different parts of speech: see **1c**.

passive voice   See **voice**.

person   The form of a verb or a pronoun which indicates whether a person is speaking (*first person*), is spoken to (*second person*), or is spoken about (*third person*).

FIRST PERSON   *I* see the boy.
SECOND PERSON   Can *you* see the boy?
THIRD PERSON   *He* sees the boy.

personal pronoun   See **pronoun**.

phrase   A group of related words without a subject and a predicate and functioning as a single part of speech.

NOUN PHRASE   *A young stranger* stepped forward.
VERB PHRASE   Ralph *will be sleeping.*
PREPOSITIONAL PHRASES   I hid *in the car.* [Used adverbially]
    The man *at the door* smiled. [Used adjectivally]

PARTICIPIAL PHRASE *Rearing its head,* the snake hissed.
GERUND PHRASE *Building a sun deck* can be fun.
INFINITIVE PHRASE Mrs. Raines went *to buy groceries.* [Used
adverbially]

See also 1d.

possessive See **case.**

predicate A basic grammatical division of a sentence. A predicate is the part of the sentence comprising what is said about the subject. The *complete predicate* consists of the main verb along with its auxiliaries (the *simple predicate*) and any complements and modifiers.

He **runs** *through the house.* [*Runs* is the simple predicate; *runs through the house* is the complete predicate.]

predicate adjective An adjective functioning as a subject complement: see **complement.**

predicate noun A noun functioning as a subject complement: see **complement.**

preposition A part of speech (often called a *function word*) that is used to show the relation of a noun or noun equivalent (the *object of the preposition*) to some other word in the sentence. Words commonly used as prepositions include *across, after, as, at, because of, before, between, by, for, from, in, in front of, in regard to, like, near, of, on, over, through, to, together with, under, until, up,* and *with.*

The portrait hung *in* the hall. [The preposition *in* shows the relationship of its object *hall* to the verb *hung.*]

See also 1c.

prepositional phrase See **phrase.**

principal clause A main clause: see **clause.**

principal parts The forms of any verb from which the various tenses are derived: *present* form (the *stem of the infinitive*), *past* form, and *past participle.*

Present stem (infinitive)	Past tense	Past participle
see	saw	seen
take	took	taken
love	loved	loved

See also Section **7**.

progressive verb   A verb form ending in *-ing* and preceded by a form of the verb *be* which is used to express continuous action or a state of being.

> I *have been playing* tennis all afternoon.
> Sally *is sleeping*.

See also Section **7**.

pronoun   A part of speech that serves the function of a noun in a sentence.

Types of pronouns

PERSONAL	*You* and *I* will see *him*.
INTERROGATIVE	*Who* is he? *Which* is it? *What* was that?
RELATIVE	The boy *who* served us is the one *that* I tipped.
DEMONSTRATIVE	*This* is better than *that*.
INDEFINITE	*Each* of you should help *someone*.
RECIPROCAL	Help *each other*. They like *one another*.
REFLEXIVE	Carl blames *himself*. Did you injure *yourself?*
INTENSIVE	We need a vacation *ourselves*. I *myself* saw the crash.

See also **inflection** and Sections **5** and **6**.

proper adjective   A capitalized adjective formed from a proper noun, as *Spanish* from *Spain*. See also **adjective**.

proper noun   See **noun**.

quotation   See **direct quotation**.

reciprocal pronoun   See **pronoun**.

grt

reflexive pronoun See **pronoun**.

regular verb Any verb that forms its past tense and past participle by adding *-d* or *-ed* to the stem of the infinitive: *love, loved; laugh, laughed.*

relative pronoun One of a small group of noun substitutes (*who, whom, whose, that, which, what, whoever, whomever, whichever, whatever*) used to introduce subordinate clauses; sometimes called a *subordinate-clause marker.*

> He has a son *who is a genius.* [Adjective clause introduced by the relative pronoun *who*]
> *Whoever wins the prize* must have talent. [Noun clause introduced by the relative pronoun *whoever.*]

See also **adjective** and **pronoun**.

restrictive Essential to sentence meaning. A phrase or clause is restrictive when it is necessary to the meaning of the main clause and cannot be omitted: see **12d**.

> Every drug *condemned by doctors* should be taken off the market. [Phrase]
> Every drug *that doctors condemn* should be taken off the market. [Clause]

See also **nonrestrictive**.

sentence An independent unit of expression. A simple sentence follows the pattern **SUBJECT—PREDICATE**. Sentences are often classified according to structure as *simple, compound, complex,* or *compound-complex.*

> SIMPLE The final game disappointed us. [One subject, one predicate]
> COMPOUND He lost the game, but he had done his best. [Two main clauses]
> COMPLEX When the whistle blew, the parade began. [One subordinate clause and one main clause]
> COMPOUND-COMPLEX The work stops when it rains, but the tools are kept in readiness. [Two main clauses and one subordinate clause]

See also Section **1**.

subject A basic grammatical division of a sentence. A subject is a noun or noun substitute about which something is asserted or asked. It usually precedes the predicate and answers the question *Who?* or *What?* in front of the predicate. (Imperative sentences have subjects that are not stated but are implied.) The *complete subject* consists of the *simple subject* and the words associated with it.

> The **dog** at the front of the house barked at the car. [*Dog* is the simple subject; *the dog at the front of the house* is the complete subject.]

subject complement See **complement**.

subjective See **case**.

subjunctive See **mood**.

subordinate clause A dependent clause: see **clause**.

substantive Any word or group of words used as a noun. Substantives may be nouns, pronouns, phrases (especially gerund or infinitive phrases), or noun clauses. See also **noun substitute**.

syntax (construction) Sentence structure. The grammatical functions of words, phrases, clauses.

tense The form of the verb which indicates its relation to time. Inflection (*eat, eats, eating, ate, eaten*) and the use of auxiliaries (*will* eat, *have* eaten, *had* eaten, *will have* eaten, and so on) show the tense of a verb. See also **inflection** and Section 7.

transformation A construction that is derived by converting a basic structure (simple, affirmative, declarative, with a subject preceding a verb in the indicative mood, active voice) to another structure with similar meaning. Below are three examples.

> John locked the office.
> The office was locked by John.
> [Active voice changed to passive]

> A stranger stood at the door.
> At the door stood a stranger. [Shift in word order]

> Honey is in the bread.
> There is honey in the bread. [The expletive *there* added]

transitive See **verb**.

verb A part of speech used to make a statement, to ask a question, or to give a command or direction. Inflections indicate tense (and sometimes person and number) and mood of a verb: see **inflection, voice,** and Section 7.

A *transitive verb* is a verb that requires an object to complete its meaning. Transitive verbs can usually be changed from the active to the passive voice: see **object** and **voice**.

> Sid *laid* a wreath on the tomb.   [Direct object: *wreath*]

An *intransitive verb* is a verb (such as *go* or *sit*) that does not have an object to complete its meaning. Linking verbs, which take subject complements, are intransitive.

> She *has been waiting* patiently for hours.
> I *was* sick last Christmas.

The same verb may be transitive in one sentence and intransitive in another.

> TRANSITIVE Lydia *reads* novels.   [Direct object: *novels*]
> INTRANSITIVE Lydia *reads* well.

verbal Like a verb. A gerund (often called a *verbal noun*), a participle (often called a *verbal adjective*), or an infinitive: see **nonfinite verb**.

verbal phrase A participial phrase, a gerund phrase, or an infinitive phrase. See also **gerund, infinitive, participle,** and **phrase**.

verb phrase See **phrase**.

verb with particle A word group equivalent in meaning to a single-word verb.

> The parade *held up* traffic.   [Compare "The parade stopped traffic."]
> Please *turn on* the motor.   [Compare "Please start the motor."]

vocabulary words Nouns, verbs, and most modifiers—those words found in vocabulary-building lists. See also **function words**.

voice Only verbs have voice. A verb with a direct object is in the *active voice*. When the direct object is converted into a subject, as is done in the sentences below, the verb is in the *passive voice*. A passive verb is always a verb phrase consisting of a form of the verb *be* followed by a past participle. The subject of an active verb acts. The subject of a passive verb does not act.

ACTIVE VOICE	PASSIVE VOICE
Priscilla *chose* John.	John *was chosen* by Priscilla.
Ed *must learn* that.	That *must be learned.*

word order The arrangement of words in sentences. Because of lost inflections, modern English depends heavily upon word order to convey meaning.

Bill wanted some milk chocolate.
Bill wanted some chocolate milk.

Nancy gave Henry $14,000.
Henry gave Nancy $14,000.

Index

In the following index, boldface numbers refer to rules; other numbers refer to pages. A colon is used after each boldface number to indicate that the following pages refer to the rule or the pertinent part of the discussion of the rule.

d

f

Manuscript form (*Cont.*)
revising, grading symbols as a guide to, **8d(2)**: 89–91
title, **8b(4)**: 83
typewritten papers, **8a(2)**: 82, **8c(2)**: 85, **33e**: 421–55
word division, at ends of lines, **8b(8)**: 84–85
Markers
defined, 480–81
of modifiers, **4**: 39, 480
of nouns, **1b**: 7–8, 480
of subordinate clauses, **1d**: 19, 481
of verbs, **1a**: 4–5, **7**: 69, 480
May be, maybe, **19i**: 219
May, can, **19i**: 210
Meanwhile, as a conjunctive adverb, **3b**: 36, **14a**: 133, 474–75
Mechanics, **8–11**: 82–108
Merely, position of, **25a(1)**: 274
Metaphor, **20a(4)**: 235–36
Middle English, **19a(5)**: 194–95
Mighty, **19i**: 219
Misplaced parts, **25a**: 274–77
clauses, **25a(3)**: 276
phrases, **25a(2)**: 275–76
words, **25a(1)**: 274–75
Mispronunciation, as cause of misspelling, **18a**: 170–71
Misreading, caused by omission of comma, **12e**: 125–26
Misspelling, **18**: 168–87
Mixed figures of speech and other mixed constructions, **23c**: 262–64
Modal auxiliary, defined, 471
Mode. *See* Mood
Modifiers
clauses used as, **1d(4)**: 20–21

coordinate adjectives, **12c(2)**: 116–18
dangling, **25b**: 277–81
defined, 481
markers of, **4**: 39, 480
misplaced, **25a**: 274–77
nonrestrictive, **12d(1)**: 119–21
phrases used as, **1d(2)**: 17–18
position of, **25a**: 274–77
restrictive, **12d(1)**: 119–21
"squinting," **25a(4)**: 276
Modify, defined, 481
Mood
defined, 481–82
imperative, 474, 481
indicative, 473, 481
shift in, **7d**: 77–79, **27b**: 291
subjunctive, **7c**: 75–77, 474, 482
Moral, morale, **19i**: 219
More, most, agreement of verb with, **6a(6)**: 57
Moreover, as a conjunctive adverb, **3b**: 36, **14a**: 133, 475
Most, for *almost,* **19i**: 207
Motion pictures, italics for titles of, **10c**: 100
Mr., Dr., etc., **11a**: 103
Mrs., in signature of letter, **34a(6)**: 463
Ms., use of, **34a(3)**: 462
Myself, for *I* or *me,* **5a(2)**: 48, **19i**: 219–20
Mythology, guides to, **33b(3)**: 411–12

n

Names, proper
capitalization of, **9a(1)**: 93–94
titles before, **11a**: 103–04
titles or degrees after, **11e**: 105

517

p

L
M
N
O 5
P 6
Q 7
R 8
S 9
T 0

GRAMMAR

1 ss — Sentence Sense
- a Verbs
- b Subjects and objects
- c All parts of speech
- d Phrases and subordinate clauses
- e Main clauses and sentence types

2 frag — Sentence Fragment
- a Phrases
- b Subordinate clauses
- c Other fragments

5 ca — Case
- a Appositives and compounds
- b Use of pronoun in own clause
- c *Whom* in formal writing
- d Possessive before gerund
- e Objective with infinitive
- f Subjective for complement of *be*

6 agr
- a Subject and verb
  - (1) Intervening words; pronunciation
  - (2) Subjects joined by *and*
  - (3) Singular subjects joined by *or*, etc.
  - (4) Subject following verb
  - (5) Relative pronoun as subject
  - (6) *Each*, etc., as subject
  - (7) Collective noun as subject

MECHANICS

8 ms — Manuscript Form
- a Proper materials
- b Arrangement; word division
- c Legibility
- d Proofreading and revising

9 cap — Capitals
- a Proper names
- b Titles preceding proper names
- c Titles of books, plays, etc.
- d *I* and *O*
- e First word of sentence
- f Unnecessary capitals

PUNCTUATION

12 ,/ — The Comma
- a Main clauses
- b Introductory elements
- c Items in series
- d Nonrestrictive elements
- e Misreading

13 o — Superfluous Commas
- a Subject and verb, verb and object
- b Misuse with coordinating conjunction
- c Slight parenthesis
- d Restrictive elements
- e First and last items of series

16 ""/ — Quotation Marks
- a Direct quotations
- b Minor titles
- c Special sense
- d Overuse
- e Position with other marks

17 — The Period and
- a ./ Period
- b ?/ Question mark
- c !/ Exclamation point
- d :/ Colon
- e —/ Dash

DICTION

19 g — Good Use
- a Use of dictionary
- b Informal words
- c Slang; jargon
- d Regional words
- e Nonstandard words
- f Archaic and obsolete words
- g Technical words
- h "Fine" writing, etc.
- i **Glossary of Usage**

20 e — Exactness
- a Exact words
- b Idiomatic words
- c Fresh expressions

EFFECTIVE SENTENCES

23 u — Unity and Logical Thinking
- a Related thoughts
- b Excessive detail and excessive subordination
- c Mixed or illogical constructions
- d Sound logic

24 sub — Subordination
- a Related series of short sentences
- b Ideas of unequal weight
- c Illogical subordination

27 pv — Point of View
- a Tense
- b Mood
- c Subject and voice
- d Person
- e Number
- f Indirect and direct discourse
- g Tone or style
- h Perspective

28 ref — Reference of Pronouns
- a Ambiguous
- b Remote
- c Broad
- d Pronoun *it* with expletive *it*